"This book goes beyond the many primers and explainers of bisexuality and gets to the fascinating nuances, challenges, and joys that Bi+ people experience beyond just fluid attractions. Diving into next-level topics like non-monogamy, kink, sex work, disability, and aging, Dr. Lisa Speidel clearly and expertly lays out the complexity and diversity of the Bi+ community before turning it over in each chapter to the community itself. Hearing from these voices directly was engaging and invaluable, and paired with Dr. Speidel's analysis, this is the most layered and insightful work on bisexuality that I've ever read—and I've read a lot!"

Robert Cohen, *host of the podcast* Two Bi Guys *and author of* Bisexual Married Men: Stories of Relationships, Acceptance and Authenticity

"This book offers personal testimony and solutions from those most impacted, which is always a welcome addition to conversations and learning about sexuality topics. To be guided by those most impacted is one of the paths to liberation for all of us! Join the community members who are envisioning a world where radical healing love is the path that will set us free."

Bianca Laureano, *author of* The People's Book of Human Sexuality: Expanding the Sexology Archive

"Grateful that the bisexual diaspora's emergence since the turn of the century is shown so well. This collection highlights how the global majority and gender-divergent people are most disproportionately hurt. Resistance is fertile. Bi passion eternal."

Loraine Hutchins, *co-editor* Bi Any Other Name: Bisexual People Speak Out, *co-founder—BiNet USA*

"This book is a must read for anyone in the field of Women, Gender and Sexuality Studies interested in how bisexuality is lived in everyday life. Speidel uses compelling personal stories to convey the pleasure and pain of inhabiting a sexuality that is largely marginalized and misunderstood in the contemporary world. Deeply rooted in intersectionality, the book spans crucial topics and addresses the relationships between bisexuality and: history, religion, media representation, race, gender, age, disability, and so much more. Since Speidel has a unique way of making theory accessible and complex ideas relatable, this book is perfect for undergraduate classes and lay readers alike!"

Andre Cavalcante, *Associate Professor of Media Studies/Women, Gender and Sexuality, University of Virginia and author of* Struggling for Ordinary: Media and Transgender Belonging in Everyday Life

BISEXUALITY BEYOND BINARIES

This book brings together a collection of diverse contributors to discuss bisexual erasure and biphobia and how this intersects with racism, sexism, ableism, and transphobia.

Amplifying the voices of a group often unheard and erased, this book explores and celebrates the experiences, stories, and complexities of bisexual identity, providing tools to help dismantle the dehumanization of erasure, move beyond the gender binary, and increase visibility of multiple bisexualities. Beginning by outlining key definitions, labels, and context, each chapter addresses an identity or experience that intersects with bisexual identity, such as disability, masculinity, femininity, gender-diverse identities, media, religion, dating apps, porn, non-monogamy, intimate partner violence, aging, kink, and sex work. Each chapter begins with theoretical research before illuminating the personal narratives of bisexual people, especially people of color, that reflect the negative impact of bisexual erasure as well as the joy, beauty, and resilience of bisexuality.

Engaging and powerful, this book will help sex therapists, students, and educators enhance their inclusive and supportive practices. It will also be of immense interest to bisexual people so they may see diverse realities, celebrating stories of resistance and joy.

Lisa Speidel, Ph.D., is an associate professor in the Women, Gender and Sexuality Department at the University of Virginia and a Certified Sexuality Educator (CSE) through the American Association of Sexuality Educators, Counselors and Therapists (AASECT). She is a co-editor of *The Edge of Sex: Navigating a Sexually Confusing Culture from the Margins* (Routledge, 2019).

BISEXUALITY BEYOND BINARIES

Celebrating Multiple Bisexual Identities in a World of Erasure

Lisa Speidel

Routledge
Taylor & Francis Group

NEW YORK AND LONDON

Designed cover image: By Emma Terry

First published 2025
by Routledge
605 Third Avenue, New York, NY 10158

and by Routledge
4 Park Square, Milton Park, Abingdon, Oxon, OX14 4RN

Routledge is an imprint of the Taylor & Francis Group, an informa business

ISBN: 978-1-032-15130-4 (hbk)
ISBN: 978-1-032-15129-8 (pbk)
ISBN: 978-1-003-24265-9 (ebk)

DOI: 10.4324/9781003242659

Typeset in Minion
by Apex CoVantage, LLC

Dedicated to Mom and Dad: Dementia has taken so much away from you, Dad, but your lessons are not lost. Your commitment and care Mom, is a testament to your unwavering strength. If only I could be half as strong as you.

Many bi voices
Sharing our truths and stories
Defy erasure

—Tania Israel
#biku

CONTENTS

ABOUT THE AUTHOR

Lisa Speidel (she/her), Ph.D., CSE, is a white, cisgender, bisexual, 54-year-old woman who is an associate professor in the Women, Gender and Sexuality Department at the University of Virginia. She is also a Certified Sexuality Educator (CSE) through the American Association of Sexuality Educators, Counselors and Therapists (AASECT). Lisa teaches Human Sexualities, Pleasure Activism, Men and Masculinities, and Gender Violence and Social Justice among other classes. She has worked locally and nationally as an educator for over 30 years, with a focus on the examination of joyful sexuality, masculinity, violence, and the intersection of systemic oppressions. She has also been teaching women's self-defense for over 30 years in the Charlottesville community and at the University of Virginia. She is the co-author of *The Edge of Sex: Navigating a Sexually Confusing Culture from the Margins.*

CONTRIBUTORS

J. Bhattacharyya (she/her) is a 24-year-old South Asian, bisexual, cisgender woman who grew up the Washington, DC area. She graduated from the University of Virginia in 2021 with Bachelor of Arts degrees in cognitive science and global public health, and she is now in graduate school at Columbia University studying epidemiology and population mental health. She is deeply passionate about global mental health research, and she hopes to use her research skills to uplift queer and other marginalized populations around the world.

Jazmin Bolan-Williamson (she/her) is a 33-year-old bi-racial, Black, queer woman living in Michigan. She came out in 2019 as a bisexual woman but over the course of the last few years has determined the over-arching term Queer fits better. She is a 2015 graduate from Michigan State University with a degree in food industry management and has focused most of her career on local food systems work to help elevate BIPOC, women, and queer farmers and producers. Currently she is working for a woman -led curly hair care company called Original Moxie as Production Manager.

Robert Brooks Cohen (he/him) is a 39-year-old white, Jewish, bisexual/ queer, cisgender man living in Los Angeles. Robert is a writer and content creator who spent seven seasons writing for *Law & Order: SVU*, among other shows. In 2019, he appeared on camera in Viceland's *Slutever* in an episode about male bisexuality, and soon after he created *Two Bi Guys*, a podcast about sexual fluidity, masculinity, and the gender spectrum, which he continues to host and produce. His first book, *Bisexual Married Men: Stories of Relationships, Acceptance, and Authenticity* was published by Routledge in 2024.

Marissa Conniff (she/her) is a 34-year-old white, bisexual, cisgender female who is married to a cisgender man. Marissa came out as bisexual after being married to her husband for five years and also uses the term queer to describe her sexuality. Marissa's bisexuality is reflected in her attraction to her gender and other genders. Marissa is a professional marketer and specializes in strategy and social media. She is also an accomplished singer who performs locally in the Detroit area. Marissa's most tremendous pride is her son, who is full of wit and love.

Emilia Couture (she/her) is in her early twenties and is a white, queer, cisgender woman. She recently graduated with high distinction from the University of Virginia with a Bachelor of Arts in Psychology and Women, Gender, and Sexuality Studies. Her thesis was entitled *Stigmatized, Objectified & Erased: The Impact of Biphobia and Sexism on Bisexual Women's Mental Health*. She hopes to continue studying to explore how psychology can be used as a tool for care and liberation.

Adrian Cruz (he/him) is a 26-year-old Cuban/Colombian first generation immigrant, bisexual, cisgender man who grew up in a predominantly Hispanic dominated hometown in Miami, Florida. He graduated from the University of Florida with a Bachelor of Science degree in industrial and systems engineering and is now working for a top technology innovation consulting firm. In his free time, Adrian enjoys weightlifting, traveling, photography, dancing, happy hours, and a good rom com.

Dani (she/her) is a 34-year-old Black, queer, femme, and University of Virginia alumna with her bachelor's degree in women, gender and sexuality studies. She is a sex worker and entrepreneur who is passionate about amplifying the voices of those from marginalized communities.

Hillary Duah (she/her) is a 23-year-old African-American, bisexual woman who grew up in the Northern Virginia area. She graduated from the University of Virginia in 2023 with a Bachelor of Arts in Sociology and minors in economics and finance. She is now pursuing her JD/MBA at the University of Virginia Law School and the Darden School of Business. She is deeply passionate about using the law as a tool to serve underprivileged communities throughout the country. In her free time, Hillary enjoys playing volleyball competitively and hiking in Charlottesville, Virginia with her dog, Coco.

Shiri Eisner (they/them) is a 40-year-old Mizrahi, bisexual, genderqueer, feminist, anarchist, and vegan activist and writer living in Occupied Palestine. They are the author of the book *Bi: Notes for a Bisexual Revolution*, a longtime organizer in a multitude of radical and intersectional movements, and the founder of (now defunct) anarchabisexual group *Panorama—Bi and Pansexual Feminist Community*. Most of their English-language writing is currently on Twitter, where they can be found under @ShiriEisner.

Anastasia Fonseca-Carvalhais (she/her) is a 23-year-old Portuguese-American, queer, cisgender woman with a Bachelor of Arts in biology, Bachelor of Science in cognitive science, and a minor in women, gender and sexuality from the University of Virginia.

Katelyn Friedline (she/her) is a 27-year-old, physically disabled, chronically ill, white, bisexual person who is currently a Ph.D. student at the University of Pennsylvania within the History and Sociology of Science Department. Her research interests center around disability, digital infrastructure, history of electronic medical records, and digital privacy. She recently graduated with an MA in media studies from the University of Virginia where she served as the '23–'24 Graduate Fellow in the John L. Nau III History and Principles of Democracy Lab, '23–'24 Graduate Teaching Assistant for the Dept. of Media Studies, member of the University of Virginia's Disability Studies Initiative, Graduate Assistant at the Student Disability Access Center, was involved with the Student Disability Alliance, and was the 2022 recipient of the Stillfried-Godsey Award, which is given to a physically disabled student that demonstrates strong intellectual potential and motivation. Prior to entering graduate school, Katelyn received her BA from the University of Alabama and worked in Washington, DC for three years in various political communication roles.

Cris Jones-Hennin (he/him) was born in 1950 in Mainz, Germany and immigrated with his French family first to Ontario, Canada in 1951 and later to Buffalo, New York in 1956. He is educated with degrees in international affairs, economics, and education from Antioch University, Federal Universities of Rio de Janeiro and Brasilia and the Juarez-Lincoln Center. He has had an extensive career as economic development expert promoting projects in Africa, Asia, and Latin America. He is currently retired and dedicated to full-time care to his partner of 46 years as well as to mosaic and stained glass work in Chetumal, Quintana Roo, Mexico.

Hope (she/her) and Katie (she/her) are both in their early twenties white, queer women. They are friends of many years who frequently discuss their experiences surrounding bisexuality.

Wolf Hudson (he/him) is a 39-year-old Latino, cisgender man, openly bisexual adult performer, and 18-year veteran in the porn industry since 2006. He's performed in all genres: straight, gay, bisexual, trans, and BDSM.

He is an advocate for inclusivity and breaking down stereotypes and stigma associated with men in gay and bi porn who also perform in straight porn, specifically with regards to HIV and the lack of education about "U=U," undetectable equals untransmittable. He is also credited with reviving the bisexual M/M/F genre as a content creator and has broadened the genre to mainstream attention and acclaim.

Loraine Hutchins (she/her) co-edited the 1991 anthology *Bi Any Other Name: Bisexual People Speak Out* and co-founded BiNet USA, a national network of bisexual groups, as well as AMBi, the Alliance of Multicultural Bisexuals in Washington, DC. A fourth generation Washingtonian, she taught multi-disciplinary sexuality studies and holds a Ph.D. in cultural studies. She is retired, age 76, and an active part of her continuing care retirement community in Maryland.

Tania Israel (she/her) is a biracial, bisexual, Jewish, Buddhist, currently able-bodied, U.S.-born, cisgender woman. She is 58 years old and has identified as bisexual since her mid-20s. A professor of counseling psychology at the University of California, Santa Barbara, she conducts research relevant to scholarship, policy, and practice with sexual and gender minorities. Her professional contributions on bisexuality include the TEDx Talk *Bisexuality and Beyond* (viewed over 100,000 times) and other public speaking, journal editorships for special issues on bisexuality, development of psychological interventions and measures related to internalized binegativity, and co-founding Bialogue (a bisexual discussion group). She tweets bisexual haiku (#biku).

Pinay Jones (she/her) is a 20-something, Black, queer, cisgender woman. While she regularly identifies as bisexual, Pinay prefers the term "queer," as it speaks not only to her sexual way of being in the world but also her political and social commitment to queer liberation. She graduated from the University of Virginia in 2022 and her areas of study/interest include race, gender, sexuality (particularly non-normative forms and practices of sexuality such as kink and BDSM), political theory, history, and the Spanish language. Currently, she is living in Spain as an English teaching and cultural assistant. Ultimately, she plans to pursue a Ph.D. in either history or Black studies and become a professor.

ABilly S. Jones-Hennin (he/him) is an 81-year-old, Black, bisexual, cisgender man. ABilly served in the U.S. Marine Corps and graduated from Virginia State University in 1967. In 1978, ABilly helped launch the National Coalition of Black Gays (NCBG) in Columbia, Maryland, the first national advocacy organization for African American gay men and lesbians. A year later, ABilly helped to mobilize the first March on Washington for Lesbian and Gay

Rights—and helped to convene the National Third World LGBT Conference at Howard University, which gave rise to Howard University's Lambda Student Alliance, the first openly LGBT organization at an HBCU. Over the subsequent decades, ABilly had multiple leadership roles including minority affairs director of the National AIDS Network, founding member and co-chair of the National Coalition of Black Lesbians and Gays, board member of the National Gay and Lesbian Task Force (today known as The Task Force), and board member of BiNet USA. Along the way, ABilly earned his master's degree in social work at Howard University. ABilly and his partner **Cris Jones-Hennin,** have been together for 46 years, married for nine years, and have five children, ten grandchildren, and ten great grandchildren. (*ABilly passed away in January, 2024. Please see this beautiful tribute to ABilly in the Washington Post: www.washingtonpost.com/obituaries/2024/01/24/abilly-jones-hennin-dead/).*

Bianca Laureano (dr/she/ella) is a first-generation Puerto Rican, queer femme and is an award-winning educator, curriculum writer, and sexologist who turned 46 years old in 2024. She is a co-foundress of the Women of Color Sexual Health Network and ANTE UP!, a virtual freedom school. She has written curricula and led the curriculum development for the award-winning Netflix film *Crip Camp* and PBS documentary *I Didn't See You There,* both guided by disability justice principles. She is an AASECT certified sexuality educator and supervisor and was awarded an honorary doctorate from the California Institute for Integral Studies for her work in expanding the U.S. sexuality field. She is the editor of *The People's Book of Human Sexuality: Expanding the Sexology Archive* (2023). Find out more about Bianca at her website BiancaLaureano.com and about ANTE UP! at www.AnteUpPD.com

Janis Luna (they/she) is a 35year-old, mixed race, queer, two-spirit (qari-warmi) somatic therapist, writer, former stripper, and single mom. They have been writing about sex and sexuality since 2014 and in 2020 self-published *Death to Whorephobia: A Guide to Sex Worker Affirming Care,* an eBook adaptation of their Masters of Social Work thesis researching sex worker cultural competency in social work practice. They can be found on IG at @ janisxluna and @socialworkbookclub, and links to their work can also be found at www.janistherapy.com.

Ishita R. Mahajan (she/her) is a 23-year-old Indian, bisexual woman who was born in New Jersey but spent her childhood in Seoul, South Korea, and Singapore. She moved back to the U.S. at 17 to pursue her undergraduate education at the University of Virginia, where she majored in biology and double-minored in bioethics and psychology. As a recent college graduate, she is pursuing her career in health care and life sciences consulting, back in Singapore. In her free time, she loves reading, going on spontaneous adventures, being outdoors, spending time with friends and family, cooking, traveling, and weightlifting (@fitandfuelledwithishh)!

Ray Maxwell (they/them) is a 24-year-old, white, queer, trans, non-binary person who graduated from the University of Virginia in 2023. They participated in the Distinguished Majors Program for Women, Gender, and Sexuality Studies, producing a thesis paper titled, "Unmasking the Impacts of COVID-19 on the Communication of Gender Identity: A Survey of Transgender, Non-binary, and Gender-Diverse Individuals." They have spent many summers getting to know queer and trans youth through their job as a camp counselor and they look forward to continuing to support and advocate for these communities.

River McMican (they/them) is a 41-year-old white, queer, nonbinary, kinky, polyamorous, neurodivergent, and disabled artist/designer living in central MA. Although they never planned to be an activist, they've settled into it quite nicely. Their work includes bi and trans health care advocacy; educational content and presentations that support LGBTQ+ communities; and formerly serving as President of the Board of the Bisexual Resource Center.

Barbara Mona (she/her) is a 25-year-old Greek-American, bisexual, cisgender woman and graduate of the University of Virginia. She dreams of uplifting, empowering, and advocating for women, trans, and queer people around the world.

Noreen (she/her) is a 22-year-old Muslim Pakistani-American, bisexual, cisgender woman. She is a pre-med student with a Bachelors of Art in biology and minor in religious studies with a concentration in Buddhism from University of Virginia. She is currently doing research in a biology lab and hopes to get into medical school and continue doing research.

Ti'Asia Parker (she/her) is a 23-year-old Black, bisexual, cisgender woman originally from Poughkeepsie, NY. She graduated from the University of Virginia in 2023 and has decided to take a gap year between applying for psychology graduate programs as she is still figuring out her professional interests. As for her more casual interests, Ti'Asia is an avid video-gamer and songwriter.

Jessica Podkalicki (she/her) is a 33-year-old, Polish-American, bisexual woman. She is a bisexual advocate and Program and Operations Coordinator at the Bisexual Resource Center. Jessica has devoted her life to not-for-profit work and works to protect and support bisexual+ folks through support and educational resources. She holds a master's in public policy and administration from John Jay College School of Criminal Justice in New York. She lives in Malden, MA with her orange cat, Nala.

Ryan Powell (He/him/they/them) is a 24-year-old white, bisexual, cisgender man who was born in southern Virginia and grew up in a military family moving from Texas, to New York, and back to southern Virginia to live with family. He graduated from the University of Virginia in December of 2023 with a bachelor's degree in sociology. He plans to get his masters in clinical psychology and to become a clinical therapist working with general patients and working with people that were in the military and military families.

Livia Sauvage (she/her) is a 24-year-old French-American, Jewish, white, queer, cisgender woman who grew up in Northern Virginia. She graduated from the University of Virginia in 2021 with a Bachelor of Arts in Women, Gender and Sexuality and Global Studies-Security and Justice. While at the University of Virginia, she focused her studies on the intersections of gender, intimate-partner violence, and sexuality violence, which she plans to continue studying as she applies to law schools. She currently lives right by the Luxembourg Gardens in Paris, France working as an English teacher (and yes, she eats as much cheese as she can).

Bryant Staff Jr. (they/them) is a 28-year-old, Black, nonbinary filmmaker who currently resides in Hawaii. Bryant grew up among Virginia, Pennsylvania, and Southern Spain, where their mother served in the military and their father worked as an artist. This gave Bryant the opportunity to travel the world and witness many different walks of life. Bryant worked as a premier drag performer in the state of New Mexico where they also acted in films, as well as television shows. Aside from performing, Bryant graduated from The University of New Mexico with a degree in cinematography, where they premiered their senior thesis short film *Gold Fish*. They hope to continue creating wholesome films that center black, queer, and trans coming-of-age stories.

Zora Stone (she/her) is a 27-year-old Black, biracial, bisexual, cisgender woman. In pursuit of attaining her degree in hospitality, she decided to change direction in her career due to the various traumas she experienced throughout her high school and college years. Jada is now conquering the path of achieving a master's in social work while continuing her life's passion in supporting local youth of color in interpersonal violence prevention work. She sees herself as a passionate advocate towards a more ideal community where people can feel safe to love themselves and thus be able to love in liberation together.

Ash Ward (they/them) is a 22-year-old multiracial, bisexual, neurodivergent, non-binary person who studied Women, Gender, and Sexuality

Studies. They have been openly bisexual since childhood and began exploring their gender identity in 2021, during the COVID-19 pandemic. Ash has PTSD, ADHD, and depression and hates writing biographies because they don't know how to condense their identity into a palatable paragraph.

Yaiza (she/ella) is a 26-year-old Latina, originally from Cuba, bisexual, and cisgender. She is a recent college graduate currently living in the East Coast of the U.S. and works in a consulting company. She hopes to create positive change through emerging technology and is passionate about inclusion and diversity work. She also partakes in volunteering opportunities both at work and in her community.

ACKNOWLEDGMENTS

A special thank you to my incredible editing and transcribing team:

Micah Jones

Emilia Couture

Charlotte Gimlin

Blood, sweat, and tears. Maybe not the blood part, but there was plenty of sweat and lots of tears. And insomnia, a pandemic, my dad's decline with dementia. The tragic loss of UVA students Devin Chandler, Lavel Davis Jr., and D'Sean Perry. A hip injury that made it painful to sit and write. Menopause. Teaching and having a family. It is astonishing how difficult it is to get a book done. Despite all of the struggles, it has been such an incredible ride.

Three things motivated the creation of this book. My former editor at Routledge, the fantastic Heather Evans, was looking for someone to write about bisexuality. Second, many of my students were writing about being bisexual and revealed multiple challenges and isolation. And third, my own bisexuality. Producing this book was life changing as I discovered more of my own truth.

The project took off with my review of a proposal for Routledge by Rob Cohen, the host of *Two Bi Guys*. In the proposal, he mentioned a class called Bisexuality from Margin to Center. I searched online and learned it was taught by Tania Israel at UC Santa Barbara. Was this *THE* Tania Israel? Who went to high school with my sister Kiki and together they were in a production of *The Crucible*? Whose dad was a China historian like my dad and spent time at my house? It turned out it was *THE* Tania who was writing, teaching, and did a TedTalk about bisexuality! Tania agreed to be interviewed and connected me with River McMican at the Bisexual Resource Center. I reached out to Rob Cohen, who introduced me to Shiri Eisner and ABilly Jones-Hennin and his husband Cris. ABilly linked me to Loraine Hutchins, and the wonderful Dani Rose hooked me up with Wolf Hudson. It was so cool to watch this network build and meet these extraordinary people. I totally fangirled with all of you! I feel so much gratitude for your shared wisdom, thoughtful insight, and your endless efforts advocating for bisexual people. This book would not exist without you all. I am so sad, ABilly, that you are not with us anymore and that you couldn't see the final product, but you will forever be a part of me.

Thank you, my incredible students, for trusting me with your life stories. I feel so lucky to learn from so many cool people. So grateful to all of the contributors, for your courage to speak your truth in a world full of bi-erasure. This book wouldn't exist without any of you either!

I feel such gratitude for Janis Luna and Bianca Laureano and look up to both of you. You are always in my corner and never stop answering my texts or emails.

A specific shout out to Emilia Couture and Katelyn Friedline, for writing chapters in this book and bringing your own lived expertise to the pages.

Micah Jones, thank you so much for your editing expertise, friendship, laughter, and love. I am so lucky to know you. It was almost like doing *The Edge of Sex* together again!

To my former editor Heather Evans, thank you for supporting my ideas and handing me off to my new editor Julia Giordano, who is incredibly kind and patient, just like you Heather!

To Chappell Roan, your career skyrocketed during my grueling completion of this manuscript, and your amazing music motivated and inspired me to dance through to the finish line! Thank you!

I truly needed my amazing friends and family to finish this book. Thank you to my tiny yoga Zoom family, Amanda Topping, Kristen McCurry, and my sister Robyn, for the hour-long support sessions each week before we actually do any yoga. Andre Cavalcante, Jenifer Marshall, Bonnie Hagerman, and Bridget Walsh, thanks for continuously asking how the book was going and for being my friends. Thank you, Benjamin Randolph, for actively listening so well when I monologue on our daily walks. Kiki, Joe, Robyn, and Mom, I love you all dearly. Mom—you are my hero. I wish Dad could really be cognizant, but his enthusiastic response every time I tell him I am working on a book, because it is new to him each time I say it, is pretty endearing. Andy and Elena, your unconditional love and patience has not been taken for granted. I am so proud of you Elena, but the best reward has been you telling me that you are proud of me too. I love you both so much.

INTRODUCTION

Bisexual visibility has grown significantly through activism, social media, and entertainment over the last few decades. On television, multiple bisexual characters have appeared on such shows as *Will and Grace*, *How to Get Away with Murder*, *My Crazy Ex-Girlfriend*, *Sex Education*, *Euphoria*, *Queen Sugar*, *Grey's Anatomy*, *A Million Little Things*, *Brooklyn Nine-Nine*, *Shitts Creek*, *Good Trouble*, and, most recently, *911*. Although we see an expansion in representation, rarely do these characters actually use the term *bisexual* or discuss *being* bisexual. Ideally this would not be an issue, if only bisexuality was normalized, fully accepted as a valid sexuality and the harm caused by bisexual erasure did not exist. Increased visibility is just not enough.

Even though the acronym LGBTQ+ is commonplace in social media, academics, and our cultural discourse, the "B" is regularly misrepresented, misunderstood, or simply not included.[1] It is estimated that bisexual identities total over 52% of the LGB community, however, they are labelled "the invisible majority" due to bisexual erasure, biphobia, and monosexism.[2] Bisexual people are regularly told they must be confused, are going through a phase, are transphobic and problematic for "perpetuating the gender binary," or are using the label "bisexual" as a stepping stone to coming out as gay.[3] Their sexual identity is commonly stereotyped as unreal, greedy, experimenting, having difficulty with monogamy, hypersexual, or extremely promiscuous.[4] The legitimacy of this identity is frequently questioned or denied outright by both straight and queer people alike, which is often described as a "double discrimination" or a "double closet" that "leads some to hide their bisexual identity, thereby 'erasing' their specific sexual identification."[5] In addition, much of sex education in America is so lacking in LGBTQ+ inclusivity that queer people in general get little to no information. Moreover, sexualities

DOI: 10.4324/9781003242659-1

scholarship has historically marginalized bisexual people by conducting research to disprove the validity of bisexuality or underrepresenting the bisexual experience and perpetuating invisibility.[6]

What research does exist often fails to capture the nuance of bisexuality by focusing mostly on white, cisgender, young, able-bodied people; particularly cisgender women. Robyn Ochs and H. Sharif Williams assert in their book on bisexual men, "People with identities that are non-binary or non-monosexual are simply not seen enough, and men are even more underrepresented, even among bisexuals."[7] This is even worse for bisexual people of color, who make up more than half of the bisexual community.[8] As Ghabrial and Ross found a

> Scarcity of intersectional research that attends to the specific needs and experiences of BPOC [bisexual people of color] . . . the available research often does not include adequate proportions of people of color, or groups all races/ethnicities together, neglecting the impact that unique cultural identities can have on bisexual identity development and well-being.[9]

Lim and Hewitt second this by noting that the participant pools are all White and the "discussions pertaining to ethnoracial identity and or/racism are largely absent."[10] What other issues are not being addressed about people of color who are bisexual? What might non-binary or transgender bisexual people encounter when navigating bisexual erasure? How do sexism, racism, transphobia, or ableism intersect with bisexual erasure and biphobia? What are the experiences of older adults who are bisexual?

The aim of this book is to expand the discourse about bisexuality and to amplify the voices that are traditionally not heard. Bisexual people are not a monolithic group but rather full of multiple intersecting identities beyond the typical dominant culture representation. In addition, that the experience of bi-erasure, biphobia, and monosexism can be impacted by other forms of oppression and intersectionality—a theory of oppression and framework created and expanded on by Black feminisms in the United States—is essential. The intersection of biphobia, bi-erasure, and monosexism with sexism, racism, ableism, ageism, and transphobia is explored throughout the book. Furthermore, personal narratives and interviews in each chapter enhance this intersectional analysis and work to dismantle the dehumanization of bisexual erasure, move beyond the binaries of gender and sexuality, and increase visibility of multiple bisexualities. These voices are the core of this book, as they reveal the realities of bisexuality and how joy and resilience are a key component to fighting these oppressions.

Multiple Bisexual Identities

The history of the term bisexual (addressed in more detail in Chapter 1: "What Even Is Bisexuality?") starts with a few early definitions, such as simply "attraction to both men and women." This had its limitations given how it was rooted in a gender binary and a more inclusive description evolved: "attraction to one's own gender and another gender"[11] and then more recently "attraction to *two or more genders*."[12] The definition commonly used today comes from bisexual activist Robyn Ochs: "the potential to be attracted romantically and/ or sexually to people of more than one gender, not necessarily simultaneously, in the same way or to the same degree."[13] In many bisexual communities and online spaces the label Bi+ has emerged, which is used as an umbrella term to include not only bisexual but other multi-sexual identities[14] such as *pansexual* (attraction to people *regardless* of gender), *omnisexual* (attraction to all genders) and *polysexual* (attraction to multiple genders but not necessarily all genders).[15] Another umbrella term that has recently emerged is *m-spec*—"multigender attracted spectrum"—which "covers all of the various identities where their attraction is not limited to a single gender."[16]

These umbrella terms allow for differences in *sexual orientation*— attraction that includes the desire to have sexual contact with a person—and *romantic orientation*—attraction that fuels the desire to have an emotional connection based on personal traits and character.[17] Typically, the dominant culture expectation is that the two orientations always equally overlap, but often they do not. For example, a person can be *biromantic* (romantic attraction to two or more genders) and *asexual* (experiencing little to no sexual attraction/sexual desire or the need to be sexually partnered). As porn star Wolf Hudson discusses in Chapter 7: "Pornography and Sex Work," as a cisgender man he is *hetero-romantic* (romantic attraction to and having relationships with women) and bisexual, which means being sexual with more genders but not having romantic connections with them.

It is important to note that there is much debate between the label *bisexual* versus *pansexual*. Some people use the terms interchangeably, where others may distinguish bisexual as very different from pansexual. Many of the personal narratives in this book are from people who are bisexual, but some are pansexual. Some are exploring what fits best, while others feel that pansexual is more who they are but it is easier to publicly define themselves as bisexual. The distinctions that people may make between these two terms is explored further in Chapter 1: "What is Bisexuality?" in an interview with sex educator Bianca Laureano. Others may argue that identifying as *bisexual* is inherently transphobic, which will be challenged in Chapter 3: "Gender-diverse Identities." The purpose of this book is not to use one specific definition throughout but to acknowledge that there are multiple bisexualities and it is a very individualistic decision how to self-identify. As Tania Israel writes in her article about being both biracial and bisexual,

> *Only recently have I started to emerge into an experience of my ethnicity that seems internally derived rather than externally imposed. My identities intersect to reveal the complexity of bi-ness, the impact of*

> *community at various points in development, and the importance of*
> *self-definition. My understanding of these intersections continues to grow*
> *as I bring them into a professional context.*[18]

Creating a space for self-definition allows for the fluidity of sexuality, and bisexuality is no stranger to this fluidity. Regardless of how someone defines their bisexuality or pansexuality, what is shared under the Bi+ umbrella are the various challenges and struggles of erasure, biphobia, and monosexism.

Bisexual Erasure, Biphobia, Monosexism, and the Obsession with Binaries

The Gay and Lesbian Alliance Against Defamation (GLAAD) defines *bisexual erasure* as "the existence or legitimacy of bisexuality (either in general or in regard to an individual) is questioned or denied outright."[19] Another component is *biphobia*, the "prejudice, fear or hatred directed towards bisexual people,"[20] which intersects regularly with bisexual erasure. These are integral parts of *monosexism*, which Shiri Eisner describes as "a social structure operating through the presumption that everyone is, or should be, mono-sexual, a structure that privileges monosexuality and monosexual people, and that systematically punishes people who are non-monosexual."[21] Eisner contends that both monosexism and biphobia are heavily disputed concepts even within bisexual activism and research. Some theorists proclaim that bisexual people do not actually suffer from a unique form of oppression that is separate from homophobia.[22] As Eisner asserts,

> *In fact, very often, simply raising the issue of biphobia (in any setting) is perceived as an affront to gay and lesbian politics and is ridiculed, often with the ubiquitous 'bisexuals are privileged' argument . . . to claim that bisexuals do not experience oppression differently from gays or lesbians is to subsume bisexual experience into homosexuality, thus eliminating its unique existence. For if no unique bisexual experience is to be found, then certainly the category of bisexuality itself is null. The second half of the argument ('privilege') acknowledges the existence of bisexuality, but connects it with the notion of privilege and thus oppressor status, again nullifying the unique oppression that bisexuals experience and the need for specific attention to it.*[23]

Often times biphobia is described as interpersonal behaviors fueled by stereotypes, such as telling someone who is bisexual that it is just a phase, that they need to decide what their "true sexuality" is, assuming that two men who are involved are both gay, or if a man and woman are married that they are both straight. Eisner argues that monosexism and biphobia are not just about personal attitudes or mistreatments but are part of a system of oppression "originating from and upholding heteropatriarchal structures."[24] Recognizing monosexism as a form of oppression enables us to "read between the lines of culture in order to delineate where it is that bisexuality is forbidden, denied, or erased, and why."[25]

A component of monosexism is Western culture's obsession with binaries, many of which have historically oppressed the queer community, such as male/female, man/woman, straight/gay, cisgender/transgender, monogamous/non-monogamous.[26] Barker and Iantaffi, in their powerful publication *Life Isn't Binary*, address this further by stating,

> *When we turn to the wider world, we see a good deal of binary thinking. Politicians and journalists tend to frame everything as a 'debate' between two sides. People divide into 'us' and 'them' in conflicts at every level from the micro to the macro. Boundaries and borders are drawn between inside and outside.*[27]

Autumn Elizabeth found through her research on the impact of binaries that this "imposes multiple vectors of oppression on many people in the queer community. Given the constraints of these binary systems of thought, it is no surprise that new concepts and identities challenge these dualities."[28] American society is so invested in the binary of straight/gay that bisexuality is a threat to many people's world order, causing doubt and discomfort "which as humans we frequently mistake for danger and lack of safety."[29] This also impacts what it means to be out as a bisexual person. As Barker and Iantaffi explain,

> *Being out seems to become almost irrelevant, especially if someone is in a relationship with a person of the 'opposite gender.' No matter how open about their sexuality a bi person is, they tend to be read as straight or gay by the world around them on the basis of their relationships, or as not having a sexuality at all if they're single and do not 'appear gay'. Of course, 'appearing gay' is often another coded way to indicate not being gender conforming in some way.*[30]

This mindset reinforces distrust of bisexual people because they might "turn" to either side of being straight or gay. This is often confirmed when there is a break-up and someone "turns" to the "opposite gender." This can be considered a threat instead of just being a reality of bisexuality.[31] The "end point" of a relationship is also used to define bisexual people in relationships, as Michael Amherst claims,

> *It is all too easy for bisexuality to be erased when in a long-term relationship. At this point the confusion or fluidity of earlier seems moot.*

> *An individual is presumed to have reconciled to whichever gender they are in a relationship with now. This is coupled with a presumption that any previous relationship with the other gender was merely a phase, now left behind. This is to mistake a settled life and a stable relationship for an abandonment of bisexuality.*[32]

There is a refusal for many to recognize sexual fluidity, because it means denying the binary of straight and gay.[33] This disbelief in bisexuality pressures people to prove their identities against a heteronormative benchmark that makes their sexuality a public platform for debate.[34] Furthermore, they are often expected to quantify the degree to which they are bisexual by explaining their attractions as percentages of gay versus straight. For Amherst, there is comfort and safety in using the label *queer* (an umbrella term used to express a spectrum of identities and orientations that are counter to the mainstream), because it does not force bisexual people to have to constantly justify their existence.

The binaries of sex and gender also impact the understanding of bisexuality. *Sex*, which is assigned at birth and based on a person's biological makeup, creates the binary of male/female. *Gender* refers to the societally enforced roles and behaviors associated with male/female, which is the masculine/feminine binary. Even though these binaries have constantly been challenged in recent years, stereotypical masculine and feminine expectations still are prevalent and require navigation. Dominant culture masculinity reinforces anti-femininity and homophobia, as men's sexuality is expected to not be associated with anything feminine, like having sex with men.[35] Stereotypical expectations of feminine sexuality are mired in the male gaze, where women are positioned as objects of heterosexual male desire. As Amherst states,

> Social attitudes towards bisexuality are starkly different, none more so than the different responses to men and women. The 'taint of homosexuality' often means that even a single same-sex encounter can be levelled against a man as proof that he is 'really' gay. A man who has debased himself by not conforming to the masculine paradigm is forever other. On the other hand, a woman is often perceived to be performing same-sex activity for the titillation of a male subject. Our society's intrinsic misogyny means her sexuality, her very agency, can only be seen through this prism. She demeans herself, not through same-sex desire, but only when she dismisses men altogether.[36]

Clearly the investment in these binaries only perpetuate biphobia, bi-erasure, and monosexism, so it is imperative to move beyond binaries to fully understand, explore, and support the multiple realities of bisexuality.

Another challenge is that much of sexuality and queer studies is a space where biphobia, bi-erasure, and monosexism are often perpetuated. As

Hemmings contends, bisexuality's invisibility "is fundamental to ensuring that lesbians and gay men remain the *de facto* subjects of queer studies."[37] Not only does bi-erasure in general play a role, but bisexuality is often defined as "pre-oedipal potential or androgyny, rather than sexual identity—to understandings of how a gendered queer subject position is formed."[38] Mosely et al. assert that in scholarly research "bisexuality is further made invisible and erased through monosexism, or the tendency to privilege attraction to one sex or gender, while discrediting non-monosexual identities including bisexual identities."[39] In addition, a review of sexualities scholarship from 1970–2015 revealed "uneven" representation of bisexuality in the literature. For example, biphobia received far less attention than homophobia or transphobia. Furthermore, actual biphobia of the researchers impacts the research itself since they are not free from the influence of monosexism in American culture.[40] Historically research was conducted by combining all identities under the title of LGBTQ but, as Rodriguez affirms, "when bisexuals are not separated out in investigative data or critical analysis, we simply disappear."[41] When mainstream focus is actually on bisexual identities, much of the research addresses HIV and AIDS transmission, thus "amplifying heterosexual and lesbian anxieties about sexual contamination caused by border crossers."[42] More recently research has improved, particularly work published in the *Journal of Bisexuality*, but there is clearly a need for more inclusive work on bisexuality.

Bi-Erasure, Biphobia, and Monosexism in Queer Spaces

The personal narratives and interviews in this book reveal a common experience of bi-erasure, biphobia, and monosexism in queer spaces. Queer communities often show some acceptance for sexual fluidity, but even that fluidity tends to be on a binary of straight and gay. Bisexual individuals are often made to question whether they are "queer enough," which leads to alienation and overall erasure. There is often pressure to explain themselves, particularly when they are in straight-looking relationships that somehow eradicate their bisexual or queer identity. It is important to emphasize that this does not mean queer communities are inherently biphobic and are more so than heterosexual society but that the impact of experiencing the discrimination in what is perceived as a safe space can be worse. The feeling of rejection can be central to the development of bisexual identities and can add to the potential experience of struggle.[43]

Julia Shaw's work presents the long history of biphobia and bi-erasure in gay and lesbian communities. Many queer activists have long perceived bisexual people as "appearing heterosexual by day and homosexual by night" and were privileged by a "sexual camouflage" because of their supposed ability to blend into both homosexual and heterosexual spaces.[44] Shaw critiques the history of Gay Liberation Front (GLF) organizations who were often portrayed as "radically inclusive" and "proudly having a rainbow philosophy" but didn't "live up to its rainbow image, especially when it came to bisexual people."[45] GLF politics equated bisexuality with different gender attraction instead of same gender attraction, which was perceived as "regressive politics" and associated with heterosexual politics.[46] As Shaw asserts, "Here bisexual people were being edged out of the organization rather than being absorbed by it. Bisexual people were seen as sleeping with the enemy."[47] Shaw partly faults the Kinsey scale (this is discussed further in Chapter 1: "What Even is Bisexuality?") for using language like "predominantly heterosexual, but more than incidentally homosexual," which was weaponized against bisexuality because it was seen as still linked to heterosexuality.[48]

With the start of the AIDS epidemic in the 1980s, bisexuality became particularly stigmatized in dominant culture because of the fear of bisexual men spreading HIV, specifically to heterosexual women.[49] This enabled some community building with the queer community since there was a common cause to fight against, but for bisexual women, this was not the case. The growth of the feminist movement meant for some a kind of lesbian feminism that did not include bisexual women because they were "perceived as a threat to the feminist cause."[50] This led to the creation of a bisexual movement, including organizing and holding conferences that enabled spaces to address the unique needs of bisexual people; however, this history still contributes to the biphobia, bi-erasure, and monosexism that can exist in queer spaces today. For more on the creation of the bisexual movement, see Chapter 1: "What Even Is Bisexuality?"

The Harm Caused by Bi-erasure, Biphobia, and Monosexism

There are multiple ways bi-erasure, biphobia, and monosexism cause harm, including higher rates of mental distress, suicide, and sexual and relationship violence, not feeling a part of either straight or queer communities, and discrimination in the workplace.[51] Barker and and Iantaffi argue, "even when people are open about their bisexuality, they still encounter marginalization and often bullying in both straight and gay environments. This can lead to feeling a lack of belonging, until they are able to access bisexual or queer communities, and a lack of safety."[52] The exposure to biphobia and bi-erasure can also result in anxiety and depression with bisexual people exhibiting "higher or equivalent rates in comparison to lesbian/gay people."[53] In addition, bisexual people are at a higher risk of experiencing sexual violence, with one study showing that 46% of bisexual women report being rape survivors, followed by 17% of heterosexual women and 13% of lesbians.[54] Furthermore, 75% of bisexual women in the United States experienced other forms of sexual violence.[55] Shiri Eisner sums up these harmful realities when they state,

> *Monosexism kills. Biphobia kills. Bisexual people commit suicide, bisexual people get sick, bisexual people lose our homes, our families, our friends, our communities, our support, our jobs, our money, our education; bisexual people suffer violence and sexual violence; we are beaten, brutalized, bullied, bashed, raped, and sexually assaulted; we get STIs, no information, and no treatment; we get exploited, alienated, marginalized, disempowered, dismissed, erased, derided. And after all of this, we are told that it's all in our heads, that monosexism and biphobia do not exist, that those problems are our personal problems: We are pathologized. Our experiences, our lives, our pain, and our oppression are written out and wiped clean of history, culture, and community. But this is not our "personal" problem, this is not "just in our heads." It is not a figment of the imagination. It is real, and we see it and feel it in our bones, as we struggle to survive and as we struggle to live.[56]*

Chapter 10: "Mental Health Issues and The Impact of Violence" explores these complexities in more depth.

Celebrating Multiple Bisexual Identities in a World of Erasure

The following pages include an intersectional examination of the exclusion, discrimination, and misunderstanding of bisexuality along with many examples of joy and resilience. The first chapter, "What Even is Bisexuality?" consists of a brief history of the term *bisexual* along with separate conversations with professor Tania Israel, bi porn star Wolf Hudson, and AASECT Certified Sexuality Educator Bianca Laureano, all of whom explore the meaning of gender, sexuality, bisexuality, pansexuality, and intersections of oppression. Chapter 2: "The Joy of Bisexuality" addresses the power of exploring bisexual joy and resilience. The importance of this is emphasized by Tania Israel when she declares,

> *If we want to engender bisexual visibility, community and pride, we need to speak, not only of invisibility, discrimination and health disparities, we must also shine a light on bisexual history, community and resources. If we want to celebrate bisexuality, we need to know about the positive and powerful aspects of it.[57]*

The rest of the book consists of ten topical chapters, including gender-diverse identities; cisgender women and femininities; cisgender men and masculinities; media representation; pornography and sex work; different kinds of relationships including consensual non-monogamy; kink and

BDSM; mental health and violence; disabilities; and aging and older adults. Each chapter comprises an analysis of the topic designed to challenge biphobia, bi-erasure, and monosexism. In addition, personal narratives and one-on-one conversations are included in every chapter from a total of 34 bisexual and pansexual people, the majority of whom are people of color, people with disabilities, trans and non-binary people, survivors, or of different generations. These powerful written creations and perspectives enhance this intersectional analysis, create a platform for the voices typically not heard, and allow for the celebration of the resistance, resilience, and joy of multiple bisexual identities. Recognize the validity of bisexuality, move beyond the binaries, and witness the authenticity of the colorful spectrum of bisexual people.

Notes

1 Nikki Hayfield, "Introduction," in *Bisexual and Pansexual Identities: Exploring and Challenging Invisibility and Invalidation* (New York: Routledge, 2021).
2 Movement Advancement Project, "Invisible Majority: The Disparities Facing Bisexual People and How to Remedy Them," (September 2016), 1, www.lgbtmap.org/file/invisible-majority.pdf.
3 Movement Advancement Project, "Invisible Majority," 5.
4 Movement Advancement Project, "Invisible Majority," 5.
5 Katheryn Morrison, Jordan Gruenhage and Cory Pedersen, "Challenging Binaries by Saying Good Bi: Perceptions of Bisexual Men's Identity Legitimacy," *Journal of Bisexuality*, Vol. 16, No. 3 (2016), 361.
6 Surya Monro, Sally Hines and Antony Osborne, "Is Bisexuality Invisible? A Review of Sexuality Scholarship 1970–2015," *The Sociological Review*, Vol. 65, No. 4 (2017), 663–681.
7 Robyn Ochs and H. Sharif Williams, "Introduction," in *Recognize: The Voices of Bisexual Men* (Boston: Bisexual Resource Center, 2014), xvii.
8 Monica A. Ghabrial and Lori E. Ross, "Representation and Erasure of Bisexual People of Color: A Content Analysis of Quantitative Bisexual Mental Health Research," *Psychology of Sexual Orientation and Gender Diversity*, Vol. 5, No. 2 (2018), 132–142.
9 Ghabrial and Ross, "Representation and Erasure of Bisexual People of Color," 140.
10 G. Lim and B. Hewitt, "Discrimination at the Intersections: Experiences of Community and Belonging in Nonmonosexual Persons of Color," *Journal of Bisexuality*, Vol. 18, No. 2 (2018), 318.
11 "A Short History of the Word 'Bisexual,'" *Stonewall.org*, January 13, 2022, www.stonewall.org.uk/about-us/news/short-history-word-bisexuality.
12 "A Short History of the Word 'Bisexual.'"
13 Robyn Ochs, "Bisexual: A Few Quotes from Robyn Ochs," https://robynochs.com/bisexual/.

14 "Bi+ Info: What It Means to Be a B(ee)," Bisexual Resource Center, https://biresource.org/bi-info/.

15 Vaneet Mehta, "Introduction," in *Bisexual Men Exist: A Handbook for Bisexual, Pansexual and M-Spec Men* (London: Jessica Kingsley Publishers, 2023), 11.

16 Mehta, "Introduction," 10.

17 "Asexuality, Attraction and Romantic Orientation," LGBT Resource Center UNC Chapel Hill, https://lgbtq.unc.edu/resources/exploring-identities/asexuality-attraction-and-romantic-orientation/.

18 Tania Israel, "Conversations, Not Categories: The Intersectional of Biracial and Bisexual Identities," *Women and Therapy*, Vol. 27, No. 1–2 (2004), 181.

19 "Erasure of Bisexuality," Gay and Lesbian Alliance Against Defamation Website, www.glaad.org.

20 "Bisexual FAQ," Human Rights Campaign Website, www.hrc.org/resources/bisexual-faq.

21 Shiri Eisner, "Monosexism and Biphobia," in *Bi: Notes for a Bisexual Revolution* (Berkeley, CA: Seal Press, 2013), 63.

22 Eisner, "Monosexism and Biphobia," 59.

23 Eisner, "Monosexism and Biphobia," 59–60.

24 Eisner, "Monosexism and Biphobia," 63.

25 Eisner, "Monosexism and Biphobia," 63.

26 Autumn Elizabeth, "Challenging the Binary: Sexual Identity That Is Not Duality," *Journal of Bisexuality*, Vol. 13, No. 3 (2013), 329–337.

27 Meg-John Barker and Alex Iantaffi, "Introduction," in *Life Isn't Binary: On Being Both, Beyond and In-Between* (London: Jessica Kingsley Publishers, 2019), 16.

28 Elizabeth, "Challenging the Binary," 330.

29 Barker and Iantaffi, "Introduction," 27.

30 Barker and Iantaffi, "Introduction," 25.

31 Barker and Iantaffi, "Introduction," 26.

32 Michael Amherst, *Go the Way Your Blood Beats: On Truth, Bisexuality and Desire* (London: Repeater Books, 2018), 11, Kindle.

33 Amherst, *Go the Way Your Blood Beats*, 1.

34 Amherst, *Go the Way Your Blood Beats*, 1.

35 Chris Kilmartin and Andrew P. Smiler, *The Masculine Self* (New York: Sloan Publishing, 2015), 222.

36 Amherst, *Go the Way Your Blood Beats*, 2.

37 Clare Hemmings, "What's in a Name? Bisexuality, Transnational Sexuality Studies and Western Colonial Legacies," *The International Journal of Human Rights*, Vol. 11, No. 1–2 (2007), 14.

38 Hemmings, "What's in a Name?" 14.

39 Della V. Mosley, Kirsten A. Gonzalez, Roberto L. Abreu and Nahal C. Kaivan, "Unseen and Underserved: A Content Analysis of Wellness

Support Services for Bi + People of Color and Indigenous People on U.S. Campuses," *Journal of Bisexuality*, Vol. 19, No. 2 (2019), 278.

40 Monro et al., "Is Bisexuality Invisible?" 663–681.

41 Juana Maria Rodriguez, "Queer Politics, Bisexual Erasure: Sexuality at the Nexus of Race, Gender, and Statistics," *Lambda Nordica*, Vol. 21, No. 1–2 (2018), 172.

42 Rodriguez, "Queer Politics, Bisexual Erasure," 172.

43 Shiri Eisner, *Bi: Notes for a Bisexual Revolution* (Berkeley, CA: Seal Press, 2013).

44 Julia Shaw, "Our History," in *Bi: The Hidden Culture, History, and Science of Bisexuality* (New York: Abrams Press, 2022), 43.

45 Shaw, "Our History," 43.

46 Martha Robinson Rhodes, "Bisexuality, Multiple-Gender-Attraction, and Gay Liberation Politics in the 1970s," *Twentieth Century British History*, Vol. 32, No. 1 (March 2021), 119–142.

47 Shaw, "Our History," 44.

48 Shaw, "Our History," 44.

49 Shaw, "Our History," 44.

50 Shaw, "Our History," 45.

51 Movement Advancement Project, "Invisible Majority."

52 Meg-John Barker and Alex Iantaffi, "Chapter 1: Sexualities," in *Life Isn't Binary: On Being Both, Beyond, and In-Between* (London: Jessica Kingsley Publishers, 2019), 23.

53 Lori E. Ross, Travis Salway, Lesley Tarasoff, Jenna MacKay, Blake Hawkins and Charles Fehr, "Prevalence of Depression and Anxiety Among Bisexual People Compared to Gay, Lesbian, and Heterosexual Individuals: A Systematic Review and Meta-Analysis," *The Journal of Sex Research*, Vol. 55 (2018), 435.

54 Movement Advancement Project, "Invisible Majority," ii.

55 Movement Advancement Project, "Invisible Majority," 20.

56 Shiri Eisner, "Monosexism and Biphobia," in *Bi: Notes for a Bisexual Revolution* (Berkeley, CA: Seal Press, 2013), 64.

57 Tania Israel, "Concluding Remarks: A Perspective on Envisioning Bisexuality as Inclusive, Celebratory and Liberatory," in *Bisexuality: Theory, Research and Recommendations for the Invisible Sexuality*, ed. D. Joye Swan and Shani Habibi (New York: Springer, 2018), 192.

1

WHAT EVEN IS BISEXUALITY?

A Brief Intersectional Account of Historical and Contemporary Perspectives

The History of the Term Bisexual

Over the centuries there have been multiple accounts of sexual interactions that are considered bisexual, but the term *bisexuality* as we know it today was not commonly used until the early 20th century. In the mid-19th century, the European study of anatomy and physiology used *bisexuality* to describe "forms of life that are sexually undifferentiated or thought to exhibit characteristics of both sexes"[1] but not to define a sexual orientation. During the late 19th century, European and Northern American white, cisgender male researchers perceived sexuality as a perversion or an immoral act medically diagnosed as an "innate morbid condition."[2] These researchers quantified same-gender loving sexual contact as an illness and a crime.[3] In his 1886 work *Psychopathia Sexualis*, Austrian psychiatrist Rich Von Kraff-Ebbing identified a "sexual condition" called *psychosexual hermaphroditism*, a diagnosis for those who were either sexually attracted to and/or were sexual with "both sexes" (the problem with the language of "both sexes" or "both genders" will be addressed more in Chapter 3: "Gender-diverse Identities").[4] British sexologist and eugenicist Havelock Ellis followed suit by supporting this theory in his work *Studies in the Psychology of Sex*, a six-volume series first published in 1897.[5] For both Kraff-Ebbing and Ellis, the explanation of homosexuality and bisexuality fell under "inversion theory" and Ellis's second volume of the series was entitled *Sexual Inversion*. As Shiri Eisner explains, inversion theory meant "gay and lesbians were 'inverts'—people who were physically male or female, but internally the 'opposite sex.' Same-gender desire was explained as latent heterosexuality: gays and lesbians were really just heterosexual people born in

DOI: 10.4324/9781003242659-2

the wrong body."[6] Marjorie Garber describes this as an understanding that "the male invert's feminine side desired men; the female invert's masculine side desired women. Thus, human sexuality could still be imagined according to a heterosexual model."[7]

Contrary to the times, Ellis was actually not interested in demonizing queerness and addressed sexual inversion as a "curious and unthreatening variance of human sexuality—which is what made his book scandalous at the time."[8] He felt homosexuality should be "treated as a natural phenomenon and not as a sin or disease" and his work "aimed to portray sexual inverts as normal individuals and not as degenerates."[9] Given how controversial his work was, he faced many challenges trying to get his book published. He was, however, credited as one of the first to use the term *bisexuality* as a sexual orientation in his 1927 edition when he claimed: "Those persons who are attracted to both sexes are now usually termed 'bisexual,' a more convenient term than 'psycho-sexual hermaphrodite,' which was formerly used."[10]

Even if Ellis was not vilifying queerness, his work tied in closely to his scientific beliefs in eugenics, a movement that focused on hereditary traits as determining certain qualities and behaviors in people. Ellis believed that sexuality was a biologically determined trait and that people were born bisexual,[11] however, he was invested in eugenics' racist, sexist, classist, cissexist,[12] and ableist fundamental values that studied "how to arrange reproduction within a human population to increase the occurrence of heritable characteristics regarded as 'desirable.'"[13] It may seem out of place to discuss eugenics in a book about bisexuality, but it is actually an important component of an intersectional understanding of how sexual "deviance" was part of a white supremacy agenda. For example, eugenicist R.W. Shufeldt wrote about racial purity, but he also researched queerness, which he described as both "inversion" and "perversion." Like Ellis, Shufeldt believed that sexuality was hardwired into the body and could not be changed, but he also believed that queerness could be prevented by closely controlling heterosexuality. He argued in one of his papers that America "will continue to breed millions of sexual perverts and inverts—psychopathic types—just so long as any ignorant priest, justice of the peace or other party, is permitted to give people permission to breed them."[14] In every way eugenicists believed that a white "racial purity" could be obtained through controlled "breeding"; so could heterosexuality.

Many American eugenicists also linked sexual degeneracy to the perceived inferiority of people of color and "historically amplified cultural anxieties about race and sex, yoked these anxieties together, criminalized Blackness as sexual non-normativity, and forcibly ungendered Black flesh to facilitate white self-definition."[15] Indigenous people—seen for centuries as "savages" and "designated as inherently sinful and dirty"[16]—were also targeted. Many indigenous cultures did not have gendered norms or sexual practices that coincided with the European settler mentality, and the label *berdache* was often used "to mark Indigenous difference" in order "to teach both colonial and Indigenous subjects the relational terms of colonial *hetero-patriarchy*."[17] Balestrery describes this as "compounded colonization," when sexologists "intertwine theories of racial degeneracy and sexual pathology, theories bound up in racism, homophobia, and heterosexism."[18] Those who did not fit in the dominant culture norms of cisgender, heterosexual, white or able-bodied were "labeled in some form as degenerate and stigmatized, thereby construed as a threat to the propagation and progress of the human population."[19]

By 1915, the meaning of bisexuality had shifted to include a "combination of masculinity and femininity in an individual—psychical rather than physical traits—and had also come to signify a sexual attraction to individuals of both sexes."[20] Sigmund Freud is credited as one of the first to use the word *bisexuality* to describe sexual attraction, instead of just a physical or psychological state.[21] Even though Freud viewed bisexuality as an attraction to "both sexes," his analysis consisted of "bisexuality not being a stable, enduring sexual identity."[22] As Rapaport affirms,

> *For* Freud, the mental world of a European child was equivalent to that of a savage, that is, an African or American Indian native. A neurotic was conceptualized as a person who had not developed fully; hence, his world, too, was the same as the child's and the savage's. Homosexuality, as a developmental arrest, also represented lagging behind in evolutionary time. In short, anything that did not match the male European ideals of mastery, autonomy and rationality was associated with the primitive past, the childhood of the individual and the species.[23]

Once again, white scientists perpetuated their beliefs of the intersection between sexual deviance and racial inferiority. Stoute reveals that this was a common practice of psychoanalysts who often published with such language as "the 'Negroes' development is lower than the white race and . . . similar to those of the savage" and "their psychological activities are analogous with those of the child."[24]

Despite white scientists' racist interpretations of sexuality and infantilization of people of color, there are multiple accounts during this time of queer people of color although they often felt great pressure to hide these identities. Some famous examples of bisexual people of color include blues singers and performers Bessie Smith and Ma Rainey. Smith is described as being "unapologetically herself" and "drank and was open about her romantic relationships with both men and women."[25] Ma Rainey, who was married twice to men, had a few songs that referenced her bisexuality and being involved with women, in particular the 1928 song *Prove It on Me Blues*.[26]

By the time World War II ended, the popularity of eugenics waned, but racism still permeated the general discourse around "normal" sexuality. This was still a time of promoting dominant white sexuality and American citizenship, which was symbolized through the creation of two naked statues put on display in 1945 named "Norma" and "Normann." These statues revealed a man and woman that, As Carter contends, "represented an ideal of specifically heterosexual whiteness, not simply a statistical composite of the American people. The statues dramatize the connection between "normal" modes of erotic intimacy and important cultural meanings of 'whiteness . . .'"[27] Against this backdrop of white supremacy, Alfred Kinsey published research on bisexuality in the 1940s and 50s that "railed against the pathologization and the monosexual view of sexuality" and asserted that "all individuals are capable of a range of sexual interests and behaviors."[28]

Kinsey created a scale of sexual orientation from zero to six, zero being exclusively heterosexual and six exclusively homosexual. He argued against the binary of just heterosexual and homosexual, stating, "The world is not to be divided into sheep and goats. Not all things are black nor all things white"[29] and discovered that self-reported bisexual attraction and behavior was common.[30] Although this was revolutionary for the time, the scale is criticized for not ever using the term *bisexual*. Elia et al. argue that

> *The term* bisexual *or* bisexuality *never appears; it is everywhere (1–5) yet nowhere. Despite Kinsey's acknowledgement of bisexuality, his scale is yet another way bisexuality is erased—as ironic as this might seem given Kinsey's inclusive and nonjudgmental approach with people exhibited varied sexual behaviors.*[31]

He was also controversial because his subjects were mostly white people and "his data probably erred in the direction of the sexually active and adventurous. . . . Those most eager to talk about their sex lives—perhaps because they *had* sex lives—were probably overrepresented."[32] Regardless, Shaw affirms, "Kinsey flipped around sexual norms; instead of heterosexuality being the default, he thought that bisexuality was. . . . His approach changed the conversation about sexuality, and the significance of this shift didn't go unnoticed."[33]

The work of Kinsey did not automatically end the societal perception of queer sexualities as deviant and the Diagnostic and Statistical Manual of Mental Disorders had homosexuality as a diagnosable disorder until 1973.[34] Bisexuality did, however, start to slowly become part of the general discourse when LGBTQ activism began to flourish, but there were still struggles for bisexual people to feel included in both queer and straight communities. In 1978 psychiatrist Fritz Klein was credited as conducting groundbreaking research that was an expansion of the Kinsey Scale. He published *The*

Bisexual Option and the *Klein Grid* evolved from his support groups for bisexual men. According to Shaw, "While the Kinsey Scale was created to help scientists classify sexual behavior for research purposes, the Klein Grid was created for psychologists and their patients to help structure a conversation about sexuality."[35] The grid explores seven variables: sexual attraction, sexual behavior, sexual fantasies, emotional preference, social preference, het/homo lifestyle, and self-identification. Each person can determine how they feel about these variables in the past, present, or the ideal based on variations of attraction, such as "other sex only," "other sex mostly," "both sexes equally," "hetero only," "hetero mostly," "gay/lesbian somewhat more," etc.[36] Klein also founded the American Institute of Bisexuality and *Journal of Bisexuality*, which still conducts research on bisexuality today.

It is important to note that much of the history of the studies of bisexuality focuses on white, cisgender men as scientists, researchers and sexologists, without recognizing the work of women and people of color, let alone queer people. Bianca Laureano, in her new book *The People's Book of Human Sexuality: Expanding the Sexology Archive*, addresses this issue when she states:

> *It is unacceptable that the US sexuality field and its training programs rarely cite sexologists of Color. This is a dehumanizing practice, one that is violent through its erasure. This practice is corrected when relationships are prioritized with care. Yet, what has manifested are relationships of a select few scholars of Color; the idea that we are a checklist that once you have a Black queer scholar teaching or lecturing or on a panel you've built a relationship with Black queer community. This is part of the scam of white supremacy and settler colonialism.*[37]

An example of a researcher not often addressed in sexuality studies is June Dobbs Butts, a Black professor of psychology whose career started at Fisk University in 1950. Butts was a researcher who became the first Black sex therapist trained by Masters and Johnson in the 1970s. She also wrote four book chapters on human sexuality and "advocated honest discussion of topics like masturbation, bisexuality and gender reassignment."[38] Her work included content that promoted dialogue within Black communities about sex education, conversations about sexuality with children, safety during the AIDS epidemic, and the problematic reality of the lack of clinical and scientific research on Black sexuality.[39] In addition, she hosted a radio call-in show in Washington, wrote articles for magazines like *Jet* and *Ebony* and a column, *Our Sexual Health*, for *Essence* in the late 1970s.[40]

Today, the topic of bisexuality and the intersection of multiple identities and forms of oppression could not be addressed without the tireless work of activism. The activists of the 1970s fought against biphobia and bi-erasure's harmful impact, which led to the development of different organizations through the 1980s and 1990s, such as The New York Area Bisexual Network,

The National Bisexual Liberation Group, the San Francisco Bisexual Center, BiPOL, BiNET USA, and the Bi+ Resource Center. (See the resource section for more on these programs today.) As the HIV/AIDS epidemic devasted the LGBTQ community, advocacy included the work of bisexual activists, particularly since bisexual men where often unfairly blamed for the spread of HIV. *Newsweek* magazine in 1987 went so far as to call bisexual men "the ultimate pariahs" of the AIDS epidemic.[41] According to Eisner, the bisexual movement evolved as a feminist movement, with such activists as Maggie Rubenstein, Naomi Tucker, Lani Ka'ahumanu, and Loraine Hutchins (her interview is included in Chapter 12: "Aging and Older Adults") as leaders who "insisted on emphasizing the importance of feminism to the bisexual movement, as well as bisexuality's feminist potential."[42] These leaders fought to have bisexuality included in the discourse on gay and lesbian rights, and particularly in the 1990s multiple efforts were made to include representation of bisexual people in the gay and lesbian community, including the 1993 March on Washington for Lesbian, Gay and Bi Equal Rights and Liberation. Also in 1993, Ron Fox conducted the first large-scale research study on bisexuality.[43]

The Meaning of Bisexuality, Pansexuality, and More

Throughout contemporary bisexual activism the definition of bisexuality has been ever changing. As described in the introduction chapter, there is a history of defining bisexuality that has evolved into one that is more inclusive and not perpetuating the gender binary. One of the most popular definitions is from bisexual activist Robyn Ochs, who describes bisexuality as "the potential to be attracted romantically and/or sexually to people of more than one gender, not necessarily simultaneously, in the same way or to the same degree."[44] Eisner asserts that there is no one definition of bisexuality, since all the variations are still used today, but they emphasize the importance of Ochs's definition:

> *In a world in which bisexuality is usually very narrowly defined, many people who experience bisexual desire, and want to identify as bi, often feel afraid to start (or keep) identifying as such, as they feel as though they "don't qualify." The role that an enabling definition for bisexuality can fulfill to counter these feelings of internalized biphobia is invaluable—and I feel that Ochs's definition does just that. It reassures people that they are "allowed" to identify as bisexual if they wish to do so.*[45]

Moreover, umbrella terms such as Bi+ or m-spec—"multigender attracted spectrum"—allow for the inclusion of *pansexual* (attraction to people *regardless* of gender), *omnisexual* (attraction to all genders), and *polysexual* (attraction to multiple genders but not necessarily all genders).[46]

In order to examine the meaning of bisexuality and these labels even further, the following conversations allow for exploration of the significance of bisexual self-identity. First is a conversation with Professor Tania Israel, then bi porn star Wolf Hudson, and next Sex Educator Bianca Laureano, as they discuss their various definitions of and experiences with bisexuality. Bisexuality does not fit perfectly and neatly into one box but rather exists in a world of different histories and complexities often impacted by multiple forms of oppressions. The following interviews reveal how it is up to each individual to make sense of how bisexuality works best for them.

A Conversation with Tania Israel

LISA:
My first question is how do you define bisexuality for
yourself.

TANIA:
So, for me, bisexuality means that gender's not
the most important characteristic, in terms of my
romantic and sexual attractions to people.

L:
There seems to be a lot of debate around whether
people should just be using pansexuality so they're
not reinforcing a binary. Why does bisexuality fit
for you as far as an identity label?

T:
To me, bisexual doesn't mean that I think that
gender is binary. Bisexual is a term that came to
prominence before there was a lot of cultural conversation about non-binary gender, and so bisexual
was actually pretty revolutionary at the time, just
by saying that you could be attracted to more than
one gender. Just saying that dismantles binary gender in a lot of ways by saying that, you know, men
and women are not necessarily such completely different entities that you can only be attracted to
one. Bisexuality is a revolutionary term that's got
a lot of historical significance.
    It also is how I started identifying when I came
out in my twenties. Whatever identity label works
for people, whether it's bisexual or pansexual, or

something else, I think that bisexual is one of the few terms that people argue about what it means. We let people define their own identities in other ways, we don't say, oh, well if you're gay, then that means you must be happy. If someone says, I'm bisexual for someone else to say, well, then that means that you believe that gender is binary . . . I don't think that that's a useful argument or conversation to have. I think we accept the terms that people use to define their own sexual orientation.

L:

Regardless of label there are some universal experiences when it comes to biphobia and bi-erasure.

T:

Yeah, there's so much bi-erasure and bi-negativity out there. I would say it is impossible not to encounter it. Certainly, people assume my sexual orientation based on the gender of my partner when I'm in a relationship. People will assume that I am lesbian if I'm with a woman and straight if I'm with a man. That's all bi-erasure and involves a lot of just repeatedly coming out, in ways that monosexual people don't have to do.

One of the challenges is that when I've been in a relationship with a woman and people assume I'm lesbian, for me to object to that and say, "Oh, no, no, I'm bisexual," feels out of solidarity with a marginalized group. I find it doesn't feel that way if people assume I'm straight and I say, "oh no, I'm bisexual." That feels sort of more radical and like I'm aligning myself with marginalization and it feels braver in a way to do that. But no matter what, it's still bi-erasure and certainly there's bias. I face people having negative stereotypes, oversexualizing my bisexuality, like there's just a lot that I face.

L:

And bi-erasure is potentially happening in both queer spaces and non-queer spaces.

T:

Oh, unquestionably. In fact, I would say more so in queer spaces. It's not only that I encounter it more in queer spaces, but that it always feels more disappointing to experience it in queer spaces, because there's sort of a hope that that is my community and it will be accepting and embracing. And certainly, for lesbian and gay people, it's been such a protective factor against all of the negative outcomes that lesbian and gay people can otherwise have, that having that community is really important. It's really one of the hardest things, I think, for bisexual people is the isolation and the invisibility.

L:

Why is there such a lack of understanding bisexuality?

T:

We just assume that people are monosexual unless proven otherwise. Even if people state it, people assume that you are just in transition to another monosexual identity. There's certainly something where some lesbian and gay people identified as bisexual for whatever reasons that they did, and then later went on to identify as lesbian or gay, and saw that in their own history and generalized that trajectory to other people. So, they say, "I remember when I identified as bisexual and now, I identify as lesbian or gay." But there are also certainly people who identified as lesbian or gay and then later identify as bisexual.

There's a whole different journey that people are on and some, whenever they came out, just came out as bisexual and stayed that way, or came out as lesbian or gay and stayed that way. So, all of those things are a possibility. I think some of it is people generalizing from their own experience.

There is something also about how bisexual women were treated within lesbian communities. And certainly, sort of more political lesbian feminism in the seventies, there was a sort of more separatist take on things. Not just, "We need to be away from the patriarchy," but we need to be away from men in order to fully develop ourselves as women and not be influenced by the patriarchy. Also, we need to celebrate women and femininity and goddesses and, all the seventies stuff. For women to then say, actually I'm not just attracted to women, I'm also attracted to men, felt like a betrayal of the community, of the beliefs of the whole solidarity. Bisexuality sort of has a different role, I would say, in queer men's communities.

L:

It's interesting you talked about people coming out as gay or lesbian and then identifying as bisexual. You don't hear much about that.

T:

No, we don't hear much about it. There's that invisibility again. I also know plenty of people who are bisexual, when in a long-term monogamous relationship or a long-term relationship start to be identified as lesbian, gay, or heterosexual and it just gets too exhausting to keep objecting to it. I know lots of bisexual women who are in relationships with other women and now, are like, okay, well I'll just be a lesbian then, you know? They still fit the definition of bisexual. It's not like they're not bisexual anymore, it's just swimming upstream and it gets exhausting.

For more of the interview with Tania, check out Chapter 3: "The Joy of Bisexuality."

A Conversation with Wolf Hudson

LISA:

How do you define bisexuality?

WOLF:

The Bi+ community is probably the most fluid sexual community that exists. There are so many different spectrums you have, like say, cis men who identify as straight, but every now and then want to be with men physically. You have gay men who live their lives as gay men, but every now and then they want to be with a cis female, and there are people who are in between. The only definition is the one that applies to you. Nobody should really have a say in what bisexuality is. Some pansexuals look down at bisexuals because they're attracted to gender. There's nothing wrong with being attracted to gender the same way that there's nothing wrong with looking past gender.

L:
How do you differentiate that for yourself?

W:
I'm attracted to gender and not even just gender, I'm also attracted to non-binary people. I'm not excluding anybody in that equation. But I am not wrong in being attracted to gender. If you're saying that being attracted to gender is wrong, you're also saying being homosexual and heterosexual is wrong because they're clearly attracted to a gender. There is nothing wrong with being attracted to gender. But if you can look past gender and just like the person, that's awesome too. I find that the infighting between bisexuals and pansexuals is that it really comes down to the attraction. And you can be pansexual and bisexual at the same time. You can be bi, you can be pan, you can be demi, you can be polysexual, you can be anything that you want that defines you in that moment, that defines you as a whole. It has to make sense for you and not for everybody else. The only thing that's expected from everybody else is the acceptance.

Accept me for who I am. I am going to accept you for who you are. Let's move on with our lives. It's not rocket science, but some people, they have a sort of tribal mentality and if something is going against what they know is right, they have to defend it. My question is, how is it really hurting? Because if it's hurting somebody, then we can have the discussion of like, okay, does that need to be defended?

You have to defend it if the opportunity is there to defend. But just because I am attracted to a gender and that goes against you not being attracted to gender and you feel the need to attack me, I'm not hurting anybody by being attracted to gender. The same way that I respect somebody who identifies as non-conforming, non-binary or gender fluid, someone who's trans, I respect that the same way. To be attracted to anybody should not come into question, because there's a whole segment of people who are attracted to one particular gender, and you're discrediting them by saying, that shouldn't matter.

For more of this interview with Wolf go to Chapter 5: "Cisgender Men and Masculinities" and also Chapter 7: "Pornography and Sex Work."

A Conversation with Bianca Laureano

BIANCA:
I think for me growing up in the U.S., the sexual identities and orientations that I knew about were being gay, lesbian or heterosexual. So, when I learned about bisexuality, I was like, oh, that's different than all the other identities that I knew about or experienced.

And in the nineties, it felt like the right one that I wanted to claim for myself, it felt genuine in how my attraction and my understanding of gender at that time worked and how it made sense to me. I was a teenager in the nineties, but I also became an adult at the end of the nineties. And so, what that looked like was working within a gender binary as well.

The definition of bisexuality for me, the way I was introduced to it, was being attracted to both genders. And I was like, yeah, I'm attracted to men/women, masculinity/femininity. I really grew up in that binary of understanding the world and our attractions. And even when I was trained in the nineties as a sexuality educator.

And then in 2000 I went into a graduate program at NYU. The conversation, the training was still upholding a binary. There was nothing that was challenging that. Even the way that I was trained to think about certain topics was completely different than the way that I understand them today. And I think claiming the identity of bisexual was really important for me, even if it was done quietly where I didn't share it with other people or felt like I had to out myself. I would just agree, be like, oh yeah, that person is beautiful. There was definitely some protection of being a feminine presenting person and saying, oh yeah, women are beautiful. Or, this woman looks amazing in this, or that's a really sexy outfit. And then being able to say the same things for people who are masculine. It never was questioned. It very much was a part of building community and being in community of loving my friends and people that we were like, "wow, that's a beautiful person."

Things didn't really change for me until the language started to expand a lot more. And that was probably in the 2010s. Literally almost 30 years of the language still being what I would consider limited and very much in a binary. That language expanded when I started to do a lot more activism and community building online, like on Tumblr and on my blogging spaces. I went outside of the traditional training that I had, which was very white, Western ideas of coming out, of being queer, of being bisexual. And when that happened, I started to expand the work that I was doing. I realized, oh, people are defining bisexuality beyond this binary of liking both genders.

When I began to understand that, bisexual people were like, no, no, no, no . . . the definition for bisexuality is: I'm attracted to my gender and others. So, we're not upholding a binary. I was like, oh, that's really interesting. It was really in those moments of building community, virtually being more exposed to a range of other people, especially young people, who remain on the forefront of shifting these terms.

That was an opportunity for me to really understand. I think I made the right choice. And then other words came about like queer, pansexual, demi-sexual, a really more expansive micro label, which allowed me to pause and really think about why am I choosing this label? What does it mean for me? And what does it not mean for me? Why am I attracted to other labels? Why do those other terms feel more accurate for me where I'm at currently? I really went from being like a 16-year-old to being like a 30-year-old and really being challenged in the ways that I was choosing certain terms.

It wasn't difficult. It wasn't shocking or scary. A good example that I can offer is that it was almost like shifting from using the term Hispanic as a self-identifier to then using Latina. I was always Puerto Rican. That was always my ethnic identity. But the way that the terms changed for me, especially growing up in the Washington DC area and being there for my undergrad and also my second round of graduate school, that being a very political space, I began to move away from using Hispanic and today I don't, even though it's reemerged as a term that people are using. So, for me, that changing language, wasn't a shock. I really had to think about why would I want to change a label that I've used for so long that felt okay? And I think it was more of a queering for me. Like I had a more queering adulthood once I got a more stable internet connection. And I started doing work beyond this Western scope that I was trained to do the work in and started building my own community.

That was when I was like, oh, I'm learning from more people and building more community. There are more community collaborations. These limiting terms aren't necessarily feeling as comfortable as they were prior to where I was at then. I feel for me that when I was thinking about claiming the term pansexual, it was really rooted in where I was intellectually learning more, reading more, engaging more with queer theory as it's presented in the academy primarily. But I was also doing a lot of queering of gender and of coming into my own gender identity too. So, not just saying, I'm a woman or, I'm a Latina, but I instead say I'm femme.

So that being an example of claiming a certain level of what people understand to be femininity, but also complicating it and queering it in a way where it says, I'm not just a girl. I'm not a woman in the way that you think I am. I felt that similar connection with sexual attraction and orientation, and I also saw that pansexual as an attraction and identity was welcomed a lot more freely and openly than bisexual was by the queer community.

To this day, bi erasure is real. I actively see it. None of that stuff makes sense to me. What do [you] mean what makes me feel most femme? It's me doing whatever the fuck I want. That's what makes me feel most queer. That's what makes me feel most present. I think that's what really attracted me to pansexuality and shifting away from bisexuality was where I was at intellectually and also in healing parts of myself that I didn't realize needed attention because I had been in such a limited space with certain terms and identities.

But I had to have a long talk with myself, a lot of inner dialogue to really ask myself. Would this be because it is easier to claim pansexuality than bisexuality? Am I choosing a more privileged route? What do I lose by claiming pansexuality and not bisexuality? What do I gain? And who has power in those moments? Do I still have any power in certain contexts? For me, it's hard to separate sexual attraction from all my other lived realities and identities. I can't separate it from being femme, fat, disabled or a racialized person in this country. And I think today looking back, it's been over 12 years that I've made that decision to claim pansexuality. It is the term that I think offers me the most liberation. It brings me closest to my idea of gender utopia. And it also welcomes in bisexuality. It wasn't a throwing away of it. I didn't dispose of bisexuality by claiming pansexuality. I feel like I became more into myself in a way that wasn't possible with how I understood and was in bisexual community. That was just how it was for me.

I don't know what it's going be like in the future, but a lot of the things I experienced with bisexuality—constantly coming out, being in what people thought was a heteronormative relationship and constantly having to correct people—that still exists for me as a pansexual femme. And the queering part really became a lot more solid across other interests that I had and other experiences that I had. The difference is very minimal, but it really is deeply rooted in my ideas of what does liberation feels like for me, someone who is displaced from their homeland because of Puerto Rico's economy and impact of colonization. What does it mean for me to choose to be guided by young people who are expanding language and recognizing that there's not necessarily a right or wrong because binaries are a scam? I think today learning from young people about how they expanded this definition or corrected the definition of bisexuality is also really important for me too.

L:

I am curious if you teach anything about sexuality scales. There are so many different ones and different limitations and issues, but do you feel like there's value in talking about them?

B:

I think there can be. For the work that I do as a sex educator, I really try to divest in telling people you have to do this in order to be a sex educator. I don't believe in that, even though I'm a member of these national organizations that tell you exactly that. It's not my personal philosophy of moving forward. I think for me, usually how I teach these new emergent terms, or even just terms in general, is to remind people that being a good sexuality professional isn't about memorizing what these words mean and their definition. Instead, it's about being able to figure out where you can find that information and make it accessible to people who have never heard those terms before.

I personally don't teach scales. I used to, when I taught sociology and people had questions like, how do we even know this is real? Then I would talk about Masters and Johnson's and the Kinsey scale. But those are very linear concepts and that's not how I view life or time or being a human being. It's not a linear experience. My idea of time and expression is different from what these scales offer. It's also a part of me doing the work of what people today would probably call a decolonial approach where I want to ask, why is this scale useful? Why was it created? Why do I need to know about it or use it?

And so far, my answer has been, I don't need to. It can be helpful for some people in certain parts of their lives. But for me, I was forced to use these scales because I was trained in the nineties and the early two-thousands. They did not help me do my work any better. They did not help me connect people to resources. Those scales didn't help me at all. I think today, a scale that's really useful is a spectrum around asexuality and that it's not this all or nothing spectrum. There are a lot of different experiences, like you can be a bisexual asexual person. And my ability to understand what that means is because I am in community with bisexual and asexual people. And because I've understood what's useful for both communities to be able to share their experiences.

I also just don't read a lot of the work by white people who I don't already have a relationship with. And that's an agreement that I made with myself when I was 40. I was like, I need to stop reading the work of white people who I don't know, or who don't do good work or whatever it may be. Because I can find other people who are doing the work better in a different way.

L:
How do you see different oppressions intersect with biphobia and bi-erasure?

B:
That is a good question. One of the ways I explain oppression, like misogyny and racism . . . we may have different terms for them and they impact certain

aspects of our lives, but they are all friends. They hang out, they go to happy hour. They talk shit. Like they are constantly moving together. They don't move in isolation. They inform each other and that's how they really become this breeding ground for maintaining more oppression. I think it's important to acknowledge the roots of bi-erasure, biphobia, homophobia, all being deeply rooted in this idea that there is only one right way to be a human being. And that has to be someone who is lighter skinned, who has a more athletic body, whose body moves in a particular way, who can reproduce more people that look like them, without injury or impact. I think we're going to see a lot more of that conversation masked under a language of health or wellness in the coming months and years.

Because we're going to have a lot more disabled people because of long Covid. Bisexual people are a part of that community that are also going to be negatively impacted. And if this is a community that we already know doesn't have access to quality care and health insurance, that's going to be a major impact for that community. That's one of the things that intersectionality helps us understand: how can we reimagine how to lessen that oppression and alleviate that negative impact altogether. That requires us to work together and be creative, and we don't always get the opportunity to be creative if we're working within a white supremacist, heterosexist, ableist lens or framework. It's very limiting, I don't even know who it helps at the end of the day.

I think white supremacy hurts everyone, including the people who benefit the most from it, because it doesn't allow them to be their full selves or to even acknowledge that they're having fuller experiences that don't have a name or that they feel shame for. And that I think is a really important thing for us to think about. How are white men being negatively impacted by white supremacy? When we look and dive into that research of what attracts people to white supremacist militias in this country, it's always about wanting to feel connected, wanting to be in community, not be alone. That's a human experience. And why is it that we are in a generation right now where there's so many young white people who feel so lonely that they're willing to dehumanize other people in order to not feel lonely? That to me is a really important question, but also allows us to think about, well, what are solutions?

How can we ensure that people don't feel that lonely or isolated anymore? Which requires us to talk about disability, which requires us to talk about segregation. To me, it's all interconnected. It all informs each other and it can feel overwhelming. But I think when we get really into the messiness of it, the chaos can really help us feel grounded and knowing that whatever path we take, there's going to be an impact. There is no one right way necessarily. It's going to be a multi approach. So, I'm hopeful for that type of future. I believe that the young people are already doing that kind of work. I'm excited to be guided by them and to no longer be the leader of certain things. I love the idea of being able to witness other people lead in a different direction.

L:

Yes! What other ways does bi-erasure intersect with other forms of oppression?

B:

What I witnessed in Black community was this label of "down low." A Black man who is having sex with women and men. This is still a stereotype that follows certain people. But it's not because that's what Black people still believe all the time. I think that language has evolved, but non-Black people are learning about it and then still writing about it as outsiders. And we used that term in the nineties. We're not really using it anymore in community. To me, that's also a re-traumatizing for Black queer people and Black queerness.

We also witness the stereotype of femininity demonstrating or revealing bisexuality. Thinking across race and gender when attraction or orientation is celebrated, encouraged, and eroticized by masculine people of all races and ages, that is also, to me, about consumption, right? It's about, oh, I want to watch two women that I find attractive do things together and it's like, actually you don't. You don't want to see us do a crossword puzzle together or play UNO. You want to see us have sex, right? You don't want to see us love each other by snuggling and watching whatever TV show. You don't want to see us celebrating our birthdays and eating cake and singing songs. That is another example of the oppression of erasing the joy that people experience in life and really compartmentalizing it just for sexual fulfillment.

I think the oppression part, it exists for sure. The way that intersects with other communities. I mean, we're still seeing it with the way that racialization impacts people's idea of attraction of desirability, and of what people believe is worthy. I know that there's still this language of no fats, no femmes, no Asians. Well, what if you're a fat femme Asian, right? We all know what that means. And those individuals are some of the most brilliant, amazing people in our communities. Why are we isolating them? Why are we allowing that language to still thrive?

The Role of Religion and Spirituality

Another major factor is the historical role of religion, but an extensive analysis of religion and bisexuality is beyond the scope of this book. It is, however, imperative to introduce some religious concepts that do play a role. Many LGBTQ+ people find comfort in religion, but it can also be a great source of suffering from ostracization, banishment, or pressure to choose between their faith and authentic selves.[47] Mainstream discussions typically focus on such important concerns as same-gender loving marriage and gay men in religious leadership positions, but it "signifies the prominence of homosexuality in such a discourse, and the continued erasure of bisexuality within it."[48] This is particularly evident in the institutions of Christianity, Islam, and Judaism but less so in New Age, Buddhism, Sufism, and Paganism which, according to Yip and Toft, allows "bisexual individuals to accommodate their sexual and religious identities more harmoniously."[49] A more detailed analysis of these complexities around religion and bisexuality is explored in newer texts such as: *Blessed Bi Spirit: Bisexual People of Faith* by Debra Kolodny;

Sexuality, Religion and the Sacred: Bisexual, Pansexual and Polysexual Perspectives by Loraine Hutchins and H. Sharif Williams; *Bisexuality and The Western Church: The Damage of Silence* by Carol Shepherd; and *Bisexuality, Religion and Spirituality* by Alex Toft and Andrew Kam-Tuck Yip.

Why is bisexual erasure *so* common in mainstream religious institutions? As seen throughout this book, bisexual erasure, biphobia, and monosexism permeate many aspects of society, so it is no surprise that this exists in religion. Many religions have a long history of being gatekeepers of sexual norms, morals, practices, and beliefs that promote heterosexuality, abstinence until marriage, monogamy, and cissexism.[50] LBGTQ+ people who may be outside of these cultural norms are often targets of "sacramental shame," which makes "being recognized as a person—in the eyes of God and others—contingent on constant displays of will to change things most LGBTI people cannot change, instilling shame as an enduring, conscious mental state."[51]

Since most religious doctrines consist of gender complementarianism, where gender is seen as dichotomous, "incomplete halves to be completed in heterosexual marriage,"[52] sacramental shame heavily stigmatizes and psychologically harms LGBTQ+ people when they do not fit into these strict gendered expectations.[53] Levy and Harr found in their study that the participants discussed how they were told bisexuality was a sin, that they needed to repent, and that they should "simply pick someone of the opposite sex."[54] The shame also manifests as unsupportive families, rejection, and being put into "conversion" therapy, in addition to the internalization of this messaging that can lead to depression, anxiety, isolation, and suicidal ideation.[55]

Despite bisexual erasure and the pain of sacramental shame, there are plenty of bisexual people who are religious and their faith is an integral part of who they are.[56] Religion for many is about guidance around struggles, morality, and life decisions, and for many people of color, it may be a support system "to cope with crippling racist ideologies that, at best, regarded them as second-class citizens."[57] It is an important part of life, so instead of choosing religion over bisexuality or vice versa, many adapt their faith and sexuality rather than leave their religion.[58] Alex Toft found in his research that some participants began a "process of desexualisation in which their own sexuality and sexual behaviours took a back seat to their faith" while other chose celibacy or figured out a way for bisexuality to be more congruous.[59] Others felt it necessary to find different congregations that were more supportive or worked to enact social change within their own faith communities.[60] External resources, such as social media, bisexual community resources, and relevant readings were also essential, along with exploring the integration of religion and their authentic selves, not only in order to accept their own identities but to "share their lives with others as a way to promote understanding and acceptance" about bisexuality.[61]

Not all bisexual people are able to access these options, when there may be other barriers such as systemic racism. For example, Jefferies et al. discovered that bisexual Black men had certain ways to make sense of religious and spiritual experiences and they typically did not reveal their same-sex attractions in their religious communities.[62] Religion and spirituality were a vital part of their lives, which was not just about the influence of the doctrine but also the reality that church and religion were "deeply intertwined with family and community life."[63] Jefferies argues that what makes bisexual Black men unique in their relationship to religion is that they are "socially marginal to White communities and White gay communities" while also not fully accepted in Black or Black gay communities, so they may "be even more likely than even Black gays and lesbians to seek solace in religion" and feel empowered by their faith communities.[64]

Recent research has shown that accepting one's bisexuality should not have to be at the cost of one's faith, so how does society rethink what bisexuality actually contributes to this discourse on sexuality and religion? Yip and Toft passionately offer these thoughts:

> *We believe that, bisexuality—with its queering spirt of liminality and fluidity—can serve as a catalyst to liberate us from the shackles of sexual and gender binarism, and help us envision a world beyond binary that celebrates the kaleidoscope of humanity. It sounds like a dream. But who says we can't dare to dream?*[65]

Adding to this dream are the following three personal narratives, starting with Anastasia Fonseca-Carvalhais discussing her first love and what role Catholicism played in making sense of this. Noreen writes about being Muslim and finding a place for bisexuality on her own terms within her religion. And finally, Jessica Podcaliki writes about discovering paganism and witchcraft as the perfect balance for her bisexuality and spirituality.

Lost in the Gray Space by Anastasia Fonseca-Carvalhais

I grew up embracing the Church before I could ever embrace a romantic partner. My parents are both Catholic and were raised in the traditional-Portuguese church, so when it came to their children, it was second nature to pass on their faith. When I was younger, I didn't mind, it was all that I knew. I found comfort in the prayers that my older sister—Briana—and I would recite with our parents before bed. Even now, years after I have stopped reciting them along with my parents, I can still hear my mother's soothing voice almost singing, "Anjo da Guarda/Minha companhia/Guardai a minha alma de noite e dia. Amen." Guardian angel, my companion/Protect my soul/night and day. I thought that the Catholic church—and God specifically—would always protect me and put my needs and well-being first. After all, God wanted us all to be happy, right? Christ was the embodiment of all love and, as his children, we were expected to embody his loving ways. As a result, my family never shied away from intimacy, in fact, they welcomed it. I grew up in a world where telling someone you loved them was normal, and the act of loving someone was welcomed. However, like everything else, things change once you begin to grow up.

When I turned 13, I was expected to take the biggest step in my Catholic faith: Confirmation. It was finally time in my religious journey when I chose to become a Catholic for myself. While I technically became Catholic at the ripe age of one, when a priest dunked my head in holy water at Baptism, Confirmation was finally my choice. I started going to Sunday school and learned more about Catholicism than I had ever known before. This was the first time that I was brought face to face with every ideal and belief that the Church held, including their beliefs on "same-sex" relationships and intimacy. We were taught that any individuals of the same sex that engaged in romantic or sexual relationships were committing a sin. I would leave every Sunday session feeling less secure in my faith, questioning more and more if I agreed with the ideals I was being taught. So, as a soft-spoken middle schooler, I decided to reach out to those that I trusted instead of voicing my opinion in class.

One Sunday night, after we had recited our nightly prayers, I turned to my sister in bed and asked her if she believed that same-sex relationships were a sin. It was not irregular for Briana and I to talk late into the night about everything—and anything—on our minds. Briana didn't even open her eyes when she said "no." This one word both bothered me and sent butterflies twirling around in my stomach. I wasn't entirely sure what I wanted her answer to be, but somehow, I felt comforted. But then, from the other side of my childhood bedroom came her real answer, "I personally think it's stupid. But, it's not really something that involves me though, so I don't really think it matters either way." The comforting feeling I had held in my stomach moments before vanished. But she was right, wasn't she? I would never have to deal with that small little caveat of being Catholic, so why was I worrying myself now?

I went on to become confirmed in the eyes of the Catholic church even though I didn't truly believe in everything I was supposed to. I felt like a prized pig being shown off at the county fair. If I didn't come home with a blue ribbon around my neck, then what was the point of priming me and sending me off in the first place? Who was I to break my parents' hearts and refuse to be confirmed? I wasn't going to be a disappointment to them or to God. So, I pushed away my worries, affirmed the Catholic faith, and became an official member of the Church. And when I finally thought that all of this "catholic business" was over, a new development came about: My parents were sending me to a private Catholic high school. In their eyes they were giving me a better education and a fresh new start to learn about who I wanted to be. However, having transferred from a public school, it felt as if they had just blindly thrown me into the ocean expecting me to swim, when in reality I began to drown. I walked the halls with my new collared shirt tucked into my khaki kilt, feeling like a fraud. Everyone around me was a stranger, and I felt like the black sheep constantly wandering, hoping to finally find their place. And finally, I did find my place, because I found my person.

"Is this seat taken?" She looked up at me, almost shocked that someone was speaking to her. I recognized her from my English and Theology classes, always sitting in the back with her friends. But I had also noticed over the last couple weeks that she usually sat by herself during study hall, listening to music and reading. Her green eyes seemed to be quietly asking me what the hell I was doing. "I was just wondering if I could sit here," I said as I dropped my laptop onto the table next to her. That seemed to break her from her silence. "Oh yeah, umm—yeah go ahead, why not."

That's all that we said to each other that day. And every day during study hall, like clockwork, I would plant myself next to this complete stranger. It was something so simple, but it was a small comfort to me. I would notice her make quick glances at my computer to see what I was up to, and if I was being honest, I was doing the same. After a while, we started to make conversation during study hall. It was nothing remarkable or noteworthy, but it was someone to talk to. And over time I began to realize that I wasn't the only black sheep wandering these god-awful echoey halls. It almost seemed humorous how alike we were once we got to know each other. This newfound friendship came so naturally I swore to Briana that it must have been fate that I wound up at this school.

Months went by and there wasn't a single weekend that Isabella wasn't at my house re-watching *Sherlock* on BBC or I at hers listening to her father's old records in their living room. We would share everything with one another, especially how much we hated going to Catholic school and how it made us feel suffocated. Finding Isabella allowed my inner self to finally have some reprieve. Others would probably hear our conversations and say we were just trying to be "rebellious" teenagers, but I would say quite the opposite. I would say that we were finally being ourselves and finally opening up to the fact that it was okay to have our own original thoughts. Finally realizing that we didn't have to always look over our shoulder for the "man upstairs," scared that He might strike us down with a lightning bolt if we were disobedient. This was our little piece of heaven we created for ourselves.

Before we knew it, we were sophomores and Homecoming was just around the corner. Even if you didn't like the idea of school dances you couldn't help but keep up with the theatrics. What were people going to wear? What group of friends were you going to go with? And more importantly, who was asking whom to the dance? But, no matter how good our guesses were, Isabella and

I were completely shocked when we walked out of school to a guy holding a "Homecoming?" sign for me. To say he was a friend of mine just looking for a date would be an overstatement; I think I had maybe spoken to him a handful of times outside of an academic setting. But he was nice, and I was not going to make an awkward situation even worse by saying no. So, I left school that day with a date to the homecoming and feeling of disappointment I couldn't quite shake.

All of the girls in our group decided to get ready together. I helped Isabella with her makeup and she helped me straighten all of the pieces of hair at the back of my head I couldn't seem to reach. The night was honestly nothing memorable. Just a bunch of awkward high school students attempting to let loose for the night in their school's gym, with teachers on the lookout for dresses that were too short and couples that weren't dancing with enough room for the "Holy Spirit." The highlight of the night was the afterparty. My afterparty wasn't like the ones in the movies with underage drinking and an open house. I went over to Isabella's just like every other weekend. Except this weekend we had a new topic to talk about: how horrible Homecoming was.

"I don't really know what I was expecting, but I definitely wasn't expecting him to be so uncomfortable. He practically avoided me the entire night!" I shrieked, dramatically rolling back and forth on her bed. A sharp "Shh" came from upstairs as her mother trekked off to bed for the night. Isabella jumped up and quietly closed her bedroom door, "I mean how bad was it really? Do you like him?"

"No! Oh god no," I hardly could articulate the words as I attempted to muffle my laughter with her pillows. "I mean it's not that it was horrible. I just don't really like him that much honestly. I feel like I put in a lot of effort for very little in return. I can't believe I was stressed over how I looked to not even get a compliment from him," I said motioning to my black dress crumpled on her floor.

"Well, I think you looked beautiful," Isabella said as she turned off her light and slid under the covers next to me. I leaned my head against her shoulder, "I thought you looked beautiful too." Her bedroom fell silent as if the walls were holding their breath knowing what would come next. "Maybe it would have been better if you went with someone who really liked you," Isabella whispered, breaking the silence. "Maybe it would have been better if you went with me." And there it was. The words that I was subconsciously hoping and praying for.

Isabella fidgeted with her duvet cover and I began to stroke my hair, both of us not knowing what to do with our hands. And finally, after what felt like too long, we both turned and went in to kiss the other. We failed miserably, bonking our noses into one another. But then I could feel both of our bodies relax and fall into the kiss. I was kissing my best friend and it just felt right. While there was still a little bit of teenage awkwardness it felt safe, comfortable, and natural. My mind fell silent. We pulled away and both didn't know what to say. I turned and wrapped my arms around her like I did every weekend when we would fall asleep.

"Goodnight, Isabella."

"Goodnight, Anastasia."

The room fell silent again, but this time it was the silence only a secret could create.

"I love you."

"I love you too."

And that's when my mind broke the beautiful peaceful silence with the horrible, ever-present voice of Catholic guilt. It said, "You might as well have signed and kissed your ticket to heaven goodbye young lady. Because you are a sinner." Except deep down I wasn't sure if I believed that dumb little voice. Isabella was the person that made me the happiest, made me feel like my best self. She wasn't a bad influence over me, if anything she was one of the many good influences in my life. Why would someone that made me feel so whole be the reason that God saw me as broken?

The next couple weeks were both confusing and enlightening for me. I was angry at God for letting this happen. If God really did make us in his "perfect image" then why was I somehow stuck in the gray space where I wasn't gay but I wasn't straight? What did my feelings towards Isabella really mean? I kept trying to convince myself that it was all because of my heightened emotions of the night that made me physically attracted to her, but deep down I knew that was a lie. So, I finally decided that if I was going to sin, why would I waste my sins on lying to myself?

Isabella and I dated for the rest of high school. I broke up with her the summer before college because I wanted to "be free." If I am being honest with myself, I broke up with her because I was also scared about not being able to experience the other side of my sexuality. I craved to finally know if I was actually bisexual or if this was all a little rebellious fantasy I cooked up in my brain. The first few months of college were thrilling as I began to explore every side of my sexuality. A fresh environment that allowed me to begin as the version of myself that I had always wished to be. And while I may have taken a few wrong turns here and there, I finally found my place and my person. Like Isabella, he is my best friend. He has always been accepting of me and makes it feel as though he is just an extension of myself.

Maybe people won't understand it, but even though I am not with Isabella anymore I still love her. She helped me figure out who I wanted to be. I still think of her on my walks to class when I am listening to "Strawberry Fields Forever" by the Beatles, and I smile every time I take a sip of her favorite Hot Cinnamon Sunset black tea. These are moments that I never want to give up, memories that will stick with me forever. Human beings are just collections of experiences and memories, and these small simple moments have shaped the beautiful and empowered bisexual woman I am today. And while I am no longer a traditionally practicing Catholic, I am still grateful for my upbringing and faith. I haven't fully figured out how I want to identify religiously, but I continue to keep my mind open to any possibilities that come my way. I no longer feel trapped in this gray space, rather I have learned it's where I thrive. According to the National Library of Medicine, the human eye can perceive about 900 shades of gray. There are always numerous unexpected outcomes to every situation as long as you are brave enough to search for them.

My Faith and Bisexuality by Noreen

When I think about sexuality, I am flooded with a range of emotions from my childhood trauma to my weird teen years to now, in the present. The emotions linked to my sexual orientation are what have kept me up at odd hours of the night; they made me question myself and my identity in all its forms. I thought I knew who I was. I was a Pakistani American Muslim, but there was something else too, which I was not ready to accept. I remember thinking about who I was attracted to, what feelings I had for someone I liked, and what it meant about me. Growing up with South Asian Muslim parents who never talked about sexuality or gender made it difficult to understand these concepts and left me unaware of what this meant for myself.

When I think about Islam and sexuality, I remember my first conversation with my mom when I was five years old about the Islamic rules we had to follow and what was essential for us to do as good Muslims; being caring, helping people, giving charity, and not saying bad words. My mother taught me everything I knew about Islam but never uttered a word about liking the opposite gender, men, or sex. I assumed when we watched Disney movies, and she turned the movie off when the prince kissed the princess, it was wrong and something we didn't do as "Muslims" (which is completely false). I learned that Allah (God) made everyone in pairs in Islam, so each person had a partner they were eternally linked to. They would spend their entire life together, have children, and live happily ever after. I understood growing up that heterosexual relationships were the only ones allowed, as that was the only type of relation I ever witnessed. My parents, grandparents, and family members all had partnerships between a man and a woman. But that soon changed as I got older and started to use the internet more and watch different TV shows. The first homosexual and bisexual relationship I saw on screen was in shows like *Glee*, *Gossip Girl*, and *Modern Family*. But I had never seen a real-life homosexual or bisexual or other sexual orientations.

I was in middle school, and my parents decided to move to Pakistan for a few years. I faced a major culture shock; I felt so out of place as an American girl dropped in the middle of Pakistan. I didn't know how to speak the language and didn't feel like I fit in with the culture or religion. I remember going to one of my physics classes and meeting this girl who was shy and sat next to me. She and I soon started talking and became friends. I saw her in each class, and we got to know each other better. One day this girl decided to tell me something about herself that changed the way I thought about sexuality and Islam altogether. This girl told me she was attracted to women and she had a girlfriend. The girl shared how she had never told anyone because it was wrong in Islam to be in a relationship with anyone other than a man. She told me how she loved her girlfriend, wanted to marry her, spend their lives together, and move away from Pakistan. The laws and stigma of not being heterosexual and the disapproval of the LGBTQ+ community were too challenging to live with. Her family, however, would never let that happen and would force her to marry a man. I was in utter shock. I had never met a Muslim who was in a homosexual relationship. This person, who was my friend, trusted me and told me her secret about her sexuality. I didn't know how to react besides being so sad that she had to hide her relationship and live in fear of being forced into a marriage. I met this girl a few times in class, and we always talked about sexuality and attraction. I shared how I didn't think I liked anyone or knew what my sexuality even was, and she shared how she knew she liked girls from the moment she was young and went to grade school. There was something she said that stuck with me for a very long time, which determined how I felt about my sexuality and validated my attraction towards anyone. She said, "It doesn't take long for us to fall into what others want us to do, so when we have one life to live, why wouldn't I go love the person I want." Unfortunately, after a few weeks, she stopped coming to class, and I didn't have any contact information to ask where she went. All I can remember is that she shared how she feared her parents would force her to get married to a man and would make her never see her girlfriend ever again. I often think about her and pray that she is happy and healthy with her partner, living the life she always wanted.

I moved back to the United States after a few years of living in Pakistan, and once I had completed high school, I decided to go to community college. Being back in America, I saw people embracing their sexuality. It was so freeing to see after being in Pakistan, where so many people hid themselves in fear. I was so focused on school that I didn't want to distract myself by thinking about boys or girls and who I liked, so I pushed it down further. I had moments throughout my first year of college where I felt like I was someone I couldn't recognize, probably because I was trying so hard to be like everyone else. I cared so much about what people thought about me that it stopped me from doing what I wanted and expressing myself the way I wanted to. I stayed focused on school and studied hard to get into UVA. I knew if I did anything but study, I would let my parents down, and all their hard work would have been wasted.

I eventually got into UVA, and I felt like everything would start feeling better, but it didn't. I used to walk past the LGBTQ center and think about walking in and talking about the feelings I have and what they mean. But I didn't feel like I belonged there, and for the first few semesters, I stayed quiet and kept to myself. Slowly, things began to change. For example, one time in my Buddhist philosophy class, my TA shared her experience being part of the LGBTQ+ community, and it made me feel like I wanted to be free like her too. In addition, I had a friend in that class, and she and I got very close. I enjoyed spending time with her, as we had all these fun conversations about life and traveling. I definitely had a crush on her; I felt my heart race every time she was near, and I would get so nervous I would get sweaty palms just thinking her; I knew I had fallen a little for her. I had a dream about kissing her, and when I woke up, I couldn't stop thinking about her, her lips and how it felt in my dream, and how it would have felt if it had happened in real life. That very week I met my family and saw my grandparents, and I obviously couldn't stop thinking about her, but I realized my family would never be happy knowing I was thinking about being with a girl. I was flooded with memories about how much my parents taught me to abstain from these "dirty thoughts," about how wrong it would be with someone of the same sex and what would Allah (God) think of me. I knew I didn't want to lose my family, but I didn't even know what I felt and what it meant, so I should keep it to myself and move on, which is exactly what I did. The girl and I stopped talking after the class ended, and I moved on.

That summer, I decided to take a course in the Women, Gender and Sexuality department, and I chose to take Men and Masculinities. In this class, I was open to my misconceptions about gender and sexuality. It was the first time I learned about how complex your identity could be, and it made me realize I wasn't alone. I was able to explore ways I wanted to express myself and found words that described the feelings I had kept inside for so long. Throughout every class, I would feel more and more comfortable in my skin, feel more confident in myself, and start accepting my emotions instead of keeping them hidden inside. In my last autobiographical essay, I was able to share how I felt and how I saw myself as bisexual. For the first time in my life, I accepted those feelings, and the validation brought a sense of contentment within myself.

This acceptance of my identity made me so proud of who I was and how long it took me to be able to say those things to myself. I knew it wasn't going to be easy to continue accepting myself and telling people about my sexuality. I am a very private person, and I like keeping my feelings to myself. I knew my sexuality was something I would only tell people I trusted. I was in a relationship with a man while accepting myself and coming to terms with my sexuality. I was really afraid that my boyfriend would be upset or angry at me for sharing these feelings, and I didn't want him to feel like I tricked him or even lied to get him into this relationship. To my surprise, when I told him I was bi, he was understanding and supportive. My boyfriend was really happy I could get through the feelings, and he made me feel like this relationship was still as strong as before. He and I did have more conversations about being bi. He had questions and some misconceptions I tried to answer, and we kept educating each other along the way. I thought I would feel better about my identity once I told my boyfriend and some friends. But I questioned my feelings again, second-guessing them all because I am bi and have romantic feelings for women and men, but I haven't even kissed a girl. I don't know how that feels; what if someone says I'm not bi and I'm making this all up? These thoughts haunt me and make me feel like I needed to keep these feelings more to myself. I talked to Professor Speidel, and she helped me through those misconceptions about being bi and how that is a feeling many people go through.

I never opened up to strangers about my sexuality. Still, in a club organization meeting, a member from the middle eastern club talked to me about how he could never join a Muslim student group because he felt like Islam would never accept his sexuality. He believed the people in the club wouldn't accept him, just like many people he had experienced who are Muslim. I told him how I was bi and was part of these clubs, and believed I was a good Muslim for the most part. I understood where he came from because Islam taught us that men and women were the only ones who are supposed to be together. When I was going through the phase of accepting myself and where I stood in context to my faith and religion, I had a lot of thinking to do about who I was but through the lens of culture, religion, and what values I was instilled with and what I wanted to carry from my current years of finding myself and my sexuality. I went back to the basics, read the Quran, read the Hadiths (prophets' words and actions recorded), and from doing so, I saw how beautiful and accepting my religion was. Yes, there are rules, and there are people who will not accept me, but from reading everything I still had this love for my religion. I didn't want to leave my religion even though there might never be space there for many people like me. But that shouldn't mean I just leave; I felt like trying to find space and acceptance led me to find the actual peace within the religion and made me realize I needed nothing from other people and their interpretations and words about what I believe and what my religion means for me. People are so quick to call others out when they're doing something that isn't following their rules.

I truly believe Islam is such a diverse religion. What someone believes and does is so much different from what someone else does. A universal thought in Islam is that it tells its believer to never accuse someone of being bad/not a Muslim regardless of any reason/action they do; their faith is between themselves and their creator. I started to see my religion as a connection to my creator, and he made me the way I am, and he loves all his creations, and that is all I need. Recently I learned in one of my Sufi Islamic courses about Allah loving all his creations and how he loved them regardless of any flaw or mistake. I was taught growing up that Allah is merciful, forgiving, and the acceptor of all people. Things have been said in the Quran about sexuality and people interpreting them how they see fit, but I refuse to believe that people must hide their sexuality in fear. Allah (God) would never want his beings to be in pain or hurt. I know Allah (God) would never want us to hide our feelings and continue feeling pain. Islam is a complex religion with many differences in teachings in different regions of the world with different interpretations of the Quran and Hadith (Prophet's quotes). Through researching online, finding different resources, and learning more in my classes in religion, I have discovered that what is accepted in one sect of Islam may be forbidden in another, and people have chosen to accept or reject it. I also learned that there is something Islam has no opinions on and does not have a straightforward response to.

I'm a practicing Muslim; I fast every Ramadan, give zakat (charity), and pray too. I try to be the best Muslim version of myself, but I know I must be true to myself too. I do pick and choose from Islam, which is the only way I can take my religion and sexuality together. There isn't a perfect middle to both worlds. There might never be for most people, but I believe people can find their middle and happy spot on the scale. Today I am happy where I am with my faith and my sexuality. Islam is a very accepting religion, with so many words of love and joy, and I never want people to see the hate that the media spreads about Islam. Islam is a religion that spreads through every part of your life, and it is supposed to go hand in hand with everything we do. I know it's not an easy process, and I continue to struggle with both, but I believe this is a process we will always have to find a new happy spot on the acceptance scale for sexuality and religion. I know this is a never-ending process of finding peace in both aspects of life, but I am glad I found mine and hope everyone struggling can too. I also hope to spread more love and awareness about Islam and its ability to be accepting of our sexualities. Hopefully, one day everyone struggling with their faith and sexuality can find their happy spot too.

Another Bisexual Little Witch by Jessica Podkalicki

I grew up Catholic. We were "forced" to go to Catholic schools from kindergarten all through high school. Religion was part of the regular curriculum. I received all the sacraments. My grandmother would encourage us to go to church every Sunday and eventually we (my siblings and parents) made the decision to stop attending church. I did, however, sing in the choir and read from the Bible in front of everyone during mass, but that was just to make my grandmother happy.

In 7th grade, my family went through some really serious and life-altering events. We eventually lost my grandmother and with that the pressure of having to go to church.

I got really sick. Something that I live with to this very day—I am 32 as I write this. Religion became way more complicated in our house and in my life than I realized. I was raised thinking that there was a God. This all-powerful dude that controls the universe. He punishes bad people and rewards the good. That is always what was instilled in me from an early age and I sort of believed. As I got older, I did question this all-powerful God. How can one person have that much power? Why was it a him?

On top of all that, when I got sick, I felt destroyed. My concept of religion was destroyed. People would visit me and tell me "God has a reason for everything" or "this is all a part of his plan." And that just made me even sicker. What jerk would do that to a young woman, full of life, with a whole lot of life to live still? I had good grades, I didn't go out after school, I was a part of every club, heck, I even did the church thing. And just like that, my belief in God vanished.

I watched my grandmother slowly die while I sat in the bed next to her slowly healing. My belief in anything, especially a higher power, was so far from my mind. And for a while, I didn't believe in anything. Biggest atheist. I turned to science. I was thinking heck, I'll be pre-med and become my own type of God. I'll save people and have the power to do that.

I continued to go to my catholic high school. It was the safest school to go to in New York City at the time. I did have some fantastic teachers and even some great and open-minded religion teachers. The good ones preached about spirituality and being a genuine and good person. It wasn't about going to church or if you were gay or lesbian you'd go to hell. Some of my teachers were actually just good people who talked about how God led them to be good people.

When I was about 15 years old, I was a bit of a loner. I went through so much by that time that any faith that I did have in God and in the Catholic church was gone. That was the time when I got into Tarot. I would spend hours and hours at my local bookstore looking at witchy related books and cards. I had found some outside force to call upon for advice. That was my friend for a while. I would practice readings on myself nearly every day, looking for all kinds of answers. I eventually did a few readings for a few friends here and there.

As time went on, tarot and neo-paganism and basically being a witch became popular. Other people were interested in the same thing I was. I always had an affinity for mythology and would spend a lot of my time reading about all kinds of myths and goddesses. I felt connected to the ethereal. I loved seeing the tropes of the different gods and goddesses through different types of pantheons. My brain loved noticing those patterns and then going deeper to see what sets each specific god apart. For example, how is Freya different from Aphrodite? Both are women, both are connected to love, both are major goddesses within their own pantheons.

I eventually came out of the broom closet via Instagram. I created an Instagram account dedicated to exploring witchcraft and tarot in order to find some community and teach people the stuff that I spent years reading about and learning about. But this has been a journey brewing for years. I realized that I cannot NOT believe in something. I value the world around me—nature, other people, animals, the elements, everything. There has to be a world outside of the present. A power outside of our own forces.

To this day, when people ask me if I am religious or Catholic or whatever, I still don't know what to say. Well, yes, I believe in something, but to get into all of this, even mentioning my tarot practice and rituals, with some people elicits some eye rolls. What the heck is religion anyways?

Just recently, I have been listening to podcasts of all kinds. A general theme that I have been hearing is the juxtaposition of science and magic. Or to me science and religion. This has been a theme in civilizations for thousands of years. Religion and mysticism existed long before Catholicism and somehow Christianity is still one of the most popular and accepted forms of organized spirituality.

My spirituality and my neo-Pagan leanings are extremely similar to my bisexuality. I am only out to a few people that I know and trust. I still get eye-rolls from people when I talk about bisexuality. People still question the legitimacy of my sexual orientation. And yet, people have been attracted to one another REGARDLESS of their gender for centuries. I noticed that religion can be one of two things in the bi+ community: 1) this one is rare but religion can be an integral construct in their lives and they feel supported in community, or 2) their religion made them feel unwelcomed and worse because of their sexuality.

Even though I knew I was bisexual from a young age, I never really considered the intersection between my spirituality and my bisexuality. However, with the help of social media, I have connected to both the spiritual and bisexual+ community. There are a lot of bisexual+ folks that appreciate tarot and witchy things too. I am lucky to have found this community on Instagram and elsewhere. I have also met a few friends around Boston where I live that are queer and also have an interest in witchcraft and tarot. I never knew that I was missing community. And when it comes down to it, that is what religion is. A community of people who share the same values and help support each other.

Heck, even while I was starting high school, it seems like the whole world opened up to me. That is where I learned the terms "bisexual" and "lesbian." I think that, once I moved on from the constrictions of being Catholic, my world just opened up. I felt like I could explore my differences more. I know that other people have different experiences when it comes to organized religion and community, but this is my tale.

Notes

1 Lachlan MacDowall, "Historicising Contemporary Bisexuality," *Journal of Bisexuality*, Vol. 9, No. 1 (2009), 4.
2 Harry Oosterhuis, "Sexual Modernity in the Works of Richard von Krafft-Ebing and Albert Moll," *Medical History*, Vol. 56, No. 2 (2012), 133.
3 Jean Balestrery, "Intersecting Discourses on Race and Sexuality: Compounded Colonization Among AGBTQ American Indians/Alaska Natives," *Journal of Homosexuality*, Vol. 59, No. 5 (2012), 1.
4 John P. Elia, Mickey Eliason and Genny Beemyn, "Mapping Bisexual Studies: Past and Present, and Implications for the Future," in *Bisexuality: Theory, Research and Recommendations for the Invisible Sexuality*, ed. D. Joye Swan and Shani Habibi (New York: Springer, 2018), 3.
5 Elia et al., "Mapping Bisexual Studies," 3.
6 Shiri Eisner, "What Is Bisexuality?" in *Bi: Notes for a Bisexual Revolution* (Berkeley, CA: Seal Press, 2013), 14.
7 Marjorie Garber, "Ellis in Wonderland," in *Vice Versa: Bisexuality and the Eroticism of Everyday Life* (New Yor: Simon and Shuster, 1996), 239.
8 Julia Shaw, "Our History," in *Bi: The Hidden Culture, History, and Science of Bisexuality* (New York: Abrams, Inc., 2022), 36.
9 Shaw, "Our History," 36.
10 Havelock Ellis, "Sexual Inversion," in *The Studies of the Psychology of Sex: Volume II*, 3rd edition, www.gutenberg.org/files/13611/13611-h/13611-h.htm.
11 Shaw, "Our History."
12 This term will be explained further regarding gender identity in Chapter 3: Gender Diverse Identities.
13 "The Ethics of Designing Babies," https://dc.alumni.columbia.edu/designingbabies.
14 Hugh Ryan, "How Eugenics Gave Rise to Modern Homophobia," *Washington Post* (May 28, 2019), www.washingtonpost.com/outlook/2019/05/28/how-eugenics-gave-rise-modern-homophobia/.
15 Aaron J. Stone, "Toward a Black Vernacular Sexology," *A Journal of Lesbian and Gay Studies*, Vol. 29, No. 1 (2023), 28.
16 Andrea Smith, "Sexual Violence as a Tool of Genocide," in *Conquest: Sexual Violence and American Indian Genocide* (Durham, NC: Duke University Press, 2005), 10.

17 Scott Loria Morgensen, "The Biopolitics of Settler Sexuality," in *Spaces Between Us: Queer Settler Colonialism and Indigenous Decolonization* (Minneapolis, MN: University of Minnesota Press, 2011), 37.

18 Balestrery, "Intersecting Discourses on Race and Sexuality," 634.

19 Balestrery, "Intersecting Discourses on Race and Sexuality," 637.

20 MacDowall, "Historicising Contemporary Bisexuality," 4.

21 Eisner, "What Is Bisexuality?" 15.

22 Elia et al., "Mapping Bisexual Studies," 3.

23 Esther Rapoport, "Bisexuality in Psychoanalytic Theory: Interpreting the Resistance," *Journal of Bisexuality*, Vol. 9, No. 3–4 (2009), 283.

24 Beverly Stoute, "Race and Racism in Psychoanalytic Thought: The Ghosts in Our Nursery," in *The Trauma of Racism: Lessons From the Therapeutic Encounter*, ed. Beverly Stoute and Michael Slevin (New York, NY: Routledge, 2023), 17.

25 "Bessie Smith," National Museum of African American History and Culture, Smithsonian, https://nmaahc.si.edu/lgbtq/bessie-smith#:~:text=Throughout%20her%20career%2C%20Smith%20was,business%20life%20nor%20Smith's%20bisexuality.

26 "Ma Raine's Bisexuality Was a Revolutionary Act in the 1920s That Still Matters Today," *Women's Health Magazine*, www.womenshealthmag.com/life/a35014028/ma-rainey-bisexual-netflix/.

27 Julian B. Carter, "Introduction: The Search for Norma," in *The Heart of Whiteness: Normal Sexuality and Race in America, 1890–1940* (Durham, NC: Duke University Press, 2007), 2.

28 Elia et al., "Mapping Bisexual Studies," 4.

29 Alfred Kinsey, W.B. Pomeroy and C.E. Martin, *Sexual Behavior in the Human Male* (Philadelphia: W.B. Saunders, 1948), 639.

30 Elia et al., "Mapping Bisexual Studies."

31 Elia et al., "Mapping Bisexual Studies," 4.

32 Amanda Schaffer, "American Sex Portrait: Fifty Years After Alfred Kinsey, What More Do We Know?" https://slate.com/human-interest/2007/09/fifty-years-after-alfred-kinsey-what-more-do-we-know.html.

33 Julia Shaw, "The Bi Option," in *Bi: The Hidden Culture, History, and Science of Bisexuality* (New York: Abrams, Inc., 2022), 19.

34 Jack Drescher, "Out of DSM: Depathologizing Homosexuality," *Behavioral Science*, Vol. 5, No. 4 (2015).

35 Shaw, "The Bi Option," 20.

36 Shaw, "The Bi Option," 22.

37 Bianca Laureano, "Introduction," in *The People's Book of Human Sexuality: Expanding the Sexology Archive* (New York: Routledge, 2024), 2.

38 Daniel E. Slotnick, "June Dobbs Butts, Sex Therapist Who Preaches Frankness, Dies at 90," *New York Times Magazine* (2019), www.nytimes.com/2019/05/24/obituaries/june-dobbs-butts-dies.html.

39 Slotnick, "June Dobbs Butts."

40 Slotnick, "June Dobbs Butts."

41 Karen Goldsen, Sarah Jen, Theresa Clark, Hyun-Jun Kim, Hyunzee Junh and Jyan Goldsen, "Historical and Generational Forces in the Iridescent Life Course of Bisexual Women, Men and Gender Diverse Older Adults," *Sexualities*, Vol. 25, No. 1–2 (2022), 137.

42 Eisner, "What Is Bisexuality?" 33.

43 "Bi+ History," National Sexual Violence Resource Center, www.nsvrc.org/blogs/Bi-phobia-series/bi-history.

44 Robyn Ochs, "Bisexual: A Few Quotes from Robyn Ochs," https://robynochs.com/bisexual/.

45 Eisner, "What Is Bisexuality?" 22.

46 Vaneet Mehta, "Introduction," in *Bisexual Men Exist: A Handbook for Bisexual, Pansexual and M-Spec Men* (London: Jessica Kingsley Publishers, 2023), 11.

47 "Faith Positions," Human Rights Campaign Website, www.hrc.org/resources/faith-positions.

48 Andrew Kam-Tuck Yip and Alex Toft, "Bisexuality, Religion and Spirituality: Instigating a Dialogue," in *Bisexuality, Religion and Spirituality: Critical Perspectives* (New York: Routledge, 2020), 3.

49 Yip and Toft, "Bisexuality, Religion and Spirituality," 3.

50 Julia Wolf and Lisa Platt, "Religion and Sexual Identities," *Current Opinion in Psychology*, Vol. 48 (2022), 101495.

51 Dawne Moon and Theresa Weynand Tobin, "Sunsets and Solidarity: Overcoming Sacramental Shame in Conservative Christian Churches to Forge a Queer Vision of Love and Justice," *Hypatia: A Journal of Feminist Philosophy*, Vol. 33, No. 3 (2018), 2.

52 Michelle Panchuk and Michael Rea, "Sacramental Shame in Black Churches: How Racism and Respectability Politics Shape the Experiences of Black LGBTQ and Same-Gender-Loving Christians," in *Voices from the Edge: Centering Marginalized Perspectives in Analytic Theology* (Oxford: Oxford University Press, 2020), 142.

53 Panchuk and Rea, "Sacramental Shame in Black Churches," 142.

54 Denise Levy and Jennifer Harr, " 'I Never Felt Like There Was a Place for Me': Experiences of Bisexual and Pansexual Individuals with a Christian Upbringing," *Journal of Bisexuality*, Vol. 18, No. 2 (2018), 194.

55 Levy and Harr, "I Never Felt Like There Was a Place for Me," 187.

56 Rachel Murr, " 'I Became Proud of Being Gay and Proud of Being Christian': The Spiritual Journeys of Queer Christian Women," *Journal of Religion & Spirituality in Social Work*, Vol. 32, No. 4 (2013), 349–372.

57 William L. Jefferies, Brian Dodge and Theo G.M. Sandfort, "Religion and Spirituality Among Bisexual Black Men in the USA," *Culture, Health and Sexuality*, Vol. 10, No. 5 (2008), 464.

58 Alex Toft, "Re-Imagining Bisexuality and Christianity: The Negotiation of Christianity in the Lives of Bisexual Women and Men," *Sexualities*, Vol. 17, No. 5–6 (2014), 546.

59 Toft, "Re-Imagining Bisexuality and Christianity," 557.

60 Levy and Harr, "I Never Felt Like There Was a Place for Me."

61 Levy and Harr, "I Never Felt Like There Was a Place for Me," 198.

62 Jefferies et al., "Religion and Spirituality Among Bisexual Black Men."

63 Jefferies et al., "Religion and Spirituality Among Bisexual Black Men," 473.

64 Jefferies et al., "Religion and Spirituality Among Bisexual Black Men," 473.

65 Yip and Toft, "Bisexuality, Religion and Spirituality," 8.

2

THE JOYS OF BISEXUALITY

It is imperative to address the harm caused by biphobia, bi-erasure, and monosexism, as much of this book does, but it is equally important to discuss the joy and resilience of bisexual people. We often do not hear about the positivity of the bisexual experience; neither is there much research done about this. According to Rostosky et. al, it is not always an easy task to embrace the positive aspects of bisexuality, given the impact of bi-negativity that results in bisexual people being treated with suspicion, invalidation, and rejection.[1] In the concluding remarks for the book *Bisexuality: Theories, Research and Recommendations for the Invisible Sexuality*, Tania Israel addresses this concern by stating:

> *Our internal feelings about our own bisexuality can make it difficult to affiliate with other bisexual individuals and to celebrate our bisexuality. When we are repeatedly exposed to negative messages about bisexuality from family, friends and media, we might start to believe these messages about ourselves and other bisexual individuals . . . and it can contribute to isolation when we draw back from other bisexual individuals.[2]*

A key component of systemic oppressions like bi-erasure, biphobia, and monosexism is not only the invalidation and rejection described earlier but also the denial of the joy and pleasure bisexuality can bring. Positive feelings about oneself are empowering and threaten dominant power structures that perpetuate subjugation and the harmful impact of oppression. adrienne marie brown[3] describes this as *pleasure activism*, the work we do to "reclaim our whole, happy, and satisfiable selves from the impacts, delusions and limitations of oppression and/or supremacy."[4] brown also contends that pleasure

DOI: 10.4324/9781003242659-3

activism includes "work and life lived in the realms of satisfaction, joy and erotic aliveness that bring about social and political change."[5] Not everyone can feel joy given the hardships of experiencing biphobia, bi-erasure, and monosexism, in addition to the intersection of other forms oppression. It is important not to promote toxic positivity if some just are not feeling it; however, those who are able to celebrate their bisexuality and share their sense of joy create a space for others to see there can be another path that may not always have to be as full of struggle.[6] As Tania Israel states, "It is important that we unearth this internalized stigma, challenge the negativity we feel about ourselves and other bisexuals, and help others to do so. Moreover, we will need to combat the negative messages promulgated in society and encourage positive depictions of bisexuality."[7]

There are multiple ways researchers, writers, and activists have worked to raise awareness about the importance of bisexual joy. For example, the powerful research of Rostoksy et al. discovered multiple ways that bisexual folks feel positive with their identity. This evolved into 11 main categories of positivity including:

- freedom from social labels
- honesty and authenticity
- having a unique perspective
- increased levels of insight and awareness
- freedom to love without regard for sex/gender
- freedom to explore relationships
- freedom of sexual expression
- acceptance of diversity
- belonging to a community
- understanding privilege and oppression
- becoming an advocate/activist[8]

Even when facing adversity, these participants in this study found that the challenges of bi-negativity allowed for personal growth. Having access to bisexual community, positive representation in the media, family and friends who are educated about bisexuality, and psychological practitioners who understand their own biases and are well informed about the realities of bisexuality all help with this.[9] (The discussion about ways to be supportive practitioners is addressed in more detail in Chapter 11: "Mental Health Issues and The Impact of Violence").

Another example of a study about bisexual joy conducted by Galupo, Taylor, and Cole examined the positive aspects of being both bisexual and biracial. The four main categories they discovered were "(1) uniqueness of being; (2) multiplicity of experience, (3) community connections, and (4) strengths and impact."[10] Participants described their identities as providing "unique insight" that allowed for more openness to differences, diverse identities, and "defied traditional identity categories."[11] They also felt joy in the intersection of their identities, which created a space for certain kinds of connections based on the shared experience of uniqueness that allowed for close friendships. In addition, the participants reported a "multiplicity of experience" because of their ability to see many sides to identity. Furthermore, this intersection provoked feelings of strength because it allowed for a self-reflection and questioning that led to increase in self-worth, self-reliance, cultural awareness, and empathy for others.[12]

Chapter 6: "Media Representation in Television, Film, and Reality Shows" delves deeper into bisexual representation in the media, but it is important to address how the lack of positive representation directly impacts bisexual joy. One example is how many novels depict bisexual characters as stereotypes such as promiscuous or evil, but there are writers like Melissa Broder and Sally Rooney who have central characters that are bisexual.[13] Even with these novels, writer Elyse John asserts that bisexual joy "still feels new, and it still feels scarce."[14] Even "against a backdrop of pain" that bi-negativity inflicts, "narratives of triumph bloom: romance as self-love, success as a signal of hope," which is part of her own new novel, *Orphia And Eurydicius*. Her retelling of the ancient Greek story of Orpheus and Eurydice includes Orphia as a female poet

L earning to use her voice and embrace her creativity, and Eurydicius is a man—a gentle shield-maker who prefers peace to warfare. The two fall in love, finding commonality as individuals who defy gender roles and as bisexual people who finally feel understood.[15]

Her hope is that more novels will include bisexual characters and maybe, "if our real stories can't be heard, our fictional tales might be."[16]

Other spaces working on the cultivation of bisexual joy include community organizing like the conference BiCon in the United Kingdom and the BECAUSE Conference in the United States.[17] In 2011, an offshoot of BiCon, called BiReCon, held a conference with the theme of *BiTopia*. According to one of the organizers Serena Anderlini-D'Onofrio, "BiTopia" is "the utopian space where bisexuality is real and present, and also where it is the vanishing point for all the imaginative forms of amorous, erotic and sexual expression that make life healthy, creative and fun."[18] Anderlini-D'Onofrio further contends:

W hen we think of BiTopia as the energy of a global paradigm shift from binary to inclusive, from linear to complex, from erotophobic to erotophilic, we see that bisexuality functions as a portal, not a divide. When we imagine the world beyond this portal, we appreciate this complexity as an asset. Love, beyond that portal, is not a need or an instinct, but an art.

In this context, bisexuality is the subtext of a bouquet of imaginative styles of erotic expression that virtually live beyond the divide, including bi, trans, poly, swing, pan, omni, gay, lesbian, goth, metro, eco and many others.[19]

There are many other ways to foster celebratory bisexuality, by observing Bisexual Awareness Week, Celebrate Bisexuality Day, and Bisexual Health Awareness Month.[20] In addition, there are options of support and activism through the Bisexual Resource Center, BiNet USA, and the Bisexual Organizing Project.[21] Promotion of the work of the people included in this book is another option, as their biographies reveal the details of their achievements as writers, educators, entertainers, and one podcast host. In addition, Tania Israel's TED Talk called *Bisexuality and Beyond*; books from authors interviewed in this book, like Shiri Eisner, Loraine Hutchins, and Robert Brooks Cohen; and also Cohen's podcast *Two Bi Guys*, are all tools to explore both realities and accomplishments of bisexual people. Furthermore, for those who consume pornography, supporting sex workers like Wolf Hudson and Dani (interviewed in Chapter 7: "Pornography and Sex Work") allows for supporting content that celebrates the sexual side of bisexuality. And finally, there are the words of Tania Israel, who suggests to bisexual people ways to promote liberatory practices through joy:

> *However you experience and express your bisexuality, your existence contributes to our liberation, and through that liberation, we can transform society's restricted notions of gender, sexuality, and identity. Embrace your unique perspective- -speak it quietly to yourself or amplified to a crowd. Whether or not you are connected with other bisexual people, make sure you're connected with yourself. Recognize your truth, embrace your whole self, and celebrate the complexity and potential of bisexuality.*

Throughout this book there are multiple accounts of both struggle and joy, but the following personal narratives specifically address the joy of bisexuality. First is the perspective of Livia Sauvage in her piece *The Most Generous Window*. Next is a second conversation with professor Tania Israel; Robert Brooks Cohen, writer and host of the podcast *Two Bi Guys*; and, finally, the piece *What I Love About Being Bisexual Now* by Janis Luna.

The Most Generous Window by Livia Sauvage

Before I told anyone I was bisexual, I wrote it down. Before I could tell anyone else, I needed to handle seeing the words reflect back to me: *I am bisexual*. I am attracted to men, but I am attracted to women, too. It was easier to write out than speak aloud. Less judgment. Not zero judgment, as I was still judging myself for not feeling comfortable with confronting who I am. I was not afraid to share my full self and neither did I fear the reactions of my friends and family. In reality, I was surrounded by people who I knew were going to accept me for who I am, so why was I still not ready to share this part of me? I wasn't ready for my own questions about myself, let alone prepared to answer or even admit, *I don't know*, to any questions others would have. After writing down those words, it took me another four months to say them aloud just to myself. Standing in front of my bathroom mirror, eyes heavy, I struggled to recognize the paled-skin girl standing in front of me, but, still, I whispered, "I am bisexual." My stoic face needed to remain still, as I was processing the preceding words. My mind was moving too quickly for me to handle anything else at that very moment. I continued to stand still. In order to come to terms with myself, I was piecing together an unprecedented amount of vulnerability, honesty, and uncertainty within myself. I folded my trembling fingers into my palm: cold (*deep breath, Livia*). I looked back up at myself, took another deep breath, my eyes focused, my fingers uncurled, and that's when I first smiled: the first moment I felt any joy towards my sexuality. **The first time I chose myself.** The first time I chose to not just look at myself but really see myself and admit how good that smile on my face made me feel to finally admit *I am bisexual.*

Another six months later I sat in my friend's car; she had just told me she was bi, and I blurted: "Wait, I am too." I explicitly remember not saying, "I am bisexual" but rather letting her words speak for me. It was almost the word, bisexual, the idea of describing myself as something I never had described myself as before, that scared me most. At this moment in the car, I was laughing. I surprised myself. I sat in that car for another couple of hours, and I finally knew what it felt like to share my whole self with someone else. It felt as if that mirror into which I had spoken to myself was transformed into a window ready to be met with someone on the other side. Sure, still a window, an obstacle, as I realized there was still this hurdle to overcome. I continued to imagine some barrier, both within myself and between others, preventing me from feeling totally comfortable with sharing who I am so casually with someone else, but I still smiled. The mirror turned into a window, and I wasn't talking to myself anymore.

When I first told my mom I was bi, she immediately asked, "How do you know?" and I responded, "Well, how do you know you're straight?"—to which my dad promptly muttered under his breath, "We're not even sure about that." My mom remained focused on me: "Well, have you *ever* kissed a woman?" and in that moment, I knew saying "not yet" would only instigate more interrogation, so I casually said, "That's none of your business." I hadn't kissed a woman, and here's the thing, I really wanted to. There was no questioning that I'm queer, but one big thing was missing: physical experience. I knew I didn't need it to prove anything; I finally felt secure in my sexual identity, but I admitted to one of my close friends that "My next sexual experience will be with a woman," (*spoiler alert: this did not happen*).

So, after graduating from the University of Virginia (UVA), I moved to Paris, France. I needed a new space, new people, new places to explore in order to more fully explore myself. Night one: I updated who "I'm interested in" on my Hinge profile to "Everyone" (*let's goooo*). I started swiping left and right on men, women, and those who identified as non-binary. I just wanted to meet people, get to know all types of personalities, and I found myself somewhat recklessly chatting with up to 20 people at once between three dating apps (*no, I had no clue what I was doing*). I could feel my heart blossoming, genuinely excited, and I was ready to let my sexuality show me how good life could be lived. To me, this feeling is liberation—but from what, really? My own judgments. That window I transformed from my mirror became more and more approachable, almost like a door I could walk through, as I felt myself shedding those past judgments I held for myself. Through this door, I finally let myself become emotionally vulnerable with absolutely anybody I wanted to and **not just with whom society expected me to.**

Three weeks into my life here in Paris, I was going on my first ever date with a woman (!!!!). I was terrified. For me, there was no way around this feeling. I knew I was bi, I knew it, but for lack of a better explanation, I had never tested it out. I was a Women, Gender, and Sexuality studies major at UVA, so I could seriously talk about menstruation and the vulva in class, subjects so commonly avoided, but I could not personally understand what it was like to get to know a woman as a partner, not a friend. I was scared, but I was also so excited. I was afraid that after all of this emotional energy and time I had dedicated to figuring things out, what was it all for? I couldn't admit it yet, but it was for that very excitement. There's a certain, growing joy in doing things solely for the experience. That living-in-the-moment mindset I had never understood up until I was working through those pre-First Ever Date with a Woman™ thoughts. As if right back in my friend's car, I reminded myself of the laughter and joy we filled the space with, just from being ourselves. It didn't matter how the date went, let alone if there would be a second date; I was there to get to know someone, a woman, and I was there to continue getting to know myself, too. This may sound selfish, but I think you're allowed to be selfish when dating. You can be picky, and you can choose to like and dislike parts about someone: that's the entire point, right?

I gave myself one, explicit question to answer throughout the date: Could I kiss her? Could I physically put my lips on her lips? This was not a question of attraction but rather about me finding if it was possible to simply kiss a woman. It was almost operational. I had kissed two men in my life before this date, but I was processing these thoughts so much differently. This feeling was about letting myself share who I am with someone else beyond just accepting my sexuality, embracing it, and finally dating as a bisexual person.

So, that date happened. I thought it was a vibe, but she didn't feel it? I remember explicitly telling myself: *Yeah, I could kiss her.* On one hand, yes, I needed to get to know her and form some emotional connection on our mutual interests, but mainly, I just needed to meet her and imagine myself kissing her. I was at that stage of exploring my sexuality where now I knew I could genuinely enjoy conversations with a woman, but as I had yet to kiss a woman, I did not know how to fully embrace the joys of my sexuality. I guess this rejection reminded me that this particular joy was going to involve more than just me, then. This craving for physical experience with a woman drove my desire to keep dating. Here's the thing about being bi, though: I was talking to men, too. I kept repeating to my friend: The next sexual experience will be with a woman. And then I ended up hooking up with a man for a month?? To backtrack for a second, I had gone on a date with a different woman after the First Ever Date with a Woman™, but I wasn't feeling it. I had never been in that position to turn down a second date, and while it wasn't comfortable, I was beginning to build a stronger sense of security in my own feelings within the dating scene. I was beginning to trust my actions regarding who I was attracted to, physically and emotionally. **Ironically, meeting a man while in the middle of my own struggle to fully embrace my bisexuality helped me overcome that barrier towards feeling totally comfortable with casually sharing how I identify.**

I had become more confident to embrace my bisexuality, including mentioning it in passing. I felt proud to say, "Yeah, I had a date with a woman last night, but I'm talking to this man right now who I think I'm maybe more interested in, so I'll see him this weekend, hopefully." I started speaking to this man in question after those two dates, and before the first date with him, I realized how very similar my nerves felt before this first date compared to the nerves I felt before that First Ever Date with a Woman™. After speaking to random people on dating apps, the novelty of speaking to women had worn off, so, in a strange way, going on a date with a man reminded me that dating is just about getting to know each other. These first date jitters were then overwhelmed by the joy and pride I had for myself for just living in the moment and choosing to get to know someone for the sole purpose of getting to know them. I proceeded to continue seeing this man for only about a month, and I felt great. It was casual and fun, and while I had put so much pressure on myself to get to know women, this experience reminded me that I truly am attracted to men, too, both emotionally and physically.

The entire year leading up to this point, I felt that I was in a constant state of needing to convince others. Whether it was needing to explain to someone I was attracted to women without having yet kissed another or asked "Well, aren't you really just gay??" I felt stuck in this crossroads of always needing to prove my sexuality. Why weren't my feelings evidence enough? So, now you may be thinking, well, Livia, you're saying you don't need to prove anything, but you just told me that you now felt more confident in yourself after a month of hooking up with a man. Here's the thing: These are joys I am finding and holding for myself. Nobody else. **My experiences do not exist to convince you of my sexuality.** My reflections and experiences as a bisexual woman are for me to hold for myself and learn from, to smile and cry looking back on.

So, no: I had not yet kissed a woman. That fact was still weighing on me.

After that month, I was still on the dating apps, but honestly, I was emotionally exhausted. I had positioned myself on this path to explore the more physical desires of my bisexuality, and after a couple of months, I still hadn't kissed a woman (*UGH*). It was different than before, though, as I did not feel like I was missing anything, anymore. While I had never felt "less bisexual" because I hadn't kissed a woman, now I knew—oh, I didn't know how much—but I knew kissing a woman could only *add* to my life. And . . .;)

Fast forward to the beginning of 2022, I had been in Paris for four months, and as I mentioned, I was emotionally exhausted. I only opened up a dating app every couple of days, because I didn't really have a desire to get to know anybody at the moment. For me, exploring my bisexuality and dating around are one in the same, but in the moment I decided to not date around, I also found confidence and joy in who I am. With the casual comfort I discovered in passively stating, "Yeah, I'm bi," I realized it had nothing to do with my dating history. Nevertheless, the fact I had not yet kissed a woman was still looming, so after a couple of weeks messaging this one woman, we went on our first date in mid-January.

Immediately after our first date, my mouth genuinely hurt from laughing so much (*cheesy, I know*). We closed out the bar, I walked her to a taxi, and when I turned to go home, I thought to myself like *ok ok ok, that was nice.* If you haven't already figured it out, I have such limited experience dating, bi or not, so these feelings were, to put it simply, new. To feel good about a conversation, to feel heard and appreciated in such a short amount of time? I was happy. I realized I was still smiling, texting a couple of friends that it "went well??" It was a great first date, and, of course, the following 12 hours were crucial: who's texting whom first? Along with all the interacting gender norms at play in the dating scene, I had only been conditioned to hold expectations for when on dates with men. I wasn't debriefing the date with, "It was good, I mean he paid for my drinks" or "Ugh, I hope he texts me first," that 21st-century chivalry all of my straight friends still look for and depend on. Rather, my thoughts were full of, "Can't believe I might almost like olives now" and "Why was it hot when she just said, 'go on,' when I was already rambling?" Beyond a great conversation, I found myself learning more about what I find attractive in someone else. There was a sense of calm that swept over me, certifying that this excitement could be potentially reciprocated, another first for me. So, with norms out the window, I did not know the next steps. I decided to text her first (*ha!*). That *was* the next step: embracing the fact there were no societal norms to follow. We went on our second date a week later, and, according to my more experienced queer friends, this is "classic," but it lasted 20 hours? And yes, we kissed (*wooooo*)!!

I made it a point to call my friend who I first came out to, the one whose car I was sitting in almost two years prior, to tell her about my first kiss with a woman. My closest friend within the queer community, I knew she would understand what I was feeling. Like nobody else, I knew she would appreciate hearing how I felt a particular intimacy like never before and a certain tenderness I didn't recognize but only wanted to familiarize myself with more. That initial liberation from changing my Hinge profile preferences to "Everyone" only strengthened. This liberation deepened, as I actively defied societal norms like never before, kissing a woman, another person who knew what it felt like to, at one point, hide in a heteronormative world. At first, I immediately compared kissing a woman to kissing a man. I always claimed that the most continuous struggle living as a bi woman was how to be *seen* as a bisexual woman. How when kissing a man, no matter the man's sexuality, you cannot necessarily *see* the strength it has taken me to get to a point of connecting with anyone as a bisexual woman. What I realized, though, is that it is not up to the action, the kiss, or who I am kissing, that defines my strength or, simply, my sexuality. It is me. I am bisexual, and no matter who I decide to talk to, kiss, or date, this is what bisexuality can look like. And if you take the time to get to know me, then you can truly *see* bisexuality.

A Conversation with Tania Israel

LISA:
I was thinking a little bit about the intersection of racism with biphobia or bi-erasure. Do you feel like that intersection is something that you faced once you did come out as bisexual? Like being stereotyped as a bi person but also racially stereotyped?

TANIA:
Oh, sure. I mean, I'm always racially stereotyped. I have to say, one other thing I noticed [is] that when we do research and have interview questions there's a lot about leaning into the bias and the marginalization and all of that, and that's certainly been something that I've experienced. But I think that it's also so important to highlight resilience and where it's like, yeah, sure, I've navigated bias and erasure and all of that stuff

and I'm okay. It's certainly something that can be harmful and there can be very positive experiences of bisexuality as well. Yes, there's racism, there's all of that, AND there's resilience and there's joy.

L:

Well, that goes to the next question, which is, where do you personally find joy in bisexuality?

T:

You know, some people would be like, who would ever choose to be queer if they didn't have to be? And I'm like, I would! I think if I got to choose a sexual orientation, I would totally choose bisexuality. I like gender not being the highest priority for myself. I think it allows me to focus in on what are the qualities of human beings that I value and am drawn to. I think gender's a little bit arbitrary in my view.

So yeah, I love being bisexual. I also feel like bisexual community is the most diverse community I've ever been part of. And not only the most diverse but the most supportive of diversity that I've been part of. Where there's the most attention to people with disabilities and people of color and age differences and all of this. I think that there's something about being so on the margins, even of community that you feel like you should be a part of, that makes bisexual people—and especially people who have some leadership in terms of creating community—just attentive to all of the different aspects of diversity.

I love that about bisexuality. I'm a pretty happy person generally, and that happiness is also related to bisexuality. I write bisexual haiku. If there isn't a better way of expressing joy and bisexuality! It comes into my creativity and it inspires my creativity.

I didn't write haiku about other things before I started writing bisexual haiku. So, there's a lot of fun that we can have. There's a lot of community; there's connection with other bisexual

people. I love the bisexual flag colors. They suit
me very well, so I like to dress in the bisexual
flag colors.

I just taught a class with . . . undergraduate students on bisexuality and it was delightful. Seeing
them learn things and the ways that they saw things
shifted. And it wasn't just a course about being
bisexual, it was a course about all kinds of different topics, but through the lens of bisexuality.
So, it's like, okay, I want to teach about health
disparities. What if we understand that through
the lens of bisexuality? What about relationship
through the lens of bisexuality? Bisexuality offers
such complexity as it is that when we look at things
through the lens of bisexuality, it brings a complex understanding to whatever that topic is. So,
yeah, I think bisexuality is fantastic!

L:

That's awesome! I feel like it is a really important part of the conversation, so I appreciate you
bringing that up, and if we want to celebrate bisexuality, we need to know the positive and powerful
aspects of it, which is a powerful statement and
probably not something we do. You may know more than
I do, but I feel like when my students are writing
about it, there's still a lot of struggles. There's
isolation and not feeling part of community. So,
how do people find community?

T:

I think it's a great question and my answer to how
I found community is that I created it. I started a
bisexual discussion group in Santa Barbara that's
been going for seven years now at least. And we've
met like once a month for the last seven years, and
during the pandemic it was my consistent source
of community. I feel like it's been so important
to hold space for other people. Cause like every
month I don't necessarily feel the need for community, but I feel like it's equally important for me
to help hold space for other people. And we have
new people coming to that group all the time, and

people come and they'll say, "oh, this is the first bisexual thing I've ever seen in our community." And really there is that isolation and invisibility and when people see something that's for them specifically, you know, not just LGBT but for bisexual people, it's like, wow. Just knowing that it's there is healing for people. And then people have come to this group and then some people have said, yeah, because I'm in this group, I've come out to people, or because I'm in this group, I feel like I've been able to just integrate all the parts of myself, or I've made this work transition that I've wanted to make.

Things that don't even have to do with sexual orientation. It sort of helps give people a place where they can wholly be themselves. I've loved being a part of creating that and holding that space in my local community. And then also beyond that, because I do research on bisexuality and advocacy, that's connected me with bisexual people all over the U.S. and beyond.

Working on something together with other people is always such a good way of creating connection and community. So doing policy advocacy with people on bisexuality, you know, that's something that I've been trying to do, which is more bisexual community organizing. So, all of these things really helped me to feel community. I recognize people who aren't, you know, what I think of as myself as a professional bisexual . . . people who aren't professional bisexuals also need ways of finding community. It's not enough just to say, well, if you do research and advocacy . . . people who aren't activists need community as much as everybody else does.

That's where we need spaces for the everyday bisexuals. A lot of LGBT centers don't offer programs specifically for bisexual people and also don't necessarily do a lot of advertising of their programming beyond the LGBT community. And that's so much what bisexual people need. If we really want to reach people who are everyday bisexuals, we have to reach beyond LGBT community to do that.

A Conversation with Robert Brooks Cohen

LISA:
Where do you find joy in bisexuality?

ROB:
What I love about it is the potential for anything. So, if I have the potential for a spectrum of attractions in me. That to me extends beyond gender and . . . the whole experience of coming out and embracing these things that I used to be ashamed of has affected many other areas of my life too, and just helped me be able to be my more authentic self.

I'm less ashamed of lots of different things now, or if I am ashamed of something, I will notice that and try to unpack it and try to push myself to be more that. And then because of that, I've experienced all these things that I never would have come across, all these very nonconforming, diverse experiences and people and communities and settings.

I didn't know this stuff existed and now I get to be part of it. For example, I mean there's many things, but there's just a lot of queer clubs I've been to and seeing how people express themselves and how they dance with each other and all the different gender expressions and then also the kink community.

I've sort of explored the kink community a little because of my queerness. I think I wouldn't have been comfortable doing that before I came out. And just people embracing things beyond gender that there's stigma or shame around and they're embracing it and being like, *this is me*.

Even when I see stuff like that—that's not what I'm into—I just think it's so interesting and cool and I find joy in just seeing the diversity of the community and exploring new things. There's always something new in this queer world.

What I Love About Being Bisexual Now by Janis Luna

A couple of years ago, I wrote an essay for *Go Magazine* called "5 Reasons I Love Being Bisexual." In it, I wrote about how—as I navigated coming out in my early twenties—it seemed like I was the last to know I might "be kinda gay" (to quote an accidentally amnesiac Willow Rosenberg from the Season 6 episode of *Buffy the Vampire Slayer*, "Tabula Rasa"). I reflected on how I had written a love poem to a femme classmate in one of my undergrad classes, unaware that it was even a love poem. A guy friend of mine, upon hearing this, bluntly suggested to me that it seemed like maybe, just maybe, I wasn't straight.

Some of the reasons I appreciated being bisexual in 2018 included being in good company: Several famous badasses are or were bi, including Josephine Baker, Janis Joplin (from whom I take my stripper name and the name I write under), Aubrey Plaza, Anais Nin, Janelle Monae, Amy Winehouse, Frida Kahlo, Malcolm X, Billie Holiday, and none other than Buffy Summers herself (in the Season 8 comics, at least, and forever in my headcanon and heart). I wrote about how bisexual identity means whatever I want it to mean, and for me, this means being attracted to my own gender and genders other than mine, rather than thinking about it in binary terms such as "opposite" gender or in limiting terms that assume there are only two genders. Gender, after all, is a spectrum and, as one of my dear queer friends described it to me over coffee today, gender is also something way less linear than a spectrum: Gender is also a galaxy! And what could stand "opposite" a galaxy, anyway? Bisexuality, in the way I experience it, doesn't presume only *two* genders, and I chose it then (and now) simply because I like it as a word: I think it looks pretty on the page and sounds pretty to speak, and personally I prefer it to pansexual; though in form and function my orientation probably could be described as pansexual just as easily, I simply don't like "pansexual" as much, as a descriptor for me. It doesn't fit, by which I mean, it doesn't feel right in my body to describe myself that way.

I also wrote about how my dad (of all people!) suggested the possibility of my queerness to me askance. We were on a drive to visit family, and I was complaining about the end of some tragic relationship with some guy I can't even remember now. He said to me, gently and without taking his eyes off the road, "I have no doubt you're going to find a man who sees you and loves you for who you are." Then, after a very pregnant pause, he added innocently "or a woman." Remembering this, I love being bisexual for the ways that people have seen that in me before I could see it in myself, even someone as traditional as my Catholic, Sicilian American dad, who saw me and loved me and helped me give language to this part of myself.

Back in 2018, I wrote about how, when I decide to unicorn in a threesome, it's something I do of my own volition. Threesomes are a sex act I can enjoy if and when I want to, and the amalgamations of gender within the threesome are up to me (and the folks I'm sharing that experience with). I've had my fair share of experiences of unicorn hunting and had pretty much every gender assortment of threesomes (and moresomes) possible, and, admittedly, it was a learning curve. My homecoming into my own authentic embodiment of sexuality was not a journey devoid of harm—I've been fetishized for being bisexual, been treated like "a third" and "a secondary." Some of the relationships I've found myself in have had their shades of objectification and dehumanization, up to and including rape and intimate partner violence.

These days, I consider myself more biromantic than bisexual. Part of my healing from the violence I've experienced as someone of both marginalized gender and sexuality has been a journey of solo sexuality for the past couple of years. I've experienced sexual violence and intimate partner violence in part connected to my experience as a bisexual femme and an out sex worker, and currently the sex that feels most safe, empowering, healing, and joyful to me is the sex that I have with myself. In terms of sexual orientation, the label that fits the nicest to me is ace or demisexual. Within the umbrella of asexuality, too, is what seems currently to more accurately describe my sexuality: autosexuality (what I refer to as solo sexuality), that is, "people who are more attracted to themselves than to others and may prefer masturbation to sex with a partner." This definition comes from WebMD, and while I do think I'm hot shit, my experience of solo sexuality has less to do with being attracted *to* myself and more to do with enjoying sex *with* myself more than partnered sex. Whether this has to do with trauma, neurodivergence, or simple preference is still a mystery to me and generally is not a question I feel any particular pressure to answer. I'm non-binary, and the more I settle into that aspect of my identity, the more ease, comfort, and playfulness I find with the concept of both/and/neither in realms outside of gender, too. The point is, I love my embodying my erotic self, and my fantasies are not restricted by gender. Partnered sex, on the other hand, I can take or leave and I don't feel like something is missing from my life when I'm not having partnered sex. This has been an immensely liberating transformation for me, as part of the role I've played in the sexual harm I've experienced has been in holding onto the belief that there was something *wrong* with me if I wasn't having partnered sex. (I now know this to be internalized acephobia—shout out to Sherronda J. Brown, the brilliant author of *Refusing Compulsory Sexuality: A Black Asexual Lens on Our Sex Obsessed Culture*.)

As I grow into my demisexual/solo sexual identity, though, my attraction to folks of many genders hasn't abated. I appreciate beauty, sexiness, and erotic appeal from people of all genders, though again, I don't feel much moved to have partnered sex. Similarly, I have many romantic friendships with folks of all genders. There is a romance to my friendships, a platonic intimacy that encompasses much more than what we all do with and to each other's bodies if we spend time together naked. While my experience of sex and sexuality is much different now in the day-to-day than what it was in 2018, what I love about it is very much the same: I love that it is mine, for me to define and make of what I wish and desire. "Bisexual" is still a beautiful word to me, and it's still a word that feels like it fits for me. It still "sparks joy," so I'm keeping it, even though now that joy is something I experience more privately and with myself alone. Bisexuality was my way into queerness, and queerness was my way home to who I am, who I have been, and who I ever shall be, in all my mercurial fluidity. Truly *que linda*, to be bisexual still.

Notes

1 Sharon Scales Rostosky, Ellen D.B. RIggle, David Pascale-Hague and LaWanda E. McCants, "The Positive Aspects of a Bisexual Identification," *Psychology and Sexuality*, Vol. 1, No. 2 (2010).

2 Tania Israel, "Concluding Remarks: A Perspective on Envisioning Bisexuality as Inclusive, Celebratory and Liberatory," in *Bisexuality: Theory, Research and Recommendations for the Invisible Sexuality*, ed. D. Joye Swan and Shani Habibi (New York: Springer, 2018), 192.

3 She intentionally has her name all in lower case.

4 adrienne marie brown, "Introduction," in *Pleasure Activism: The Politics of Feeling Good* (Chico, CA: AK Press, 2019), 13.

5 brown, "Introduction," 13.

6 brown, "Introduction," 14.

7 Israel, "Concluding Remarks," 191.

8 Rostosky et al., "The Positive Aspects of a Bisexual Identification," 134.

9 Rotoksy et al., "The Positive Aspects of a Bisexual Identification," 142.

10 M. Paz Galupo, Son M. Taylor and David Cole Jr., "'I am Double the Bi': Positive Aspects of Being Both Bisexual and Biracial," *Journal of Bisexuality*, Vol. 19, No. 2 (2019), 158.

11 Galupo et al., "I am Double the Bi," 160.

12 Galupo et al., "I am Double the Bi," 161.

13 Elyse John, "What Does Bisexual Joy Look Like? Author of Orphia and Eurydicius, Elyse John, Tells Diva About Bi Books," (March 2024), https://diva-magazine.com/2024/03/26/what-does-bisexual-joy-look-like/.

14 John, "What Does Bisexual Joy Look Like?"

15 Elise Dumpleton, "Q and A: Elyse John, Author of Orphia and Eurydicius," *The Nerd Daily* (March 2024), https://thenerddaily.com/elyse-john-orphia-and-eurydicius-interview/#:~:text=In%20my%20version%20of%20the,people%20who%20finally%20feel%20understood.

16 John, "What Does Bisexual Joy Look Like?"

17 BECAUSE Conference, www.becauseconference.org/; Bicon in the UK, https://2023.bicon.org.uk/.

18 Serena Anderlini-D'Onofrio, "BiReConaissance: An Introduction to BiTopia, Selected Proceedings from BiReCon," *Journal of Bisexuality*, Vol. 11, No. 2–3 (2011), 146.

19 Anderlini-D'Onofrio, "BiReConaissance," 148.

20 Israel, "Concluding Remarks."

21 For more information about these programs, see the resource section of this book.

3

GENDER-DIVERSE IDENTITIES

At the time of writing, it is 2024 and far-right politicians are capitalizing on fear-mongering tactics and passing anti-transgender legislation at an alarming rate in the United States. The American Civil Liberties Union (ACLU) is tracking 515 anti-LGBTQ bills across America, most of which are attacking transgender youth[1] Gender-diverse people face the constant threat of adversity and violence in a society invested in what Shiri Eisner calls *cissexism*—"the social system to which everyone is, or should be cisgender (i.e. non-transgender), including the social system of privilege for those who are cisgender, and punishment for those who are not."[2] For the purpose of this chapter, *gender-diverse* is used as an umbrella term to describe gender expression beyond cisgender expectations of sex and gender assigned at birth or the binary framework. This includes people who are transgender, non-binary, and gender queer and allows for the fact that many transgender people do not identify as non-binary, and not all non-binary people identify as transgender.

For people who are gender-diverse *and* bisexual, there is the unique challenge of navigating the intersections of transphobia, cissexism, monosexism, biphobia, and bi-erasure. This can manifest in multiple ways, particularly around perceptions of bisexual gender-diverse people's sexuality. This chapter will address these complexities; however, it is equally important to explore the realities and experiences beyond these oppressions. The personal narratives in the second half of the chapter bear witness to Lucie Fielding's warning about transgender sexuality:

> *If our understanding of sexual health is defined primarily by health disparities and risk factors, for example, how does this serve to foreclose*

DOI: 10.4324/9781003242659-4

conversation around possibilities for embodied sexual joy? Or how does an almost exclusive focus on what a friend, activist Turner Willman, has called the narrative of "death and oppression" further limit our clinical imaginations and desiccate landscapes of experience? I'd like to invite us to consider grounding our praxis in fostering and evoking trans ingenuity, resilience, and capacities for tapping into intergenerational wisdom.[3]

First, it is essential to examine navigating sexuality as a gender-diverse person in a highly transphobic and cissexist world, particularly the "politics of desirability." This phrase and concept, created by queer, fat activists of color, describes those who do not fit into specific privileged categories of what is desirable or who is considered sexual.[4] Lucie Fielding, in her book *Trans Sex: Clinical Approaches to Trans Sexualities and Erotic Embodiments*, references Caleb Luna, who writes about desirability politics on the blog BGD:

Colonization indoctrinates us into the romantic idolization of thinness, whiteness, and masculinity—in ourselves and others. How do I, as a fat, brown, femme, decolonize my desire so I can desire myself? How do I love myself in a world that tells me I am not lovable? How can I decolonize my desire so I won't ever again compulsively glance at a skinny boy who refuses to see me as the goddess I am?[5]

These racist and ableist ideologies intersect with cissexism; as Hari Ziyad contends, "A 'fit' body is rarely disabled and never fat. 'Good' skin is often light, if not white. Ideas around masculinity and femininity and who fits into them are all directly related to cisheterosexism."[6]

Fielding describes this also as *erotic privilege*, which privileges bodies that are white, young, cisgender, monosexual, and able-bodied as erotic and those "that do not conform to—or, literally, embody—one or more of these cultural ideals are erotically marginalized and deemed 'unimaginable.'"[7] When there is so little positive media representation of gender-diverse people it is difficult not to internalize the negative messaging, as Fielding writes, that tells "us that our bodies are repulsive, that we are un-fuckable, that we are less-than, or that our desires and needs are not as important as those of other people in the world."[8]

Gender-diverse people are not only "undesirable" under these constraints but also are seen as lacking "desire-*ability*."[9] As Fielding states, "Put simply, trans and non-binary folx are not only excluded from being objects of desire, but are not imaginable as beings able to experience sexual desire."[10] There is a long history of this, such as the work of sexologist Harry Benjamin, who wrote in his 1966 work *The Transsexual Phenomenon* that transgender people "'have no overt sex life at all,' at least prior to medical interventions, and particularly bottom surgeries."[11] Benjamin's book was once considered "the transsexuals' bible" and a standard for medical care to "treat" transgender people.[12] However, according to Fielding, "Benjamin ultimately positioned hatred of the sexual body and aversion for engaging in sexual activity as a "central feature" of trans experience and as a primary diagnostic criterion for determining whether a patient is a "true transsexual."[13]

Gender-diverse people also are exposed to cisgender people's potential objectification and fetishization of their bodies. Anzani et al. define this kind of fetishization as the "sexual investment in transness as an overvalued sex object rather than holistic individual"[14] and emphasize how gender-diverse people are a "mere instrument for the attainment of a personal goal, which leads to their denial of human dignity."[15] Anzani et al. found in their own study of transgender people that 64.2% reported being fetishized in the past and 53.2% of these experiences occurred on dating apps.[16] An example of this is when cisgender people, mostly men, are "chasers." Not much research has been conducted on this, but writer Zack Zoetic eloquently addresses this when he states,

> *C*hasers aren't like . . . trans enthusiasts. They're not running down the street during Pride, giving out pamphlets on trans rights and looking to make the world a safer place for trans people. They're not concerned with workplace acceptance of pronouns, or society's perception of gender, or easy access to medical care. Chasers don't care about trans people! They only like how trans people make their genitals tingly.[17]

Furthermore, gender-diverse people of color face another layer with racial fetishization.[18] Racial fetishization is defined as "race-based fixation on a bodily part or characteristic that involves both idolization and demonization of racial difference."[19] This mindset intersects with hypersexualized stereotypes about people of color, particularly people of Asian and African descent. In addition, a recent national survey conducted in the United States found that transgender people of color "face higher levels of unequal treatment, harassment, physical attacks, sexual assault, and intimate partner violence than White transgender people."[20] (I address this further in Chapter 10: "Mental Health Issues and The Impact of Violence"). In the end, all kinds of fetishization and objectification of gender-diverse people may lead to potential fear for their safety and avoidance of sexual interactions.[21]

Sexual and romantic orientations of gender-diverse people vary widely, but a large percentage are bisexual. The 2015 U.S. Transgender Survey conducted by the National Center for Transgender Equality found that 32% of respondents identified as bisexual or pansexual, compared to 16% who identified as lesbian or gay, 21% who identified as queer, and 15% who identified as heterosexual. Transgender women were more likely to identify as bisexual than were transgender men (20% vs. 12%).[22] Approximately 35% of the individuals in this study identified primarily as non-binary. This number may be low though, given that not all non-binary people identify as transgender and may not have participated in the study.[23] In another study specifically on non-binary individuals, 31% identified as queer, but also 17% were bisexual and 17% were pansexual.[24]

There are many connections *between* gender-diverse identities and bisexuality, even though the specific experiences of being both gender diverse *and* bisexual are often not discussed. A prominent similarity is the subversion of binaries as Shiri Eisner states,

> *B*isexuality raises social anxieties concerning the hierarchical binary of gay and straight, and transgender raises anxieties concerning the hierarchical binary of woman and man . . . these subversions threaten to blur and confound—the "clear cut" borders between oppressor and oppressed classes. In addition, they also expose the fact that a hierarchy exists, since by crossing that metaphorical "border," they reveal its very existence.[25]

Eisner continues by pointing out how both groups challenge norms around understandings of identities, particularly the potential for change and fluidity.[26] There is also the perceived shared experience of "passing":

> *I*n order to survive, members of both these groups are obliged to pass as something they are not-cisgender or monosexual. People who do wish to be recognizable as trans or bi are often coercively passed off as cis or mono anyway. The price of both these things is the erasure of those particular identities from the knowledge and experience of everyday life. People who do pass as trans or bi (intentionally or not) are then forced to deal with the consequences in the form of social policing, discrimination, and other forms of violence.[27]

In addition, both groups are often accused of "seeking straight privilege."[28] There can be the perception that bisexual people want to benefit from heteronormative lives with queerness on the side, while gender-diverse people, particularly transgender people who transition on the binary, are "gay men and lesbians who change their genders in order to become straight and avoid homophobic oppression."[29] This also intersects with the accusation that both groups are perpetuating the gender binary, which contradicts the earlier analysis of how they subvert binaries.[30]

With so many shared experiences and stereotypes, one might expect there to be a strong connection between these communities, but Eisner argues that this is not always the case. The two groups are often treated as separate entities, so that people who are gender diverse and bisexual are "doubly erased as bi in trans communities and trans in bi communities."[31] For example, the frequency of language like "both sexes" or "both genders" in bisexuality discourse, erases the realities of gender-diverse people. Although the definition of bisexuality has become more inclusive, Eisner argues that the mainstream bisexuality movement itself needs to do better, along with the gender-diverse movements challenging their own biphobia. Eisner contends, "What I am trying to do is to draw attention to two things: the huge waste of revolutionary potential that these two groups could have by being allied, and the double erasure experienced by people who are both bi and trans."[32] There are more efforts in this direction, such as the publication *A Closer Look: Bisexual Transgender People*—a collaboration between the Movement Advancement Project, National Center for Transgender Equality, Bisexual Resource Center, and BiNet USA—but so much more needs to be done.[33]

As this chapter transitions to the following personal narratives, it is imperative to return to Lucie Fielding's quote at the beginning of the chapter and their call to move beyond the "death and oppression" discourse. As these narratives show, there are challenges of dealing with the intersections of transphobia, cissexism, monosexism, biphobia, and bi-erasure, but their experiences are also rich with *gender pleasure*, which Fielding describes as "the pleasure one can feel in one's embodied experience of gender, whether that's feeling affirmed in one's gender within social, sexual, or intimate contexts—or just feeling yummy in one's body at a given moment."[34] Each perspective encompasses individualistic concepts of the lived experience of both bisexuality and gender-diverse identities. There are struggles but also resilience and joy in their stories that allow for a celebration of multiple intersecting identities that are often not discussed. In addition, there are gender-diverse perspectives appearing in other chapters, including Janis Luna in Chapter 2: "The Joys of Bisexuality"; River McMican in Chapter 9: "BDSM and Kink"; and Katelyn Friedline and Shiri Eisner in Chapter 11: "Disabilities."

A Conversation with Ash Ward

LISA:
How does bisexuality intersect with being non-binary for you?

ASH:
The biggest connection in my mind is that they're always portrayed as "invisible queer identities." There's this narrative around bisexuality that it's not a visible sexuality, which, you can't know that about any sexuality. It is the same for non-binary too. I think about conversations about passing privilege for trans people or, like, how do you pass as

non-binary? There's no way to do that in a society
that doesn't recognize non-binary as a gender identity. They've just always been connected in my head
as these kind of fluid amorphous identities that
aren't really recognized by society in the same
way. They're just complete and total rejections of
binaries rather than working inside of them. I'm
multiracial as well. So, almost all the identities
I hold are in these spaces that just can't operate
the same way as other identities. They inherently
don't work within that system.

L:

That's a lot to navigate.

A:

It's definitely taken a long time to be comfortable with it. I've always known I was multiracial
because I was born that way. My entire life I've
had to navigate, well I'm not white, but I'm also
not really Indian or Bangladeshi. I wasn't raised
in that culture. It would be wrong of me to say
that there isn't part of me that's white or Italian, because that's the culture I was raised in.
But also, people look at me and don't go like, oh,
you're a white person, because that's not my skin
tone. It's hard to know if it's because I've always
had to be navigating outside of those racial binaries, if that's kind of part of where the bisexuality and non-binary came from. Identity development
is so weird. I've always had to operate outside of
how people try to place me in the box. And so, I've
always been comfortable with that.

I don't know if you've talked with anyone about
this, but a lot of non-binary people feel like they
have to be with someone who's bisexual. To be affirmed
gender wise . . . I've never personally felt like
that, but it's something I can understand . . . so
my boyfriend's straight and he's only attracted to
women or people with female bodies. And in some ways
that is reaffirming for me because I am not a woman.

I do have a female presenting body. I can understand
the sentiment of like, if my partner's attracted

to multiple genders, then there's no sort of confining my body into their sexuality. I think that's interesting how that operates in dating. Because I'm bisexual, I'm attracted to people of all different types of bodies. So, if I was dating a trans person or a non-binary person, it wouldn't matter, whatever genitalia, whatever body parts you have, I'm attracted to them regardless. And so, there's no pressure of like, oh, if you did get surgery or if you did medically transition, would you still be attracted to me?

I personally have no interest in medically transitioning, but if I did, I couldn't be with my boyfriend because if I got surgery, if I went on T, he wouldn't be attracted to my body anymore. So, I get it, especially for people who don't know if they want to transition or are in the process of transitioning, seeking out people who are bi because they feel like that pressure will be lessened.

L:
There seems to be a lot about how people are seen in their relationships and what does that mean for queer identity?

A:
Yeah. With being non-binary, people always are more likely to gender me correctly if I'm not with my boyfriend, right? Even other trans people and other people who are really gender affirming, they just get tripped up as soon as they see me with a guy, because I'm female presenting. They're like, oh, it's a straight relationship and you must be a woman because you're with a straight man. Why would my gender identity change? Because I'm with a guy and why would my sexuality change? It's so weird to me. Do people who are straight stop being attracted to other people just because they're in a relationship?

L:
That's what's supposed to happen, right!? That makes me think about how that can happen in queer spaces too, where you're not queer enough.

A:

I think so much of it comes from that pressure to prove that you're bi. Like "gold star lesbian," that targets specifically bi people . . . I've never actually been with a woman just because it never ended up working out. And then people will question, well how do you know if you're bi? And I'm like, well, regardless if I've actually slept with a woman, I know, I'm still attracted to them. Or even things like . . . I own a lot of Pride merch just because I like going to Pride marches, they make me happy. And whenever I'm by myself, I'm always assumed to be gay. Which that honestly doesn't give me that much dysphoria. But whenever my boyfriend's there, or even if I'm with a male friend, then all of a sudden, I'm read as an ally. Like, you're just here to support the community. You're not part of it. And I'm like, what? I'm the same person, I'm wearing the same pride merch. It doesn't say "Ally" anywhere. The assumption I am an ally is so invalidating in terms of like, oh, but you can't be queer.

L:

Do you identify as trans also?

A:

I do. I've always seen trans as anyone who doesn't identify with the socialization they were brought into. There are a lot of cisgender people who I think qualify as trans if they wanted to. People who are brought up as hyper-feminine but don't actually see themselves that way. I think a lot of people who are butch could identify as trans if they wanted to, even if they still identify as women. But I know that's not how everyone sees it. For me, I was raised to be a woman, that's how everyone expected me to be. And I'm not a woman. And even though I'm not a man, that's still different than what people wanted me to be or expected me to be. So, that's how I've always seen trans . . . anyone in anything that doesn't fall under the gendered expectations when they were being raised.

L:

That's the sort of the umbrella-ness of that definition. It's all inclusive. It is very individualistic, and how can we just be more accepting of that?

A:

It's policing everybody. People can be so afraid of their identity sometimes. If I let this person be queer, then what does that mean about my queerness? Or what does that mean about what my identity means? Why does it matter? Why are you threatened by other people using the same label as you or identifying the same way as you?

For another interview with Ash go to Chapter 9: "Kink and BDSM."

A Conversation with Bryant Staff

LISA:

How do you feel bisexuality intersects with being non-binary?

BRYANT:

I think that it allows me to fall in love with myself. It allows me to see myself as me and I don't have to fit those binaries of male or female. I can see that in other people too, and it makes me more attracted to the person and their energy and what they are able to give to the world. Not so much like, this is a man, he's a manly man; or this is a girl and she's so feminine and soft. We're all kind of fluid. And I'm attracted to that. Being bisexual, I'm able to see that in different people, but also see it in myself. I'm non-binary. I'm bisexual. I'm also a crossdresser and I'm a drag queen.

L:

With all of these identities, what assumptions are made about you?

B:

I think the biggest thing is when people find out that I'm non-binary and also bisexual, they assume that I'm hypersexual. Like, that's really all I care about, and that's the last thing that I care about! I'm not really that sexual of a person. I'm a more romantic person. I'm not so much into the act of sex. I enjoy it, but that's not the first thing I'm running towards. I think that's the biggest misconception of being bisexual and non-binary. My identity is very political and I'm expected to always be on the front lines, but as a Black queer person, that's exhausting. That's tiring. I don't have time for that. I'm tired. A lot of us are tired. And it's like we are not given grace, you know?

L:

If you are in a bi space do you feel like there is transphobia?

B:

I can definitely say that there is more transphobia in bisexual spaces. I can't so much speak from the trans experience because this is also kind of another topic, but obviously I am a little bit more masculine presenting because, how do I word this? I'm Black. Big surprise. But Black non-binary people aren't given the same grace that non-Black, bisexual or binary people are given. Because I don't have the passable looks, I don't pass that easy. Of course, if I shave, put on a little bit more makeup, I might be able to pass. But in my natural form, I don't pass. So, you won't really know that I'm non-binary until I tell you that. Or you can pick up on it a day where I'm dressed a little bit more feminine and not correlating with my gender that I was born with. I find more community in queer spaces because I don't really pass as straight, so I'm kind of automatically assumed gay. Not so much bisexual. When I was identifying as he/him, I had lots of people calling me up. But now that I'm a little bit more like jumping in and out . . . I'm not that sought after.

If I do date a non-Black person, whether it be a girl or a guy, they expect me to be a lot more masculine, but then me being non-binary is kind of like, okay, well wait. You knew I was non-binary before we started this, and they're expecting me to take on this very masculine role. And that's just not me. So, I've had a lot of trouble with dating, to be honest, because of that. It's very hard.

L:

We're so invested in attraction being based on these gender roles and these gender expectations.

B:

It's kind of hard, especially in Albuquerque. I mean, there are a lot of non-binary people here but a lot of them are white or Hispanic and aren't attracted to Black people; that's just the truth. Even my Black cis gay friends have trouble meeting people who are accepting. Queer Black people are fetishized. So that's kind of how it's here. But in bigger cities, it's a lot easier to meet other Black non-binary people or just non-binary people in general who are accepting of Black non-binary and bisexual people.

Honestly, I just want to be held! Being here another year does mean kind of being romantically lonely. I've kind of accepted that though. This is my time to get into my art and find out who I am, you know, self-work, got to find some way to make it positive.

L:

Good approach! What's going on that you're not pursued or that people aren't interested?

B:

Well, I think it comes down to just like me not being a sexual person, I'd rather get kind of romantic. If I go on Grindr, it's just going to be, BBC [Big Black Cock], or I'm being fetishized. They want me for my private parts. And I'm like, well, can we talk first? Obviously, I'm not going to go on the app and be like, oh, I just want to have a good conversation. Cause that's not what it's for. We all know that. Tinder or Hinge, I don't get that much attention there. It's more about, I'm fetishized.

Even when I'm in drag the chasers are all around. I still have chasers after me, but it's because I'm a Black drag queen and they automatically assume that I have a large penis, being a Black person.

L:
Can you tell me a little bit how bisexuality intersects with being a drag queen?

B:
Being bisexual allows me to help my drag persona be more attractive to men and women. I kind of know what's attractive, what men *and* women find attractive. Not that my drag is like gender fuck, because it's not, it's very high femme. But I understand how to work the crowd and do things I need to do to get my money and also have fun and put on a good show. I noticed though that when I am in drag, I am attracted more so towards women because it's just nice to see they're there for a good time. Cis gay men at drag shows, they get a little rowdy, touchy and invasive and I don't really like that. I'd rather be around girls more, but also, I find myself being more attracted to women when I'm in drag, which I don't really understand. I haven't worked through that yet.

L:
Have you ever talked to anyone about that who is also a drag queen?

B:
Yeah, my drag mom. . . . You know, obviously when you're in the club with your friends, you're like, oh, look at them! I'm always like, wow, look at that girl. She's so pretty. Like, oh my God, I want to talk to her. And then my drag mom's like, are you a lesbian? And I'm like, yeah, I think so. So, my drag mom knows that I am constantly talking about girls more so than guys in the club. It's not a weird thing. It's not like she's saying, oh my gosh! She knows that I'm bisexual and she knows that I like girls too.

When you see a drag queen, you automatically assume that they are a cis gay man outside of drag. There are a lot of drag queens that are trans but to the general public drag is considered men dressing up in wigs, putting on makeup. So, being sexualized as a Black man does seep into drag. It's kind of inevitable. A lot of the time gay men are hyper-sexual and it kind of changes their perspective of what drag is. I use drag as an art form, not so much to be super sexual, and drag is not sexual. It's an artistic expression. So, there are a lot of people we call chasers that kind of just sexual-ize drag queens and only want you because you are cross-dressing more so than respecting your art.

L:
When you use the word chaser, is that to have sex more so than to have a relationship?

B:
Yeah. I don't want to kink shame crossdressers. I don't know if that's a good term to use, but we always just say it because we're drag queens, we're cross-dressing. That is a kink for some people and it's not the same as those people who participate in that kink. It's more the disrespectful cis gay men who kind of just harass drag queens or trans people. It's like, leave me alone. So that's what I mean when I say chasers. I'm experiencing it in drag, but also the Black part . . . there's actually two specific people here in this town who only go after me and my drag mom, who's also Black; we're the only Black drag queens here, but they only go after us because they're assuming that we are cis gay Black men outside of drag.

L:
It sounds like there are assumptions associated with penis size?

B:
Yeah. It's also like, how dare you assume that I have one of those? What if I don't even have a penis? You don't know me. I haven't experienced that

so much when I'm with women. I'm not going to say
it hasn't, because it has been assumed many times,
but it's just more so with gay men than with women.

L:

Do you have other thoughts on bias and bisexuality?

B:

I will say that when I am more masculine presenting,
I'm more desirable from all genders honestly. If I'm
presenting more feminine, I'm considered not that
desirable, but I'm attracted more so to femininity
than I am masculinity. I'm deemed as more attractive when I'm buff and super masculine, but I'm also
bisexual and to some women I'm still soft, but still
a man. And then to some gay guys I'm straight passing. I notice that a lot of non-binary people tend
to dial it back, I guess, to be more attractive to
other people, to seem more attractive because they
realize once they go full throttle into the whole
gender fuck spectrum, they're not seen as desirable.

L:

One last question: where do you find joy in bisexuality?

B:

The possibility of love . . . That's my cliche answer.
The joy is that I'm able to see different sides, kind
of like the good in almost everyone. See lovable
traits, romantically and sexually in almost everyone
and just be more open to the world around me. I have
a broader perspective of what love can look like and
what love is and that's where I find joy in it. And
thank you for asking that question because honestly,
it's been very dark lately with being here and just
reminding myself that I'm able to express and see
that in other people is cool. So, thank you.

A Conversation with Ray Maxwell

LISA:

So, you are trans and non-binary . . . how does
bisexuality intersect with those identities for you?

RAY:
I think bisexuality makes the most sense for me because of my trans non-binary identities and experience . . . I identified as lesbian for four years or something like that . . . it began to feel a little bit restrictive. It's not to say you can't be a non-binary or trans lesbian because you can, and I sort of identified like that for a while, but as I started deconstructing gender identity for myself, I began to realize, it's really more person specific for me, like attraction, romantic connection, sexual connection. I want to be more inclusive with how I describe my sexuality, in relation to gender. I don't want to exclude a person on the basis of gender because I just have had great connections with people of every gender. But there's definitely a feeling of a lack of safety with cis men, for sure. I think that's why I feel safest and most comfortable and most attracted to trans and non-binary people because we have that baseline shared experience and understanding that you don't have to explain your body, or why I have a different relationship to my secondary sex characters, which is something huge.

  If I was like, I don't want you to touch my breasts, like back when I had breasts, it wasn't really a weird thing, you know? Whereas with cis people, I feel like that requires a little bit [of] handholding which is unfortunate because sex is already so intimate and requires so much communication that the added expectation of explaining my body was something I didn't love.

L:
Right! What about cis women?

R:
That is an interesting category. I have been feeling less and less of a desire to have sex with cis women because I guess the more recent experiences I've had, it hasn't been dysphoric like as a blanket statement, it's just made me feel more connected to womanhood than I like to be. And that's also

because I haven't had many sexual experiences post
top surgery. There are a lot of experiences that
were before surgery when I was sleeping with cis
women, I still had breasts, it was sort of like,
I like this, but I'm aware of the fact that our
bodies look the same and that doesn't have to mean
anything. . . . But psychologically in my head, it
still just sort of felt like we were two women having sex, which was, okay but something I have to
work through, you know?

L:
Even in your own lived experience, it's like, okay,
you had that relationship with your breasts and
what does that mean? Now, that could be something
different if you are with a cis woman.

R:
Yeah, I think there's just some reticence there
because post top surgery, I've only had sex with
someone who was already sort of a longtime partner
who understood my relationship with my body, like
very deeply. I'd been with her for like a year and
a half, sort of off and on.
So, I haven't had any sex with someone new looking
and feeling the way I do now. I guess I just don't
really know how I'm going to navigate that. The idea
of having sex with a trans and/or non-binary person
feels the most comfortable for me at the moment.
They just get it more. And I don't want to have to
worry about feeling bad about myself or explaining
my body when I'm supposed to be having a joyous
experience or being more embodied during sex than
I ever have.

L:
So how are you feeling now?

R:
I'm feeling great in terms of presentation. I almost
forget how bad I felt before because everything is
so different, like my relationship with my body,
like I don't care about how I am being perceived.

Whereas before I actively would hunch my shoulders
and try to make myself smaller. And now when I catch
myself doing that, I push back against it because
it's a bad habit that I have to now unlearn because
I like the way I feel in my body.

L:

That's cool!

R:

Yeah, it's really cool. But it's very strange, like,
I want to stand up straight.

L:

That's exciting though. It sounds like this is
still going to be a learning process as far as what
does that mean for being sexual. You had said to me
before that you are the "reluctant bisexual." Can
you explain that a little bit?

R:

Yes. So, I had joked with my friends that I'm in
my reluctant bisexual era, it's sort of tongue in
cheek to refer to the fact that some people think
of bisexuality as less queer or somehow closer in
proximity to heterosexuality and normativity than
being a lesbian per se. Like, tried and true lesbian, gold star, all that bullshit, which I never
really cared about. But there's definitely some cognitive dissonance. Being like, wait, I guess I do
identify as bisexual. I guess I do desire men, like,
you know, trans, queer, and even cis men is something that's on the table for me. And that's something to work through because I liked the distance
that I had from men when I identified as lesbian.
I think that distance was more political lesbianism
than being completely honest about my spectrum of
desire, if that makes sense.

L:

I think it's like the ongoing struggle with bisexuality as an identity and as a movement, this concept of
"not queer enough." When it's so queer in so many ways.

R:

Yeah. A lot of unlearning for me . . . I think a lot of my experiences growing up of bisexual people were very femme women who mostly had relationships with men. I do believe that they wanted to have experiences with women, but just because of their position as femme cis women, it was way easier to have relationships with cis men. And because of that I was like, oh, I don't know how applicable that is for me, because I don't see myself in these parameters.

L:

But those parameters are really huge in reality.

R:

Yeah. And actually, they're sort of fake.

L:

And it's really about making sense of it for yourself. So, what assumptions are made about you in your body?

R:

I think the best example I have is this summer when I studied abroad in Paris. When I was there, I had sex with two people who identified as non-binary, trans-ish, who were both assigned male at birth. And I told my friends about it. And that was the first time I'd had sex with anyone assigned male at birth of any identity. I told my friends about it and they were like, "Oh my God. Are you straight now? Are you not like a lesbian anymore? What does this mean?" Their reaction was like, what do these experiences now reveal about your identity? Which as a baseline, I don't think that any sexual experience has to reveal anything or change anything about your identity. But it was very confusing for me to get that reaction from people, I was like, wait, is this something I have to think about now? What the hell does this mean? And processing sort of a new sexual experience is always going to lead to questions, right? But I enjoy these experiences. These are people who identify as non-binary and/or trans. The fact that these people have penises does not have to mean anything about my identity specifically or negate anything. That is erasure of their identities and making assumptions about their bodies. It's connecting them to cis maleness more than maybe they want to be. If someone had sex with me, I wouldn't want their friends being like, oh, well you had sex with someone with a vagina. Does that mean you're into women now? Because that's sort of the underlying message of what I think that some of my friends were saying. Which was fairly complicated to unpack.

Because that's not how I think about it. If anything, those interactions were good and they just made me realize that there are certain sex acts that I enjoy and that I would want to have with people regardless of their bodies. If I'm with someone who has a vagina, maybe I want them to use a strap on. That is what I gleaned from those sexual experiences . . . Not *because* of these interactions, I am now bisexual . . . which is I think what my friends may have gotten from it because the timeline was kind of similar of me asking questions about my sexuality and what kind of sex do I enjoy? And those kinds of things became subsumed.

L:

It's fascinating. Why do we care so much about genitalia? Are there other assumptions that people may make about you as a person who's trans and non-binary and bisexual?

R:

Yeah. The other running joke in my friend group is that I like pull everyone. I have so many people on my sexual roster, which is just not true. And that I just love to have sex.

It's not as much the whole promiscuous, bisexual thing. I think it's more just like, oh, you're a WGS [Women, Gender and Sexuality] major, who's also non-binary, who's also queer and bisexual. So, because of that, I think people expect me to be having a lot of sex.

And it's usually by people close to me who don't really mean anything by it, but just the assumptions that I'm super sexual, or that I'm pursuing all these sexual interactions with people because of my queerness and transness and all of this stuff. But I think I've been lucky that I haven't been fetishized sexually that I know of. You never know what's happening in the brain of the people you're having sex with. I definitely felt more like affirmed in different sexual interactions but it hasn't felt too fetishizing.

L:
Do you feel as a bisexual person you've experienced bi-erasure in any spaces?

R:
I think that my bisexuality is the least visible queer thing about me and the first thing people see is that I am gender nonconforming, especially now that I've had surgery and different outfits that I wear that are more noticeable. People see gender nonconforming or trans or something confusing, and then they're like, oh, that person's also probably queer, probably gay. I'm not being tied to bisexuality by other people, especially people who don't know me really well. I think that's why I haven't dealt with too much bi-erasure.

L:
There's often this debate about bisexuality versus pansexuality. What do you feel about that?

R:
Pansexuality is complicated because to me pansexuality feels like sort of an unnecessary label in that it distinguishes itself from bisexuality by being like, well, we don't care about gender. We are fluid, we are progressive. And it boxes bisexuality into this cis normative definition of bisexuality when you're attracted to cis men and cis women. I think that pansexuality claims to be doing the work that bisexuality could do if we expanded it.

I think people who identify as pan are often trying to separate themselves from all of the shit and the societal baggage associated with bisexuality. I'm not going to shit on them for doing that but I think that's also indicating that we could do more work with bisexuality so that we wouldn't need a label that doesn't care about gender because bisexuality doesn't have to care about gender. It doesn't have to enforce the gender binary. But again, my close friend and kind of romantic partner identifies as pansexual. Because I think he sees it as a more fluid or a free label that's less attached to gender.

L:

If you're being specific, like "I only like cis men and cis women," that's transphobic in how you're othering and privileging who is attractive.

R:

And how much you're assuming. There are trans people I've met who I didn't know they were trans and I met them and I was like, damn. Like my radar is all off.

One time I was having sex in a group of people. And one of the people was trans. And I didn't know even during the interaction because they were sort of over here. And then later on somebody mentioned it and I was like, what? Wait . . . he had had top surgery a long time ago and scars weren't prevalent and the way that I was in this intimate setting, like literally naked, close to someone and didn't know that they were trans, you cannot tell me on the street that you know someone's trans, like, I'm sorry.

L:

So, what stereotypes are we perpetuating about trans identities in the process of claiming attraction?

R:

Exactly.

L:

Do you think there are other identities that intersect with bisexuality?

R:

When I started questioning my gender identity and
I realized that non-binary and then trans also felt
right for me, that became a window that allowed me
to question my connection to lesbianism and lesbian
identity. That opening of the gender sphere led me
to be more open and questioning of my sexuality as
well. People on the internet called it "the second
crisis." The first crisis is figuring out your sexuality and then you question your gender and then you
question your sexuality again, because if something
shifts in the way that you identify with gender, it
just fucks up all the other labels that you're using.
Which I think is good. I think it should be fucked
up. And I think you should have to question everything but it's also exhausting. It's like, damn.
Back to the drawing board, I have this figured out.

   And another thing I realize is I'm not attracted
to the idea of being perceived in a cis presenting relationship. That to me would feel like I had
abandoned queerness, which is definitely something
I have to unpack. I don't want to be perceived that
way because it would probably mean that I was being
assigned the role of "woman" in most instances.
If someone clocks me as being in a cis-presenting
relationship, it's likely going to be when I'm with
someone who is more masculine than I am. Because if
it's me and someone who's more feminine, visually
people have practiced categorizing lesbian couples
and they'd be like, oh, well, you're just masculine. You're the man. You're whatever. But still a
woman. I would be seen as the masculine woman so
I lose in both perceptions.

L:

My last question is, where do you find joy in
bisexuality?

R:

As I said, I'm in my reluctant bisexual era, but I'm
trying to reframe it and make it more of a joyous
bisexual era. I'm beginning to find joy in relearn-
ing what that could mean to be bisexual and breaking

down all the societal shit and being like, you know, no, this isn't restrictive, this isn't binary. This is very queer and I am opening myself up to different possibilities with different people. More so than I was even six months ago or like a year ago. And I think that that's really exciting for my life, it's like I can't wait to be just around more people and get to be this queer person. Saying I am bisexual is harder than saying I am trans, a non-binary queer. So, I'm working on that too.

A Conversation with River McMican

LISA:
How did bisexuality play a role for your transition?

RIVER:
To talk just briefly about the trans and bi communities, I do think there's a natural alliance between trans and bi communities. In both communities, you are navigating the in-between, right? You are navigating a space where you cannot make assumptions about someone's gender. You are navigating a space where gender matters, but it is not a fixed point. And I think that creates a natural alliance between those two communities or a natural philosophical alliance, even if it doesn't always play out that way.

L:
There could still be transphobia in bi spaces and still biphobia in trans spaces.

R:
Right, and it gets complicated. So, my girlfriend's bisexual, and my husband is the last person to know that he's bisexual. I don't want to apply a label to him that he may not fully identify with, but he's more heteroflexible than he gives himself credit for. But in theory, if you are dating people who are bisexual, transition shouldn't matter, right? That's what people think, anyway. But what I found was most challenging with my partners was their specific concerns about how I *personally* was

going to change. They might have been attracted to people of multiple genders, but when you're looking at someone that you've known for years it's a little harder to just say, *oh, I like all genders* or *I like people of multiple genders, so this is fine*. The truly challenging thing is the change. There is that fear of change that I think any trans person's partners, regardless of their personal identity, is going to experience a little bit of, and I don't think that that's necessarily transphobic. I think it goes along with any major relationship transition. When you're in a relationship with someone, in love, happy with your relationship as it is right now, there's always concern about how a big change impacts that relationship. My gender wasn't an issue to my partners, and my transition in theory was not an issue. The abstract idea of it wasn't a problem, but the actual process of it, the actual changes, took a lot of communication, navigation, and emotional energy.

Gender transition is a big disruption to everyone involved. It's really complicated to navigate the emotional and practical elements of transition. Not to mention all these physical changes and these questions of, what happens if your partner is not attracted to you in the same way anymore? Well, that's a risk, right? And in my case, one of the things that helped with that was this understanding that if my partners weren't attracted to me in the same way anymore, that was okay because there were all these other ways that we could still be attracted to each other, that we could still be intimate with each other, and that we could still have relationships with each other. That removed a lot of stress from me, knowing that maybe it wouldn't be the same afterwards, but I wouldn't have to choose between my own identity and my transition and these relationships that I was in. There was room to navigate both.

Again, I do see this philosophical alignment between bi people and trans people. But just because these communities have that natural alignment does not mean any given bi person has the emotional capacity to navigate transition. They might want to truly support a trans partner, but not every bi person wants their relationship to change in that way. But the fact that bi people have the capacity to be attracted to more than one gender can really potentially smooth out those rough edges. Hell of a lot easier to transition in a bi relationship, I think, than a straight one. But transition is always going to be challenging no matter who you're with.

L:

It's assumed about bisexuality that it should be a given.

R:

It's very individualized. I know for me as a person and the way in which I'm attracted to other people, it wouldn't make a difference for me, personally. I simply do not care, but I'm also trans. So, I also understand and recognize the challenges of transition in a way that a cis person, even a bi cis person, just cannot fully understand. I think that for anyone who is partnered to a trans person, it takes a lot of time and a lot of emotional energy to navigate that transition.

In my case being in a polyamorous relationship, it meant that my partners were leaning on each other for support at points. And you know, for me that was a really good thing because it meant that they could communicate with each other and sort of talk through some of these feelings and some of these vulnerable moments and leave me out of it. Because at that point I was way too engaged with navigating my own feelings about these changes to be able to sensitively navigate theirs. I think polyamory more so than bisexuality actually supported my transition. Which is kind of funny in its own right.

L:

Amazing! I just wish polyamory wasn't so stigmatized and we weren't so invested in monogamy. As a trans person, how do you navigate how people treat you based on how they think your relationship looks?

R:

I will say that no one looks at me and thinks I'm straight. That has not happened in a very long time. But because I'm in this polyamorous relationship, it's a coin flip. Whether people in public read me as male or female has to do with how I dress. It has to do with the context that I'm in. Over the phone, I'm always read as male. When I'm with my girlfriend, I am often read as male. With my husband, it's like a 50-50 shot, whether they read me as female or as male and read us as a gay couple. That's just sort of something where my androgyny and ambiguity is impacting other people's perceptions. And I'm very fortunate that neither of them is upset by this. They're both so comfortable with who they are and with our relationships that it's not a challenge to them as people.

L:

Sounds like they're not concerned about what other people think.

R:

Yeah, but it is an interesting thing because my husband grew up in the Midwest where straight is so much the default. He just never really saw queer people or being queer, bisexual, or heteroflexible or any of these things as an option.

He noticed over time when other people read me as male and read us as a gay couple because it does sometimes change how people interact with you. And sometimes it's more obvious than others, you know, the language that people use. But hilariously what it quite often means is that he gets hit on because it means people don't read him as straight.

We had a fantastic interaction with a flight attendant, who looked at me, clearly read me as not heterosexual, and then proceeded to spend the entire rest of the flight flirting with my husband, who was just totally unprepared for this degree of attention because he is this very shy person. He's very nice. He smiles a lot and people find him likable, but he also likes to be in the background. He's a little bit of a wallflower. But now we go into these public spaces and people see me, they see that I'm queer. They look at him, they read him as queer, and he gets all this attention that he's just not quite sure how to navigate because he grew up in the Midwest, in the straightest of suburbs. We laugh about it because it makes him feel sheepish—he's not upset by it—but you could see where someone's partner could be really uncomfortable with that.

Too Much and Not Enough: Biracial, Bisexual, and Non-binary by Janis Luna

I've known that I'm bisexual for a lot longer than I've known I'm trans. Trans, as an identity, has sat comfortably for me for less than a year—in fact, at the time of this writing, it's April 2022. I'm late on a deadline, and I've identified as trans for less than three months, I think. I'm newly 33 years old.

I've been non-binary for longer, though some within the gender non-conforming/gender expansive community will take issue with this. It's new to me, too, that non-binary is actually a subcategory, a specifier sitting neatly under the umbrella of trans. As a therapist, I'm comfortable holding this loosely: I have clients who identify as non-binary, but not trans, and I have trans clients who insist that non-binary people are trans whether they identify that way or not. From a sex education linguistic standpoint, "trans" means, most broadly, not aligned with the gender you were assigned at birth; not-cis. Nobody is assigned non-binary at birth. As a therapist, it's not my place to force labels onto anybody, but for myself, recognizing non-binary identity as transness helped something click into place for me that I'm still not certain how to describe.

My hesitation was well-intentioned but harmful: For years I've oriented towards my non-binary identity as some sort of trans-lite, not wanting to take up space among in a community where so many people experience so much more hardship and marginalization than I do. I don't take hormones. I don't have any plans to surgically alter my body—though, as of this writing, I'm waiting on clinical genetics results for the BRCA-1 gene that I may or may not have inherited from my mother. If I test positive, potential recommendations include: double mastectomy, removal of ovaries and fallopian tubes, potential removal of my uterus. The increased likelihood of breast cancer makes me eligible for the types of surgeries that other trans people often have to fight tooth and nail for, providing multiple letters from their cis doctors, psychiatrists, and therapists stating that they are of sound enough mind to choose these lifesaving, but supposedly "elective" surgeries.

I sit with the idea of inheritance as I consider my transness. It's interesting to me to trace this sequence of events, the evolutions of my identity. I've been a sex educator since 2015, and a sex worker since 2016. Both of these experiences mean that I've been surrounded by queer and trans folks for most of my adult life. I have to rack my brain to figure out if I know any cis or straight people not related to me. But for longer than this, there has existed within me a part that clings tight to imposter syndrome, that whispers to me that I'm too much of one thing and not enough of another. I have too much privilege in one area, haven't suffered enough in another. Any excuse to keep me liminal and not belonging.

Before I thought too much about gender and sexuality at all, this part of me existed. In therapy I hypothesize—is it because I grew up in a biracial family, to a white, Italian American father, and a brown, Peruvian mother. Her lineage is mixed, too: white (Spanish, Portuguese) and indigenous (Andean; though we do not know our tribe or our language. When I think of my own future daughter, my spirit bebe, I give her a name in Quecha that means "Thank you.") I trace our indigeneity via surnames and facial features, Googling images of indigenous Peruvian women and seeing the shape of my mother's eyes, her regal nose, the thick darkness of her hair, the fullness of her lips and the way her teeth crowd her mouth, strong and square, the hard angle of her jaw, the deep brown of her skin and mine, that we lose and that I mourn, nine months out of the year. I feel most like myself in the summer.

I remember as a child connecting viscerally to that moment in *Selena*, when Selena's father, Abraham Quintanilla, explains this to his daughter: too Mexican for the Americans, and too American for the Mexicans. *It's exhausting!* Navigating one's life unmoored, between worlds. When I was younger this seemed tragic. As I grew older, it seemed silly and vain—it still does, sometimes—to complain about not being noticed for being different enough, for skirting around the edges of more violent treatment. And yet, it's this, and it's not; it's this, and it's more than this, too, much like non-binary identity itself.

In sophomore year of high school, I played for one season with the soft-ball team, one of two players on an exclusively Latinx team who didn't speak Spanish. It was my eleventh and last year playing softball. All the years before that, I had played on my church team, the only public school kid surrounded by Catholic school brats. These experiences were unpleasant, deeply lonely, but I participated in them doggedly, because playing softball seemed to make my dad happy. Now, as an adult, I like the game a lot more, especially when I get to engage with it of my own volition, and recreationally. A few years ago, I co-organized a haphazard gaggle of queers in the park to play softball, perhaps unconsciously as some communal reparenting exercise. This time, for us, it was about pleasure and fun, not winning or losing and especially not some means of trying to secure . . . love? Attention? Affection? from an overburdened father navigating financial precarity who, more often than not, I experienced as an emotional void and who once asserted to me that my mother, and my brother, and I are not who we have experienced our-selves to be: "Your mother isn't a woman of color!" he insisted once out of frustration and in the middle of a dinner table argument about racism, and I wondered if he could see her, or my brother, or me, at all, or if he had always, and would always, fold us like egg whites into the flat assimilation that mid-20th-century Italians (once considered "ethnic" themselves) shape-shifted into, in order to accumulate the corresponding power, privilege, and safety that whiteness afforded them.

But I digress.

What I mean to say is, gender and sexuality aren't the first places I've experienced this uncomfortable liminality, this sense of almost-but-not-quite belonging. My identity in many ways has felt like a house of cards built on a bed of shifting sand. Am I "of color" enough? How many times do I have to be called "exotic," sexy, spicy, fiery before this quota is met? How many times must I hear from white men, "I love Hispanic girls," before being lied to, cheated on, raped, discarded, for this quota to be met? Am I indige-nous enough? Is it enough that hearing Quechua spoken and sung makes me cry, though I don't understand the words? Is it enough that the words roll off my tongue, even as I stumble over them, feeling like a home I've never been to but still, somehow, remember? Am I gay enough? Trans enough? How will I know? *It's exhausting!*

I don't know who I have in mind when I ask myself these questions. What judge? What jury? And why is it that the metric I measure myself against is one of suffering, when there is so much beauty, joy, power, and strength to all of these identities, too?

As a sex educator, I learned to make careful delineations between sexu-ality and gender. It was important not to conflate the two. It is as possible to be trans and straight as it is to be trans and gay or bi. The two—gender and sexuality—exist in parallel; one does not influence the other. They don't necessarily have to intersect. And yet, the more I sink into my transness, the more they do. Lately I've decided I only want to date other trans people of color. No cissies need apply. This does fascinating things for my sexual fanta-sies, as if by embracing my transness consciously, my unconscious has been given free range to play and is *fucking overjoyed* to oblige. I daydream of the people I'm crushing on, who, at least for the past several years, have tended towards the masculine and are often assigned male at birth. But the images in my mind shift. Our genders play—all noses and tongues, like animals getting acquainted. My body doesn't change—I still have breasts, a vulva—but the way I embody it changes. What does it mean for a masc person to fuck me like a little faggot? Why does the word, which I have never used to describe myself before and haven't tossed as an insult since I was probably nine or ten years old and learned that it's hurtful, make me shiver? Maybe it's prob-lematic, but it feels good. I don't question it. Other things become mine, too:

After spending time with a childhood friend whose marriage looks uncomfortably like my own parents' marriage did when we were growing up, I texted a different friend, "I am so FUCKING GLAD I am a dyke."

Then I shake the scene like a snow globe, and the gender dynamics shift again, and we are two femmes in love, the femme in me making love to the femme in them, all parts of us soft, luxuriating. Hardness is unnecessary. We take our time, there are no limits to this love, nothing to signify when to start and when to stop, except, of course, our wanting and its abatement. I shake it again, and my femmeness becomes hard, a dense and diamond point, leather, latex, eight-inch heels, they beg me—masc, femme, who even keeps track anymore? Who cares?—to step a little harder, to puncture, to penetrate, so I do.

As I get older the importance of these categories starts to wear on me. More often than not, I just say that I'm queer. "Ye olde English queer," my brother once said, describing himself; "as in, odd." I like this. I also like the word bisexual; I prefer it to pansexual, because the word bisexual seems prettier to me. I like to write it. I like to say it, and it fits well in my mouth. Sometimes, I joke, *pan*sexual just makes me think of bread. Right now, I follow this thread—my grandmother, tiny and frail and dying at the dinner table, asking my brother for "Pancito y mantequilla," a little bit of bread and butter, in her warbling and weakened voice. It was all she could eat, and in such tiny bird-like amounts, trapped in her own body like the Count of Monte Cristo. My mother told me they lived in a shack on the docks of Lima when she was a baby. My grandmother would sell tamales like hot cakes. Tamales take forever to make. A memory comes, standing on the chair to look over into the mixing bowl, the harsh fluorescent light of my childhood kitchen flickering over me. My childhood home is filled with shadows and flickering lights; the fluorescents, the infomercials on TV. Mom recovers from chemotherapy in the dimly lit living room, and we make tamales. It's a labor-intensive process, a lot of steps, a lot of preparation. Shelling peas. It's unclear to me now whether this is a memory or the story that arises in my mind as my mother describes the recipe to me. I've never made tamales myself. But they would sell in an instant on the docks in Lima—all my grandmother's labor gone and devoured, just in time to prepare the next batch. If my mother read this, I imagine she would say, it wasn't like that, it was like this, and doubt creeps in again. Regardless, she did tell me once, very recently, that my grandmother would sleep with my mother pinned to her coat, their bodies connected by a ribbon, my mother sleeping within the inner edges of an overturned table to keep her small body safe from the draft coming in off the water through the loose floorboards that were my grandmother's bed; my mother, pinned so that she wouldn't be stolen in the middle of the night. What about this lineage is still somehow not enough?

My grandmother's photo is the centerpiece of my altar. Laura, who I named Lala, a tiny raspy-voiced woman with cornmeal hands. Small, with a seeming delicateness that belied her strength, the exuberance of her personality that hid her immense frailty. When she is remembered to me, she is remembered as a force of nature. Simultaneously, I hear the trappings of gender: caregiving, without end. Loyalty to an abusive husband, groomed into her by her abusive family. I think about my own femmeness—formerly such a haven—and how even the make-up-as-war-paint embodiments of femininity become stifling once enough people have forced performativity on you through perception and projection. I call something new into my body, then, some tilt to femininity; I position it akimbo, allow myself a momentary abandoning of what is familiar and safe, stealing just enough time to reach for something new.

Once, after taking four grams of psilocybin mushrooms, I stared into the photo of my grandmother—her expression still and stern, short dark hair in neatly styled waves, her eyes a dark challenge—and saw her face shift and change, like flipping the pages of a book into the corners of which have been scribbled stick figure illustrations. Her gender seemed to shift, now feminine, now masculine, now unidentifiable, uncontainable, unable to be named in any language that I know. Fluid, shapeshifting. Pre-colonial Inca society recognized a third gender, qariwarmi, the word made up of the Quechua word for man (qari) and woman (warmi), a non-binary, mixed-gender role. According to *The Sun, The Moon, and Witches: Gender Ideologies and Class in Inca and Colonial Peru*, Andean social structure was carefully separated by gender roles—tasks for women, tasks for men (though it is important to note that, while these roles were created for ease and efficiency; when push came to shove, it was more important that the tasks get *done*, rather than people stay in their specific gender lanes). Qariwarmi, attendants to Jaguar spirit,

*M*ediated between the symmetrically dualistic spheres of Andean cosmology and daily life by performing rituals that at times required same-sex erotic practices. Their transvested attire served as a visible sign of a third space that negotiated between the masculine and the feminine, the present and the past, the living and the dead. Their shamanic presence invoked the androgynous creative force often represented in Andean mythology.[35]

Are they my lineage, these faces who came before my grandmother? Or is my grandmother herself this multifaceted and strange? She was a peculiar woman—the middle daughter of three girls and one among 11 children total. She was gregarious, rambunctious, intense—all words that described me, too, as a child; that still describe me. All descriptors frowned upon when found within a girl-body in Peru in the early 1900s. As such, she was the black sheep of her family (a term my therapist has used to describe my role as well and treated like a Peruvian Cinderella. They heaped chores upon her, and still she snuck out to pelt the neighborhood kids with mud cakes and run shrieking from rooftop to rooftop. I imagine her as a young woman in love, fucking with abandon, having two children out of wedlock by different fathers, losing the love of her life through the manipulation of her family and marrying my grandfather instead. I imagine her immigrating to America, alone, in her forties, only to find that the job she was promised was no longer available. I imagine the set to her jaw when she resolved for herself—I will not be going back with my tail between my legs.

I don't know where I learned these stories, but I know them. I wasn't raised speaking Spanish. She wasn't raised speaking Quechua. Lala and I never had a full conversation, but I can see her, small and wild. Her image is on my altar and I am loved by her. She is perhaps the family member I have the most in common with—I've inherited her livewire energy; her fearlessness; her devotion, often misplaced; her propensity to dance in the kitchen and demand a glass of red wine; to walk, shoulders back, tits out, hips swaying like she taught me, and save our entire family, somehow.

Notes

1 "The ACLU Is Tracking 515 Anti-LGBTQ Bills in the U.S.," 2024 Legislative Session, ACLU Website, www.aclu.org/legislative-attacks-on-lgbtq-rights-2024.

2 Shiri Eisner, "What Is Bisexuality?" in *Bi: Notes for a Bisexual Revolution* (Berkeley, CA: Seal Press, 2013), 22.

3 Lucie Fielding, "Unimaginable Bodies," in *Trans Sex: Clinical Approaches to Trans Sexualities and Erotic Embodiments* (New York: Routledge, 2021), 24.

4 Fielding, "Unimaginable Bodies," 16.

5 Caleb Luna, "On Being Fat, Brown, Femme, Ugly and Unloveable," (July 2014), www.bgdblog.org/2014/07/fat-brown-femme-ugly-unloveable/.

6 Hari Ziyad, "3 Reasons Why Dating, Attraction and Desire Are Always Political," *Everyday Feminism* (April 2016), https://everydayfeminism.com/2016/04/attraction-desire-political/.

7 Fielding, "Unimaginable Bodies," 17.

8 Fielding, "Unimaginable Bodies," 18.

9 Fielding, "Unimaginable Bodies," 17.

10 Fielding, "Unimaginable Bodies," 17.

11 Fielding, "Unimaginable Bodies," 17.

12 Richard Ekins, "Science, Politics and Clinical Intervention: Harry Benjamin, Transsexualism and the Problem of Heteronormativity," *Sexualities*, Vol. 8, No. 3 (2005), 306–328.

13 Fielding, "Unimaginable Bodies," 17.

14 Annalisa Anzani, Louis Lindley, Giacomo Tognasso, M. Paz Galupo and Antonio Prunas, "'Being Talked to Like I Was a Sex Toy, Like Being Transgender Was Simply for the Enjoyment of Someone Else': Fetishization and Sexualization of Transgender and Non-Binary Individuals," *Archives of Sexual Behavior*, Vol. 50, No. 3 (2021), 898.

15 Anzani et al., "Being Talked to Like I Was a Sex Toy, Like Being Transgender Was Simply for the Enjoyment of Someone Else," 898.

16 Anzani et al., "Being Talked to Like I Was a Sex Toy, Like Being Transgender Was Simply for the Enjoyment of Someone Else," 891.

17 Zack Zoetic, "Trans Chasers: The Good, the Bad, the Urgh," (January 2021), https://tabooless.net/stories/trans-issues/trans-chasers-the-good-the-bad-and-the-urgh/.

18 Mirella Flores, Laurel Watson, Luke Allen, Mudiwa Ford, Christine Serpe, Ping Ying Choo and Michelle Farrell, "Transgender People of Color's Experiences of Sexual Objectification: Locating Sexual Objectification Within a Matrix of Domination," *Journal of Counseling Psychology*, Vol. 65, No. 3 (2018), 308–323.

19 Lawrence Stacey and TehQuin D. Forbes, "Feeling Like a Fetish: Racialized Feelings, Fetishization, and the Contours of Sexual Racism on Gay Dating Apps," *The Journal of Sex Research*, Vol. 59, No. 3 (2022), 372.

20 Sandy James, Jody Herman, Susan Rankin, Mara Keisling, Lisa Mottet and Ma'ayan Anafi, *The Report of the 2015 U.S. Transgender Survey* (Washington, DC: National Center for Transgender Equality, 2016), https://transequality.org/sites/default/files/docs/usts/USTS-Full-Report-Dec17.pdf; Flores et al., "Transgender People of Color's Experiences of Sexual Objectification."

21 Daniel A. Griffiths and Heather L. Armstrong, "They Were Talking to an Idea They Had About Me: A Qualitative Analysis of Transgender Individuals' Experiences Using Dating Apps," *The Journal of Sex Research*, Vol. 61, No. 1 (2024), 119–132.

22 Movement Advancement Project, "A Closer Look: Bisexual Transgender People," (September 2017), 1–4, https://www.lgbtmap.org/file/A%20Closer%20Look%20Bisexual%20Transgender.pdf.

23 James et al., *The Report of the 2015 U.S. Transgender Survey*.

24 "Nonbinary LGBTQ Adults in the United States," Brief from UCLA School of Law Williams Institute (2021), https://williamsinstitute.law.ucla.edu/publications/nonbinary-lgbtq-adults-us/.

25 Shiri Eisner, "Bi and Trans," in *Bi: Notes for a Bisexual Revolution* (Berkeley, CA: Seal Press, 2013), 240.

26 Eisner, "Bi and Trans," 241.

27 Eisner, "Bi and Trans," 241.

28 Eisner, "Bi and Trans," 242.

29 Eisner, "Bi and Trans," 242.
30 Eisner, "Bi and Trans," 243.
31 Eisner, "Bi and Trans," 245.
32 Eisner, "Bi and Trans," 253.
33 Movement Advancement Project, "A Closer Look," 1–4.
34 Lucie Fielding, "Embracing Gender-Pleasure: How to Feel Yummy in Our Bodies," *Psychotherapy Networker Online Magazine* (November–December 2022), www.psychotherapynetworker.org/article/embracing-gender-pleasure/.
35 Michael J. Horswell, "Introduction: Transculturating Tropes of Sexuality, Tinkuy, and Third Gender in the Andes," in *Decolonizing the Sodomite: Queer Tropes of Sexuality in Colonial Andean Culture* (Austin: University of Texas Press, 2005), 2.

4

CISGENDER WOMEN AND FEMININITIES

Those who are socialized as women are inundated with stereotypical feminine expectations and are forced to navigate the "gender box," especially when they step outside of the box. Gender policing can be constant, from friends, family, partners, and communities, there to correct women when they do not perform gender expectations "correctly." The pressure to be "lady-like" within the context of whiteness—thin, pretty, demure, passive, sexual but not too sexual, objects of desire for men, monogamous, and adoring men—still exists as the default within patriarchal expectations of femininity. As Allan G. Johnson states, "to live in a patriarchal culture is to breathe in misogynist images of women as objectified sexual property valued primarily for their usefulness to men."[1]

For cisgender bisexual (cis-bi) women, sexist expectations of femininity intersect with stereotypes steeped in biphobia, monosexism, bi-erasure and racism, resulting in potential fetishization, alienation, and isolation. Cis-bi women are seen as hypersexual, entertainment for the straight male gaze, or as a "unicorn" for a heterosexual couple's threesome fantasy.[2] There is general discourse in society that this means cis-bi women are fairly accepted in our culture, which Eisner refutes by stating,

First, female bisexuality is appropriated and co-opted by the cisgender and heterosexual male gaze; second, social preoccupation with and prioritizing of male sexuality is the cause of this appropriation of female bisexuality; and third, these two things combined constitute and generate sexual violence against bisexual women, and against all women in general.[3]

DOI: 10.4324/9781003242659-5

Eisner also argues that cis-bi women pose a threat to patriarchy, which results in a form of bisexual erasure that neutralizes

> *The 'sting' that it carries by appropriating it into the heterosexual cis male gaze. From being a potential threat, female bisexuality is converted and rewritten into something else, something that's both palatable and convenient to patriarchy and the hetero cis male gaze, and which caters to its needs.*[4]

(Chapter 11: "Mental Health Issues and the Impact of Violence" addresses further how this leads to sexual violence).

Although all women experience objectification to a certain extent, these sexualized bisexual stereotypes create fetishized experiences distinct from monosexual counterparts. Bisexual blogger Louise MacGregor addresses this by writing,

> *You ask pretty much any non-straight woman . . . and they'll tell you the same thing. If you're a woman who's attracted to other women, someone is waiting to spring out from behind a couch and tell you that it gives them a boner.*[5]

Journalist Isabella Simonetti adds that this fetishization is perpetuated because of bi-erasure. She writes, "Most fetishes are rooted in the allure of the unfamiliar—that's what makes them enticing. Until bisexuality is more widely accepted, people will continue to force their fantasies on queer women."[6]

Additionally, racialized fetishization intersects with biphobia, bi-erasure, and monosexism with unique implications for cis-bi women of color. As writer Crystal Fleming asserts,

> *Black bisexual women are often misunderstood, excluded, or fetishized. . . . Bi black people exist at the intersections of many forms of oppression, and this difficult positionality makes it complicated for us to find love. We not only have to deal with homophobia in our families— we also have to navigate biphobia among black gays and lesbians—while dealing with racism in the broader LGBTQIA+ "community."*[7]

This ties in with the long histories of *white sexual imperialism* that "have existed and still exist through a colonized experience," which exacerbate the fetishization.[8] As Cleo Falvey explains about her own experience as an Asian American bisexual woman,

> *Just as my Tinder date leaned in to give me a hug at the end of our eight-hour long first date, 'Just so you know, I have an Asian fetish, so I'm super thrilled you're Asian' . . . Asian-American women who are queer*

are more likely to experience fetishization while dating, with one woman pointing out that she "didn't feel like Asian lesbians are taken seriously." As an Asian bisexual, I completely agree with her sentiment. In fact, I wrote this piece to bring awareness to the double standards that we face. Although these identities are important to me—I am proud of my Chinese heritage and I'm also out and proud and bisexual, these are not the only things about me. I do not want to be reduced to a submissive China doll in relationships because of these biases.[9]

Another challenge for cis-bi women of color is the enforcement of *respectability politics*. Respectability politics "describes a self-presentation strategy histori-cally adopted by African-American women to reject White stereotypes by pro-moting morality while de-emphasizing sexuality."[10] Although this concept was used in response to racism in order to promote upward mobility within Black communities, it also reinforced compulsory heterosexuality, monosexuality, and monogamy as the norm. Black queer academic Kaila Adia Story explains how respectability politics has bled into queer culture when she asserts:

Ultimately, white queers and black straights continue to silence our voices and/or sanitize our images in an attempt to make our lived experiences more palatable or respectable to the larger public. The com-mon theme that binds these two discourses is marriage in all its heter-onormative trappings. Whether it be the overwhelming push for marriage equality by white queers over and above other equally important issues facing queer people (and particularly queer people of color) or the creation of hegemonic forms of sexual representation by black straight male celeb-rities, homonormativity and heteronormativity reign supreme in today's cultural marketplace of sameness.[11]

Story continues by stating that, in order to challenge compulsory heterosex-uality, we should "dance in the delight of difference. Indeed, I want to throw shade on normativity, sashay away from a politics of respectability, and get my life from a politics of deviance."[12]

Navigating respectability politics, fetishization, and objectification all intersect with feminine expectations of what constitutes the perfect body. These ideals often lead to body dissatisfaction not only because of dominant culture expectations of white, cisgender beauty standards, but for women of color the additional pressure to adhere to various racial and cultural expecta-tions of beauty. Avery et.al. describe this as "hegemonic beauty standards."[13] Although the ideal body for Black communities may appear to be accepting of larger bodies, feminine ideals are still important.[14] Curves, or fitting into the "thick" ideal may be more accepted but "their desire for curves is limited to those that appear on slim bodies; thinness, as opposed to fatness, remains an important marker of physical attractiveness for Black women."[15]

The impact of these bodied expectations on bi-cis women is terribly under-studied, as most research on queer body image has focused on lesbians, and for bisexual women of color there is even less.[16] According to some studies, "lesbian women experience less body dissatisfaction, which researchers posit could result from lesbian women being more likely to reject heteronormative beauty ideals and accept diverse body types."[17] However, in other studies, little difference between lesbian and heterosexual women has been found.[18] For some bi-cis women discovering their bisexuality has allowed for more body acceptance, such as bisexual activist and author Robyn Ochs's account:

> *Through the firsthand experience of my own attractions, I learned that women, and their bodies, are beautiful, though I did not immediately apply this knowledge to my opinion of my own body. There was one woman friend on whom I had had a crush for more than two years. I thought she was beautiful, with her solid, powerful angles and healthy fullness. One day, with a sense of shock, I realized that her body was not so very different from mine and that I had been holding myself to a different, unattainable standard than I had been holding her and other women to. It was this experience of seeing my image reflected in another woman that fully allowed me to begin developing a positive relationship with my own body.*[19]

Chmielweskil and Yost contend that part of the body image struggle comes from a "tension" between the intellectual understanding of needing to reject hegemonic beauty standards but on the other hand also wanting to fit into those beauty standards. The lack of understanding of this tension only adds to the potential of bi-erasure, particularly in queer spaces.[20] As Chmielweskil and Yost assert,

> *Theoretically, bisexual women's attraction to women may align them with lesbians in ways that could contribute to their body image. . . . Lesbian communities have also been seen as feminist safe havens where lesbians and bisexual women can separate themselves from the dominant heterosexist culture. . . . Hence, feminist values (such as a critique of sexual objectification) may play an important role in bisexual women's perceptions of their bodies. . . . At the same time, bisexual women's attraction to men may align them with heterosexual women in some ways. Unlike lesbians, bisexual women may be interested in attracting men and, as a result, may feel the need to appeal to dominant cultural standards of appearance defined by the male gaze.*[21]

Queer communities are not always accepting of all body types either, as Oswald and Matsick argue,

> *That queer women's spaces—often hailed as havens shielding their constituents from harmful heteronormative beauty ideals . . .—tend*

to replicate the dominant devaluation of femininity and fatness demon-strates the ubiquitous challenges faced by those at the intersection of femininity, fatness, and queerness.[22]

Despite the various ways cis-bi women may make sense of their bodies, what has evolved in queer spaces as a form of resistance is the concept of *femme*. *Femme* was designed "to designate queer femininity, in a way that's often self-aware and subversive. It's both a celebration and a refiguring of femininity."[23] It is important to clarify how *femme* differs from femininity, a social construct created by a patriarchal society while *femme*

Is, in a sense, the queering of femininity—not just identifying as queer, ... but the embodiment and embracing of queerness in the full meaning of the word. This key differentiation is why it's so important for femme to stand on its own.[24]

As Chung conveys,

I see femme as the rebellious teenage daughter of femininity. . . . Femme is the process of taking the feminine words that were placed in my body, words like 'soft, weak, quiet' and transforming them into: 'wild, loud, confident'. . . . When I broke up with femininity and embraced femme, I felt strong and confident and powerful.[25]

The term *femme* first appeared in the United States around the 1920s out of a subculture of white working-class lesbians, though it became more common in the 1940s and 50s.[26] In these communities, this largely played out as a butch/femme dynamic with masculine and feminine presentations. For femmes of color, white lesbian communities were not inclusive, and bars were often segregated. Black lesbians created house parties in response to being excluded from white spaces, in addition to different terminology such as the 1960s "fishes and studs."[27] The Black/Latinx ballroom scene is another example of the creation of their own queer communities, which were designed to celebrate without feeling forced to fit into white, middle-class norms of the larger LGBTQ community. These spaces were also support systems that allowed learning about resistance and resilience in a world of discrimination and hate.[28]

The butch/femme dynamic really emerged in the 1980s, "in response to lesbian feminist politics where there was a rejection and erasure of questions of radical sexual politics, desire, and roleplaying within lesbian communities."[29] Butch/femme was heavily debated, particularly by antipornography feminists who shamed butch and femme women for perpetuating hegemonic heteronormative practices of sexuality.[30] Juana Maria Rodriguez describes her own experience in the 1980s of being bisexual within this culture:

> *C*oming of age as a bisexual Latina femme in the 1980s, I was sur-
> rounded by lesbian-feminist communities and discourses that dispar-
> aged, dismissed, and vilified bisexuality. Those of us that enthusiastically
> embraced femininity or that actively sought out masculine presenting
> butches, were deemed perpetually suspect. Femmes were imagined as being
> always on the verge of abandoning the lesbian-feminist communities that
> nurtured us for the respectability and privilege that heterosexual relations
> might afford. The label bisexuality, for those that dared to claim it, was
> viewed as the apolitical cop-out for those that were not radical enough to
> fully commit to the implied lesbian practice of feminist theory. In the bad
> old days of lesbian separatist politics, bisexuality was attached to a yearn-
> ing, not just for men, but for multifarious sexual pleasures deemed decid-
> edly anti-feminist including desires for penetration, sexual dominance and
> submission, and the wickedly perverse delights of expressive gender roles.[31]

More recently *femme* has departed from being paired in the binary construct of butch/femme.[32] Today femme is used by multiple identities in queer com-munities, including cis-bi women, trans femmes, femme dykes, gay femmes, and queer femme bois, as a way to embrace "feminine gender presentation in some form or another, which does not rely on who you are attracted to, partner with, or have sex with."[33] Although femmes may *appear* to present as tradition-ally feminine, in reality it is "understood as an *identity*, not just a *style*, and that as an identity it therefore must exceed mere appearance."[34] This can be a chal-lenge since cis femmes are often "caught in a divide," where their queerness and femininity are not recognized "as anything other than performance in the straight world," or "as legitimate in the lesbian/queer world."[35] This can invoke feelings of anxiety when they are not seen as queer enough. As one member of the Femme Hive group in Berlin exclaimed, "It's hard to be feminine and still scream out 'queer' sometimes. So, I feel like if I don't do something special then I might just be not noticed. Like people think I'm straight I guess."[36]

For cis femmes of color, the intersection of racist ideologies adds another layer of challenges, particularly trying to balance invisibility and hyper-visibility. Kaila Adia Story asserts,

> *T*he racist and heteronormative politics at work, within and outside of
> queer communities of work and leisure, continue to render Black femmes
> and others as either something they don't declare themselves to be and/or
> erases the many signifiers they adopt to be seen as who they truly are.[37]

Imani Rupert-Gordon states that an act of resistance is to live authenti-cally and openly even though Black femmes are treated as if their identities are in conflict. She describes this division as her queerness undermining her Blackness and her Blackness undermining her womanhood, which results in "an invitation to never be completely who we are. Living and loving my Blackness, my queerness, my womanhood, and all of my multiple intersecting identities is how I live boldly."[38]

Research rarely addresses cis-bi femmes who face potential bi-erasure, particularly in queer space. As bi femme writer Eva Akvol discusses about dating online, "Due to my more traditionally feminine appearance, the women I encountered online saw me as a curious straight girl instead of as someone who was 'legitimately' queer. Their judgment and disapproval was palpable when they told me things like, 'I don't date girls who are newly out, sorry,' or 'You look really straight.' This became my new normal, and I couldn't pinpoint why."[39] Writer Hannah Johnson struggles with this also as she explains, "In these situations, when I am inadvertently labeled as a lesbian or a straight woman, I simply have to advocate for myself and correct the mistake (which is not always easy)."[40] Culture and sex writer Gina Jones (aka Gina Tonic) further adds, "For me, using the word 'femme' over the descriptor 'feminine' is a key component in claiming my queerness. It's a queerness that has often, because of my bisexuality, been erased."[41] Devaluing femmes in lesbian spaces is linked to the idea that femme equals bisexual, which may be seen as a threat, particularly because of the stereotype of cis-bi women having the potential to return to heterosexual relationships.[42]

Navigating femininity, queerness, and bisexuality is fraught with many challenges, and the power of a *femme* identity cannot be denied. The following personal narratives explore many of these complexities of cis-bi women, as they make sense of the intersections of femininity, bisexuality, bi-erasure, race, and more.

Coming Out as the Daughter of Desi Immigrants
by Ishita Mahajan

I was brought up in a fairly progressive Indian household; my mom was a pioneer in her family on all fronts of social justice, advocating for gender equality, environmentalism, sexual liberation, and education. My parents took an enormous risk, leaving everything they knew behind, to raise my brother and I when they immigrated to the U.S. Ma didn't even have enough money to afford a hot shower and a sandwich at the airport after her 20+ hour flight to New Jersey from India. Together, they lived paycheck to paycheck, making raising us with an overflowing, pouring abundance of love their priority. Even though there were a lot of things for them to learn about this new place, miles away from home, my parents centralized compassion above anything else. Ma always took the time out to hear people's stories, to empathize with every tear they shed, to feel every smile they cracked, and to ultimately unlearn and learn new ways of seeing the world. Years later, we relocated to Korea and then, years after that, to Singapore. All the while, the bond we had as a family—a unit—remained the biggest pillar in my life.

Because of my upbringing, I naturally gravitated towards advocacy, introspection, art, literature, and, more broadly, the pursuit of my own truths. I started coming out to friends as bisexual in my junior year of high school and it just felt right—the way I didn't know where to look in Victoria's Secret stores as a kid (universal gay experience), how I was super drawn to certain girls who I *really* wanted to become friends with (this too), the "Am I Gay?" quizzes I took, and the way I loved wearing my dad's clothes because they just felt right on my body! Although my parents have always been my biggest cheerleaders, they were still born and brought up within a very different sociopolitical context. Deep down, I knew that they would love me irrespective of anything I could ever tell them, but I felt like I was letting them down by "being different." I was breaking away from the perfect oldest daughter they always saw me as. So, subconsciously I began policing and surveilling myself around my family, censoring parts of myself that I wasn't yet ready to confront. It was so easy to center my attraction towards men, relegating my attraction towards women into the shadows. It was a form of distrustful honesty—a byproduct of fear and socially ingrained anti-queer sentiment.

Still, I knew I was keeping such a central part of my identity from my family. I told them after my first semester of college, on January 2 (I tried on the first and had an emotional breakdown!). They reacted well, but this disclosure still shook their image of who I was—they thought it was a phase induced by being in college and that I would eventually grow out of it. "You had a massive Justin Bieber obsession when you were younger . . . and how about that guy from school you were always going out with? *Beta*, give it time—people grow in and out of these things." Although this stung, I realized that they struggled to accept my sexuality not because they had internalized particularly negative attitudes about queerness but just because it was so unfamiliar, so foreign. Even though a part of me broke in those few days, it was also rebuilt with time. A few days later, my dad came to my room with a bowl of fruits in his hands (immigrant parent love language), his eyes brimming with tears: "I can't believe you were holding all of that inside of you, on your own: that you didn't think you could trust Mom and I with it." Months later, Ma started using gender-neutral language when she was inquiring about my love life, replacing "boyfriend" with "partner." There were moments where they relapsed with ignorance, but ultimately, they wanted to understand me. Today, I'm mostly in a good place—one of acceptance and love.

I've come a long way since that period of my life. In the years that followed, I introspected further and probed deeper. I wanted to understand how my identity—as a Brown gay woman[43]—affected my journey of self-discovery. I wanted to explore how cultural and historical legacies influenced my 'coming out' process. I wanted to reflect on how traditional beliefs had infiltrated the way that I construed my own sexual being. In the earlier stages of making sense of all of this, I resented the purity culture that I thought was a byproduct of conservative Indian culture. As women, we're constantly conditioned to present ourselves as innocent, demure, and virginal. We're told to be wary of ill-intentioned men who are out to rob us of one of our most prized assets. Over time, it becomes difficult to unlearn this deeply internalized "association" among sensuality, purity, and morality and to embrace our sexual selves. Having an open channel of communication with my friends definitely provided insight on sex, virginity, and intimacy, but I still felt like there was something deeper for me to unpack. That's exactly what I gained from taking 'WGS 2600: Human Sexualities' with Lisa Speidel!

One of the biggest revelations I had through the class was regarding the function of labels in society. Although finding a label can be empowering for many folks (especially in the pursuit of community), this sort of classification is largely a product of Western colonialism and imperialism. Labels are often a device for straight, cis people to make sense of queerness. I never really analyzed my personal discomfort with these identity labels, but the idea of deconstructing the person I was into all of these social categories just didn't seem consistent with the way I was brought up. I was always taught to focus less on the little details and instead more on the macro level, big-picture things. I always appreciated the person I was for all of the little pieces that harmoniously *came together* to form my identity, the ways in which they crashed and intersected to create personhood. It was far more liberating to exist between the boundaries and along the peripheries of socially prescribed identities. I had always found strength and beauty in "femininity" and "masculinity," finding comfort and solace in both "straightness" and "queerness." It's so easy to feel consumed by and stifled by the search for the "right" label. Labeling can—in many ways—be like moving out of one box, only to force yourself into another one. Instead of focusing on categorizing identity through the lens of cultural norms and conventions, a lot of the class speakers taught me to reframe this as the pursuit of self-assertion, exploration, and authenticity. As Alok Vaid-Menon, a prominent gender non-conforming author and writer of color, said: it's useful to "remove ideas of purity and authenticity and instead, subscribe to joy."

In terms of cultural nuance, I also realized that one of the biggest lies we've collectively been fed through Eurocentric education is that the "colonized" represent regressive, backward ways of thinking, while the West is the pinnacle of racial progressiveness. Nothing is further from the truth. Colonialism pillaged physical resources, not only stripping countries of their capital but also violently robbing them of identity, history, community, and tradition, forcing them to co-opt foreign ways of being and living. This forced assimilation is yet another violent legacy of colonization—the exportation of White beliefs around the globe, with Eurocentric sexual conservativeness becoming codified in areas that were historically colonized. The Section 377 penal code in India, which outlawed gay sex, was actually a vestige of British colonial rule that was only annulled in 2018. This historical and legal artifact exemplifies how the harm and trauma from colonization live on for generations. Even on a religious front, Hinduism features countless depictions of transgender and gender-nonconforming folks. Our scriptures and artwork are inundated with erotic imagery. These artistic representations of sex and gender identity are still such novel concepts in more "first-world" Western countries: ideas that are only being brought to the public consciousness in the 21st century. In many ways, this worldview mirrors the richness of indigeneity and the ways in which a lot of Native American tribes wield some of the most radical understandings on gender, environmentalism, sustainability, and spirituality.

The answers to some of the world's most pressing concerns are nested in ancient cultures.

Above all, WGS 2600 prompted a journey of personal discovery and reflection through the various readings, guest lectures, and class forum discussions. I was able to unveil a deep appreciation for my cultural background and the ways in which it uniquely positioned me as a Brown gay woman. I was also ultimately led to the touching realization that, as queer people, we're all part of an ancient inter-generational legacy of liberation that started far before any of us were even born. We're part of a historical movement of resistance. Sometimes, it's easy to lose sight of the fact that the people who were oppressed were not passive agents without their own agency and autonomy. Rather, they were people who fought, organized, mobilized, and resisted. They deserve to be memorialized and legacized. They deserve to be celebrated for their collective resistance and resilience.

I am proud to be the daughter of Desi immigrants. I am proud to be gay. Despite the deep and profound cultural nuances associated with these intersectional identities, both liberation and radical acceptance have always coursed through the blood in our veins. They are a part of our historical legacies.

You Don't Have to Date Me but You do Have to Respect Me
by Jazmin Bolin-Williams

Coming out as queer is never an easy thing to do even in this day and age of acceptance. Most of us don't have to worry about our parents kicking us out or our friends not liking us anymore (now I am not naïve, I know that this still happens and many people are afraid of what it means to be queer or gay or trans) but the one place one should *not* be afraid of being who they are is the LGBTQIA+ community. Sadly, this isn't always the case.

I had a relatively easy coming out. I announced I was pansexual to the world and honestly no one batted an eye! Nothing! I mean, I was not entirely closeted since I had always said women were beautiful and that the personality mattered more to me than appearances. I guess it was only natural that I would swing further on the spectrum from where I am today. But while my friends and family were accepting of me, I found that the community that I thought would never shun or make me feel uncomfortable was a little less than welcoming. Now, I won't make broad definition strokes with my statements as this particular incident only involved me and one other person, but I feel many of us have been treated in a similar manner.

This interaction happened between me and a former colleague (let's call her Lucy) who I will admit I never really got to know on a personal level other than that she is a "hardcore" lesbian of color. One day back in late 2020 while I was scrolling through Facebook, I came across one of Lucy's posts. She had shared a TikTok video of another Black lesbian that basically stated that bi/pan women were fake and that she was not their "experiment." She argued that the influx of bi/pan women was due to it "being trendy" and was influenced by social media. I was flabbergasted to say the least! What made it worse was that Lucy agreed and also claimed that she would never sleep with or date a bisexual woman. I was genuinely hurt by these statements, and couldn't really understand or believe that part of my own community would have these horrible thoughts. I should state that I would be considered a "mid-life pan," meaning I didn't really accept or experience my queerness till I was 29 and my only partners up until then were men. This played a part in the interaction.

Since I was hurt by Lucy's post I replied, "I hope she didn't mean all of us that are now just accepting/experiencing our sexuality," and what happened over the course of an hour truly shocked me. It left a bad taste in my mouth that I still have today thinking about it. Instead of her being understanding or accepting she doubled down. She insisted that bi/pan women only claimed they liked women in order to hook-up and have fun but not actually be in a relationship with a woman. She also argued that bi/pan women who were involved with men/male-presenting persons were more likely to cheat on her. She had always known she was a lesbian and thus this made her more "pure and genuine." I later learned she believed in the term "Gold Star Lesbian," which means a woman that has never been with a man.

Right from the start she looked at me like I was lesser because I had allowed a man to "taint" me. She also believed that since I had sex with men that I was "unclean" because men were the ones that carried all of the STDs and thus all men were "dirty." I was FLOORED! What started as her not liking bi/pan women turned into a very misogynistic rhetoric spewing against women being with other men. I diligently stood up for myself by doubling down and stated that she can have a preference of whom she dates, but those of us that she deemed as "not pure" still deserved love and acceptance within our own fucking community! That just because I had slept with more men than women did not mean that I was automatically lesser than her or "dirty" and told her that no matter the sex of the person ALL of us can develop STDs from ANYONE, NOT JUST MEN! To say that ALL men were automatically dirty was incredibly bigoted and ignorant. Even after my comments she still held strong to her beliefs and concluded the discussion by stating she had only dated one bi woman and the only reason she had done so was because this woman hadn't been with a man for years.

Some of my other LGBTQIA+ friends that had stumbled onto the post also chimed in and began to defend me, in a way. One of my oldest friends from elementary school, who identifies as lesbian, brought up the large number of lesbians that go after "straight" girls as a mission to "turn them gay" and that many lesbians can have very predatory behaviors. Lucy's only comment was that she had never done that herself. I have heard stories that this is a very common practice in the college scene where queer people can be "predatory" and "disingenuous" and "only looking for a quick fuck." The exact same rhetoric that Lucy and that original TikToker were saying about bi/pan women! Of course, I do not believe that all queer people do this, absolutely not, and I would never make a blanketed statement that ALL GAY FOLK were only looking to "turn people gay," but there are many within my own community that will stereotype an entire section of the community to further the biphobic narrative under the guise of superiority.

The only part of our interaction that made me feel sympathy for Lucy was when she started talking about her experiences dating and how hurt she felt when some of her partners dumped her and started dating men. Now, I can understand the heart-ache that comes with break-ups and watching them move on to other people. However, while I can never understand the feeling of being such a "let down" to another woman that they had to go back to men, that is no excuse for her being biphobic. She viewed every rejection/ failed relationship with a bi/pan woman as them just "playing around" and not serious about being in a relationship with her. I reminded her that this is the risk of every relationship, not just women being involved with women. We can't blame ourselves too much for the decisions of others.

At the end of this eye opening and saddening experience all I could really say to her was: You don't have to date me, but you have to respect me. Unfortunately, this made me more wary to call myself bi/pan in order to avoid this level of confrontation, so, I merely call myself queer, and in a way, erase the "problematic" label in order to be welcome into my own community.

What this all comes down to is: RESPECT. I respect and in a way envy that Lucy has always known who she is, but that is not the same experience for many of us. Some of us take longer to come out and we should still be met with the same love and respect that we demand of others outside of the

LGBTQIA+ community no matter our sexual history. We deserve to take up space and represent the "B" in LGBTQIA+. We have always been here and have no intention of leaving and no number of "Gold Stars" are going to erase us from the community.

A Conversation with Pinay Jones

LISA:
Have you faced people thinking bisexual is not legitimate?

PINAY:
I have and I think it's been part of why, at first, I didn't want to outwardly affiliate myself with any particular sexual identity. Even though I knew I resonated with bisexuality as a term, laying claim to it was difficult. When I really began to think about why that was, having family members who are like, "will you still have a healthy attraction to men?" That was said to me, and basically with the sort of, "oh, you know, you have some attraction to people who are not cis men, but ultimately you're going to basically fall in line." And then on the other side of it, I did feel like in terms of the LGBTQ community and trying to feel a sense of community there, even that to me is kind of fraught.

I wouldn't say that I didn't feel queer enough, it was more that I see many of the struggles for people who are queer, very outwardly, like walking down the street for example, they might be harassed or called names, and I don't necessarily experience that in my day-to-day life. I didn't feel that I was in the most vulnerable place within the queer community.

I was trying to work through being honest with myself about the validity of my sexual identity. I have experienced homophobia, but also trying to be sophisticated in my thinking about it as I deepen my understanding about the struggles of the queer community.

L:
Do you still feel that's a similar struggle now?

P:

I don't think I'm as pressed about it. I don't feel like I need to prove anything really to anybody. I think I can accept the complexities within queer identities without getting too deep into it and speaking to like, oh, am I valid? It doesn't have to always get to that point.

L:

Do you think that was specific to being in college and there being sort of a known community that you could or could not access?

P:

Yeah. I did find myself not wanting to "take up too much space" in queer spaces at UVA. I volunteered at the LGBTQ Center for I think two or so years of my time there, helped with events, was an outreach intern for a year. I was doing different things and there was a moment where I also was thinking about being on the executive team for the Queer Student Union. But then I kind of held back from that. I had this moment of, am I taking up too much space as a bisexual cis woman? Some people don't have that thought, but I still just felt that sense of like, *Hmm, could someone else be in this position*?

L:

Do you identify as queer also?

P:

Yeah. I think if asked, it would be queer. And then bi kind of second. I'll use that sometimes. But queer I like more, actually. It is tied to a political orientation, rather than just my individual "I've, you know, had experiences with women and men." All that. Adding the political piece to it.

L:

Do you think as a person of color, there are things that you have faced that intersect with your bisexual identity as far as inclusion or exclusion?

                              P:
I would say a lot of queer spaces I've encountered, particularly at college, were very white.
When I was working as an intern, part of my role was
to do outreach for queer people of color to make it
known that the resources, like the LGBTQ center and
all of that, were also there for people of color.

   I think when it comes to being Black and then queer
and bisexual . . . when I have been in relationships with people or have made it known that I am
queer, I've found that because of the way I look,
I am masculinized. When I've gone on different dates
with women, I felt the sense that I was being made
to be the more masculine one, if that makes sense.
And I do think that is tied up in racialization.
Especially when going on dates with people who are
lighter, shorter, that whole thing. I found discomfort in that particular experience that I think is
deeply tied to not only my sexuality but also my
race and ethnicity.

                              L:
Based on racist ideologies, the perception of black
women as stronger, tougher, and masculine is what
has played out sometimes is what you're describing?

                              P:
Yeah. I've talked to other black women who've experienced the same thing. Even though it's a queer
relationship, there's still this unspoken sort of
gendered dynamic happening where the darker person
ends up being the one who takes on the more masculine role.

   There are masculine qualities I really enjoy,
that I do think I exhibit in my personality, but in
terms of initial impressions, I don't think I look
particularly gender queer, you know what I mean?
That's why I'm like, this the trend has to be tied
to race.

                              L:
How might you be perceived and treated when involved
with a woman versus with a man?

```
                              P:
```
I think what comes to mind—there is a social ease
in some ways being with a man. There are privileges that are afforded as a heterosexual presenting
couple in my experience. Then I think about being
with a woman—my mind goes to this trip that I went
on to New York with my best friend, and we're not
together, but we kind of have, I would say, a romantic friendship that makes sense. We were holding
hands as we were walking and we could be perceived
as two women dating. And I noticed that we got
just so much attention, specifically from men on the
street, yelling things, trying to cat call, all that
. . . versus I took a different trip to New York where
I was walking around with another close friend of
mine who's a man, and nobody said anything to me. It
sucks because it is in a lot of ways a function of
patriarchy, the sense that you are the property of
that man and therefore other men respect that. But
it also is nice to not be cat called on the street.

What's the Point? Coming Out While in a Straight-passing Relationship by Joya Bhattacharyya

When I first came out as bisexual to the important people in my life, they
were pretty confused. Everyone was accepting, which is a privilege I don't
take for granted. But they had a lot of questions. Why now? What changes
now that we know? You see, I was in a relationship at the time, and it was
with a heterosexual male. For lack of a better term, my relationship was completely "straight passing." We looked like a cis-heterosexual female dating
a cis-heterosexual male. For all intents and purposes, we looked as non-
queer as you can get. And, as a result, me coming out as bisexual seemed
extraneous.

There seems to be an expectation from people who are not queer that
coming out entails suddenly changing the way in which you present yourself to the world. Many of my friends seemed to think that, after coming
out, I would suddenly start hitting on girls, dyeing my hair rainbow, and
spending every weekend protesting. They definitely would have accepted me
if I decided to do these things. Instead, I just kind of continued on with my
life as before. If anything, the only change was that I could more openly talk
about queer issues and discrimination with my loved ones without fear that
I would out myself. I was in a committed relationship, so I had no need
to hit on girls, even if I would harmlessly flirt more openly. I had always

presented in a semi-femme manner, but I enjoyed experimenting with my look. I had always been interested in social issues and had attended a handful of protests. No hugely significant changes were made in my lifestyle, and that seemed to throw people off.

I came out to my boyfriend first, months before I even told my brother or parents. I felt that he should be the first to know, as he and I were best friends and in love. I had mentioned some possibility of being attracted to women over the years, but nothing concrete. When I told him, tears streaming down my face, he was so supportive. He thanked me for sharing this part of me with him. He needed time to process everything, which I understood. After all, I would feel confused if my partner came out as bisexual while dating me, and these thoughts would be guided by my own insecurities. I might think, *Am I not enough for them? Are they exploring other options? Were they thinking about who they are attracted to, other than me?* He definitely (and understandably) grappled with some of these questions, and this is a process I am supportive of and will be patient with.

He made a joke about how he now had twice the competition in dating me. This joke was repeated by many of the people I came out to, including my parents. Perhaps this stems from the same expectation that coming out will somehow change the way in which I date, despite the fact that I was beyond happy in my relationship. I did not want anything or anyone else—I was fulfilled. Perhaps the joke also stems from harmful stereotypes hegemonic society holds about people who are bisexual. People tend to think that since we are interested in those of our gender identity and those not of our gender identity, we must want more partners. We must sleep around more! Some people even go so far to think that being bisexual means that we are sexually interested in just about everyone, so we flirt more frequently and hit on whoever we can, guided by hedonism. They forget that just because we are attracted to a certain socially defined category doesn't mean that we are attracted to everyone within that category or even that we would express interest to those we are attracted to. In these stereotypes, bisexuality gets conflated with polyamory. Of course, there are plenty of people who are bi and poly, but the two terms mean such different things. Bisexuality is a broadly interpretable term that refers to who you are attracted to, while polyamory describes the structure in which you approach dating and relationships. It gets frustrating to think about all of the assumptions people might make about me when I tell them that I am bisexual, even if they are good people who love me and are educated about queer issues.

Regardless of the fact that nothing major changed about my relationship or life in general, coming out was still a revolutionary act for me. I have always been a very open person, and keeping this one part of me to myself was mentally and emotionally taxing. Coming out allowed me to stop censoring myself in my head, which reduces so much of my cognitive load. I can do so many things now that I could not before! One of the first things I talked to my parents about after coming out was a show that we used to watch as a family called *Schitt's Creek*. I remember when we had finished the show and watched a final behind-the-scenes episode where the show's actors discuss how a queer character, David, comes out. He has a very specific scene where he explains his sexuality to his friend by comparing it to wine. He says, "I like the wine, not the label." Although this character is pansexual, I found so much comfort in this scene and its dialogue. Watching the actor talk about this scene, I began to tear up, but I felt that I had to hide my tears because I was not out yet. The conversation I had with my parents about this scene after I came out was one that brought me great comfort, and it allowed my parents to understand a bit more about my queer identity.

After I came out, I was excited to explore queer communities and find queer friends with whom I could deeply relate. I ended up moving to New York City for graduate school about a year ago, and living here has gifted me with an amazing queer family and endless opportunities to explore my queer identity. On my first full day in the city, I signed up to go to a meetup of fellow LGBTQ+ Columbia grad students in Sheep Meadow, a large field in Central Park. I later learned that Sheep Meadow is a popular spot for queer communities to hang out, especially on Sunday afternoons in the summer. I met with a group in front of my apartment building before taking the Subway to Central Park, and I have to say that from the first minute, I knew that many of these people would be great friends of mine. We came from a place of shared identity and seemed to understand each other immediately. Not only were we queer, but we were all academics. Many of us were also Asian. These intersections helped me to feel at home with these strangers, and we found that we had so many common experiences. One of the most common experiences was trying to figure out if we should come out to our immigrant grandparents—we know they love us and would probably accept us, but do we need to go through all of the motions to explain our identity to them when many do not understand what it means to be queer? Would telling them add a lot to our relationship? This was such a relatable situation, and I still talk to some of these friends about this issue now.

After getting to Sheep Meadow and setting up our picnic blanket, everyone in our group introduced themselves, their departments, and their identity. As people went around the circle, I realized how many people were in committed relationships, and some had even brought their partners. I never really had queer relationships to look up to, so this was inspiring for me. I had role models who could be successful academics who are proudly queer and invested in their relationships. I felt comfort in seeing that what I wanted in my life was not only possible but full of joy. It has been such a pleasure getting to grow with these people over the past year, and I know that I have found some lifelong friends.

That day kicked off what has been a year of exploring my queerness publicly. I have been to my fair share of gay bars in Hell's Kitchen and Greenwich Village, and I have enough exposure to have some favorites. (Check out Industry in New York City if you can—they have incredible drag performances!) I have attended several queer performances in theatres around the city. My friend and I even attended a queer immersive art festival, where we met queer sculptors, fashion designers, photographers, and dancers. I actually bought a sticker with that amazing quote about wine from *Schitt's Creek* on it from that festival! I have learned so much about this city's history of queer activism, and I am so excited to learn and grow more.

The only negative queer experience I have had here in the city was when I tried to explore the New York City lesbian scene. This was by no fault of the scene or its members—I just found that I was repeatedly considered not queer enough. I was attending a local pop-up events for a new lesbian bar with some Columbia friends. At first, the event blew me away. There were amazing bands playing live music, great food, and a pretty venue. However, I started to feel out of place after an hour or so. I noticed that I wasn't dressed similarly to anyone there. I didn't understand some of the tongue-in-cheek jokes being made, and I didn't seem to have many similar interests to anyone I met. In my head, I felt like I was not queer enough to be at that event. Regardless of if that was true, I felt like I should leave because I couldn't keep up. I felt too queer for my straight friends and too straight for my queer friends. This was an awful feeling and one that I am still struggling with. Maybe it is just a matter of exposing myself to more lesbian events, or maybe I am most comfortable in other queer spaces.

As you might have noticed, I tend to refer to myself as "queer" rather than bisexual pretty often. This isn't because I am in denial about my bisexuality or because I am questioning it. I am really confident that this is the word that best describes my sexuality, and I am proud to tell people about it. Maybe part of me is trying to protect myself from those harmful bisexual stereotypes I find so frustrating. But, part of me feels that using "queer" helps me to relate to my community more. People of all queer identities share a common experience in feeling "othered," either by society or by their own queerphobia. I find that many of my bisexual friends feel the same way and refer to themselves as "queer." Maybe my feelings will change over time. I know figuring out your labels is a personal journey for everyone, and this is just what works for me.

In the end, I am still at the beginning of my journey of figuring out who I am as a bisexual woman. I'm still dating the same guy—we actually just celebrated our 5-year anniversary! I think he is the one I'm going to spend the rest of my life with. I know that our relationship does not negate my bisexuality in any way. I am not "effectively straight" just because my relationship is straight passing. I know I have privilege compared to people in more visibly queer relationships, and I will continue to use this privilege to advocate for queer issues and rights for the rest of my life. I am also queer enough, and I deserve to take up space in queer arenas without any apologies. I am bisexual, proud, and always enough.

On Liminal Spaces and Being Tired by Barbara Mona

In 2012, during an otherwise boring night at Barnes and Noble, a Julie Anne Peters novel nestled deep within the shelves of young adult romance caught my eye. Its cover, the blurred faces of two women with lips almost touching, excited me. *Keeping You a Secret.*

I snatched the book from its comfortable place on the shelf, bringing two others to hide it between if my parents were to find me. I sat on the floor, back pressed up against the wall, and perused the first few dozen pages. As I became immersed in the characters' world, the buzzing of the lights and quiet chatter amongst customers ceased, my breath became heavier, and my body grew warmer. I was hooked. Hurriedly yet silently, I went to the checkout counter, bought the book, and stuffed it in the waistband of my pants so no one could see. Like its title, this book was to be my secret.

That night, as I stayed up past my bedtime to read about the budding relationship between Holland and Cece, I felt my heart sink deep into my chest. Suddenly, I realized that the feelings I felt towards Haley in (the canonically queer classic) *Stick It* and Kate in *Lost*—and the lack thereof towards Justin Bieber, Zac Efron, and One Direction, unlike other girls—might mean something.[44] As I learned about the manifestation of queerness in cisgender women, what it means to be closeted versus out, and what homophobia versus acceptance can look like, I fell in love with not only the characters but also with the possibility of falling in love with a girl.

With no more pages left to flip, I came to my senses: *wait—I have a boyfriend. I'm not a tomboy. If I'm not totally straight but not totally gay, what am I?* As I questioned myself, the walls began to close in on me, a disorienting white light blurring the clarity I once had over my identity, a long hallway appearing before me with two doors, a voice behind each calling out my name. As if the ghost of Robert Frost were prompting me, I knew I had to choose one or the other—not both.

But there would be a cost. Not knowing what life would look like behind either, I hesitated, watched the hallway grow longer and the doors become out of reach, and became paralyzed when I tried to answer the most fundamental question defining any person's existence—*who am I?* I laid my head on my pillow as I thought of the answer, falling asleep to the silence of my uncertain mind.

★ ★ ★

In 2022, I sprawl on my off-white, coffee-stained, full-sized bed. With a pair of candles burning to my right, barely aromatic but nevertheless warm, and two so-called unkillable plants to my left, nevertheless wilting from too little TLC, I let out a deep sigh. Stretching my arms above my head until they contact the cold, brick wall behind me, feeling my feet graze the smooth wall opposite my gaze, I ground myself within the six-by ten-foot shoebox that I call home.

Home is unlit incense waiting for its chance to spark, piles of jeans seeping from my closet, empty coffee mugs on my desk, a bedside table piled with unread *New Yorker* magazines, and not much else, for nothing else fits. Though limited in the physical space it offers, my home is my refuge: a quiet space to breathe, relax, and uninterruptedly scroll through TikTok. As I lay on my side, my head cushioned by a freshly turned-over pillow, my finger methodically flicks the screen up and up like clockwork. Video after video, my mind tunes out of the physical world—away from my tiny New York City apartment—and into the digital realm. Suddenly, I come across a video that seems eerily familiar. My eyes squint, I turn up my volume, and an unnerving tune ensues. The screen flashes images of long, narrow hallways dimly lit by a shadowy green mist; visibly quiet airport lobbies and libraries, sans the people and books that breathe life into spaces; a muted-colored playroom with worn-out plastic toys and wooden blocks scattered on the floor, as if the playing children vanished into thin air; and a staircase leading to an unknown destination, its darkness seducing me to descend. As I look at these images, a shiver runs down my spine. For whatever reason, I feel like I know these places—but how? Where are they? When did I go to these places? Why, despite looking and feeling familiar, do these places invoke such discomfort?

According to the TikTok's comments, these are called "liminal spaces."[45] As intermediate spaces wherein familiarity and uncertainty coexist, they bleed uncertainty and discomfort. From empty and dark school hallways, seemingly never-ending airport terminals, tubular metal slides with no light passing through, all-too-familiar hotel rooms in an unfamiliar city, long wooded roads where even the crickets whisper out of fear of the unknown, these liminal spaces are temporary, meant for fleeting human interaction— places where we are welcome for only a brief moment in time, lest we remain too long, get lost, lose touch with reality, and never get home.

Scrolling past the video, my discomfort lingers. Why do these liminal spaces make me feel so lost, confused, unseen, trapped? Why do I relate so much to these feelings, like I've been stuck in a liminal space recently? I nestle my head deeper into my pillow, and as I begin dozing off, a jolt of energy awakens me and my heart sinks into my chest. I am drawn to the books lining my wall, and sure enough, it hits me: *Keeping You a Secret*. The novel sneakily pokes out from the rest, staring at me, prodding as to why I haven't yet answered the question it prompted ten years ago: *who am I?* As a femme, cisgender bisexual woman, the intersection of my gender and sexuality places me in a liminal space—a state of in-betweenness, a pit-stop on a one-way journey from being straight to gay (or maybe gay to straight)—for I am not fully understood, welcome, or celebrated in either the straight/cis or queer communities. I have not yet chosen a door—answered who I am. Until then, I am stuck in a liminal space, unable to escape.

★ ★ ★

Growing up as a femme, cisgender girl, keeping my sexuality a secret was simple. I was never perceived as anything but straight, for I did not conform to stereotypes defining queer women. I did ballet, not softball; I wore skirts and dresses, not graphic tees and basketball shorts; and I kept my hair long and sometimes wore makeup, avoiding any boyish look. In the straight, conservative, religious communities of my youth, my gender identity and performance made my sexuality invisible. My femininity protected me from those who would not understand or accept my sexuality, which was a privilege. I never questioned my pronouns, pondered whether my body felt right to me, and/or worried that I would face physical or emotional violence for my identity—harms that exist for people of color and those who are trans, nonbinary, masc., and/or disabled. At birth, I was placed into the category of Woman, and I was happy to be there. But at college, this invisibility inhibited me, and I questioned if my bisexuality might be perceived as more valid if I were not as feminine or not a cisgender woman. If I appeared queerer vis-à-vis my gender identity, expression, or otherwise, might I be more visible to the queer community—a community I so desperately wanted to join when it was safe to do so?

In middle and high school, after reading *Keeping You a Secret,* I knew in my heart that I was bisexual, but I did not yet have the vocabulary to articulate it or a community to explore my sexuality in. I also struggled to balance my attraction towards men and women when my attraction to *any* gender was quite limited. When friends asked me who my crush was, I often named a boy from our small class at random, choosing him based on his outfit, whether I liked his haircut, or some other arbitrary factor. When I made out with my middle school "boyfriend" at our lockers after school, feeling nothing but his sweaty hands on my hips and his sticky tongue in my mouth, I thought—see, *everyone? I can like boys*—all whilst imagining I was kissing a girl. In high school, I did not do so much as hold a boy's hand. The one boy I was in love with was taken, having girlfriend after girlfriend, and I had not been able to muster any comparable feelings for another boy. At both of my junior and senior proms, I cried in the bathroom, coming back to the dinner table with smudged mascara and a quiet demeanor to the chagrin of my dates. Sensing my anxiety, each asked how he could make me feel better. In my head, I screamed: *I wish I could be here with a girl!* But through clenched teeth, a tight chest, dry contacts, and puffy eyes, I smiled and said, "I'm just tired."

"I'm just tired"—not entirely untrue! I was tired because I was never able to feel the same romantic or sexual attraction towards any other boys, even if I tried (for I only liked one). I was also tired of living an incomplete existence, for—aside from the fear of being out as bisexual in my small, conservative town and to my family and church—I could not talk about girls I liked without being labeled a lesbian (and I am not one). In high school, the long hallway with two doors at its end continued persist in my mind. I stared at the doors as they taunted me, telling me to choose: behind one, you can continue to pass as straight, keeping your standing in the straight/cis community and choosing a life where you are only with men, and behind the other, you can lean into your queerness, come out, and be with women (and maybe a few men, because sure, you like them too—but not too many or else people are going to think you're straight and experimenting). Despite being dissatisfied with either option, I am told to pick a door, for one cannot last in the liminal space for too long. But alas, I remain, hopeful that I can find an escape.

As I reflect upon my place on the margins of the cis/straight and queer communities, I realize that I have experienced similar alienation as a Greek-American. Growing up with a strong ethnic, cultural, and religious heritage in a predominately white, conservative, small all-American town, I struggled to balance my Greek and American identities. From classmates gagging at the σπανακόπιτα and παστίτσιο my yiayia packed in my lunchbox, to refusing to speak Greek with my family in front of peers out of embarrassment, to pretending not to hear customers at my family's restaurant mock their accents and call them names, exhaustion became my foremost personality trait, as I worked hard to hide my Greek identity to not appear "different" from my classmates. My refuge from said exhaustion, then, should have been the Greek community. But in these spaces, I have again been ridiculed for my differences—those that they suggest align me more with Americans. Because I am half-Greek with light coloring, I am labeled as a physical and biological outsider. From asking where I dyed my (natural) bleach-blonde hair because it was so unusual, to Greeks side-eyeing me when I spoke and sang and prayed in our native tongue, to kids at church camp telling me that I'm not *really* Greek because I'm of half descent, I was surveilled and judged by people within my culture, questioned as to whether I truly belonged. I faced a constant dilemma (am I American or Greek?) requiring me to sacrifice half of myself to be wholly accepted into either community. I was prompted to choose a door, but I belonged behind both.

Just as Real Greek People question whether my identity sufficiently qualifies my existence in their spaces, Real Queer People have closely scrutinized my proximity to and association with the LGBTQ+ community, for I do not physically appear to belong. As if my presence spoils the purity of either the Greek or queer communities, despite laying legitimate claims to both, the eyes of community members divert away from me as they discuss the status of my membership amongst themselves. As a Greek-American and bisexual person, my identity—who I am—has never been a question I can answer, for the answer lies in others' hands. Those who believe they have greater stake in the community and thus greater power over me, those who are "pure" in the community, hold the key to unlocking the door they believe I should walk through. The liminal space, therefore, exists by design to trap and suppress and delegitimize. As a femme, cisgender bisexual woman, I am placed in the state of limbo I've become all too familiar with, imprisoned by the judgment of others, an infinite time-out for the sin of impurity that stains my sexuality and, therefore, identity.

To escape the liminal space, I question whether I should make changes to my identity to appeal more to one community or the other. Should I cut my hair? Get tattoos? Dress less feminine to appeal more to the LGBTQ+ community? Choose to just date women to make my sexuality more palatable to both the straight/cis and LGBTQ+ communities? Choose to just date men so that I can stop being fetishized by men? Though my answers may begin to reveal which door would be opened for me, as a perpetual sitter under Plath's fig tree,

> *I couldn't make up my mind which of the figs I would choose. I wanted each and every one of them, but choosing one meant losing all the rest, and, as I sat there, unable to decide, the figs began to wrinkle and go black, and, one by one, they plopped to the ground at my feet.*[46]

One fig is me, descending down the aisle, donning a white ballgown, linking arms with a man, planning the number of children we would have, preparing for a life that is the dream of my family; another is lying in the tall green grass, clutching the hand of a woman, planning the pottery and paintings and meals that we would make together, laughing at the absurdity of human existence. One fig is sour, another is sweet. And though I prefer sweet things at the moment, my tastes change, for sometimes sour is appealing. Why should I have to decide which I like better now, which fig I will taste for all of my life? Can I not have all of the figs I want, for they are natural, God-given fruit of Mother Nature who loves me above all? But the rule is one fig—one door, no exceptions.

During my first two years at college, I tried, tried, and tried again to enjoy the sour fig, finding a man whom I felt complete with—or, at least, not wholly anxious around. Though I was successfully engaged in a mini-romance with a grand total of one man, my desire to be with a woman wore me down again and again. Upon joining a sorority—anecdotally the most straight/cis community one could join in college—I pretended my way through conversations about loving fraternities and sex with men to conform, avoiding the topic of my bisexuality out of fear I would be ousted and ridiculed and questioned as to why I would join a sorority as a queer woman. Nevertheless, I spent those two years blasting sapphic bops through my headphones, making friends with a few open lesbian and bisexual women, and wondering when the day would come when I could escape the room in which I was trapped, freeing myself from the constraints keeping me from discussing my bisexuality with others without feeling ridicule or shame or confusion.

That day came on the first day of third year, when I was happily surprised by a sweet fig. With my signature look—a tote bag slung over my shoulder and two iced coffees in hand—I confidently strutted into class. Kicking off the fall semester in typical first-day-of-class fashion, my professor had the class go around the room to share our names, hometowns, and a fun fact or two with the class. Despite basically falling asleep minutes into the activity, a deep, sultry, assured voice abruptly woke me from my trance. Looking up and to my right, I saw a girl—legs opened wide in a non-lady-like manner (a stance my mom oft scolded me for using), feet firmly pressed on the ground, arms bent with hands behind her head, a sly smile on her face. My eyes grew wide, my breath stopped, and when it was my turn to speak, my voice shook. To prevent my face from turning bright red, I diverted my eyes from her, staring straight at our professor, sharing something about myself (but I don't know what, because I blacked out). In my heart, I thought this girl might help me escape the liminal space I felt trapped in.

For the next few months, I meticulously studied Locke and Mill and Kant and Marx and Rawls not to primarily learn philosophy—despite it being the purpose of our class—but to impress this girl with my knowledge. Not only was her brilliance palatable and her mind more complex than anyone I'd ever known, her queer confidence—from her androgynous fashion to the subtleties of her speech—made me realize that she was not someone that I just wanted to *be with* but also *be*. Despite being cisgender, she was not particularly feminine or masculine. Because I passed as straight my entire life despite wanting to appear queerer, I noted her dress and attitude, taking the things that I believed made her appear beautiful and powerful and queer and implementing some into my being. Over the semester, I too tried to talk in a lower, steadier voice; wear less feminine outfits, ditching skirts, dresses, and makeup for overalls, crewnecks, and beanies; and give off a cool, calm, confident vibe. The two of us flirted in code, her admiring my flannels and combat boots, me sharing my favorite King Princess and girl in red songs,[47] us exchanging glances in class when topics of love or relationships were discussed, walking out of class together whilst brushing arms and smiling from cheek to cheek. When she finally gave me her phone number, my heart—sunk in my chest since I first read *Keeping You a Secret*—moved back into its rightful place.

Despite being sent 1,600-miles apart due to COVID-19, we became closer, spending hours each day texting, FaceTiming, sharing movies and music, exploring our dreams, fears, goals, and worries with one another. After five long months, when we saw each other in person, we embraced as if we were the first people in the universe to discover physical touch. Our relationship was built on trust, empathy, passion for social causes and global issues, and shared experiences of being queer women from conservative communities. Through her, over the course of one year, I gained more confidence to think about, openly discuss, and celebrate my bisexuality than I had in ten years. My fear of straight/cis people finding out about my sexuality, cutting me off, judging me in disgust, or suggesting that I was going through a phase began to vanish—with her, I became blind to any repercussions of coming out, as I was unapologetically, steadfastly, deeply in love with her.

As the semester dwindled, however, we began to grow further apart, as she fell in love with another woman and my mental health severely declined. On one dark November evening, in the midst of our "is this a friendship or something more" stage, we discussed and re-watched news footage from five Junes prior, when the Supreme Court ruled in *Obergefell* that same-sex marriage was protected under the Constitution. She turned to me and semi-jokingly said: "That's when you were a gay-hating conservative, right?" My neck snapped to the right, my eyes squinted, and I practically jumped off of the couch. Upon viewing my adverse reaction, she repeated: "In high school, you were religious and conservative, right?" I responded, "Wait, when did I hate gay people? And, dude, I've known that I've been bisexual since middle school. We talked about this." Continuing, she said "Wait, I thought you became bisexual in college?"

Did she just say **became**? My head and heart throbbed, my face turned red, and unlike the first day I met her, I stared right into her eyes as mine became wider. "What the fuck?" After a long bout of silence, I left her apartment. Heavy breathing, tears streaming, I felt the walls close in on me, as if I were forced back into the liminal space, she had begun helping me escape from. The girl I called my best friend, whom I loved and looked up to, invalidated my queerness. As I tried to make sense of her comments with a mutual friend, the friend disclosed that she thought that I only identified as bisexual after falling in love with her. Unsurprisingly, she made this claim about others to me, despite my pushback. According to her, she charmed me, among other sorority girls in college—girls who she claimed were *probably* straight but who explored their sexualities with her because of her confident queerness. I am just so tired of biphobic stereotypes.

Betrayal, hurt, embarrassment, anger, guilt. Ironically, the feelings that I experienced from church, family members, and classmates just resurfaced with my best friend—my best friend who was a lesbian. The qualities that I once admired in her began to repulse me, and over the course of the following year, through tears and drawn-out conversations and awkward, passive aggressive encounters, our friendship was over. I was simply experimenting in my sexuality with her; claiming that my bisexuality was just "a phase" that she helped facilitate reinforced the most pervasive stereotype about bisexuality. To have someone I loved so deeply write off my and others' sexuality as something new, something she *created* and *controlled*, was to be a child listening to my priest scream over a bonfire, telling us to spit on the icon of Παναγία[48] if we support the sin of same-sex attraction; watch my grandfather slam his hands on a table after I said I would consider not getting married; sink into a chair as a teacher mentioned to my high school peers that she could see me being "probably gay" in college; freeze as a boy pins me up against an ice cold locker and my will, sticking his hands over and down into my pants because "I should like it."

Struggling to get over her, I turned to the other person I had been in love with years prior—the boy from my hometown—to feel comfort and friendship. Under the neon lights of the packed, dingy college bar where we had (I admit) a few drinks too many, I told an abridged version of my falling in and out of love with the girl from philosophy class, emphasizing she/her pronouns in her identification. Functioning as both a venting session and my "coming out" to a lifelong friend, I expected an emotionally mixed response, including shock and possible hesitation but, ultimately, compassion. The first responses I got—a high-five (good), a hug (great), an "I love you no matter who you are or who you want to be with" (nothing short of amazing)—made me smile as hard as I had when that girl first gave me her number. But the smile quickly wiped from my face when he became touchy in a way that we aren't normally, repeating again and again "girls liking girls is so hot," asking if I would rather hook up with him or another woman, the percentage of men versus women that I liked, if I would consider a threesome, and for explicit details about my relations with women. By crossing the line separating curiosity from fetishization, I again felt discomfort and betrayal, as he hyper-sexualized my bisexuality, suggesting that it made me more attractive to the straight male gaze, asserting power and control over me and my body in a way he hadn't before. How could I get any more tired than I already am of biphobic stereotypes?

★ ★ ★

To be a femme, cisgender bisexual woman is to be delegitimized by both of the people you love. It is to be stuck in a transitory period where I am told to be straighter or gayer depending on who I am with, a balancing act, when I am asked to tone it down in straight/cis spaces and turn it up in queer ones. It is to be invisible, existing neither here nor there, for I am in between, and people *must* choose a door to be seen. It is to be stuck in the empty and dark school hallway, walking down the seemingly never-ending airport terminal to an unknown destination, sliding down the tubular metal slide with no light passing through and thus no foreseeable future, weeping on the bed of the all-too-familiar hotel room in an unfamiliar city for I feel alone and misunderstood, driving down the long, wooded roads where the crickets are debating if I'm straight but confused or gay in denial.

In a world where binaries reign supreme and sexuality is so often viewed as black and white, I am stuck in the gray area. This gray area, this liminal space, is inherently transitory, for I am kept there until others decide where I should go. In this space, I am labeled annoying and greedy and indecisive and confused and promiscuous, called a faker and liar, told that one day I would settle down in my gay or straight identity. But that's not who I am. Lacking the privilege in and clear-cut nature of monosexuality, bisexuality is often misunderstood by those who are not bisexual, for the right questions are not asked of us and neither are the answers we give listened to.

I don't want to keep my bisexuality a secret. I want to scream from the rooftops that B is in LGBTQ+, that I don't have to renounce my femininity for my bisexuality to be valid, that my femininity and bisexuality should not predispose me to accusations of being greedy or slutty.[49] I want to be free from the liminal space in which I am trapped, a non-reality that is inherently transitory and fleeting, told that my only escape is a choice between two legitimate realities, that I am illegitimate, with the key to leaving this state of loneliness lying in the hands of the straight/cis and queer communities. I want to be accepted and understood when I answer: *who am I?*

Well, who am I? Among many things, I am a femme, cisgender, bisexual woman who spends way too much money on rent, drinks way too much coffee, (accidentally) starves my plants, works out too little, works too much, reads too little, leaves my bed unmade, watches inordinate amounts of Tik-Tok, scream-sings Greek pop followed by country and hip-hop (don't judge), calls my mom any time a minor inconvenience besieges me, checks in on my friends at all hours of the day, fantasizes about people I will meet and places I will go in the future, imagines a world where bisexuality can be at the least validated and celebrated, if not understood. As I continue to ground myself within the walls of my 60-square-foot home, finally dozing off to sleep, I dream of the day when I am free from the liminal space of misunderstood bisexuality, when we are recognized as the beautiful, complex, dynamic, and, most of all, *real* human beings that we are.

Until then, I sleep to escape, for I am tired.

A Conversation Between Friends: Hope and Katie

HOPE:
What does it mean to be a "feminine, bisexual" person?

KATIE:
I feel like to be bisexual and feminine—technically
I might be both of those things in the dictionary
definition. I honestly feel like I resonate more
with being feminine than I do with being bisexual. I feel more empowerment—or perhaps community—
within that word than with bisexuality. But, even
at that, I don't feel like femininity exactly fits.
And part of that might be due to the bisexuality or
the queerness that I have. . . . Especially since
I started realizing I was not just attracted to men,
it's like, what does that mean for my femininity?
People expect a certain thing of me as a woman or
someone who they perceive as a woman.

H:
I feel like with queerness or bisexuality particularly, I know your identity shouldn't be necessarily connected to who is attracted to you and who
you're attracted to and who you're with. But I feel
like they are so intertwined.

K:
No, they are. And also, I feel like there's such
a connection between gender and sexuality too. You
know, gendered expectations for someone's sexuality. I feel like I'm more attached to my femininity
than my bisexuality.
But I also feel like both are so fluid too. When it
comes to gender, it has more to do with the choices
I make every day to signal things versus my bisexuality, which can be invisible or like someone might
not know. Why would they know? I don't make choices
necessarily that show it, even though my choices in
my gender presentation might signal my sexuality.

H:
Exactly. I feel like so much of my femininity is
lived experience, but it's also what's done to me.

And the way you're treated and perceived, both of them are so internal but also so external. And the external is, I feel like where you get those names that don't quite line up. And then I feel like the internal doesn't have a title in the same way. I'll have moments where I'll be like, oh, that felt very feminine. I mean obviously like something that is confounded by different identities besides gender. Not to be like, "oh, the sisterhood". . . . But there's a trustingness associated with my femininity. That I really like.

K:
Yeah. Where do our views of femininity and masculinity come from? And why is it like that?

H:
I don't think that changes based on my partner. But it's kind of hard to tell if, when I'm with a person who that type of thing doesn't come as naturally to, which in my experience tends to be masculine people.

K:
That type of thing in terms of openness and stuff, right?

H:
Yeah. Which of course is not across the board, but it is a general trend that I've noticed. So, then I wonder if that sort of makes me have to embody that sort of feminine more.

K:
I feel like there are just so many shared experiences you might have if you are clocked as a woman, versus with bisexuality. Unless you're necessarily stepping out with another woman or someone who people don't expect you to be in a relationship with.

H:
But then also when you do that, you're not clocked as bi or queer. You're clocked as a lesbian. It's

such a weird thing—you're always seen as feminine no matter who you're with, but then like straight or gay . . .

K:

There is not the "bi" in between. I feel like there's sometimes a general sentiment like, "Oh, I don't like men. I hate men." All these things which I feel can make people lean more into the sexuality side of their queerness. . . . There's that, and then there's also the trope of the "bi girl with a boyfriend." But, then also I know people who say "I like women so much more than men" you know? But maybe that's just how your sexuality goes?

H:

Exactly. And then it's also like, okay, I like women so much more than men, but I'm dating a guy.

K:

I guess we've talked about being clocked as gay or straight. . . . Do you feel like that changes for you when you're in more queer spaces? Like how do you feel as a "bisexual" person in queer spaces?

H:

In general, I think, fine. When I'm in the QC [Queer Center] or at Pride, I feel like most of the time people aren't thinking too hard about it, but I do think there is, at least for my boyfriend—I don't think he feels super accepted in it. Which is fine because he's not queer. But then it's a weird thing where I'm at Pride, which is a space for me and my partner, but then to go there and present superficially as a straight couple. Or to be like half of the couple is straight, then I feel like you lose a lot of that safety and ambiguity, even though my identity is the same.

K:

I've talked a lot about that with my partner too. I feel like there are different ways people operate in private and public spheres. Because technically,

we are in a very queer relationship. But I would
kind of joke that we are "straight" because if someone saw us on the street, they could totally clock
us as a straight couple. But also, people's truths
are ever evolving, you know? I'm also trying to
think now about how many true all-queer spaces I'm
in. And I feel like that's not usually often.

H:

Because there's a bunch of places that are queer
coded, right?

K:

Especially in college, it's like a lot of people
are having awakenings and realizations and stuff
like that. To a certain degree people don't necessarily care, but they do assume, you know? I assume
that you are this or that, but it's not like, from
another queer person, it doesn't feel as loaded,
even though it's still problematic or like, "don't
assume my sexuality or whatever." They're like,
"Oh, I thought you were gay" or something like that.

H:

Right. When I'm sitting in a queer space by myself,
I think the general assumption is just oh, she's
a lesbian. And I'm not really that pressed about
it, even though it's not true. But then when you're
trying to be a part of any sort of queer community
with your non-opposite-sex-presenting partner. I am
not sure how to qualify the shift but it's really
significant.

K:

You mean for you and your boyfriend? Yeah. I feel
like it also is challenging too, especially with
boyfriend, capital B boyfriend. Because there's a
reason that it's not accepted usually in that space.

H:

Exactly, so I'm like okay, it's an LGBTQ space. It's
a queer space. But it's like what's really meant is
it's a gay space? Or really, it's that my queerness

doesn't "cover" my boyfriend. Which is fine. I don't want it to look like queer spaces are being co-opted by a het couple or like I'm co-opting or taking up space that isn't ours. But there are lots of times where I would like to share the parts of my life that are associated with queerness with my partner but either I don't want to bring him into the space or he feels uncomfortable being in a space that becomes "not for us" when we look like a straight couple. I feel like that is a weird thing, at least in my experience of bisexuality—but also coming off as straight—there is so much safety and convenience to it. So, it's not like that's the only space we have. And I really want it to feel safe for people who don't have the luxury of passing as a straight couple.

It's just an interesting dynamic—because queer is the word that I most prefer. And I understand why queer is an umbrella term, and I feel like if you talk to people about it, they would be like, oh yeah, like bi- women, bi- everyone, are welcome. It's a queer space! But that changes based on the presentation of who you're with.

H:

Because people are like, "Why is a straight couple here?" I've actually never been in a straight relationship, I guess "fully" straight, so I wouldn't know. But being in that space and a partner being in that space, especially one who identifies as straight, at least for my partner, I would never expect to be invited or welcomed necessarily into a trans space, for example, even though I am queer. But I also understand. If you have someone who you're with or someone who you want to come along with you to things, but they can't, that can be tough.

And there's just the weird repeated, "coming out" of it all. But also, even that term is wrapped up in a bunch of weird feelings for me.

K:

I've gone through different phases where sometimes I'll tell people just to be visible. And also, sometimes it's a through the grapevine kind of thing.

H:
I feel like that's a lot of how it goes, particularly in college.

K:
One time during my first year of college, I shared that I was queer with someone, and we were with their—not their girlfriend but, just, their person for that night. And then later in the night, he came up to me and he was like, oh, it would be really hot if you kiss this girl right now. And I was like, oh, like is this what I get for being vulnerable? I shared it as—not even being super vulnerable, right? Cuz honestly, I am open about it. But to share and then to be asked that. I don't know. I was just like, Oh my god.

H:
The sexualization is just always lurking. I have had partners be like, oh, *really*? (suggestive)

K:
It's like slow your roll. It's also interesting to see that play out at bars and stuff. Sometimes I'll see two feminine presenting people with two guys, and then the girls will make out and then go back to the guys. Not looking upon that necessarily in judgment, but it's interesting, like, what is going on.

H:
Part of it can be people exploring in college. Sexuality is fluid, doesn't need to be named. All of that. Some people are like, I'll make out with a girl cause that guy thinks it's hot. And it seems like there are people who it's just really that simple for them.

K:
I also feel like I am a big proponent of "you should use the labels that empower you." And people have different understandings of their own sexuality. That's how I think of sexuality. But I feel like if you're a feminine person and you kiss a girl and you like it? That's a little gay. You must be at least a

little bi then or something. Which again might be an
unfair assumption and couldn't necessarily always
be true. But if you're attracted to someone of the
same gender and then you are kissing them, and that
turns you on. . . .

K:

Yeah. The male gaze is so strong. It's crazy.

H:

I think that about femininity too. I don't know
about you but I feel like there's always an outside
observation. I could be alone or just hook up with
my partner, and I'll be seeing or thinking about
myself from that kind of external view. Even if my
partner isn't a man. There's this impulse of, oh
I should arch my back.

K:

Right? I should do this. What would—

H:—

look the sexiest, right?

K:

I feel like my attraction lies primarily with
women, but—what does that even mean? Who knows?
I am attracted to many men. Many cis men, trans
men, or just whoever. But I want people to think
I'm attractive, right? I want people to think I'm
hot. And I'm always like, why? I feel like the
majority of people I have felt sexualized by in
my life have been men. Mostly cis men. So, I think
that affects it too. When I go out, usually the
people who flirt with me aggressively are men.
And there's a weird fear component there. Even
if feminine people are *really* coming onto you, it
doesn't have that power dynamic baked into it. And
so, I'm not scared.

H:

Yeah. Those moments where a feminine person is
aggressively flirting with you, I think, one, they

are rarer, and two, they don't stick out as much looking back because it's not saved in my head as a time where I was genuinely afraid or really having to think about my safety.

K:

It can often be way more ambiguous. Even with me and not even regarding flirtation in like a super express way. But being like, "oh, you look really cute today." Is someone gonna clock that as a flirt or a friendship thing?

H:

Right, how sexuality or intention is assumed differently depending on the gender or presentation of the person talking.

K:

I love women. This is totally a mass generalization, but the more negative thing that I think tends to happen with women is overthinking or that, "Are we friends? Are we flirting? What's going on?" Obviously, *anyone* of *any gender* can be harmful at any time, especially on an individual level, but as a whole, the thing with women is more confusion about intention.

H:

It is more nebulousness. Have we been on five dates or have we just been hanging out as friends?

K:

Also, if we have mutual friends . . . I had a threesome with someone and I see them around all the time. And it's not really that sexual even. We're just chilling. But we did have sex so, I don't know. But if it was a guy, I could imagine that playing out very differently. If it was different gendered dynamics or being more of a thing.

H:

It's so hard to untangle big macro trends from personal experiences with individuals. I feel like these big labels and ways of ordering the world shape how I define and categorize myself and the ways I feel queer or femme. And I have so many moments or interactions with people or even things that are kind of seemingly small and mundane that I'm sure other people don't remember but have been so huge in shaping those identities and what those categories mean to me or who feels like they are "allowed" to occupy them.

K:

The labels for all of it aren't so helpful. I want to say they aren't specific enough, but I also feel like it is kind of a generational thing as well. People's relationships to terminology, it ebbs and flows.

H:

Along with just the definition and way we use the terms themselves.

K:

Some people do find a lot of power in labels like bisexual. I don't want to take any of that away from them or be like, "oh, why don't you just say queer" or whatever. I would never say that to anyone, never.

H:

Me neither. I hope no one would ever say, "don't call yourself queer," to me. Right? Like, I think that has to be the—

K:

— understanding, the exchange. I hope, honestly, I feel like that's something that's not in my life as much as I would want it to be. I wish I was in more queer spaces. So, I hope to carve that out more wherever I end up.

Notes

1 Alan G. Johnson, "Patriarchy, The System," in *The Gender Knot: Unraveling Our Patriarchal Legacy* (Philadelphia: Temple University Press, 2014), 41.

2 Samantha R. DeCapua, "Bisexual Women's Experiences with Binegativity in Romantic Relationships," *Journal of Bisexuality*, Vol. 17, No. 4 (2017), 451–472.

3 Shiri Eisner, "Bisexuality, Feminism and Women," in *Bi: Notes for a Bisexual Revolution* (Berkeley, CA: Seal Press, 2013), 142.

4 Eisner, "Bisexuality, Feminism and Women," 143.

5 Louise MacGregor, "Hot Bisexuals, the Safety of Sexiness and the Fetishization of Queer Women," https://thethreepennyguignol.com/2020/06/08/hot-bisexuals-the-safety-of-sexiness-and-the-fetishization-of-queer-women/.

6 Isabella Simonetti, "Bisexuality Is More Than Just a Pornhub Category," *The Daily Pennsylvanian* (October 2018), www.thedp.com/article/2018/10/porn-bisexual-fetish-college-upenn-isabella-simonetti.

7 Crystal Fleming, "Being Black and Bisexual Comes with Extra Obstacles: But They Can Also Be Overcome," Everyday Feminism Website (June 2015), https://everydayfeminism.com/2015/06/a-black-bisexual-manifesto/.

8 Sunny Woan, "White Sexual Imperialism: A Theory of Asian Feminist Jurisprudence," *Washington and Lee Journal of Civil Rights and Social Justice*, Vol. 14, No. 2 (2008), 284.

9 Cleo Falvey, "Bisexual and Biracial: The Challenges of Dating While Fetishized," Bisexual Resource Center (March 2020), https://biresource.org/bisexual-and-biracial-the-challenges-of-dating-while-fetishized/.

10 Mikaela Pitcan, Alice Marwick and Danah Boyd, "Performing a Vanilla Self: Respectability Politics, Social Class and the Digital World," *Journal of Computer Mediated Communication*, Vol. 23 (2018), 163.

11 Kaila Adia Story, "On the Cusp of Deviance," in *No Tea, No Shade: Writings in Queer Black Studies*, ed. Patrick E. Johnson (Durham: Duke University Press, 2016), 364.

12 Story, "On the Cusp of Deviance," 364.

13 Lanice Avery, Alexis Stanton, L. Monique Ward, Elizabeth Cole, Sarah Trinh and Morgan Jerald, " 'Pretty Hurts': Acceptance of Hegemonic Feminine Beauty Ideals and Reduced Sexual Well-Being Among Black Women," *Body Image*, Vol. 38 (2021), 182.

14 Avery et al., "Pretty Hurts," 182.

15 Avery et al., "Pretty Hurts," 182.

16 Sarah Steele, Lisa Belvy, Cindy Veldhuis, Kelly Martin, Robyn Nisi and Tonda Hughes, "Femininity, Masculinity and Body Image in a Community Based Sample of Lesbian and Bisexual Women," *Women and Health*, Vol. 59, No. 8 (2019), 829–844.

17 C. Blaire Burnett, Melissa Kwitowski, Michael Trujillo and Paul Perrin, "Body Appreciation in Lesbian, Bisexual and Queer Women: Examining a Model of Social Support, Resilience and Self-Esteem," *Health Equity*, Vol. 3, No. 1 (2019) 238.

18 Burnett et al., "Body Appreciation in Lesbian, Bisexual and Queer Women," 238.

19 Robyn Ochs, "Bisexuality, Feminism and Me," https://robynochs.com/bisexuality-feminism-men-and-me/.

20 Jennifer F. Chmielewski and Megan R. Yost, "Psychosocial Influences on Bisexual Women's Body Image: Negotiating Gender and Sexuality," *Psychology of Women Quarterly*, Vol. 37, No. 2 (2012), 224–225.

21 Chmielewski and Yost, "Psychosocial Influences on Bisexual Women's Body Image," 224–225.

22 Flora Oswald and Jes L. Matsick, "Understanding Body Size and Bisexuality via Femme Theory: An Investigation of Self-and Meta-perceptions of Gender Expression," *Fat Studies*, Vol. 12, No. 1 (2023), 101.

23 Cassie Donish, "Five Queer People on What 'Femme' Means to Them," *Vice* (2017), www.vice.com/en/article/d3x8m7/five-queer-people-on-what-femme-means-to-them

24 Briana Shewan, "Are You Femme? What Femme Isn't and What It Is," The Affirmative Couch Website (2019), https://affirmativecouch.com/are-you-femme-what-femme-isnt-and-what-it-is/.

25 Cecila Chung, "What We Mean We Say 'Femme': A Roundtable," (2016), www.autostraddle.com/what-we-mean-when-we-say-femme-a-roundtable-341842/.

26 Hannah McCann, "The Invisible Femme," in *Queering Femininity: Sexuality, Feminism and the Politics of Presentation* (New York: Routledge, 2018), 84.

27 Jamie Geneve Davis, "The Evolution of Femme," DePaul University, https://depaul.digication.com/davis-hon-100/femme-as-it-intertwines-with-class-race-and-othe-1.

28 Davis, "The Evolution of Femme."

29 McCann, "The Invisible Femme," 84.

30 McCann, "The Invisible Femme," 84.

31 Juana Maria Rodriguez, "Queer Politics, Bisexual Erasure: Sexuality at the Nexus of Race, Gender and Statistics," *Lambda Nordica*, Vol. 21, No. 1–2 (2016), 169.

32 McCann, The Invisible Femme."

33 McCann, "The Invisible Femme," 88.

34 McCann, "The Invisible Femme," 90.

35 McCann, "The Invisible Femme," 91.

36 McCann, "The Invisible Femme," 91.

37 Kaila Adia Story, "Fear of a Black Femme: The Existential Conundrum of Embodying a Black Femme Identity While Being a Professor of Black, Queer and Feminist Studies," *Journal of Lesbian Studies*, Vol. 21, No. 4 (2016), 408.

38 Imani Rupert Gordon, "For Black Queer Femmes, Redefining Blackness and Queerness Are Revolutionary Acts," Interview by Vilissa Thompson,

Prism Website (February 2022), https://prismreports.org/2022/02/03/for-black-queer-femmes-redefining-blackness-and-queerness-are-revolutionary-acts/.

39 Eva Akvol, "The In-Between: Femme Bisexuality," Queer Majority Website (April 2022), www.queermajority.com/essays-all/tibfemme bisexuality.

40 Hannah Johnson, "How I Maintain Visibility as a Bi Femme," bi.org Website (November 2016), https://bi.org/en/articles/how-i-maintain-visibility-as-a-bi-femme.

41 Gina Jones, "The Difference Between Being Femme and Feminine," *Bustle*, www.bustle.com/articles/166081-what-does-femme-mean-the-difference-between-being-femme-being-feminine.

42 Oswald and Matsick, "Understanding Body Size and Bisexuality via Femme Theory."

43 I prefer the label "gay" as it feels less restrictive, more fluid, and comfortable!

44 My online history—a combination of "girls kissing" searches and "Am I gay?" *Buzzfeed* quizzes—serves as further evidence of this "something." But I digress.

45 Liminal (adj.): "of, relating to, or being an intermediate state, phase, or condition" (Dictionary, Merriam-Webster).

46 Sylvia Plath, *The Bell Jar* (London: Faber & Faber, 2005), 73.

47 Real talk—do any of us actually like them, or are we obligated as queer women to listen to them? Again, I digress.

48 Greek for "the Virgin Mary."

49 Okay but ladies, seriously, let's reclaim "slut."

5

CISGENDER MEN AND MASCULINITIES

Although cisgender (cis) men benefit in multiple ways from the privileging of masculinity and it being more valued than femininity in a misogynist, patriarchal society, there is still the pressure to fit into the masculine "gender box." Gender policing of cis men can result in bullying, violence, and self-harm, as many try to adhere to the unobtainable ideals of masculinity.[1] In addition, masculinity is fraught with cis heterosexual expectations that reinforce homophobia, transphobia, and anti-femininity, a view that avoids anything feminine, including feeling emotions.[2] Cis men are also socialized to believe that even the smallest sexual interaction with another man is automatically considered gay, which dismisses the realities of what it means to be bisexual.[3] Furthermore, this can lead to a negative understanding of bisexuality within cis male communities while contributing to bisexual erasure within both queer and straight communities.

While cis-bi women's identities are often considered less controversial because of appropriation by the heterosexual male gaze, cis-bi men particularly face skepticism and are believed to *really* be either straight or gay.[4] From the work of Kinsey in the 1940s to recent studies of bisexual men, there is a plethora of evidence that reveals that cis men can be bisexual. Studies are still being done to substantiate this, even one as recently as 2020, which confirmed "Results provided compelling evidence that bisexual-identified men tend to show bisexual genital and subjective arousal patterns. Male sexual orientation is expressed on a continuum rather than dichotomously."[5] The struggle to prove the validity of cis male bisexuality continues to this day.

Additionally, cis-bi men face an ample amount of biphobia and binegativity. According to Helmes and Waters, bisexual men are regarded more negatively than all other sexual orientations, partly due to "the perceived

DOI: 10.4324/9781003242659-6

androgyny of bisexual individuals. This fluidity may play havoc with some people's need to dichotomize the world."[6] Many argue that these negative attitudes are simply a form of homophobia, since bisexual men can be involved with men; however, the fact that people in queer communities can also have bi-negative attitudes demonstrates that biphobia stands alone.[7] Another contributing factor is the lack of representation of cis-bi men in research. According to Eisner, when cis-bi men are included, it usually focuses on three themes, medical (usually focused on HIV), sexual behaviors, or denial.[8]

Multiple stereotypes prevail about cis-bi men, particularly because mainstream media portrayals are almost non-existent (see Chapter 6: "Media Representation in Television, Film, and Reality Shows" for more on this). Zivony and Lobel discovered that cis-bi men, compared to heterosexual and gay men, are considered "more confused, untrustworthy, open to new experiences, as well as less inclined towards monogamous relationships and not as able to maintain a long-term relationship."[9] Many believe cis-bi men have "sexual orientation instability" defined by the "denial of their sexual orientation, that bisexuality is 'just a phase'" and that they are afraid of embracing their true identity as gay.[10] There is also the stereotype of "sexual irresponsibility" and that cis-bi men are more likely to contract and spread HIV along with other STIs.[11] These stereotypes also decrease the desire for many people to be involved with cis-bi men.[12]

Another challenge for cis-bi men is the constant questioning by society of their gender performance, particularly how they should fit on the binary of masculine and feminine. Because cis-bi men can be involved with women, there is the expectation that they have to be masculine presenting, since it is assumed that women (whether they are straight or bi) only want to be involved with masculine men. As Eliel Cruz states,

> *There are spaces for gay men, lesbian women, bisexual women, and trans women to express femininity. There are few, if any, arenas in which bisexual men, queer in our own right, have the space to express femininity without fear of our sexuality being nullified.*[13]

Rio Veradonir, a lead organizer for the world's largest bi social club, amBi, writes about his own experience with assumptions about masculinity when a gay man at Pride asked him: "Are these the colors of the bi flag? Pink, purple, and . . . lavender? Because I would have thought you guys would choose more 'manly' colors—you know like green and brown or something like that."[14] The stereotype that cis-bi men should be masculine, Veradonir argues, can cause fetishization, particularly by gay men who may feel that masculinity is what makes men the most attractive. He reacts to this notion by exclaiming,

Bisexuality is about liking more than one gender. That's it. If you've never met a 'feminine' bi guy, you haven't been looking. Just like not all lesbians are 'butch' and not all gay men are 'queens,' not all bi guys are a fantasy of 'masculinity.' Our sexual orientation is more than your porn fetish. Sorry.[15]

This assumption that cis-bi men are *supposed* to be masculine adds to Shiri Eisner's assertion that there is general confusion about cis-bi men's masculinity. Heterosexuality and monosexuality are masculine, rendering bisexuality unmasculine. Monosexuality promotes "decisiveness and stability" while bisexuality consists of "instability, confusion, and indecisiveness," traits associated with femininity.[16] In addition, masculinity requires men "to comply with the patriarchal single standard, and any deviation from it is perceived as a defect in one's masculinity."[17] These gendered expectations can make it difficult for cis-bi men to make sense of their own gender presentation.[18] Furthermore, this can impact body image, particularly with the pressure to fit the ideal westernized muscular body that is often unobtainable.[19] Little research has been conducted on cis-bi men and body image, but one study describes findings that cis-bi men felt pressure not to "engage in modifications that are culturally coded as gay," which may be a form of internalized homophobia, as they were "demeaning and separating themselves from the perceived 'gay' appearance, while simultaneously identifying with the culturally valued 'masculine' appearance."[20] Given the unique challenges cis-bi men face, it is not surprising that there may be pressure to conform to masculine presentation in behavior and bodies.

Bi-negativity, bi-erasure, and denial of cis-bi men's identity has resulted in cis-bi men being "one of the most closeted populations among LGBT communities."[21] According to the 2013 Pew Research Center report on LGBTQ Americans, 77% of gay men said they were out in comparison to only 12% of cis-bi men.[22] This fact is what motivated bisexual activists and writers Robyn Ochs and H. Sharif Williams to write the anthology *Recognize: The Voices of Bisexual Men* in 2014, in addition to Robert Cohen writing his 2024 book *Bisexual Married Men*. Vaneet Mehta also authored the book *Bisexual Men Exist* in 2023, because of his own experiences of "being questioned, erased, ridiculed and rejected from numerous different angles," which did not improve in queer spaces.[23] Mehta felt that growing up he was "uninformed and ignorant," which led to some hard work to unlearn his internalized biphobia.[24] As a result of these experiences, Mehta created the hashtag #BisexualMenExist to raise awareness and combat the bi-erasure and bi-negativity with bi-positivity.

For cis-bi men of color, the intersection of racism compounds this reality. Given how little research and understanding there is about bisexual men in general, there is even less conducted about cis-bi men of color. For Black cis-bi men, there are many stereotypes to navigate around Black manhood. Given the history of racism, *Cool Pose* author Richard Majors describes being a Black man in the United States as being "psychologically castrated—rendered impotent in the economic, political, and social arenas that whites have historically dominated."[25] Obtaining masculinity in this context means maintaining a "cool pose," comprised of the suppression of deep feelings, in addition to upholding a balancing act. As Majors explains,

> *People are drawn to the power of the cool black male because he epitomizes control, strength, and pride. He presents a mysterious challenge. He is charismatic, suave, debonair, entertaining. On the other hand, being cool can become more important than life itself. Unfortunately, it can exact a price that seems destructively high.*[26]

Masculinity is again associated with heterosexuality, and for many Black cis-bi men, this can further reinforce not being out. As Alexander Otusajo explains,

> *Gay men embrace their femininity and the Black community sees that as being weak because it doesn't fit into their definition of masculinity. But if you're a bisexual man in the Black community, then you're seen as gay. Your masculinity is stripped away from you completely because you can have sexual and/or romantic relations with both males and females.*[27]

Clinical psychologist Dr. Marcus Patterson adds, "It's where you have to be hard, tough, hyper masculine or you're not real. You're not one of us."[28]

Cis-bi men of color can also feel a particular sense of isolation, when many queer spaces are dominated by white people, and bi-erasure and racism may thrive. Applebee found in his work with cis-bi men of color that heteronormative and masculine cultural expectations led to fearing family rejection or being disowned.[29] Mehta describes his own experiences growing up in a British Indian household:

> *I found myself constantly surrounded with the expectations of what it meant to be a man. Many South Asian cultures are steeped in heteronormativity and with this come certain expectations on how people behave, which often means enforcing strict, traditional and archaic gender roles. For men, the expectation is to be the provider, to be strong and unemotional, to be rich and successful in order to support your wife and kids. This creates an air of toxic masculinity.*[30]

He further explains the collectivist culture that he grew up in maintained a "culture of shame" created to "encourage people to follow the unwritten rules of the community and fall in line with expectations, or else risk bringing shame on their family and ruining their social standing."[31] Similar to the respectability politics for cis-bi Black women discussed in Chapter 4, within the context of racism and white supremacy there can also be even more pressure for cis-bi men of color to uphold certain cultural norms, such as traditional masculinity, heteronormativity, monosexuality, and monogamy.

Another intersection of biphobia and racism is the stereotype associated with Black cis-bi men on the "down low" (DL). Interestingly, what little research exists about Black cis-bi men focuses mostly on the rates of spreading HIV, AIDS, and the DL. According to Layli Phillips, the DL is defined as:

*B*lack men who secretly have sex with other men while maintaining heterosexual relationships with women and presenting themselves as masculine rather than effeminate. Thus, the key components of the DL as it currently functions are: a) Blackness, b) sex with men, c) secrecy, d) the appearance of heterosexuality, and e) masculinity.[32]

In reality, homophobia and biphobia could make anyone, regardless of racial identity, feel the need to hide their sexual activity. The term "down low" specifically targets Black men and "vilifies these men as being dishonest, both with others and themselves, and as the main spreaders of sexual diseases within the community. This is, of course, false, and it refuses to grasp the concept that multiple sexualities exist."[33] The myth about Black men on the DL spreading HIV first erupted in 2004, when author J.L. King published his autobiographical book *On the Down Low: A Journey into the Lives of "Straight" Black Men Who Sleep with Men*. Although the rates of HIV among straight Black women are on the rise, research has shown that Black men on the DL only account for a small percentage of the spread of HIV. According to Sandfort and Dodge, this kind of discourse on the DL has "renewed demonization not only of bisexuality but of Black male sexuality."[34]

The impact of binegativity and bi-erasure for cis-bi men means a lack of access to support, potential risk-taking behaviors, higher rates of experiencing sexual violence, and mental health struggles.[35] (This is addressed in more detail in Chapter 11: "Mental Health Issues and The Impact of Violence"). There clearly needs to be more research done on cis-bi men, where their voices are central, respected, and heard, especially for cis-bi men of color. There are, however, still ways that they are privileged as cis men. According to Eisner, cis-bi men could strategically use their privileges to enact social change and challenge toxic masculinity as they state:

*I*n general, it appears that the concept of male bisexuality is so inconceivable in the eyes of society that it constantly denies that it even exists. Bisexual men "fail" at dominant masculinity; they are perceived as deficient because of the "crack" that their bisexuality creates. . . . In the face *of biphobia, monosexism, and sexism, bisexual men have a "way out" of patriarchy, and a "way in" to creating new, "postpatriachal" masculinities. Male bisexuality gives them the opportunity to step away from dominant masculinity, to refuse to be oppressors and to instead participate in the deconstruction of patriarchy. Instead of trying to "do better" at being men, bisexual men have the opportunity to create a sexual and gender revolution.*[36]

This is not an easy task, given all the pressures and expectations of masculinity. There are, however, cis-bi men working to make sense of masculinity and to challenge the toxic aspects, as seen in the following four personal narratives. There are so many different ways bisexual men do exist, and this discourse is essential to decrease the harm caused by a society thinking otherwise.

A Conversation with Wolf Hudson

LISA:
What do you think about the intersection of bisexuality and masculinity?

WOLF:
Masculinity is a huge part in bisexuality because there's already the thought process that to be masculine, you have to be straight. You cannot be a homosexual and be masculine. But when there are so many people who are surprised to find very masculine, homosexual men . . . one of the biggest struggles with men who have curiosities and desires is that they're equating weakness with gayness. There's this denial of their bisexuality because they don't want to be pinned to what is perceived as weakness. And so, you find cis men who have to be ultra-masculine. They have to assert themselves in a manner that fits what society has already dictated you were supposed to be.
Which is one of the reasons I think that there is bi erasure; it has to do a lot with masculinity. As opposed to a cis woman or someone who is female assigned at birth who can freely be that. I have sort of a theory that female sexuality is viewed as weakness, and because it's viewed as weakness, lesbianism and female bisexuality . . . [are] acceptable because that is what you're supposed to do as

a woman. But a man can't do that. A man has to be masculine. You cannot cross that boundary. And for me it always comes down to, who gives a damn? You can be straight and be effeminate. You can be homosexual and be masculine. You can be any gender and assume any traits and not have it dictated by your own desire, by your appearance.

L:

Have you struggled with that yourself at all? Trying to find that balance when coming out?

W:

No, well, first of all, I never came out because I was never in. I had always identified as a heterosexual. That viewpoint has evolved over time in the sense that, in my personal life, I am heteroromantic. I've never dated a cis male. Not opposed, but I've never dated a cis male. I've always had more of an intimate relationship with cis females. But my desire to be with people has always been very open. I've never hid that fact. It was never, do I like that or don't I like that. It was more of well, let me try it.

I've always been an open book. And actually, my early porn career was the truest representation of me exploring my sexuality for the first time. Most of the stuff that I was doing on film was my first time. So, I've never had to conform. I've never been about what society tells me to do. I mean, even as a little boy, I always challenged authority. I challenged my mother, especially when it came to religion. I always had a curiosity and I could always see the man behind the curtain. I'm like, wait a minute. That doesn't make sense.

L:

Did you feel like there were pressures and expectations of masculinity?

W:

The pressures were always there and still are. I just never gave into people's expectations. I never try to be anything other. I have a masculine side, but I also have a feminine side and both work hand in hand. It's something that took time to embrace, but I never denied it because I knew it was there. In my earlier years, I never really explored or tried to find what that really meant for me. And once I figured it out, then I reveled in it. I think most people have both in them, one more than the other. The issue is that they don't accept it because of what somebody else is saying. The thing is, everybody has an insecurity. Everybody's feeling a certain way and feels like they're going to be judged by the other.

L:

Yeah. What is that? It's pluralistic ignorance, I think.

W:

That's the perfect word. Which is why it goes to what I said earlier; I always saw the man behind the curtain. For me it was like, wait a minute. You realize that it is all bullshit. We're all just playing a game. And once you can figure out that game, then you can have fun. Part of why I've been able to stand out like a sore thumb is because I'm willing to push the buttons that people won't. And when it comes to my masculinity, I know when to use it and I know when not to abuse it. The same thing with my femininity. And it's served me well. It's also had some backlash, but the backlash had nothing to really do with me. It had to do with the structure of society telling me, oh, you can't do that and we're going punish you for that. Being able to embrace all aspects of myself. Being able to express myself sexually, being able to showcase my desires to be with both genders. And also, non-binary people. So, I've been punished for that, especially in the porn industry.

For more conversation with Wolf Hudson go to Chapter 7: "Pornography and Sex Work."

If I Have to Use a Label by Ryan Powell

I'm not too fond of labels. If I had to identify myself as something, I am a cis male using he/him and they/them pronouns, and I am also bisexual. I hate labels because there is so much more to a person than just trying to put our identities into a box, and I understand this even better after taking a class with Dr. Speidel. I have talked about how it is odd living as a bisexual man many times with her, which is why I wanted to help her with this book. She told me that it was surprisingly hard to find cisgender bisexual men and I understand why, because as soon someone identifying as a cis male says that they are bisexual, it is immediately dismissed, and they are thought of as gay.

I realized that I wasn't straight in high school when I started to have feelings for men. I didn't know how to react because I knew I liked women but not like everyone else did. I was also scared of being gay. After all, my family was kind of religious. However, it was mainly just me, my mom, and my dad who was in the military. Since I didn't know who to talk to about my sexuality, I tried talking to one of my friends, who said she was pansexual. This is how I remember our conversation going:

```
"Do you like girls?"
"Yeah, I think so."
"Ok, well, do you like guys?"
"Yeah, I think so."
"Ok, would you date someone if they were trans?"
"I never really thought about it, but sure."
"Well, okay, then you're pansexual."
```

So, for a while, I said I was pansexual, saying that I didn't really care how someone identified, I would still love them. But whenever I told people this, they would make jokes saying I would have sex with anything. I ignored the jokes and insults, but then I thought about it more. The more I thought about potential relationships, the more I realized I had never really been in a romantic relationship. The only people I dated at the time were women, and even then, we never did anything sexual because I was either scared for some reason or I just wasn't interested. Also, I hadn't been attracted to anyone who was trans so far, so I guessed that meant I was actually bisexual.

Around this time, I had moved schools because my dad had medically retired from the military, so we moved back to southern Virginia because that is where my mom and dad's family is. Since it was the south, many people around me were Baptist Christians. When I went to my new school, most of the people there were homophobic, racist, xenophobic, transphobic, and so on. This was also the first time I had experienced these things since I grew up in city areas with diverse types of people. When I would try talking to people and they questioned me about my crushes, or the guys at my school would talk about girls they found hot or had sex with, I would nod my head and agree. But eventually, the question of sexuality would come up. Then I just said that I was bisexual. People would automatically assume that I was gay, completely ignoring how I also liked girls. It was frustrating before, but now I just ignored it, if that makes sense. Whenever I would talk with my friends I met while my dad was still in the military, Mom would make jokes about how I was gay but ignore how I also like girls. But the people at my new school would forget that I was interested in guys and still be homophobic. However the fuck that works, I don't know. The people in my class or on the football team would try to hook me up with other women, but I felt awkward and would deny it. But there were also times when they were genuinely curious about it, asking me, "wait, so you would have sex with a dude?" and I just said, "yeah, it doesn't really matter to me."

There was also a time when three guys on the football team came up to me while I was getting stuff ready for the game that night, laughing. The conversation went like this:

```
"Hey Ryan, do you watch straight porn?"
"Uh yeah, sometimes I do."
"Okay, so do you watch gay porn?"
"Yeah, I watch gay porn sometimes too."
"Well, maybe you should watch lesbian porn because
that's not gay."
At this point, I stopped putting the coolers on the
cart and said, "are you a fucking idiot?"
```

It was so stupid to me that they thought lesbian porn wasn't gay, even though it's in the name. I understand it was probably because they felt uncomfortable seeing a guy cum and only wanted to see a woman climax. Sometimes they seemed supportive of my sexuality, like when one of the football players asked me, "if you could have sex with one of the guys in here, who would it be?" I didn't like any of them like that, but I just said one of my friends because that felt the least awkward. Even with this supposed support, they still made fun of me for my sexuality because later, people in my class tried to hook me up with girls or use me as a joke by saying stuff like, "Hey Ryan, don't you think that that person is hot?" while that person was in the room. They obviously were trying to make both of us uncomfortable.

There have been plenty of other times when people would be surprised when I told them I was bisexual. I apparently don't look, talk, or act like I'm bisexual. Is it because I feel better presenting more masculine? Is it because I look like a typical man? I think that as soon as I tell people that I'm bisexual, they dismiss that part and just assume I'm straight, while at the same time saying that they don't want me to hit on them.

This was probably most evident during my senior trip when I was called to the room of one of the infamous guys in my class who had tried to hook me up with girls but also made fun of me in order to make other people uncomfortable. He made my friend call me to their room so he could tie me to the bed to make sure I didn't touch anyone in the middle of the night. He also recorded it and sent it to everyone in my class because they thought it was funny. After this incident, the whole school showed their true colors. The school didn't want to punish anyone except my friend, who was pressured into calling me over to the room. It took fighting with the school board for them to do something about everyone in the room, which was barely anything. They only gave the person who tied me to the bed and recorded it out-of-school suspension for the rest of the year and everyone else was suspended for three days.

At this point, people at my school started hating me because of my sexuality and saying that I "couldn't take a joke" or asking, "why is that faggot even going here?" It even got to the point where even the school staff was treating me poorly. One of my teachers accused me of cheating on an exam, treated me more coldly, and acted like I was a nuisance when I asked for help on an assignment, which wasn't a problem before the incident. In addition, the person that helped with student accommodations would go out of her way to not help me after everything happened.

Once I graduated, I didn't really have to deal with those people anymore, which was a relief. Even though it was a small town and I could see anyone from high school, I didn't have to interact with them every day. I was better off going to the local community college because most people there were more accepting of different people.

Sometimes I had to deal with biphobia, such as this time when I skated with an old friend. There were times when he talked to me about a girl he hooked up with, and then when I talked about a guy I was talking with, he immediately changed the subject. Sometimes he would say that bisexuality didn't exist and that people who were bisexual needed to choose if they were either straight or gay because they couldn't do both. Basically, he believed that anyone who was bisexual would eventually cheat because they couldn't stay faithful to their partner. I tuned it out at the time because I didn't think one of my friends would say something like that, but I don't know why I let that kind of thing slide at the time.

During another interaction with him, we were checking out an indoor skatepark and discussing times we had sex. I brought up that I had a threesome with two of my friends, and I didn't really enjoy it because I found out that I didn't like women that way. He asked me what I didn't like about it, and I just said I don't know; I just wasn't really enjoying it. So, he tried to make me picture having sex with a woman to make me want it, and I told him to stop because it made me feel uncomfortable.

People constantly question my bisexuality. When I participated in a study at the university about hook-up culture, the researcher asked me about my sexual experiences. I said that I was bisexual but had only had a good time with men. She stopped me and asked me why I don't just say that I'm gay, and I replied, "then that ignores the fact that I still like women." Another example is when I was talking to a friend about my theory that everyone is at least one percent bisexual. I was not saying that everyone is at least a little bit horny for the same gender but that most people have the ability to recognize someone is attractive. The higher that attraction, the more likely someone is bisexual. I also brought up how if someone was a hundred percent straight or a hundred percent gay, they have some form of internalized homophobia, something that I used to talk about with my psychology professors and in my classes. But whenever I would bring it up with this friend, he would immediately shut it down and say you must pick.

So, if I have to identify as something, I say I am bisexual. I have been dating my boyfriend for over a year now. While, yes, my sexuality will change and morph, I still will like both men and women. Right now, I am probably some form of asexual because, lately, I don't feel like having sex; just lying in bed and playing video games with my boyfriend is enough for me. If someone does ask about my bisexuality, I will I say that I like both men and women, but my dick only likes guys. How does that work? I don't know, but I am most comfortable with that explanation.

A Conversation with Adrian Cruz

LISA:
Tell me a little bit about this idea of "straight passing" in the context of masculinity.

ADRIAN:
It's just what people tell me, like within the queer community, they're like, you're so straight passing. And I'm like, well, you don't know until you ask about my story. But I can see that firsthand just because my last relationship was with a female for a year and a half. She felt comfortable knowing that I was bisexual. Her whole family knew . . . I was very close to her sister. But I guess because I had [the] privilege of being a cis male, I was straight passing. The integration for me to get into that relationship within the family dynamic was very easy

because I feel like I can be that masculine man, you know, what's within a male-to-female relationship, versus if I wasn't, I feel like it would've been a little bit different to get accustomed to.

L:
It's so fascinating how much we are invested in masculinity as a society representing sexual orientation. It's so arbitrary.

A:
Yeah. I feel like anybody could be masculine. My ex-girlfriend, she played sports. She watched more sports than I did. That's the attribute I didn't have. I'll play sports, but I won't be like a super huge fanatic. She followed up a lot of those sports. So even the female could tailor some of that masculine perspective too. But even within the gay community, there's a who's a masculine top, or who's a masculine bottom type of thing.

L:
What does masculinity mean to you?

A:
It's very big in Hispanic culture that the man of the house is the one that provides, does all the yard work, takes care of the family, provides the roof. But within my personal experience, my parents divorced so it was flipped. But before that it was my mom working the long hours. It was my mom providing, it was my dad being the one to cook because he finished work early. But within the realm of Hispanic culture and machismo, I saw it firsthand within a lot of my family, you provide in one sense, but you also get provided for, so I always saw all my aunts serve my uncles first and then serve themselves.

There was this thing, I am the man of the house, the one that says what has to happen, the one that provides, brings in the money. That was my first perspective and introduction to masculinity. Then once I got into the queer world, I've realized for me, because I enjoy sports or I enjoy the gym or I have a deep voice . . . like I can say bro and all this stuff, like it's part of my lingo within the queer community. That's what's defined within masculinities. So, I feel like they go hand in hand, but one is very different within the queer community versus the Hispanic community. But at the end of the day, they have an overlap.

L:

Have you felt pressure to perform masculinity a certain way in different spaces? Within the queer space, do you feel pressure to not be as masculine or, at home, [to] be more masculine?

A:

Definitely at home, be a little bit more masculine . . . but there are times where I'm like, I don't feel like doing that yard work because I'm just lazy. But then you'll see me prioritize watching a romcom over a sports broadcast or something. I don't want to tie everything about masculinity to sports, but it is related to that, versus once getting myself integrated within the queer community, I feel like I started letting go a little bit of my masculinity in some spaces. I still carried it as my first presence, but get me a good cocktail and get me on the dance floor . . . I'll be dancing with whomever! I feel like at first, I was kind of siloed and then didn't want to do that. I just feel like actually within integrating myself, having more queer friends and having more of that relationship and dynamic, I've been able to let it go myself and get new perspectives or new hobbies or new ideas. Like watching RuPaul's *Drag Race*. I won't say I'm a big fanatic and watch it every time, but I wouldn't mind sitting there versus like a typical straight male would rather watch a whole sports game.

L:

How have you made sense of masculinity and bisexuality?

A:

I feel like they kind of go hand in hand just because if you do want to bounce into the female dating pool, you do have to present yourself as more masculine just because at the end of the day, I feel like that's part of the straight attributes. I guess nowadays we're starting to see some straight cis males venturing into makeup and stuff like that. And maybe masculinity is not a top priority within the current generation, but I do think they kind of do go hand in hand . . . I was kind of excited to do this interview because it's also my point to reflect and see how much growth has happened. If you would've asked me to have done this interview fresh-man year, I would've not been able to speak to this at all because I didn't know how to comprehend it.

L:
It's so fascinating to me how there are expectations of how masculinity is supposed to look but the way we each navigate gender every day can look so different.

A:
Here in the U.S. and even in Hispanic culture, like the toxic masculinity piece . . . I've even heard girls say, I'd rather date a bi man because he is able to give me more attention or he is able to com-pensate with me, or I'm able to take that, wear the jeans in the relationship and say also what goes. It also ties into even just the dynamic you have within the relationships as well.

L:
That's interesting to think about, for a bi man and his own experience of navigating masculinity in a different way could be attractive to women.

A:
I think now it's becoming more common where actu-ally people are able to understand you more or just understand those different experiences.

L:
So, you've talked a little bit about being Hispanic intersecting with identity, but are there other identities that intersect with bisexuality?

A:

That's a good question. I would say top of mind is definitely Hispanic. I don't consider myself a religious person. I didn't grow up religious, so I know that could have been another intersection. But I think the main one that comes to mind, I wake up every morning like, how can I navigate this Hispanic world. . . . Now my dad, every time he drops me off and we talk about like, me potentially buying a house, and every time he is like, "Hey, you'll get to that point where you'll have a girlfriend, you can settle down." Like, how do I tell him, "Hey, just try to use general terms." You don't know what I'm going to end up with. I appreciate you not asking questions when I came out to you. Try to get to that space. So, it's my main intersection is always gonna be being Hispanic and then being bisexual. You know, I just want to be labeled as Adrian Cruz, who is Hispanic, who is first generation, who is bisexual. . . . But I don't want that to be like the main sticker I get because that is one of the main things that a lot of people face when they're coming out. They just get slapped with that identity and everything revolves around that at the end of the day.

L:

Do you think there are ways in which you've experienced an intersection of racism and biphobia or bi-erasure?

A:

Yeah, I will say that probably came a lot during college. They were like, so what are you into? Questioning what my preferences are like because I'm Hispanic and that biphobia type of thing. They would ask, are you going to snatch my girlfriend or are you going snatch me? And it's like, I'm not going snatch any of you. I'm just here to be your friend.

But growing up in Florida, especially Miami and around a lot of Hispanics, I didn't see a lot of that racism. If anything, I saw biphobia, but I've also learned to take it as if the person doesn't know. I take it as an opportunity to educate and share my experiences so that they can become a better person and just become more educated.

L:

I was just thinking of racist stereotypes of Hispanic men, like hypersexual or super into machismo.

A:

I've had situations where people have asked, "How are you so masculine?" And it's like, well, I think that's just who I am. I feel like even within the queer community there are these hashtags called "masc for masc." Like, masculine for masculine, because I feel at the end of the day, I might prefer to be with a masculine man because if I want the femininity piece, because of my bi privilege, I can go ahead and be with a female. So that's why it kind of depends on what dynamic I want during different time periods of my life.

A Conversation with Robert Brooks Cohen

LISA:

So, tell me what masculinity means to you or how you've navigated those pressures and expectations.

ROB:

It's a tough question because masculinity is a concept I'm still trying to wrap my head around and what that means for me has shifted a lot over time. I think some of it was just the basic cultural things that were ingrained in me early. You know, being athletic and good at sports . . . made me feel masculine and being tough and strong and things like that. And some of that fit me. I liked some of that, but I think I'm starting to unpack that it also meant being in a dominant role because of patriarchy. I guess without realizing it, I saw that that was the way the world was structured. In relationships, I just often saw men as the dominant ones and women as not. I really didn't like that, even before I noticed or was aware of that.

Even when I saw myself as straight and didn't think about same-sex attractions, I ended up gravitating more towards dominant women. I liked not being in that dominant position, or at least not being forced into that dominant role. I think . . . you could subvert that and have equal partnerships, which is what I've been trying to do in my life and talking to people about.

But for a lot of people, they associate masculinity with patriarchy and with being in a dominant role. And I think it's scary to think about sexual fluidity because then you're not automatically in the dominant role. If you're outside of a heterosexual relationship, then you have to sort of figure it out and discuss who wants to be in a dominant role or maybe neither of you, and suddenly you have to rethink that. I think that's scary for people who have never done it before. That's one reason why bisexuality conflicts with many people's perceptions of masculinity.

L:

In the context of gay culture for men, there can be these expectations of masculinity and that you're not attractive if you're not fitting certain masculine norms. Do you think that's something different for bisexual men at all?

R:

I do think bi men are more open to different types of gender expression. The *masc for masc* thing, it's a turn off when I see it, because I don't exactly even know what that means. I know what I think that might mean, which is more masculine presenting features: facial hair, body hair, muscles or a certain build or something. Maybe some of those guys mean your personality or how you talk. Maybe some of that is internalized homophobia too; seems like they don't want gay guys who "act gay." I feel like in some sense that *masc for masc* is about conformity.

And personally, I've always been attracted to non-conformity. Maybe because that signals something to me about the way the person thinks, and that's more interesting to me than the way a person looks. Although I also care about the way a person looks, I think I've always been most attracted to more feminine men and more masculine women because it's non-conforming and interesting and takes a certain level of confidence to be that. And so sometimes when I see *masc for masc*, I think, oh, that's a boring person.

L:

In many ways, bisexuality is non-conformity because it's fucking with the binary, right? Do you think that allows for more flexibility around gender?

R:

Oh, absolutely. In some ways my bisexuality came from a specific place of curiosity about sex with men, but it has become more of a new conception of gender. And it's more about seeing gender as a spectrum. And for me, there's a big range—but if there's even a little range, to me, that's sexual fluidity and that's bi. In our culture there's a lot more trans and non-binary identities and it's becoming more visible and accepted. There's the backlash, but it has become more visible in the last ten years. And that's when I've also come out as bi. I don't think that's a coincidence.

I think I was seeing that and learning and starting to meet people who were moving on the gender spectrum. And I thought, well, if they're still the same person they were before as they're transitioning, why would that affect how I would feel about someone? That's happened with my wife who's transitioned. When we met, she presented as a man and she has transitioned and like a lot of other things have affected our relationship, but her gender hasn't. To me that makes a lot of sense. I sometimes don't understand when that would make such a big deal to other people. I'm like, why?

L

Since coming out, has there been pressure to be masculine in a certain way?

R:

Since coming out, it's gotten a lot better. It's really opened me up and allowed me to be more honest about what I'm interested in. I had a lot of shame for many years about my same-sex attractions and had a lot of internalized homophobia. And so, overcoming that is really helpful. And that also helped me have less shame about other things too, like my gender presentation. I wear nail polish now, and other things that made me feel vulnerable and I used to be pretty closed off about. It's almost like once I overcame the hump of coming out that I liked men, everything else felt a little easier to talk about. But I will say the one area where I still feel pressure to perform masculinity is in straight spaces.

With cis women, if I am on a date or wanting to be with a cis woman, especially a cis straight woman, I still feel like there's an expectation to be in a certain box for me. And maybe that's not true because many cis women could be open-minded also. But I guess maybe a lot of doing that in my life as a straight guy and putting myself in that box and staying there was traumatic. And I think about that and it's still hard to break out of that in those situations.

L:

It has a lot of power!

R:

Yeah. I mean, memories of people I dated in my teens and early twenties will just come back to me, and things one woman said to me will make me feel self-conscious about how I am as a 37-year-old. Which I know intellectually is dumb, but you know— you feel it. You can't help it.

L:

Not being able to be your authentic self is really harmful.

R:

That's definitely been a big thing I've noticed in my book and in everything since coming out. How closely associated masculinity is with not having feelings or how feelings are considered feminine and so many men repress not just their sexuality but all their feelings. And they have trouble figuring them out and expressing them and communicating them. That was me for a long time. When I started seeing a therapist, I couldn't even figure out how I felt half the time. My therapist and I had to work on identifying feelings and where they are in my body and how to put words on them.

I think there are so many men in that situation. For most of the men in my book, the stories are about relationships and bisexuality and coming out, but almost all of them have a turning point or they hinge on repressing stuff and then there's the moment where they started coming out and being more open and honest. All of them talk about being their authentic selves and how different it is when they can't do that versus when they can. Some of them still can't, because marriage is complicated and they want to stay together and still want to repress certain things, but it makes such a difference to feel like you can identify and express your feelings, especially to a partner. And when you can't do that, you often don't realize how hard it is, because you don't have much to compare it to. And it feels that this is the norm, but it's actually very difficult.

L:

Just because someone is born with a penis, that doesn't mean that you have this superpower to not feel. You're human. You're complex, caring human beings who want to connect.

R:

Right. Before I came out, I started going to a bi discussion group in New York City called *BiRequest*. That was a big turning point for me in terms of feeling like a normal person. There were other real live bi people—but I was surprised that there were more men in the room on a consistent basis than women, even though statistically there are more bi women than bi men. More men were showing up to this group, and there may be many reasons, but I think one of the reasons is men feel like they can't talk to anyone else. I think women more often have friends or family or other women they feel they can talk to about stuff like this and get support.

L:

It is okay if you want to talk to somebody about your feelings and to feel things besides anger!

R:

Yeah. I was locked into that way of thinking, and now it's a total 180. If I see someone who is aware of their emotions and talking about things they're struggling with, that to me signals strength and confidence and awareness and all positive things. I see it a lot more clearly now, like men, especially straight men doing the "everything's fine" routine. I see through it a little more than I used to. When somebody never talks about anything difficult in their lives, I don't automatically view that as a sign of strength anymore. I sometimes think, what are they ignoring or unwilling to talk about?

L:

Yeah. Vulnerability is actually a strength.

R:

I agree. The future is a world without any of these boxes, but in the present moment, a workaround like that is really nice. Let's redefine vulnerability as courage. That makes a lot of sense to me. And it's just a quick way to get people to rethink this stuff, because you have to start somewhere. It's hard to tell people to throw it all away. You have to start with trying vulnerability and see how it feels.

For more conversations with Rob, see Chapter 2: "The Joy of Bisexuality";
Chapter 6: "Media Representation in Television, Film, and Reality Shows";
and Chapter 8: "Relationships: Dating, Marriage, Monogamy, and Consensual
Non-monogamy."

Notes

1 Chris Kilmartin and Andrew P. Smiler, *The Masculine Self* (New York: Sloan Publishing, 2015).
2 Kilmartin and Smiler, *The Masculine Self.*
3 Jeremy Jabbour, Luke Holmes, David Sylva, Kevin Hsu, Theodore Semon, A.M. Rosenthal, Adam Safron, Erlend Slettevold, Tuesday Watts, Verall, Ritch Savin-Williams, John Sylla, Gerulf Rieger and J. Micahel Bailey, "Robust Evidence for Bisexual Orientation Among Men," *Proceedings of the National Academy of Sciences of the United States of America*, Vol. 117, No. 31 (2020), 18369–18377.
4 Jabbour et al., "Robust Evidence for Bisexual Orientation Among Men."
5 Jabbour et al., "Robust Evidence for Bisexual Orientation Among Men," 18369.
6 Jeffrey L. Helms and Ashley M. Waters, "Attitudes Toward Bisexual Men and Women," *Journal of Bisexuality*, Vol. 16, No. 4 (2016), 461.
7 Mickey Eliason, "Bi-Negativity: The Stigma Facing Bisexual Men," *Journal of Bisexuality*, Vol. 1, No. 2–3 (2000).
8 Shiri Eisner, "Bisexuality, Feminism and Men," in *Bi: Notes for a Bisexual Revolution* (Berkeley, CA: Seal Press, 2013).
9 Alon Zivony and Thalma Lobel, "The Invisible Stereotypes of Bisexual Men," *Archives of Sexual Behavior*, Vol. 43, No. 6 (2014), 1165.
10 Elissa Sarno, Micahel Newcomb, Brian Feinstein and Brian Mustanski, "Bisexual Men's Experiences with Discrimination, Internalized Binegativity, and Identity Affirmation: Differences by Partner Gender," *Archives of Sexual Behavior*, Vol. 49, No. 5 (2020), 1784.
11 Sarno et al., "Bisexual Men's Experiences with Discrimination," 1787.
12 Sarno et al., "Bisexual Men's Experiences with Discrimination."
13 Eliel Cruz, "Being 'Feminine' Can Be a Double-Edged Sword for Bisexual Men," *Slate* (August 2015), https://slate.com/human-interest/2015/08/bisexual-men-and-femininity-when-sexuality-and-gender-expression-collide.html.
14 Rio Veradonir, "Being a Bi Man Isn't About Being a 'Masculine' Fantasy," bi.org Website (July 2016), https://bi.org/en/articles/being-a-bi-man-isnt-about-being-a-masculine-fantasy.
15 Veradonir, "Being a Bi Man Isn't About Being a 'Masculine' Fantasy."
16 Eisner, "Bisexuality, Feminism and Men," 201.
17 Eisner, "Bisexuality, Feminism and Men," 202.
18 Tyler Curry, "Op-Ed: A Second Look at Bisexuality," Advocate Website (March 2014), www.advocate.com/commentary/tyler-curry/2014/03/07/op-ed-second-look-bisexuality.
19 Shaun M. Filiault, Murray J.N. Drummond and Eric Anderson, "Bisexual Men and Body Image," *Psychology and Sexuality*, Vol. 5, No. 3 (2012), 1–10.

20 Filiault et al., "Bisexual Men and Body Image," 8.
21 Eisner, "Bisexuality, Feminism and Men," 201.
22 "A Survey of LGBT Americans," Pew Research Center (June 2013), www.pewresearch.org/social-trends/2013/06/13/a-survey-of-lgbt-americans/.
23 Vaneet Mehta, "Introduction," in *Bisexual Men Exist: A Handbook for Bisexual, Pansexual and M-Spec Men* (London: Jessica Kingsley Publishers, 2023), 9.
24 Mehta, "Introduction," 9.
25 Richard Majors, "Expression and Survival," in *Cool Pose: The Dilemmas of Black Manhood in America* (New York: Simon and Schuster, 1992), 1.
26 Majors, "Expression and Survival," 2.
27 Alexander Otusajo, Bi-Standards: The Double Standards of Bisexual Men in the Black Community," McDaniel Free Press (November 2019), www.mcdanielfreepress.com/2019/11/15/bi-standards-the-double-standards-of-bisexual-men-in-the-black-community/.
28 "How Biphobia Impacts Black Bisexual Men's Health," Black Youth Project (April 2019), https://blackyouthproject.com/how-biphobia-impacts-black-bisexual-mens-health/.
29 Jacq Applebee, "The Bi's of Colour History Survey Report," (June 2015), https://bisexualresearch.wordpress.com/wp-content/uploads/2015/06/bis-of-colour-survey-report.pdf.
30 Vaneet Mehta, "Intersectionality," in *Bisexual Men Exist: A Handbook for Bisexual, Pansexual and M-Spec Men* (London: Jessica Kingsley Publishers, 2023), 168, Kindle.
31 Mehta, "Intersectionality," 170.
32 Layli Phillips, "Deconstructing 'Down Low' Discourse: The Politics of Sexuality, Gender, Race, AIDS and Anxiety," *Journal of African American Studies*, Vol. 9, No. 2 (2005), 4.
33 "How Biphobia Impacts Black Bisexual Men's Health."
34 Theo Sandfort and Brian Dodge, ". . . And Then There Was the Down Low: Introduction to Black and Latino Male Bisexualities," *The Archives of Sexual Behavior*, Vol. 37, No. 5 (2008), 676.
35 Robyn Ochs and H. Sharif Williams, *Recognize: The Voices of Bisexual Men* (Boston: Bisexual Resource Center, 2014).
36 Eisner, "Bisexuality, Feminism and Men," 230–234.

6

MEDIA REPRESENTATION IN TELEVISION, FILM, AND REALITY SHOWS

Many bisexual activist and researchers agree that bisexual representation in the media continues to be "rendered invisible by the cultural hegemony of monosexuality."[1] In general, queer characters in scripted shows on mainstream television networks, cable, and streaming sites have decreased from 596 in the 2022–2023 season to 468 for the 2023–2024 season.[2] Out of the 468 characters, only 113 (24%) were bisexual[3] (despite the fact that bisexual people make up 52% of the LBGT population).[4] This is a decrease from the previous season by 36 characters and one percentage point.[5] Monosexuality is still most prominent on shows with heterosexual relationships primarily and gay and lesbian relationships second.[6] In addition, the lack of accurate bisexual representation perpetuates stereotypes through characters that are mostly cis, conventionally attractive, young, and able-bodied. According to the LGBTQ *Where We Are on TV* report for 2023–2024, "A recurring problem that is still seen today is bi+ erasure, where a character does not label themselves as bi, pan, queer, or any word to self-describe."[7] This does not reflect the real world, where bisexual people far outnumber the representation seen on television.[8]

When bisexual characters are created, they are often portrayed as torn between two lovers, on a journey from straight to gay, or as a cheater struggling with monogamy due to immense, uncontrollable attractions.[9] Madison argues that one of the most common depictions is the "triad" where "three people convey the (mis)representation of bisexuality as a sexuality in the 'middle' of heterosexuality and homosexuality."[10] Corey describes this as the bisexual "love triangle," which perpetuates "the stereotype that bisexuals cannot be trusted; that they will never be satisfied with a single sexual partner, or a single gender. The partner of the bisexual is constantly

DOI: 10.4324/9781003242659-7

at risk of being replaced with a partner of a different sex."[11] For example, in 2023, during Season 6 of the ABC show *Station 19*, female firefighter Andy is pursued by Eli, the male campaign manager for fellow firefighter Travis, a gay man running for mayor. Andy and Eli flirt a lot, go on a date, and kiss; however, after an exciting moment during the campaign, Travis and Eli have sex. The love triangle story continues, as Travis and Andy realize what has happened and discuss who can be involved with Eli.[12] As Madison contends, this kind of depiction of bisexuality

> *R*eifies the notion that bisexuals are torn between two polar desires and experience equal and concurrent attraction to more than one partner simultaneously. Furthermore, the triad represented in this way suggests that the essential bisexual is having simultaneous liaisons with heterosexual and homosexual partners.[13]

Returning to Robyn Och's definition of bisexuality, it specifically states "attraction to people of more than one gender" that is "not necessarily *simultaneously*, in the same way or to the same degree,"[14] but television shows often fail to address the realities of bisexuality by perpetuating the triad trope.

Additionally, a regular trope is what Vaneet Mehta defines as "ambiguously bi." Many supposed bisexual characters are shown as *not* having attractions simultaneously so that there is debate about whether the characters "now identify as gay like countless other characters before them."[15] Although some bisexuality may be presented accurately, most character's identities are shown as ambiguous so that there is room for debate, which perpetuates bi-erasure. Mehta gives the example of Eleanor on the show *The Good Place*, when he declares:

> *C*an we really say that she provides m-spec [multigender attracted spectrum] representation? She shows attraction to Tahani, and in one of the reboots is partnered up with her, but we never see their relationship. We don't see her express attraction for any other women and we don't see any former relationships that aren't with a man. Of course, none of this means that she can't be m-spec; this is all entirely valid. But that, coupled with the fact that she doesn't state her sexuality outright, means people may read her attraction to Tahani in different ways.[16]

This kind of storyline leaves the sexuality up to the interpretation of the viewers, thus reinforcing ambiguity, the stereotype that bisexuality is about confusion or, as previously mentioned, being stuck deciding between heterosexuality and homosexuality.

It is particularly problematic how the word *bisexuality* is rarely used or discussed in television shows, even though there are some characters involved with one gender, then another.[17] On *The Rookie Feds*, Niecy Nash-Betts' character Simone is involved with DJ—played by Nash's real-life wife

Jessica Betts—but when that relationship ends, Simone finds herself single again. In 2023 in Season 1, Episode 16, Simone is discussing relationships with a new character, LAPD Detective Naomi Voss. Simone laments, "I don't have an excuse as to why I am single. I date men and women, so you would think that my odds would be much better."[18] A queer woman of color on a television show is significant and essential, and in an ideal world, it would be great not to label someone's sexual orientation if they chose not to. In real life, Niecy Nash-Betts does not use a label for her sexual orientation;[19] however, given the amount of misrepresentation, misinformation, stereotyping, and bi-erasure, it is unfortunate how rarely *bisexual* is used. As Corey conveys,

> *Naming a sexual identity gives the identity credibility. . . . By failing to name 'bisexuality,' the media reinforces the heterosexual/homosexual binary. It fortifies the concept that sexual identity is solely defined by current sexual activity and that individuals shift between heterosexual or homosexual, rather than maintaining their bisexual identity regardless of the composition of their romantic or sexual relationships. . . . Failing to have bisexual characters self-identify as bisexual contributes to bisexual invisibility. Characters who exhibit sexual or romantic attraction to more than one gender but do not self-identify as bisexual cement the cultural belief that bisexuality is not a real identity.[20]*

There are other problematic tropes that Mehta names "just an experiment," "anything that moves," and "depraved."[21] "Just an experiment" is when a character appears to be bisexual but then goes back to the monosexual identities of straight or gay. Experimenting is of course a legitimate practice when exploring sexual fluidity, but when bisexual characters are continuously portrayed this way, it can be harmful.[22] "Anything that moves" is pretty self-explanatory but reinforces the stereotype that bisexual people are highly promiscuous, hypersexual, and without boundaries. This ties in closely to "depraved" where the bisexual characters are "cold-blooded, manipulative and murderous and are willing to do anything to achieve their goals, which includes using sex."[23]

Both cis-bi men and women characters are pigeonholed, but there are some gendered differences. For cis-bi women, a recurrent theme is what Eisner defines as the "femme fatale," who is "highly seductive and very dangerous" and "often the source of trouble or conflict in the plot of the film."[24] Such films as *Basic Instinct*, *Bound*, and *Femme Fatale* all have cis women characters who are "behaviorally" bisexual but also duplicitous, and it is unclear where their loyalties lie. According to Eisner,

> *Their plots invariably situate them where they must make a choice between a man and a woman in a way that creates the conflicts,*

mysteries and riddles on which these plots are based. The bi characters' choice is both detrimental to the plot and is the source of the threat the she poses.[25]

For example, the antagonist Catherine in the film *Basic Instinct* has a girlfriend but also seduces male Detective Nick Curran and uses her sexuality to obtain what she wants. One review proclaims the movie's message was that "sex is war. It can be mysterious, tantalizing, even temporarily rewarding. But a woman with power can't be trusted. If she is strong, she could be fierce enough to castrate you."[26] Catherine fits all of the biphobic stereotypes of being untrustworthy, a villain, and a target of Nick's male gaze, as he falls under her "spell."[27]

One of the first cis-bi women television characters is Callie Torres—played by bisexual actor Sara Ramirez—who began questioning her sexuality on ABC's *Grey's Anatomy* in 2008. *Grey's Anatomy* is credited as one of the few shows that regularly includes queer characters, but it is not until Season 11 that Callie actually *says* she is bisexual after being involved with different genders for multiple seasons. When she does speak about it, she exclaims, "So I'm bisexual. So what? It's a thing and it's real. I mean, it's called LGBTQ for a reason. There's a B in there and it doesn't mean 'badass.' Okay, it kind of does, but it also means bi."[28] She had been involved with George, Erica Hahn, slept with Mark Sloane, married Arizona, and had a child with Mark,[29] but it took years for Callie to actually say *bisexual*.

Another frequent portrayal of cis-bi women is characters who are straight but then switch to being with a woman as the show progresses. Again, there is typically no discussion about bisexuality or the use of the word *bisexual*. Some examples include Annalise Keating on *How to Get Away with Murder*, Valencia on *My Crazy Ex-Girlfriend*, Petra Solano on *Jane the Virgin*, Nova Bordelon on *Queen Sugar*, Toni Topaz on *Riverdale*, and, most recently, the beloved Keely Jones on *Ted Lasso*. An additional example from 2023 is the character Katherine Kim on *A Million Little Things*—previously married to the male character Eddie Saville—who marries her lesbian partner, Greta Strobe, towards the end of the series, with no mention about bisexuality. Also in 2023, *Grey's Anatomy* closed their nineteenth season with Amelia Shepherd, formerly involved with the male characters Owen Hunt and Atticus "Linc" Lincoln, realizing her true feelings for her non-binary partner Kai Bartley but being heartbroken when Kai takes a job overseas. Once more, *Grey's Anatomy* challenges the norms by showing variations in how bisexuality can exist, but they never use the term *bisexual* to describe Amelia's identity.

Meyer argues that an additional recurrent practice is to cast women of color as bisexual in order to position other characters as "more accepting, tolerant and enlightened."[30] Various shows have cis-bi women of color characters "originally introduced as heterosexual, whose identity journey is aided by (or mostly ignored by) their surrounding cast" and are used to "stabilize heterosexuality and open discourse for White characters."[31] In addition, the cis-bi women of color characters are never the leads but rather the "foils to White, heterosexual women protagonists."[32] Interestingly enough, just from the eight shows listed above, six of the bisexual characters are women of color. Two shows, however, have Black main characters—Annalise Keating on *How to Get Away with Murder* and Nova Bordelon on *Queen Sugar* — who do start off in straight relationships and never actually use the word *bisexual*, but their bisexuality is not used in contrast to white characters.

Meyer claims that bisexual characters are written differently than gay or lesbian characters, whose storylines usually included struggles with their identities or coming out, then being accepted or rejected. Bisexual identities are "introduced casually, usually as a secondary plot device" which some may see as positive representation of sexual fluidity, but Meyer argues that is not the intent.[33] The casual approach to the topic and lack of actual discussion of bisexuality rather stabilizes "hegemonic discourses" of heterosexual and homosexual as "valid, nondebatable identities."[34] Meyer asserts that bisexuality today is the "contested terrain" that gay and lesbian representation was in the 1990s and audiences "understand the gay, lesbian or heterosexual person by their stable, serially monogamous desire and behavior in relation to the unstable, confused bisexual."[35] Monosexism is reinforced through this trope as the bisexual character's multi-gender attractions are still seen as invalid and problematic.

For cis-bi male characters there are other issues. Of the 113 bisexual characters counted in the *Where We Are on TV Report 2023–2024*, 69 were women, 38 were men, and six were non-binary.[36] Although this is an eight-point increase in the percentage of bi+ men since the previous year, "many biphobic tropes persist around bi+ men, including that they are 'secretly gay' and being untruthful about their sexuality, or only using sexuality for personal gain."[37] As discussed in Chapter 5, bisexuality for cis men has long been disputed and television and film are not free from this debate. Take the infamous Carrie Bradshaw quote on *Sex in The City* when she stated about dating a bisexual man, "I'm not even sure bisexuality exists. I think it's just a layover on the way to Gaytown."[38] Or in 2016, when Molly Carter on HBO's *Insecure* finds out that Jered, with whom she is involved, had sex with another man after she just told him about making out with other women. Molly is uncomfortable with this disclosure, and while discussing it with her friends, one friend pronounces Jered gay and Molly ends the relationship with him. Her compulsory monosexuality proves to be an obstacle, despite the connection she has with Jered.[39] Maria San Filippo, author of *The B Word: Bisexuality in Contemporary Film and Television*, further adds, "Bi+ male representation has always been the biggest challenge," as it "threatens heteropatriarchy and phallic authority, and so must be hidden or, if acknowledged, desexualized and disparaged through mockery."[40]

A typical portrayal of cis-bi men is also the "depraved" trope mentioned earlier. Frank Underwood in *The House of Cards* is one such example. Although the creator of the show, Beau Willimon, specifically stated that he wanted the audience to experience Frank without labels, Frank and his wife Claire Underwood have a threesome with their Secret Service agent Edward Meechum; he also reconnects with a lover from his military academy days and becomes involved with the biographer Thomas Yates. And Frank is pure, murderous evil.[41] Another show, HBO's *Euphoria*, credited with four bisexual characters, has two cis-bi men Nate Jacobs and his father Cal Jacobs. Filled with anger issues and a knack for mistreating people, Nate realizes his attraction to Jules, a transgender girl, and blackmails her to hide his sexuality. His dad, Cal, cheats on his wife and has attractions to men and women, including Jules, and while struggling with his identity he "creates a toxic web of lies."[42] Father and son both represent a form of toxic masculinity that feeds into many negative stereotypes about male bisexuality. As writer and bisexual activist Damian Emba states, these characters "lie, cheat, manipulate, and are incapable of honesty with themselves or others."[43]

For cis-bi men of color there is even less representation. Unlike the women of color often being cast as bisexual characters, (as problematic as those storylines often are), cis-bi men of color are hard to find on television or film. Little research has been done on this issue, but it may closely relate to the Chapter 5 analysis on the intersection of biphobia, bi-erasure, monosexism, and racism that render cis-bi men of color nonexistent. There have been some creations that are worth noting, such as the film *Moonlight*. This film is often heralded as a powerful film about being Black and gay, but Kevin, the character that Chiron gets involved with, is bisexual, a fact that is rarely discussed.[44] One show on Amazon Prime, *Harlem*, is credited as accurately showing a Black man as bisexual. Angie Wilson, one of the main characters, befriends Eric while they are castmates for an off-Broadway play. Angie discovers that Eric is bisexual, and when he admits his attraction to her, they get involved. Even with this positive portrayal, he is only on the show for eight episodes, which reinforces the fact that there is rarely a "robust, fully developed, humanity-validating, modern-day depiction of Black bisexual men."[45]

There are even fewer gender-diverse bisexual characters. Of the 468 LGBTQ characters addressed earlier, 24 are transgender with six bisexual characters who identify as non-binary and one as a trans woman.[46] This is not surprising given the onslaught of anti-transgender legislation and rhetoric in American culture right now and how rarely gender-diverse characters are created in general. One example that does exist is Jules on HBO's *Euphoria*, who is a bisexual trans girl, but her interactions with cisgender men are often fraught with mistreatment and violence. Jules is a damaged character who finds gender affirmation by being treated poorly by men, because this is something she witnesses as a norm for cis-women. Another example is Che

Diaz, (played once again by Sara Ramirez) on the *Sex in the City* reboot, *And Just Like That*. Che is "one of the most polarizing characters" on television, but they are a non-binary character who openly exclaims about coming out as bisexual, "I stood up in the living room and I was like, 'Family, I love you, and just want you to know that I am queer and non-binary and bisexual', . . . And they were like: 'That's nice, can you move? You're blocking the game.'"[47]

Reality shows are often heralded as a groundbreaking space for the validation of gay and lesbian identities,[48] but the portrayal of bisexuality tends to perpetuate stereotypes. The first reality show to focus on bisexuality was *A Shot at Love* with Tila Tequila in 2007. Tila Tequila self-identified as bisexual, and the show had 16 straight men and 16 lesbian women who were unaware of Tila's bisexuality or that they had to compete against different genders to win. Each episode consisted of a "battle of the sexes" where a contestant would then earn the "key to her heart."[49] According to Rebecca Beirne, this emphasized "the unfortunately common perception that bisexuals need to 'pick a team,' and that audiences should feel personally invested in what 'team' that might be."[50] Reality shows also frequently focus on sexually charged conflict in order to increase ratings, which associates bisexuality with hypersexuality.[51] Although this show was very popular and another season followed, Tila Tequilla ended up becoming an alt right supporter and admitted in 2018 that her bisexuality was a façade.[52]

Many reality shows use the formula of adding bisexual people to create "an extra set of dimensions and complications."[53] An example of a more recent show is Season 8 of the MTV show *Are You the One?* This show placed a group of people together in a house to find their perfect match among their housemates. Each episode would include a "matchup ceremony" where the contestants pick who they believe is their perfect match and, if guessed correctly, they could eventually win $1 million to share. The Season 8 cast had 16 male and female contestants who all identified as sexually fluid and had the potential to be attracted to any of the other contestants. When bisexual writer Hannah Harris Green first started watching Season 8, she was excited to see so many bisexual, pansexual, and m-spec people represented. She writes, "And then, rarest of rarities, these people are actually happy about their sexual orientations! Within the first few minutes of the show, contestant Kari declares, 'I'm bisexual and I fucking love it.' Another contestant Justin echoes her: 'I am very proud of being bisexual, I think of it as a superpower.'"[54] Sadly, the show did not continue in this positive fashion and reverted to the usual "messy trysts" and reinforced stereotypes of bisexual people as greedy and untrustworthy.[55]

There are some reality shows designed to explore sexuality, like Demi Burnett on *Bachelor in Paradise*. In the 2019 Season 6 premiere, Demi revealed to another castmate about dating a woman but didn't know for sure how to define her identity, which she processed throughout the show. In 2021, an offshoot of the American franchise *The Bachelor* and *Bachelorette*—called

The Bachelorette Australia—cast an indigenous bisexual Australian named Brooke Blurton. This was a first for the franchise, both casting male and female contestants and having an indigenous main contestant. This format looked different than Tila Tequila's show, particularly since Brooke stated at the start that she was interested in connections with people rather than their gender.[56] This was supposed to create less of the dynamic of "both sexes" and "teams" but sadly, in the first episode the men and women were grouped in separate gazebos, and Blurton was constantly expected to make comparisons between the "boys" and "girls."[57] As Beirne contends, while some shows are starting to create better representation of bisexuality, "the broad-brush strokes of reality dating series are probably still a way off being able to imagine a world where gender is not an 'issue' of dating."[58]

The harmful impact of these misrepresentations, stereotypes, and lack of positive, accurate portrayals of bisexuality is multilayered. There is ample evidence that bi-erasure, biphobia, and monosexism "are omnipresent in media, reinforcing the idea that attraction to more than one gender is inherently unnatural, immoral, disingenuous, and/or invalid."[59] This can be a contributing factor to mental health struggles (which is examined further in Chapter 10: "Mental Health Issues and the Impact of Violence"), and more research is needed on how the media influences people's understanding about bisexuality, in addition to how it affects people who are bisexual.[60] In addition, as Corey argues, the key to this "rests in portraying bisexual characters in a more dynamic, nuanced, and less stereotypical light."[61] Furthermore, bisexuality should not presented just through the act of sex. As Shiri Eisner recently posted on Twitter, "Substantial bi representation doesn't require characters to display their sexuality visually on screen. In fact, one of the most problematic misconceptions of bi representation is that it can't be represented in any way other than sex."[62]

It is not all doom and gloom, as more positive examples of bisexuality keep emerging. One media assessment tool that bisexual activist and writer Lois Shearing created is what she calls the Ramirez Test, named for the actor Sara Ramirez who has played two bisexual characters discussed in this chapter. Modeled after the famed Bechdel Test that was designed as a metric for how well women are portrayed in television and film, the Ramirez Test asks these three questions:

1. Is the character recognizable as bisexual within the media itself?
2. Is the character's bisexuality presented as a joke or flaw?
3. Does the character ever say that they're bi/pansexual?[63]

Very few characters complete all three, but some do. Darryl Whitefeather, on the musical comedy *Crazy Ex-Girlfriend*, not only uses the word *bisexual* to describe himself, he sings a whole song dedicated to his bisexuality called "Gettin' Bi."[64] Rosa Diaz on *Brooklyn 99*, played by bisexual actor Stephanie

Beatriz, is also credited as positive representation as she comes out as bisexual on the show.[65] Another example is the British show *Heartstopper*, where the teen character Nick Nelson, having experienced attraction to more than one gender, comes out to his mom as bisexual in an incredibly heartwarming scene of acceptance and love.[66] *Good Trouble*'s Gael openly identifies as bisexual from the series beginning and his character is hailed as the "kind of representation that's all too rare on television."[67] Writer Alison Stine credits the character Ava on *Hacks* who not only says she is bisexual, but "It's part of her. It's not the whole character. It just *is*."[68] There is also the web series *Insomnia*, written by South Asian-American and bisexual creator Vishaal Reddy. Reddy stars as Nikhil, a bisexual character who becomes an escort during his sleepless nights in order to support his aunt who has been diagnosed with multiple sclerosis.[69] In addition, there is some representation of pansexuality, such as Jazz Jennings's life story as a transgender girl on *I Am Jazz* or Ola stating she is pansexual on *Sex Education*. One of the most famous pansexual characters is David Rose on *Schitt's Creek*, whose quote has been made into multiple memes: "Um, I do drink red wine," says David. "But I also drink white wine. And I've been known to sample the occasional rosé. And a couple summers back, I tried a Merlot that used to be a Chardonnay, which got a bit complicated . . . I like the wine and not the label. Does that make sense?"[70]

It is essential that more positive bisexual representation exist in the media in order to decrease the harm caused by the misrepresentation, misinformation, and perpetuation of stereotypes. It is hopeful that some improvements have been made, but there is still so much more to do. What follows are two very different pieces adding to this discourse: one is a conversation with Robert Brooks Cohen—a host on the Podcast *Two Bi Guys* and author of *Bisexual Married Men: Stories of Relationships, Acceptance, and Authenticity*—who is extremely familiar with the media industry as a former television writer. This discussion explores further issues in the media and what is needed for the future. The second is a personal narrative written by T'Asia Parker that addresses her own experience with consuming media and what role it played in making sense of her own bisexuality.

A Conversation with Robert Brooks Cohen

```
                    LISA:
It is cool to see bisexual characters in various
show[s], however, people rarely talk about actually
being bisexual.


                     ROB:
I do think it's getting a little better recently.
I have seen more bi characters here and there, but
a lot of it is on shows that are a flash in the pan
```

because there's so much streaming now. All these little niche shows that have had pretty good bi representation. There's some younger queer shows that have younger queer characters, which is great. But nobody is watching them.

I think it's positive that Gen Z is even more queer and bisexual than millennials, and I hope that trend continues. But we're not seeing the most common bi experience, which is bi people, married to someone of a different gender. That's the majority of bi people. I also haven't seen a polyamorous marriage that is successfully navigating polyamory. Too often when bisexuality is introduced, it's introduced as a conflict or an obstacle. And in some ways, that was my life. It was a difficult thing to come out. But there's so much more than the struggle or just coming out.

I worked on *Law & Order SVU* on NBC. On network shows, they don't want to turn anyone off. They don't even really want to make viewers uncomfortable. I had pitched bisexual storylines but those pitches didn't go. I just think it's because there's a hesitancy at these big companies to not do that. There's probably not much bisexual representation in those writers' rooms and at those networks or a lot of closeted bi people who haven't worked through their own shame and confusion about this, so they don't want to represent it because they're not comfortable with it yet themselves.

If 88% of bi men are not out, some of those people must be TV writers and network executives. But if they're not out, it's hard to write about bisexuality if you are not able to say, this is my authentic experience.

L:

There are a lot more bi women represented in shows than bi men. I can't think of many, but there is *Heartstopper* . . .

R:

Heartstopper was great because it was about the experience that a lot of bi men have had, which was first identifying as straight and then coming out as bi. When that character used the word bi and came out to his mom, she took it really well. One of the best scenes in a long time, it makes me cry just to think about it. There are a few others. *Schitt's Creek* had Dan Levy play a pansexual character. They used the word pansexual I think at some point, although not the word bisexual. And then the most recent one that's really good that I've seen is *Interview with a Vampire*. It's great bi representation in my opinion, and it feels really authentic and an interesting metaphor about these vampires and how it relates to sexuality. But nobody's watching it.

L:

How can we do it better?

R:

It's a tough question. What I want to see is more authentic representation. I just think there's a lot of married bi people who are either only out to their partner or not out to a lot of people. I think a lot of people would connect with a show like that. But then I also think it would be great to represent the spectrum of bisexuality and gender diversity and to expose everyone to the furthest corners and the queerest people out there. But I don't know if everyone will want to watch that. Especially with all the anti-trans and anti-queer rhetoric, half the country is going to balk at stuff like that at the moment, and therefore the networks are going to be hesitant to have shows that are about those things.

I would like to see more bi characters who embrace this stuff as opposed to it creating conflict out of the stigma of bisexuality. For example, there was a show called *I May Destroy You* that had pretty good bi representation. There were bi women. There was a gay man character who was sort of exploring his bisexuality, so maybe a bi man character, but he was gay identified. The conflict was when women didn't want to date him because he had been with men. On the one hand, I think that's an accurate portrayal of the bi male experience—cis women may be turned off by the fact that you're bi or you have dated men.

But I haven't seen any show where a guy comes out as bi and a woman says, oh, wow, that's hot, let's see that. Or let's see two guys make out and the women hoot and holler at them. Let's twist some of this and subvert it and show people that male bisexuality is hot too. I almost want to fetishize men because I know women have been fetishized and that's not great, but we could use a little bit of fetishization to even the playing field.

L:
Tell me about the role porn plays.

R:
In the interviews in my book and also my personal experience, so many bi men realize they were bi or first explored their fluidity with porn because it's a very low stakes way to see how you feel and how your body responds. Nobody has to know, you can go down any rabbit hole you want and it's completely safe. You don't have to get on prep, to tell your doctor, get tested, or talk to anyone about it. Most straight guys who want to explore a little, that's the most safe way to do it at first. And when you look at PornHub each year they release the categories that were the top categories and top performers the last few years. One of the top categories for gay porn is straight guys. And I understand it because that's what I watched. Before I came out, I watched a lot of gay porn that featured straight men and that was what I was attracted to because maybe it's a little twisted, but in my mind at the time I wanted to maintain my straight identity, but I also was interested in gay sex. And so those videos, in addition to being hot to me, also allowed me to maintain the straight identity because the guys in the videos were straight.

I was terrified of being gay and thinking I was gay. I knew I liked women and I didn't want to have to lose that in my life. And I didn't want to identify as gay and I didn't see bi as an option. So, to me the straight porn where they had sex with each other was the best.

Actually, I remember in the SVU writer's room, my second year, we were doing an episode about a married guy with his wife who went out at night to cruise for gay sex. And all the writers in the room talked about him as a gay character. And I didn't know any better than to just go along with that at the time. And I remember someone saying *once you suck a dick, you're gay*. I remember where I was sitting and where he was standing and the weather, it was stuck in my memory—that sentence. And for years I internalized that—if you step over the line once, you're gay. And I think so many people think that way.

L:

They do! Can you tell me about starting the *Two Bi Guys* podcast and what moved you to do that?

R:

Alex and I started the podcast in 2019. We had met in the bi discussion group *BiRequest*, and I had identified as straight until I was 31, 32. At the time, Alex had always identified as gay and was sort of coming at it from the other side. And yet, every time either of us spoke in the room, the other one would be nodding along. We had all the same feelings and views, even though we had almost opposite upbringings and experiences with sex up to that point.

We just kind of became friends and talked about this stuff a lot. We got selected through this discussion group to be on a show called *Slutever*, hosted by Karley Sciortino on Vice. It lasted two seasons. It's gone now. The episodes are online and they did an episode about bisexual men and it was great.

We recorded 90 minutes of footage with them. They used five minutes. And so, when it aired, we were like, this is great. We feel really good about putting this out there. And this was the first time I had been publicly bisexual. I had come out to my friends at that point, but I had never posted anything on Facebook or written a blog post. I posted this video and that was like my social media coming out and it was really positive. Everyone had nice things to say. But it also was only five minutes and we have a lot more to say. That was when we decided to keep going and do something ourselves. At the time, there wasn't anything I could find that was really worthwhile about male bisexuality. There were podcasts out there, but all hosted by women and then there were one or two podcasts about the male bi experience, but they weren't good. So, we started it in 2019. Half of it was us talking to each other and telling our stories, and half of it was interviewing other bi people. We kind of did it to fill that gap. I wanted to listen to other guys talk about this, like guys specifically. It didn't exist, so we just created it. Then the pandemic happened before the second season, and Alex sort of continued to help a little bit, but then he got a job at The Trevor Project, which is a great job. He's doing great work there, but he has sort of become pretty busy and focused on that. So, I have continued the podcast without him, and pretty much every episode is an interview with a bi person or someone who's done research on the bisexual experience.

For more conversations with Rob, see Chapter 2: "The Joys of Bisexuality"; Chapter 5: "Cisgender Men and Masculinities"; and Chapter 8: "Relationships: Dating, Marriage, Monogamy and Consensual Non-monogamy."

Virginity as a Bisexual by Ti'Asia Parker

I am 21 years old. In many ways, I have regressed and I have evolved; there have been instances where I have changed very little and instances where I have changed very much. Yet, immutably, the fact still remains that I have *always* loved *love*. From the expressions of affection, to the promises of deep, soul-stirring intimacy, I've long adored what love looks like, what love sounds like, and I've always enjoyed the fluttery feeling that I got whenever I thought about love.

Eagerly, I've anticipated what love could mean for *me*.

Romance movies, TV shows, songs, and books were a couple of the things that increased my anticipation. On a Friday night in the early 2000s, my mother, sister, and I bonded around the TV, eating baked chicken and rice while watching BET romance movies. *ATL,* a film directed by Chris Robinson, is most prominent in my memory, as I remember yearning for the love that existed between T.I. and Lauryn London's characters, feeling an indescribable pull to both of them and wondering what it would be like if I had taken the other one's place. At that time, the "pull" that I was feeling was indecipherable, but I would come to understand why exactly I wanted to kiss "New-New" just as much as I wanted to kiss "Rashad" in later years.

Still, my conception of love was reductive. In my elementary school days, I thought love would be like those movies. I would fall in love with a boy—he would be cute and my parents would approve and we would live happily ever after. I had no idea that love could be different—that I may *want* it to be different. I was only aware of what I heard and saw the most: *two folks in love = man and woman.* So, despite what my natural inclinations were leading me toward, I had made and *accepted* the implicit association that, in order for love to be real and legit, it had to operate under the prior condition.

So, year after year, I would survey my classrooms in the hopes that I would be so lucky as to meet my future husband. But third, fourth, and fifth grade went on without any of the boys I liked expressing interest in me, and so the desire for love remained.

I was 12 years old when I started thinking about sex *as* love. By that point, I was already reading Wattpad e-books and had found myself waist-deep in angsty articulations of teen love. But it quickly became apparent to me that (aside from the heteronormativity) all of these teen love stories shared one thing in common: every single one incorporated sex. Whether it was the main couple having sex or the characters around them, for some reason sex made a consistent appearance in these e-books. Sometimes, the sex was awkward—sometimes the characters fumbled. But more often than not, the male characters were written as 16- and 17-year-old sexual savants with eons of sexual experience who knew just what to do to give their virgin partners the time of their lives. Not to mention, Wattpad sex was *always* used as a vehicle to express love, feel loved, or repair love.

Two partners fighting? Expect the next chapter to feature a confusing scene of them sweeping relationship problems under the rug by fucking each other on the floor.

Or, better yet, the ever-present trope of the insecure but attractive teenage girl who uses her wits, her lips, and the space between her hips to fill the void of not having been loved. And I don't make these comparisons to shame those who have been in situations like these. The main point that I wish to drive home is that sex and love were always related to each other in the books that I read; they were always connected.

So, as a virgin who had never been in a relationship before, it was easy to equate sex to love and love to sex. And since my views on love were heteronormative, this new ideological association made it even easier to define sex as heteronormative, too.

Despite this, 12 years old was around the age when I officially recognized myself as bisexual. After years of a perplexing stomach-turning arousal at the sight of various women, I finally came to understand that my attraction to boys applied to girls too. This acknowledgment I largely credit to the majority-queer friend group that I had in my earlier years of middle school.

Aside from my sister, however, they were the only people who knew. I didn't have a come-out discussion with the rest of my family; neither did I attempt to clue them in to the true nature of my sexuality. But make no mistake; this decision wasn't made out of fear or hesitancy. My bisexuality just wasn't something I saw as relevant. At the end of the day, I liked boys more and I *knew* that I would ultimately end up with a boy. And even when I entered high school and discussions of sex became more frequent, I firmly maintained this stance. Indeed, I can remember having a conversation with one of my best friends where we both acknowledged that we could "fuck around" with girls, but we couldn't *seriously* date them; eventually, we would end up with men. And by that same logic, we also decided that our first time *had* to be with a man.

Honestly, this was a strange conclusion as we both desired men *and* women. However, whenever we talked about sex, we never knew what to consider girl-on-girl intercourse. To us, it didn't feel like sex because penetration was rarely the focal point and, if it occurred, wasn't with a "real" penis. In that sense, we invalidated girl-on-girl intercourse because we still subscribed to the notion of heterosexual intercourse as the only form of "real" sex. This was the only way we thought we could imagine losing our virginities.

Though, this isn't to say that I didn't experience dissonance when I considered non-heterosexual sex. I want to make it clear that my definition of sex did *not* feel secure, and I always wondered if my first partner was a girl and we interacted sexually, whether that indicated a loss of my virginity. Yet, I didn't have the confidence or the open mindedness to challenge my perspective more, so it remained.

Thinking back, I can understand why this perspective made sense to me. As I stated earlier, I noticed that all relationships that were deemed legitimate by most others were between men and women, whereas relationships between girls or guys were situated almost exclusively as sexual. Exclusively sexual relationships weren't "real"—they were invalid. Movies such as *The Color Purple* illustrate this concept perfectly, as Celie and Shug's relationship amounts to nothing more than sexual tension, despite the obvious partnership that is highlighted in the book. All things considered, it was difficult for me to view same-sex relationships as actual relationships.

Still, it wasn't until my fourth year of college when I truly began to interrogate my ideals a bit more. During that time, I was taking a course titled Human Sexualities, which questioned the current existing concepts surrounding virginity. Through Human Sexualities, I was introduced to various resources such as *The Purity Myth*—a film that discusses the fallacy of virginity equating to purity and Valenti's "The Cult of Virginity"—a text that illustrates why women subscribe to the idea of virginities. These resources along with the relationships I was cultivating encouraged me to be more intentional when thinking about the concept of virginity. Specifically, whether virginity was a concept worthy of my subscription.

Which begs the following questions: Why was it necessary for my first time to involve a penis? Why couldn't I date women seriously? Was sex really love? What is "real" sex?

Nowadays, I have come to realize that my former belief in the concept of "necessary penises" has a lot to do with how I and other folks were socialized. As I have demonstrated, romance media was a consistent figure in my childhood. I was surrounded by interpretations of love, yet those interpretations still clung to patriarchal norms and messaging. Considering this environment and my impressionable age, it's no wonder I adopted the belief that penises/men had to be present in order for sex to occur. It's what all relationships looked like! And while my heteronormative ideas about sex and love developed in these early years, I think it's important to note that they were sustained until I was 21. This illustrates just how influential the messaging we receive during socialization can be.

I think this also explains why I felt that I couldn't date women seriously. Without examples of genuine partnerships between women, I struggled to articulate and accept what that may look like for myself. Of course, I no longer endorse this sentiment. As time has gone on, my bisexuality has become a more salient identity that I hold and I'm now able to recognize the faulty schemas I created pertaining to same-sex relationships. Not to mention, society has become increasingly more accepting of the LGBTQ+ community, which has allowed for further representations of same-sex partnerships to appear in the public sphere.

But what does love currently mean to me? What does virginity mean to me? For one, I now understand that sex and love aren't the same. I credit "All About Love" by bell hooks for these realizations, as she has helped me better understand what love is and what love isn't. Love is not care; neither is it affection or respect. Rather, I am learning that love is the sum total of all these things and *then some*. Though, I'm still reading the book, so I expect and have accepted that my definition of love will evolve.

Additionally, I understand that my ideas around sex and virginity are also evolving. I have had sexual interactions (oral, for instance), but I have not had vaginally penetrative sex yet. By those standards, I still consider myself a virgin. Yet, I'm no longer sold on this penis-centric definition of virginity, and I wonder if my self-proclaimed status as a virgin is one I want to continue to identify with.

Life experiences, Human Sexualities, Valenti, and "The Purity Myth" are just some of the things that have coaxed me into being more open with what I consider sex. For instance, "The Purity Myth" illustrated how damaging the concept of virginity can be to mine and other women's personal development. Surely I can recognize how the purity myth has colored my perception of virginity, as a part of me has secretly feared the loss of my innocence after I have sex. And Valenti helped me realize how restrictive and invalidating I was acting towards fellow LGBTQ+ folks. Clearly, I demonstrate that one is not above falling victim to harmful patriarchal beliefs no matter how non-straight they might be. I think that's why it's so important that folks remain open to different perspectives and critical of their own. In the end, this really does help us become better people.

So no, I don't have a concrete definition of love or sex or virginity to give. When reduced, I'm a section in a book, and aren't books supposed to offer concrete answers? Perhaps, but my humanity makes me just as fallible as the next person–still learning and still growing. In fact, all of these realizations are concepts I'm *still* sitting with, and I'm not sure whether or not I should consider myself a virgin anymore. Ideally, my other experiences offer just as much importance to me as the idea of losing my virginity, and I now know there is nothing *truly* stopping me from recognizing those experiences as sex, too.

Notes

1 Nora Madison, "The Bisexual Seen: Countering Media Representation," *M/C Journal*, Vol. 20, No. 4 (2017), https://journal.media-culture.org.au/index.php/mcjournal/article/view/1271.
2 "Where We Are on TV 2023–2024: Representation of Bisexual+ Characters," GLAAD Webpage, https://glaad.org/whereweareontv23/representation-of-bisexual-characters/.
3 "Where We Are on TV 2023–2024."
4 Movement Advancement Project, "Invisible Majority: The Disparities Facing Bisexual People and How to Remedy Them," (September 2016), 1, www.lgbtmap.org/file/invisible-majority.pdf.
5 "Where We Are on TV 2023–2024."
6 Madison, "The Bisexual Seen."
7 "Where We Are on TV 2023–2024."
8 "Where We Are on TV 2023–2024."
9 Madison, "The Bisexual Seen."
10 Madison, "The Bisexual Seen."

11 Sarah Corey, "All Bi Myself: Analyzing Television's Presentation of Female Bisexuality," *Journal of Bisexuality*, Vol. 17, No. 2 (2017), 198.

12 Station 19, Season 6, Episode 14, "Get It All Out," directed by Stacey K. Black, written by Stacy McKee, Shonda Rhimes and Peter Paige, first aired April 13, 2023 on ABC.

13 Madison, "The Bisexual Seen."

14 Robyn Ochs, "Bisexual: A Few Quotes from Robyn Ochs," https://robynochs.com/bisexual/.

15 Vaneet Mehta, "Representation and Education," in *Bisexual Men Exist: A Handbook for Bisexual, Pansexual and M-Spec Men* (London: Jessica Kingsley Publishers, 2023), 18, Kindle.

16 Mehta, "Representation and Education," 19.

17 Corey, "All Bi Myself," 198.

18 The Rookie Feds, Season 1, Episode 16, "For Love and Money," directed by Jean E. Lee, written by Stacy A. Littlejohn and Nick Hurtwitz, first aired February 21, 2023 on ABC.

19 "Niecy Nash Rejected Sexual Identity Labels, Told Her Daughter She's 'Jess-Sexual,'" The Grio Website (October 2022), https://thegrio.com/2022/10/04/niecy-nash-rejected-sexual-identity-labels/.

20 Corey, "All Bi Myself," 197.

21 Mehta, "Representation and Education."

22 Mehta, "Representation and Education," 24.

23 Mehta, "Representation and Education," 27.

24 Shiri Eisner, "Bisexuality, Feminism and Women," in *Bi: Notes for a Bisexual Revolution* (Berkeley, CA: Seal Press, 2013), 152.

25 Eisner, "Bisexuality, Feminism and Women," 153.

26 Mimi Avins, "Feminism After the Fact," *Los Angeles Times* (March 26, 2006), www.latimes.com/archives/la-xpm-2006-mar-26-ca-basic26-story.html.

27 Eisner, "Bisexuality, Feminism and Women," 153.

28 Grey's Anatomy, Season 11, Episode 5, "Bend and Break," directed by Jesse Bochco, written by Meg Marinis, first aired October 23, 2014 on ABC.

29 Corey, "All Bi Myself," 196.

30 Michaela D. Meyer, "Representing Bisexuality on Television: The Case for Intersectional Hybrids," *Journal of Bisexuality*, Vol. 10, No. 4 (2010), 373.

31 Meyer, "Representing Bisexuality on Television," 373.

32 Meyer, "Representing Bisexuality on Television," 379.

33 Meyer, "Representing Bisexuality on Television," 380.

34 Meyer, "Representing Bisexuality on Television," 380.

35 Meyer, "Representing Bisexuality on Television," 380.

36 "Where We Are on TV 2023–2024."

37 "Where We Are on TV 2023–2024."

38 Caroline Framke, "How TV Failed Me on Bisexuality, and Then Got It Together," Variety Online (June 2019), https://variety.com/2019/tv/news/tv-failed-bisexuality-1203249798/.

39 Michel Ghanem, "Where Are All the Bisexual Men on Television," Dame Website (January 2023), www.damemagazine.com/2023/01/30/where-are-all-the-bisexual-men-on-television/.

40 Maria San Filippo, quoted in email interview in Ghanem, "Where Are All the Bisexual Men on Television."

41 Michelle Garcia, "Sex Is Power: Frank Underwood, Hollywood's First Bi President," Advocate Website (March 2015), www.advocate.com/spotlight/2015/03/05/sex-power-frank-underwood-hollywoods-first-bi-president.

42 Damian Emba, "The Unicorn Scale: Euphoria," bi.org Website (September 2019), https://bi.org/en/articles/the-unicorn-scale-euphoria.

43 Emba, "The Unicorn Scale."

44 Muhammad Modibo Shareef, "The Unicorn Scale: Moonlight," bi.org Website (March 2020), https://bi.org/en/articles/the-unicorn-scale-moonlight.

45 Janell Haezelwood, "'Harlem' Presents a Refreshing New Take on Black Male Bisexuality," To Necole Website (January 2020), www.xonecole.com/black-bisexuality-on-screen/.

46 "Where We Are Now 2023–2024: Representation of Trans Characters," GLAAD Webpage, https://glaad.org/whereweareontv23/representation-of-transgender-characters/.

47 Julia Jacobs, "Sara Ramirez Is Not Che Diaz," *New York Times* (February 2022), www.nytimes.com/2022/02/02/arts/television/che-diaz-and-just-like-that.html.

48 Nicole Richter, "Ambiguous Bisexuality: The Case of a Shot at Love with Tila Tequila," *Journal of Bisexuality*, Vol. 11, No. 1 (2011).

49 Richter, "Ambiguous Bisexuality," 1.

50 Rebecca Beirne, "The Messy History of Bisexual Representation on Reality TV," *The Sydney Morning Herald* (October 2021), www.smh.com.au/culture/tv-and-radio/the-messy-history-of-bisexual-representation-on-reality-tv-20211027-p593k1.html.

51 Beirne, "The Messy History of Bisexual Representation on Reality TV."

52 Ally Parker, "Whatever Happened to Tila Tequila AKA MTV's OG Bisexual Reality Dating Show Lead?" *Nova Sydney*, https://novafm.com.au/article/whatever-happened-to-tila-tequila-aka-mtvs-og-bisexual-reality-dating-show-lead.

53 Beirne, "The Messy History of Bisexual Representation on Reality TV."

54 Hannah Harris Green, "New Season of MTV's Are You the One?" *Slate* (July 2019), https://slate.com/human-interest/2019/07/mtv-are-you-one-bisexual-representation.html.

55 Green, "New Season of MTV's Are You the One?"

56 Beirne, "The Messy History of Bisexual Representation on Reality TV."

57 Beirne, "The Messy History of Bisexual Representation on Reality TV."

58 Beirne, "The Messy History of Bisexual Representation on Reality TV."

59 Hannah J. Johnson, "Bisexuality, Mental Health and Media Representation," *Journal of Bisexuality*, Vol. 16, No. 3 (2016), 379.

60 Corey, "All Bi Myself."

61 Corey, "All Bi Myself," 203.

62 Shiri Eisner (@ShiriEisner), "I Don't Know Who Needs to Hear This, but Substantial Bi Representation Doesn't Require Characters to Display Their Sexuality Visually on the Screen," X (formerly known as Twitter) (May 26, 2023), https://x.com/shirieisner/status/1662121024010215426?s=42&t=abBfF0SrJi_FS6GwBPDS5w.

63 Lois Shearing, "Introducing the Ramirez Test," *Medium* (February 2019), https://medium.com/@lois.shearing/introducing-the-ramirez-test-b91e98b57d1d.

64 "Darryl Whitefeather: Bi Characters," bi.org Website, https://bi.org/en/bi-characters/darryl-whitefeather.

65 "Rosa Diaz: Bi Characters," bi.org Website, https://bi.org/en/bi-characters/rosa-diaz.

66 "Nick Nelson: Bi Characters," bi.org Website, https://bi.org/en/bi-characters/nick-nelson.

67 Tom Smyth, "'Good Trouble' Is the Representation Bisexual Men Need," *Teen Vogue* (February 2021), www.teenvogue.com/story/good-trouble-bisexual-men-representation.

68 Alison Stine, "Celebrating the Casual Bisexuality in 'Hacks,'" *Salon* (June, 2022), https://www.salon.com/2022/06/09/hacks-ava-bisexuality-pride/.

69 Samantha Riedel, "Can't Sleep? Follow the Adventures of a Bi South Asian Escort in the New Web Series," *Them* (June 2019), www.them.us/story/insomnia-vishaal-reddy-interview.

70 Schitt's Creek, "The Wine, Not the Label," *Identiversity* [Video], YouTube, www.youtube.com/watch?v=gdcmhvLaNUswww.identiversity.org/topics/bisexuality/i-like-the-wine-and-not-the-label#:~:text=In%20a%20particularly%20iconic%20scene,kind%20of%20wine%20David%20prefers.

7

PORNOGRAPHY AND SEX WORK

Professionals in academic, legal, medical, societal, feminist, and religious studies consistently debate about sex work.[1] Much of the research focuses on a binary analysis of exploitation versus empowerment, with little nuanced understanding of the complexities of the sex workers' real lived experiences. *Sex work*—the trading of sex or sexual services for money, food, shelter, or other commodities between consenting adults—is a centuries old profession, consisting of a spectrum of labor that started with full-service options and in present day includes stripping, web-cam work, and internet pornography. It has an equally long history of society, government, and religion attempting to eradicate and solve the "problem" of sex work.[2]

The largest body of research on sex work has focused mostly on cisgender straight men purchasing sex from cisgender straight women, be it on the street, at a strip club, through escort services, online websites, or social media.[3] In addition, research often conflates sex work with *sex trafficking*, the crime of using force, abduction, deception, or coercion to induce someone into a commercial sex act.[4] Some feminist theories examine how the patriarchy contributes to the "inherently" exploitative nature of sex work and the potential for gender-based violence. Other feminist perspectives advocate for sex workers' individual agency, the potential for empowerment, and decriminalization. While these discussions are imperative and valuable, LGBTQ+ identities are rarely addressed as an essential part of discourse on sex work. According to Laing, Pitcher, and Smith in their book *Queer Sex Work*, this kind of erasure "not only restricts the potentialities of the political agency of queer and trans* sex workers" but also perpetuates "heteronormative assumptions that there is a 'natural' gender order in which women are sexual objects and men are sexual subjects."[5]

DOI: 10.4324/9781003242659-8

As little research as there is on LGBTQ+ sex workers, barely any exists specifically about those who are bisexual. When there is discussion on bisexuality it is typically blended in with LGBTQ+ identities in general. Although some analysis on bisexuality has been conducted in the context of pornography, often the focus is on the impact of the bisexual nature of the pornography, not the actual bisexual identity of the porn performer. Interestingly, a recent poll conducted about porn performers in the United States concluded that 44% identified as bisexual and 22% as pansexual.[6] Where do bisexual sex workers fit into this climate of debate? What are the experiences that are unique? Are there certain ways they may thrive in this work? Or face specific discrimination that is at the intersection of biphobia and monosexism?

Sex Work Is Work

Work is necessary to survive in this capitalist culture, and sex work can be a viable option for a job. It takes on many forms, and there are multiple reasons why adults do sex work. For some it is empowering and fulfilling, for others it may be the only possibility and feel like any other crappy job out there. Whatever the motivation, a major factor is that people are struggling to make money in a society that continues to maintain a federal minimum wage of only $7.25.[7] Even though there are states who have raised the minimum wage—Virginia's is $12—this is not high enough to obtain a "housing wage," which means fulltime pay that could actually cover an average rent with two-thirds left over.[8] Approximately 12% of people live in poverty in the United States and a middle class lifestyle is proving more difficult to obtain because incomes are not growing as fast as the cost of health care, housing, childcare, higher education, student loans, and other monthly costs.[9] The Covid pandemic, the recession, and inflation make it difficult for a number of Americans to make ends meet, leaving many to scramble for wages, sometimes by working several jobs.

Sex work may be a viable option; as Bicker and Ditmore assert, "There are so many ways in which capitalism limits our lives, but sex work offers some space to make capitalism pay off."[10] Not that all sex workers are making "easy" money, and neither is it feasible or of interest for everyone, but it can offer a flexible schedule and a pricing range for services that are always above minimum wage and allow for a lucrative supplemental income.[11] In addition, Bicker and Ditmore ask, if someone is open to being sexual with strangers, why not get paid for it?[12] Furthermore, the internet has enabled more ways to access sex work, such as connecting to customers through websites or internet-based sex work. For those who may not want to actually interact with someone in person or have sex with a stranger, digital sex work has created new opportunities.[13]

Sex work is a job, and like other jobs, there are challenges—bosses who are jerks, customers who are a pain, slow nights with low tips—and it can be hard, taxing work.[14] Like any form of work, there is always the possibility of exploitation. Sex work, however, has the added challenge of stigma, which often silences any actual discussion about the work. It is often stigmatized as dirty, degrading, and threatening to the conventional family structure. As Christina Tesoro writes,

> *Sex workers, by their very existence, reject the norm that sex should only exist within the bounds of heterosexual marriage. Perhaps even more subversive, sex work illustrates the frankness of the transactional nature of feminized aspects of relationships under capitalism; not merely sex, but also intimacy, fantasy, and emotional labor.*[15]

Not only does it promote sex outside of marriage, but money is being earned for it, and when a woman "chooses to capitalize on her sexuality in service only of herself and her survival, rather than in love, relation, or service to another (cisgender, straight, male) person, the entire fabric of society is perceived to be threatened."[16] Thus, criminalization of sex work has been maintained for centuries as the moral high ground and a way to deal with the "problem" of sex work.[17]

Sex workers face additional challenges due to political agendas that associate sex work with sex trafficking. In the last 25 years, much of the discussion of sex work has been framed around antitrafficking legislation.[18] In 2018 this particularly impacted sex workers with the passing of SESTA/FOSTA, a set of laws implemented during the Trump administration: the Stop Enabling Sex Traffickers Act (SESTA) and the Fight Online Sex Trafficking Act (FOSTA). So far, these laws have proven to have the opposite intent of prevention.[19] One of the main stipulations of these laws is the federal crime for owning, managing, or operating an "interactive computer service" with "the intent to promote or facilitate the prostitution of another person."[20] There is little evidence of SESTA/FOSTA decreasing sex trafficking, but rather these laws have increased vulnerability to violence for sex workers through limiting safety protocols.

LGBTQ+ Sex Work

Sex work has been a long standing, albeit often erased, part of the LGBTQ+ community.[21] Both the LGBTQ+ and sex work movements have had overlapping members and crossover on various concerns, such as insisting that the state not infringe on the rights of consenting adults to use their bodies how they choose.[22] Sex workers were an integral part of the start of queer activism and often played a role in creating the climate that made uprisings possible.[23] For example, a San Francisco group of mostly transgender and queer street youth who were sex workers organized in 1966 to create the group called Vanguard. Vanguard published a newsletter, met with city officials, and participated in such activism as marches and speeches that raised awareness about issues they faced on the streets. Their fight against the criminalization of sex work also intersected with their resistance to anti-queer harassment.[24]

Regardless of the similarities of issues in these movements, this relationship was fraught with tension and challenges. For example, the famous Stonewall Riots of 1969 included many transgender sex workers of color who were prominently involved in the protest, but the mainstream LGBTQ+ movement rarely highlighted the fact that sex workers were pivotal participants.[25] There was also reluctance on the part of gay liberation groups to include sex workers and transgender people in the movement, claiming "sexual respectability" as a core tenant of the movement.[26] Tension continued to escalate. During the 1973 gay pride rally in Washington Square Park, Jean O'Leary of the Gay Activists Alliance publicly condemned drag queen Sylvia Rivera—a former sex worker of color who was a key figure in the start of the LGBTQ+ rights movement—for "parodying" womanhood.[27] Rivera had to fight to speak at this event due to so many attendants' refusal to hear from a transgender sex worker of color.[28]

As different LGBTQ+ rights organizations obtained more "respectability," these groups typically distanced themselves from the sex workers who helped lay the groundwork for queer rights. Recently there has been some involvement of LGBTQ+ groups working towards decriminalization of sex work, but there is still some reluctance.[29] This unwillingness to address sex worker rights means neglecting a whole population of LGBTQ+ people. Although there is not an exact count of the number of LGBTQ+ people who are sex workers, there are multiple factors that may lead to sex work for this population. For LGBTQ+ youth, *survival sex work*—a term coined to describe "queer and trans youth engaging in street-based sex work while facing homelessness due to discrimination against their gender identities"[30]—is fairly common for queer youth who need to run away from home for their safety.

According to research from The Trevor Project, 28% of LGBTQ+ youth experience being unhoused at some point in their lives.[31] Another comprehensive study found that many LGBTQ+ youth who are unhoused turn to survival sex work because of "social-service barriers that leave few other options, the difficulties that a lack of services presents to getting out, and the complicated purposes—beyond allowing basic subsistence—that it serves."[32] As one respondent described in the study, "All I know is just that I was starving. I was hungry, I was cold, so I did it."[33] The question of choice often arises in the discussion of survival sex work, but Meredith Dank, author of the book *The Commercial Sexual Exploitation of Children* states, "To the extent this can be considered a choice, it is born out of the fact that there are no other choices," she says. "Language when it comes to this is so difficult; if you say they have a choice, that implies full agency, that they had other options. This is very much about resilience."[34]

For adult LGBTQ+ sex workers there may be different motivations. Recent research shows that full-time LGBTQ+ workers earn less than those who are not queer and make approximately 90 cents for every dollar earned by the typical worker.[35] For those who are transgender men and gender-diverse identities it is 70 cents and for transgender women 60 cents. It is also estimated that 25% of bisexual men and 29% of bisexual women live in poverty,[36] along with 29% of transgender people.[37] Furthermore, 40% of Black transgender adults and 45% of Latinx transgender adults are living in poverty.[38] For those who do have jobs, one 2020 study revealed that 36% of LGBTQ+ adults experienced discrimination in the workplace within the last year which increases the risk of poverty and economic struggle.[39] In this same study, the groups who had experienced discrimination —29% of LGBTQ+ people, 37% of Black respondents, and more than 50% of transgender respondents—expressed that discrimination significantly affected their financial well-being.[40] Given these realities, some may turn to sex work to make ends meet.

Bisexual Sex Work

The exact numbers of bisexual sex workers are unknown; however, there are some unique realities of the intersection of biphobia, bi-erasure, monosexism, and *whorephobia*. Tesoro describes *whorephobia* as "the fear and hatred of sex workers, which presents at the institutional, cultural and interpersonal level as violence against sex workers, and as social and cultural exclusion of sex workers from dominant/mainstream "respectable" ways of being in the world."[41] These layers of oppressions perpetuate shame and stigma in a culture that values white sexual purity, heterosexuality, marriage, monosexuality, monogamy, and "sexual respectability" politics. As shown in previous chapters, part of monosexism is the belief in certain bisexual stereotypes, including that bisexual people are hypersexual. This correlates with mainstream perceptions of sex work, which is often misunderstood as a job that requires someone to be hypersexual. The belief that any group is hypersexual is a risk factor for violence, but for bisexual sex workers, the intersection of monosexism and whorephobia increases the vulnerability to violence, along with other forms of oppression such as racism and ableism.

For some cis-bi women sex workers this intersection may be a deterrent from revealing their bisexual identities because it will attract certain types of customers, particularly cis straight men who may be obsessed with the fantasy of being involved with two women at once. For other cis-bi women this could be viewed as beneficial, as Capiola et al. found in their research on cis-bi escorts. Those who advertised as bisexual were able to charge more and had higher rates of calls for services because of this cis male obsession.[42] Customers who believed that bisexual people were promiscuous, particularly cis male customers interested in short-term sexual encounters, possibly found promiscuity appealing.[43] In addition, knowing the escort was bisexual allowed for the fulfillment in fantasies for customers, particularly "scenes of varied or forbidden sexual imagery that included questionable partners and atypical sexual acts."[44] Another possible explanation is the commodity theory, which means that a commodity "will increase in value when it is perceived to be scarce."[45] For cis-bi women sex workers in particular, the rarity of what they symbolized enhanced the interest in their services and increased what they were able to charge for their services.[46]

There can be potential criticism that cis-bi women sex workers are feeding into the patriarchy and traditional gender roles,[47] particularly if they are femme presenting. Their gender presentation can be perceived as heterosexual, which Sexsmith argues is a form of gender discrimination. Sexsmith states, "when someone refuses to recognize a femme as queer, that person is saying, straight women are feminine, dykes are not, therefore your gender presentation trumps anything that might come out of your mouth about how you identify or who you are."[48] As Blewett and Law contend, often times cis-bi women sex workers are read as

Too gender-conforming and too straight, and perhaps not even as femmes but merely as conventionally feminine; our queerness as bisexuals, femmes, and, we contend, as sex workers is erased. Such assumptions force us to out ourselves over and over to justify our queerness.[49]

According to Pendelton, "there is nothing straight about sex work," because sex work itself is a queer act.[50] Pendelton describes queerness as the "diverse oppositional politics of 'dissent from the dominant organization of sex and gender,'" which is exactly what sex work is doing. Pendelton further conveys that many femme sex workers' experience of the "repeated performances of heterosexuality" allows for their ability to actually critique compulsory heterosexuality. Blewett and Law address how the performance aspect of sex work could relate to their identities or not. In addition, sex work performance is actually "queering" because "it disrupts the taken-for-granted assumptions that heteronormative gender/sexual relations are naturally occurring, rather than something that is 'put on,' created, purchased, and consumed in the marketplace."[51]

Cis-bi men who are sex workers experience additional challenges, particularly the fight against stereotypes that their profession automatically spreads STIs and HIV. Cis-bi men in general are stereotyped as sexually irresponsible and more likely to contract and spread HIV along with other STIs.

Bisexuality alone does not determine the spread of HIV or other STIs; neither is sex work inherently the cause of this, but rather, the lack of safer sex practices is. If there are safer sex practices and regular testing, this decreases the chances of spreading any STI, but some sex workers do not have access to these services or are afraid that their occupation would be revealed if they do.[52] For others, negotiating condom use may be a challenge if the customer prefers condomless sex or if the customer will pay more for a condom not to be used.[53] Furthermore, the criminalization of sex work decreases general safety where decriminalization would allow for safety and support, the option of legal action against violence when needed, and access to health care services openly without judgment.[54] There is also a growing body of research that reveals most male sex workers who have sex with men actually do use condoms and are refuting the stereotype that they are the sole cause of the spreading of HIV and other STIs to large numbers of people.[55]

The sex work where bisexuality is the most visible and well known by mainstream culture is in the context of pornography. Similar to mainstream media, pornography can manifest stereotypes and misrepresentation but also be a potential space for *positive* representation and the normalizing of bisexuality. Finding the positive representation can be a challenge, when the fetishized, hypersexualized imagery dominates the mainstream porn industry. In particular, cis-bi women are portrayed as always willing to have sex with and desiring to be in a threesome.[56] Another common trope is for the storyline to include bisexual characters as cheaters, forcing others to have sex with them, or bisexual men "turning" lesbian women straight.[57] Furthermore, the intersection of racialized stereotypes adds to this fetishization and objectification. For example, Black women are often cast as prostitutes in videos like *Ebony Sex Workers* and *Black Girls Working the Streets* or are called *Black Ghetto Freaks* and *Inner City Sluts*, which are often filmed in urban settings, rundown buildings, and trash-filled alleys.[58] Black men are often featured under the term "ebony" or "BBC" (Big Black Cock) or the trope of the "Big Black Beast."[59] The list continues, as Asian women are portrayed as passive, submissive, with little sexual agency and "somewhat like exotic children or rare birds."[60] In addition, Latinas are generally portrayed as shy, virginal immigrants until "a real man (usually white) unleashes their hot and spicy firecracker side."[61] These racialized fetishes have roots in colonization and are based in the mindset of the oppressor "always romanticizing and fetishizing the oppressed."[62]

This is problematic for multiple reasons, but one in particular is the fact that our sex education in the United States is so lacking,[63] that many use porn to learn sexual scripts that may be perpetuating certain forms of oppression.[64] Given that mainstream porn is a form of entertainment based in fantasy, it is clearly not always the best resource for sex education.[65] For LGBTQ+ people though, it may be the only place where they can find validation and representation of their own identities. While so many states continue to try to implement laws against inclusive sex education like the "no promo homo laws,"—which still exist in such states as Texas, Oklahoma, Louisiana, and Mississippi[66]—or the "don't say gay" legislation that passed in Florida, porn may be a safe haven.[67] In the research of McCormack and Wignall, they found that "most participants found that pornography was helpful in intellectually processing their sexual desires, it also provided a safe space to explore sexual desires . . . pornography provides a platform for self-confirmation and self-validation about one's sexual identity."[68] According to Bowling and Fritz, research has shown that pornography can empower queer people, especially bisexual people who may not be represented in other forms of media, to identify and communicate their own sexual wants and dislikes, in addition to finding and forming community.[69]

There is also a growing number of better options for porn, particularly ethically produced porn sites that are feminist, queer, or created by people of color. As the authors of *The Feminist Porn Book* argue, feminist porn "uses sexually explicit imagery to contest and complicate representations" of identity and "explores concepts of desire, agency, power, beauty and pleasure at their most confounding and difficult, including pleasure within and across inequality, in the face of injustice, and against the limits of gender hierarchy and both heteronormativity and homonormativity."[70] Ethically produced porn allows for better representation of LGBTQ+ identities and people of color and also works to take care of the performers, many of whom are LGBTQ+ and people of color themselves. One example is Royal Fetish Films, created by real-life couple and adult performers Jet-Setting Jasmine and King Noire, which is an inclusive, ethical, and safe space for performers of color.[71] As Jet-Setting Jasmine explains,

> *There is a high turnover rate for people in industry, especially for Black and brown performers because of that pigeon hole that we get placed in. And you can only deal with that for so long, especially at the expense of your body and emotional labor. The expense of the sacrifice you make from your friends, your family and all of the things that come with this stigmatization [of sex work]. . . . So our work will be really helping [BIPOC] people explore other ways of creating a sustainable career in porn.*[72]

It is important to have more discourse and understanding of the realities of sex work. The following three personal narratives add to this exploration specifically for bisexual and pansexual people and reveals the human side to sex work. Janis Luna, a former sex worker, reveals their experiences in the piece *Spoiling the Fantasy*, in addition to conversations with bi porn star Wolf Hudson and pansexual sex worker Dani Rose.

Spoiling the Fantasy by Janis Luna

My experiences with bisexuality and sex work and my experiences as a bisexual sex worker are two different things. My experiences with bisexuality as an aspect of sex work are somewhat limited; as a stripper, I never marketed myself, so I never marketed myself as bisexual in an effort to attract clients, though sometimes I would flirt with my coworkers on stage, pantomime pinching a nipple, licking pussy, eating ass. Sometimes it would get a rousing cheer; most of the time, at the dive that I worked at, the sullen middle-aged customers didn't seem to want a reminder that strippers could have eyes for anyone other than them. That would spoil the fantasy. It was more lucrative to keep eye contact on stage: One of my coworkers was known for it, the way she would hold eye contact from across the room, pull her legs behind her head, stroke her pussy over her slingshot bikini slowly. Unblinking. Magnetic. Customers would fall into her gaze like it was a force of gravity. Sometimes I got sucked into it too, and in true bisexual fashion it provoked the age-old question: Do I want to be her, or do I want to be on her? That might have been the question that prompted me to become a stripper in the first place.

Bisexuality at the club strikes me as different from bisexuality in other aspects of the sex industry. Is a Mommy Domme tapping into queerness, just by virtue of how she inhabits the erotic space? When I connect to dominance, it's so rarely about sexual gratification or desire for me. It's about my will to power. It's about this tiny seed of sadism that is buried deep within me, some kind of Kali Mother, destroyer deity; Demeter, weeping and enraged; Ereshkigal, I want to hurt you, and I want to make you like it, but mostly, I want to hurt you. I feel that way about dominance regardless of the gender of the person I'm playing with. If I were straight, and if I were a cis woman, would I feel that way only about cis men? There's no way for me to know.

My experience with full-service work is pretty limited. In grad school, during slow months at the club, I would occasionally go on dates with 1–2 other workers, always with a regular who was well-vetted by my more experienced friend. He liked us to enact the same fantasy with him, every time: That we were all teenagers having sex for the first time, and he was a wise, kind, gentle older man teaching us how to "experience our bodies" and "connect to our pleasure." Though there were several of us, he never seemed particularly interested in us fucking each other (though, I'll admit, sometimes I was). It was always about how *we* interacted with *him*; how *he* could teach *us* to be in our bodies.

When I told my boyfriend at the time about this—an older man who would spend the last five months of our relationship cheating on me with a woman younger than me—I told him that I found it absurd, but almost sweet and pretty harmless, as far as sexual fantasies go. After all, my coworkers and I, though young, were in our mid-to-late twenties, not teenagers; we made men cum, professionally, and had been making ourselves cum, recreationally and professionally, for at least a decade each, and an entire lifetime, cumulatively. Before the date we would drink a glass of wine in our lingerie and make up, chat, catch up, and as I write this, I honestly couldn't tell you anymore what our constellations of gender were or what they are now. But they were all beautiful, and I loved them, the dry humor, the eye contact made over a rubber-encased, middle-aged penis, the breaking of the fourth wall, in those moments, and biting back laughter that this old man could suspend enough disbelief to dream that he had something new to teach these millennial sex workers about a blowjob.

My then-boyfriend was less amused by the fantasy; he thought it was pathological. But it's worth noting: This customer never hurt me, never betrayed my trust, never violated my sexual boundaries by fucking me raw while starting a whole new relationship with another woman, and probably fucking her raw, too. So, who, really, is the pathological one?

At the club, it seemed like most of my coworkers were queer, and many of us were non-binary. It's such a conundrum of correlation and causation. Are queers more likely to seek out sex work? Probably—both from the standpoint of already being perceived as sexually deviant to mainstream culture, so what's the big deal? And also out of pure economic necessity: bisexual men and women make less money than gay men[73] (who make more money than straight men), and 29% of bisexual women are living in poverty, according to the American Psychological Association.[74] Trans people are also overrepresented within the sex industry, especially Black and brown workers; unsurprising, given that same study showed that trans people were four times as likely to have a household income of less than $10,000 per year compared to the general population.[75]

Still, when I started stripping, I thought I was a cis woman. The persistent exposure to the absurdity that is cis het beauty standards and desirability politics quickly forced me to question that. Who was this femme goddess, glittering and smelling like cinnamon, gloss on her lips like honey; glowing, soft, almost innocent—except when her head was in your lap, miming fellatio, teasing, suggesting; creating, for you to indulge in, that very same magnetic pull I felt when watching my coworker on stage. The pull of the tide. The force that holds planets bound up in their orbit. She both was, and she wasn't, me.

Once during a lap dance, the façade vanished when I whirled around to elbow a man in the trachea in reaction to him trying to grab me by the throat. On another night, the music in the main room paused just as I slapped a man in the face across the bar for trying to shove a dirty single dollar into the front of my thong; the leering smile stayed on his face even as a print of my hand bloomed on his cheek. The etherealness of the fantasy is just that, a sheer veneer; High Femme gender identity runs bone deep and vicious. Come hither, but beware. Like a carnivorous plant.

This has become a meditation on gender, and as a sex educator, we were always instructed to make neat, clean distinctions between gender and sexual orientation. Yet, in my experience of sex work, there are no such clear distinctions. There is only my body and the energy that is expressed through it, which takes whatever form it takes in the moment. Most often, it delights me.

When I think about this delight, I think about the cis women I've encountered at the club, as well. The motorcycle gang of lesbians who made it rain and cheered at every inversion on the pole, on one of the most magical nights I've ever danced. Not every lesbian who walks into a strip club is that happy to be there; certainly, I've encountered the lesbians who sit silent at the bar with a sneer on their faces. I assign a story to the expression in their eyes and entertain briefly the narratives of second wave feminism and gold star baby dyke rhetoric: How I must be betraying women by making my money dancing for men, performing queerness before cis het masculinity. But on this night and with this group, it was a brief, shining moment of femmeness on stage—true femmeness, embodied and expressed, for myself and for other non-men, one glorious glimpse into the world I would most like to live in.

Cis straight women at the club are another beast entirely.

Some strippers know how to handle couples. Some strippers like couples, but I never did. I gave them a wide berth, usually, because even the couples made up of a straight man and a queer woman tended to feel awkward to me. The adoration from cis women at the club—*you're so brave, you're so strong, I could never do what you do*—felt fetishizing in a way that was almost more uncomfortable than the run-of-the-mill objectification I've come to expect from men in the club. The cool competitiveness of recreational pole dancers, the ones who you know tag their videos with #notastripper: *Do you know how to do jade monkey? Snap dragon? Shooting star?* No, bitch, I know how to make money!

Then there was the moment when offering a dance to a couple, of not knowing what the outcome would be—a stiffening of her shoulders? A twist to her lips? A hollow, cheery assertion that it was *totally okay* for him to get a dance? And hearty acquiescence, with the stipulation that I dance only on her (fine), while he watched, and she ran her hands over my body with enthusiasm that, sometimes, I shared, but which also sometimes pushed my boundaries even more relentlessly than when I danced for a single, cis het man (less fine). Girl-on-girl, so hot. Couples at the club meant navigating the disdain of femmephobia and femme competition or the slightly manic grasping at a performance of queer femme sexuality, not because we delight in each other but because her boyfriend was watching, a dynamic not unlike the one I experienced with the first woman I ever dated, who had a boyfriend who would watch, and sometimes touch me even though I had made it clear that while I was okay with him being there, I only wanted to be touched by her.

It doesn't surprise me that the place I have landed is a place of violence. Think about gender, sexuality, or sex work for any length of time, and it is inevitable that we will land here, which has little to do with gender, sexuality, or sex work and everything to do with patriarchy, colonialism, and capitalism. According to recent research, bi women are at greater risk of domestic abuse: one in ten bi women experience it, as compared to 6% of straight women.[76] Sixty-one percent of bi women have been raped by their partners or experienced physical violence or stalking.[77] Did the men who abused me in our intimate relationships do so because I was a sex worker and therefore was in some way "asking for it"? Because I was bisexual and therefore perceived as hypersexual? Because I was perceived to be a woman? Because I insisted I was not one? Does it matter? They harmed me. I suffered for it. I am healing.

Part of it, too, is my lineage of intergenerational trauma: I come from a family whose cultures include machismo, of the Peruvian and Sicilian variety. Was there ever a femme in my family who didn't experience this type of violence?

The violence that I experienced in these relationships also played out with sex work stigma and fetishization as two of its central organizing principles: my ex's jealousy. His lack of understanding about the relationship between sex worker and customer; his unwillingness to believe that, more often than not, my interactions with customers drained and irritated me, and that almost all the pleasure I experienced on the job was experienced in the dressing room, with my coworkers. Or was that a threat, too, because I am queer?

His public-facing support of sex workers and his private insistence that he be allowed to visit the club, even though it could get me fired, which would threaten my economic independence and stability, such as it was. Sex work made up two-thirds of my income, despite having graduated with an MSW and working in a psychotherapy clinic. His repeated demands that I wear my work outfits and lap dance for him, even though those actions were associated with work and not play. I tried to explain that I could sometimes access play at work on good nights—or even, out of desperate necessity, on bad, slow ones—but that I didn't really feel like doing that on my off-hours, because I didn't want my romantic partnership to feel like sex work. This seemed to insult him, as though he felt he was entitled to every expression and performance of my sexuality, all the time, simply because other men had access to them when they paid for it. I tried to explain: I loved him, and because I loved him, I didn't want to perform.

His inability to hear or respect my "No," whether it be in response to a request for sex or touch more generally. The way he repeatedly groped me, murmuring "Come on, just let me touch a little," until I relented. The way I had to say, "Please don't grab me that way outside of a sexual context, it reminds me of work." The way I couldn't find the words to say, I don't want to associate you with that place, with those men. I want to love you. If you do this, I cannot love you. The way it didn't get through to him until I was frozen on his bed, non-verbal and furious, and still unable to feel like I had a right to tell him to go sleep on the couch, even when he offered to do so.

As a bisexual femme and sex worker, violence is the net thrown over every aspect of my life, every intersection of my identity. It is useless to ask, why did you hurt me in this way? They don't know, won't let themselves know, and so they wouldn't be able to answer, though I hope that one day, they become curious. The wound they act from is not found within sex work or queer sexuality. Nor is it related to femmeness or transness. It is about whiteness; patriarchy and how it warps masculinity; colonialism, capitalism, control. Fear. Fear of what they cannot control. Fear of who they could become, if they could relinquish that insecure impulse to control. Again, I hope they become curious.

I am not afraid; at least, not always. Not anymore. I have been hurt over and over, for being bisexual, for being femme, for being a sex worker, for existing in this trans indigenous body under racialized capitalism and colonialism, in relationship after relationship. Never for a moment have I regretted my queerness, my transness, my place among sex workers and femmes. I am unwavering in who I am and whoever I am becoming, loyal without end to how these identities allow me to experience *being*, deeper, and clearer, and more.

A Conversation with Wolf Hudson

LISA:
Tell me a little bit about how you make bisexual porn.

WOLF:
The one thing I always tell performers once that camera's on, I don't care what we do. I don't care if we have soft, intimate, rough, aggressive, or kinky sex. I don't want to plan anything or do positions that are impossible. I just want to have fun because this is my true expression when it comes to sex. I don't get to have a lot of bi sex in my personal life. This is my outlet to really have a good time. So, I don't want it to be contrived. And that's the thing that has come across for a lot of people. It's given people a sense of security because they're seeing people who are not only secure with themselves, but they're in a safe place

and it's inspired them to explore their sexuality and even come out as bisexual.

I get messages all the time from men and even women from around the world. "Thank you for doing this. I've finally been able to realize who I really am. I came out to my wife. I came out to my family." I'm not thinking that when I make these films, I'm just having a good time. But that's the impact of that sort of medium. That you can reach across and have an effect on it. Once I really had that knowledge, it was imperative for me that what I represent in my films, it's just plain honesty, consent, and nothing that goes against oneself. I don't want somebody to be ultra-masculine. I don't want somebody to be ultra-feminine if it's not who they are.

L:

That's cool. I read in an article about you that authenticity was important, since typical bisexual presenting porn is too staged and contrived.

W:

There's so much more gay/straight porn. The bi porn community is very small, not just in scope of people but in scope of scenes and films. It has not been heavily produced over the decades and there hasn't been a true exploration of it. What you've had is people not really understanding bisexuality, these scenes being produced by people who are not bisexual. Everything has been contrived and mechanical. It's like, okay, let's follow a formula. And so here I come and I'm just putting my own spin based off of not seeing what I want to see in bi scenes, so let me do it the way I want to see it. That became a concept that shocked people. They didn't think it could be like that. I do recognize that the authenticity, the chemistry, the passion is pivotal into making a successful scene. And that starts immediately when I engage with the performers, just by contacting them and then being on set. And establishing a very safe place, especially for a cis female because they're so used to being on sets where they don't really have a say and they have to do things that are uncomfortable. It is part of the job, but I always make it so that they know they're going to be taken care of. Like, we have your back, and in turn we know you're going to have our back.

L:

Right on! Are you intentional in finding people who identify as bi for you[r] films?

W:

I'm open to anybody who is open. I've dealt with gay men who have had curiosities. They didn't have the intention, but they've seen my stuff and they wanted to try it. It always comes down to, as long as you want to be there, let's shoot it. I don't care how you identify. Gay, straight, bi, pan. I don't care if you identify as a male or female, if you iden- tify as trans, non-binary, gender fluid, as long as you want to be in that space and you want to have a good time, let's do that.

L:

Sounds like you are describing ethically produced porn. In another article you mentioned challenging racial stereotypes, how do you do that?

W:

The biggest way to challenge it is by not fetishiz- ing it. If I work with a person of color, I don't have to emphasize that I'm working with a person of color. If you have vision, you can clearly see I am with a person of color and so I don't need to emphasize the stereotype of Ebony, BBC, and all that other stuff that goes with it. I don't treat people like an "other." To me, everyone is equal while still recognizing that we look different. Just because we look different doesn't mean that we have to treat each other differently. I also have to respect that we don't have shared experiences, so I have to be very mindful of my interactions with people who look different from me.

I'm not going to use derogatory words, I'm not going to play on stereotypes in the film. And for

me, I'm actually multiracial, but I'm white passing. I've gotten a perspective that a lot of people don't get. So, I've heard the conversations in
the white community in regards to Black people, and
so knowing that, I am much more diligent in making
sure that people of color are represented fairly,
are treated with respect, but are not treated differently because they're a person of color.

L:
Have you faced the stereotyping or fitting into a
certain fetish based on your racial identities?

W:
Absolutely. Because I'm white presenting, I would
not be considered Hispanic, which I am. People's
perception of Hispanic is brown, Mexican. You would
not consider a black or white person Latino, which
is bullshit because we come in many different colors. On the one hand I had the privilege of being
able to have more access to scenes because of my
complexion. On the other hand, because I don't fit
with the narrative of being Hispanic, I won't get
cast in certain roles, like if they're doing an
all-Hispanic film, I would not be on the top of that
list because I don't fit that mold. Even within communities, I don't fit being Hispanic or Black. And
with a lot of white people, I don't fit the white
mold. I'm kind of in an island of myself, but that's
okay. I There is no set mold of how you're supposed
to act, of how a bisexual or Hispanic person is supposed to act. You're just supposed to be yourself.

L:
I would assume it would be a challenge to not get
sucked into the racialized categorizations in porn.

W:
It's not a challenge for me in that I don't see
the problem of treating every scene equally. By not
categorizing it as interracial or categorizing it
with the click words. The stereotypes, the click
words, by not doing that, it's not really hurting

me. If anything, I'm more likely to be hurting
somebody else. Whether it's consciously or subconsciously, the fact that, I could make more money if
I categorize it, that to me is ridiculous.

L:

Is that true?

W:

To some extent it is true. If I put it in a category,
the people who want that need to be able to search
for it. If you go to PornHub, what you're primarily
bombarded with is straight Caucasians having sex.
But if that's not what you want to see in a sea of
white people, we're told you have to have a category
to be able to search that. Well, I'll tell you what,
I did a bi scene with two African Americans, did not
categorize it, and guess what? It was one of the top
scenes for that week. On PornHub. And I didn't have
to categorize it.

L:

This is what social activists are encouraging people to do, not to participate in this, right?

W:

Well, if I have to call out a social activist
moment, during the BLM protests there were a lot of
conversations in the porn industry about equity and
breaking down a lot of the stereotypes that have
been permeating for years. A group of us, people of
color, had conversations with AVN (Adult Video Network), the biggest trade organization we built for
the industry, and we were voicing the changes that
we wanted to see.

They have the AVN awards, which is like the Oscars
of porn. But they have a trade magazine that exclusively talks about news and porn and have advertisements for porn, so they're a big deal in the
industry. They are the pinnacle of porn greatness
in terms of recognition.

And we voiced our opinions. Some of which they were
open to and others they were not, which disappointed

us. The stuff that they were not open to was probably the smallest thing. But one of the things we told them is to not have advertisements from racist companies or people that promote stereotypes. And they had said that they would be open to that. I knew they would not be. And so, weeks later, it was brought to my attention that they were promoting a website, I forget the name of the website, but it had spades on the title. When it comes down to it, green is the only color they see.

They're going to take it from anybody and they clearly do not care. In the beginning, they cared about the optics, and then when things calmed down, they felt they can go back to business. It had taken me about 14, maybe 15 years to gain two AVN awards. I had just won two AVN awards.

I gave it back. I said I cannot look at these trophies collecting dust on my shelf and feel good about myself knowing what they're doing. I just gave them back. I went to their headquarters and I returned the statues. Just like that. And I have no qualms about it. They're just statues; I was grateful [for] what they represented. But that representation has been tainted by what *they* represent.

L:

Wow. That was a big deal to get those awards though?

W:

Yeah. Within the industry, that's a very huge deal. And for someone like me, I'm not one to win AVN awards. It's just not in my future of things to receive. To have received those accolades was a very big deal, especially for the projects that I had worked on. Which meant a lot to me. I was very proud to have won those at the time but once I saw that they just didn't care about representation or who they could possibly be hurting, that changed everything for me. I wasn't expecting anybody to follow suits. For me it was, I can't support you. I'm not sorry. And I'm doing just fine without having those trophies. I really am.

L:

That's awesome! You talked previously about being biracial and bisexual and navigating the in between. Can you talk about that a little more?

W:

Put the bisexuality aside, just being biracial is hard enough. I've had to deal with finding my own identity and where I fit. Am I truly Hispanic? Am I American because I'm the first born American in my family? There's a lot of things growing up that I couldn't make sense of. And it was very confusing. And now I've gotten to the point where I am Hispanic, I am white, I am mixed, I am bisexual. But that has to make sense for me. My identity is what I molded it to be. And that is the right way to be. The same way that what you are is the right way you're supposed to be. So long as you're not hurting anybody, there is no rule about how you should act and look.

A Conversation with Dani

LISA:

What does pansexuality mean to you?

DANI:

I'm attracted to people and their energy and personalities. It's less about anything physical. It ends up that I'm attracted to a lot of different people in different ways, and it's not always just a sexual thing, I just feel like pan is the best term to describe how I move in the world with regards to other people romantically or sexually.

L:

Have you always identified as pan or did you have a time of identifying with other labels?

D:

Oh yeah. I legitimately thought I was a lesbian. And then, I was like, well, no, I think I do like boys.

I wish that there were more resources available at that time for educating ourselves . . . just driving home the importance of having more comprehensive sex education in schools. I didn't know any of the terms. I had to go on queer sites, well I'm calling them queer, but at the time it was just lesbian or women who like women kind of things, you know what I mean? And I would go and research and that's how I was like, oh, maybe I'm bisexual. I kind of flipped back and forth . . . I actually don't like men. I like penetration. And then I was like, no, fuck. I think I do like men.

L:

A lot to navigate, isn't it?

D:

Yeah. With the help of the internet, as with many other things in my life, that's when I learned about the term pan and I was like, oh yeah, that actually resonates with me more than bisexuality.

L:

There's a lot of crossover. Sometimes people use those terms sort of interchangeably. Bisexual can be sort of a broad definition too. It's like attraction to more than one gender or multiple genders.

D:

For me, I like pansexual better because I'm attracted to all kinds of people who may be gender nonconforming, who identify all different ways, and I think breaking out of the binary of women and men, pansexuality encompasses more.

L:

That's cool! Do you think you've ever felt people being biased towards pansexuality?

D:

I don't really think about it that much. I typically don't talk to people about it who are not already part of the LGBTQI+ community. I don't want to do all this labor to educate you about what it is. I have heard shitty jokes though, for example, pansexuals are attracted to everything, like everything including the pans. It's a terrible joke.

L:
Has pansexuality come up at all in doing sex work?

D:
It comes up sometimes. Most of my clientele are cishet men, so it doesn't come up that much because that's just my clientele. If I could find more queer spaces to post ads, I totally would. I don't know of any right now. But I do make sure to mark that I'm available to anybody who wants to book me. But even on the ads, it's not like they have real spaces to expand on that necessarily. They don't do it in your profile, and it also doesn't really come up that often other than in the strip clubs. We're always making comments about how hot someone else looks. We're all just like being very sexual towards each other. It's just like, "Oh my gosh, girl, your ass looks so good in that!" And then like, "Can I smack it?" You know what I mean? And we're all just like very like touchy feely, lovey dovey with each other. There was one time where a girl was like, be careful joking with me. I'm actually a lesbian. And I was like, oh. I'm queer. What's up? You know what I mean? But I used queer as an umbrella term. I don't necessarily specifically say pan . . . queer is the thing that I feel like I use just because I feel that's what people will understand in those situations.

L:
What identities do you use in your ads?

D:
My ads are pretty much catered to cishet men. Lemme pull up one of my ads. I just want to see how they have it structured. So yeah, caters to male, female, non-binary and couples . . . those are my options on this particular site. So, I just click all of them.

This is on the site *Tryst*. I really like *Tryst*. And then underneath, they say, "if there's an option you'd like to see, please let us know." Oh, that's nice. I appreciate that. I wouldn't mind writing for *Tryst*. I could talk about going from doing vanilla work and then sex work and how my business lost contracts when I came out of the sex worker closet.

L:

Can you tell me that story?

D:

I started working as a cam girl around 2009. I've been in the industry for a long time, but I also was in school and waiting tables. And it's something that I hid for a long time knowing that people wouldn't necessarily get it. I did that for a while, stopped and started other things and then shifted into other forms of sex work but also keeping that hush hush except with people that I was close to. My sex work was becoming a bigger part of my life, and I felt like I was living kind of a double life in a way, and it didn't feel right to hide it. I had to reckon with my own shame around being a sex worker and also some whorearchy bullshit that I had to process. I eventually decided to come out of the sex worker closet and I lost some contracts in the process. I literally heard verbatim, "we are a family company and we can't be in association with that, but we wish you all the best." I lost money because of that and it sucked. But I feel freer being out of the sex worker closet. I recognize that there's much more to gain than what I'm going to lose by being my full self and being more authentic.

L:

Can you explain what whorearchy is?

D:

Let me look it up. . . . It's the "hierarchical system by which sex workers too often order themselves from elite to inferior." The woman who walks the streets is always at the bottom of this hierarchy, which I don't think they're right to use "women" because there are all kinds of people who do full-service sex work. The order from top to bottom is: camgirl, strippers, sugar babies, adult performers, and dominatrixes, and then full-service sex workers at the bottom. Damn.

L:
Seems like some internalized purity bullshit going on there.

D:
Yes. It's all bullshit because I've even been in on it, when I was doing just cam work and OnlyFans stuff for a little bit. I went on a date with someone from like Hinge or Bumble, and he still said that I was selling myself. Even though I'm selling a fantasy online, in his mind, I was selling myself. Needless to say, I did not go on another date with him, but that's what he perceived me as doing.

L:
Have you dated folks that aren't cishet men, and if so, what were their perspectives on sex work?

D:
The only time I'll date others now, it's more like other sex workers. And then I don't have to explain that. It's like they get it, you know?

L:
That makes sense. What are some challenges that you're facing in sex work that may or may not have to do with your sexuality but other identities?

D:
Ninety-nine percent of my clients are men, who have not done any work on themselves. Some of the conversations that come up, they might want to talk about the news, like trans rights. Mind you, I'm trying to sell a fucking fantasy, but I take that shit very seriously. When they do that, I am now trying to

speak and advocate for this issue that I care a lot
about while not trying to break the fantasy of performing femininity. It's like I'm trying to still be
this sex kitten while also saying, we do not share
the same views on that and trying not to get angry
about it because what I want to be, is like that's
ignorant shit, grow up! I'm trying to challenge it in
a way that I'm still able to finish the date and get
my money because I need money. It puts me in an uncomfortable position. I feel like I'm betraying my queer
side when I have to try to tiptoe around it. I do make
sure to challenge them, but I think also that's kind
of where my autism plays a role too. It depends on
what is said, but I can go a little non-verbal too.
I notice that I have all the thoughts going and then
I don't know what to say. I feel like I need to prepare prompts for myself, for when some of these problematic things do come up. But so far, it's just been
me trying to check myself and still sell this fantasy
while also showing that I do not have the same feelings about certain issues that these men have.

L:

Yeah. Do you face racism also?

D:

Less so, since a lot of my clients recently have
been Black men, so I don't have to navigate that.
But in the strip club, I'm constantly dealing with
racist bullshit. They might not say it outright,
but like, I sit down to talk to customers. They
don't want to look at me, they're looking at another
girl. They're very dismissive, ignoring me. And
then I get up and then the white girl that sits
down, they get a champagne room. But they don't want
to spend money on me.

L:

That sounds really hard. When people from the outside are looking in at sex work, there may be this
question of, why don't you just go get some other
job? Why are you putting yourself through all of
this? What would be your response to that?

D:

I do have other jobs. I work at an adult toy store part-time; they only pay $11.50 an hour. I also have a marketing business. I just haven't been working with clients in that same capacity because it's horrible for my mental health. I am autistic, ADHD, chronically depressed, and also have severe anxiety. I'm taking medication for some of these things and seeing a therapist consistently, but these are disabilities. I am actually a disabled person. So, when I work these regular jobs, I might be okay for a little bit, but when I start to not feel good . . . I've been fired from so many jobs because certain days I cannot do the work. I've lost contracts, where I'm very gung-ho in the beginning. I can show up and then when I don't feel well, when my brain is very unkind to me, it throws a wrench in the whole thing. I've lost multiple jobs this way. It makes me sad because I'm super capable. I'm a super intelligent person. I know this, but sex work gives me a little bit more flexibility. I've tried working regular jobs.

L:

Yeah. And they're not paying very much.

D:

They really are not paying. I've tried applying for different companies, client support services, whatever. I can't get a job. I don't know why, I'm super accomplished. My resume looks amazing. I've been a fellow at a prestigious university. I've been part of amazing projects. My resume is incredible. I've applied to so many jobs and have not heard anything back. I think the hard thing is my disabilities are invisible. People think that I'm making it up. When I say that I can't do it, they don't believe me.

I think that's why a lot of people with various disabilities kind of stick with sex work. Especially once it starts working, like what other job can you work at home and maybe work two days or three days a week and pay your mortgage. Some people are able to do that. Not a lot of people; it doesn't happen for everyone. And I think for me, what I'm holding on to hope for is that I can let my body rest more and I can also hopefully start to afford what I need.

L:
Sounds like a good plan. From your own experience, do you feel like there are a lot of sex workers who are LGBTQ+?

D:
In my online communities, a lot of us are part of the alphabet brigade in some way. Like Kira Noir, she's a Black lesbian porn star. And she is doing scenes with men. You know, there's a saying "Gay for pay," she's being "straight for pay," but she's very openly lesbian. I feel like a lot of folks in the adult industry are queer.

L:
What is something you would like everyone to know about sex workers?

D:
We're people trying to survive capitalism. What we do to make money doesn't mean we are less-than, or dirty, or untrustworthy. And just like there are good and bad days at your vanilla job, sex workers experience that too. Granted, this work comes with its risks, stigma, and harmful legislation that differs from other forms of work. However, it is a valid form of labor and deserves respect. Decriminalize sex work!

Notes

1 Nicola Smith, Mary Laing and Katy Pilcher, "Being, Thinking and Doing 'Queer' in Debates About Commercial Sex," in *Queer Sex Work* (New York: Routledge, 2015).
2 Matilda Bickers, peech breshers and Janis Luna, *Working It: Sex Workers on the Work of Sex* (Oakland: PM Press, 2023).
3 Smith et al., "Being, Thinking and Doing 'Queer.'"
4 Smith et al., "Being, Thinking and Doing 'Queer.'"

5 Smith et al., "Being, Thinking and Doing 'Queer,'" 1.
6 "Survey: Only One in Four Porn Performers Identify as 'Straight,'" GAYVN (April 2019), https://avn.com/business/articles/gay/survey-only-one-in-four-porn-performers-identify-as-straight-830960.html.
7 "Your 2024 Guide to Every State's Minimum Wage," (December 2023), www.paycom.com/resources/blog/minimum-wage-rate-by-state/.
8 Bickers et al., *Working It.*
9 John Creamer, Emily A. Shrider, Kalee Burns and Frances Chen, "Poverty in the United States: 2021," (September 2022), www.census.gov/content/dam/Census/library/publications/2022/demo/p60-277.pdf.
10 Matilda Bickers and Melissa Ditmore, "Introduction," in *Working It: Sex Workers on the Work of Sex*, ed. Matilda Bickers, peech breshers and Janis Luna (Oakland: PM Press, 2023), 10.
11 Bickers and Ditmore, "Introduction," 10.
12 Bickers and Ditmore, "Introduction," 10.
13 Allison Garvey, "The Digital Age: Giving Sex Work a New Meaning," *Journal of Feminist Scholarship*, Vol. 20, No. 20 (2022), 80–81, https://digitalcommons.uri.edu/cgi/viewcontent.cgi?article=1259&context=jfs.
14 Bickers and Ditmore, "Introduction," 10.
15 Chritina Tesoro, *Death to Whorephobia: A Guide to Sex Worker Affirming Care* (Self published E-book, 2020), 9.
16 Tesoro, *Death to Whorephobia*, 10.
17 Tesoro, *Death to Whorephobia*, 10.
18 Bickers and Ditmore, "Introduction," 5.
19 "What Is SESTA/FOSTA?" *Decriminalize Sex Work*, https://decriminalizesex.work.
20 Elizabeth Nolan Brown, "Appeals Court Panel Seems Skeptical That FOSTA Doesn't Violate the First Amendment," (January 2023), https://reason.com/2023/01/18/appeals-court-panel-seems-skeptical-that-fosta-doesnt-violate-the-first-amendment/.
21 "GBTQ Communities and Sex Work," *#SurvivorsAgainstSesta*, https://survivorsagainstsesta.org/lgbtq/.
22 Scott W. Stern, "Sex Workers Are an Important Part of the Stonewall Story, But Their Role Has Been Forgotten," *Time Magazine* (June 2019), https://time.com/5604224/stonewall-lgbt-sex-worker-history/.
23 Stern, "Sex Workers Are an Important Part of the Stonewall Story."
24 Stern, "Sex Workers Are an Important Part of the Stonewall Story."
25 Melina Chateauvert, *Sex Workers Unite: A History of the Movement from Stonewall to Slutwalk* (Boston, MA: Beacon Press, 2013).
26 Chateauvert, *Sex Workers Unite.*
27 Jessi Gan, "'Still at the Back of the Bus': Sylvia Rivera's Struggle," *Centro Journal*, Vol. 19, No. 1 (2007), 133.

28 Chateauvert, *Sex Workers Unite*.
29 Lou Chibbaro Jr., "LGBT Groups Cautious Over Decriminalizing Sex Work," *Washington Blade* (January 2016), www.washingtonblade.com/2016/01/13/lgbt-groups-cautious-over-decriminalizing-sex-work/.
30 Tesoro, *Death to Whorephobia*, 2.
31 "Homelessness and Housing Instability Among LGBTQ Youth," The Trevor Project Executive Summary (February 2022), www.thetrevorproject.org/research-briefs/homelessness-and-housing-instability-among-lgbtq-youth-feb-2022/.
32 Shauna Miller, "When Sex Work Means Survival for LGBTQ Youth," *Bloomberg* (February 2015), www.bloomberg.com/news/articles/2015-02-25/a-groundbreaking-new-study-reveals-how-lgbtq-teens-engage-in-survival-sex.
33 Miller, "When Sex Work Means Survival for LGBTQ Youth."
34 Miller, "When Sex Work Means Survival for LGBTQ Youth."
35 "Understanding Poverty in the LGBTQ+ Community," Human Right Campaign, www.hrc.org/resources/understanding-poverty-in-the-lgbtq-community.
36 "New Patterns of Poverty in the Lesbian, Gay and Bisexual Community," UCLA School of Law Williams Institute, https://williamsinstitute.law.ucla.edu/publications/lgb-patterns-of-poverty/.
37 "New Patterns of Poverty in the Lesbian, Gay and Bisexual Community."
38 "The Wage Gap Among LGBTQ+ Workers in the United States," Human Rights Campaign Website, www.hrc.org/resources/the-wage-gap-among-lgbtq-workers-in-the-united-states.
39 "Understanding Poverty in the LGBTQ+ Community."
40 "Understanding Poverty in the LGBTQ+ Community."
41 Tesoro, *Death to Whorephobia*, 67.
42 August Capiola, James D. Griffith, Brandon Balotti, Ryan Turner and Mark Sharrah, "Online Escorts: The Influence of Advertised Sexual Orientation," *Journal of Bisexuality*, Vol. 14, No. 2 (2014), 222–235.
43 Capiola et al., "Online Escorts."
44 Capiola et al., "Online Escorts," 231.
45 Capiola et al., "Online Escorts," 231.
46 Capiola et al., "Online Escorts."
47 Lindsy Blewett and Tuulia Law, "Sex Work and Allyship: Reflections on Femme-, Bi- and Whorephobia in Queer Communities," *Feral Feminisms*, No. 7 (2018), https://feralfeminisms.com/wp-content/uploads/2019/04/7-BlewettLaw.pdf.
48 Sinclair Sexsmith, "On Femme In/Visibility," *Sugarbush Chronicles* (November 2009), www.sugarbutch.net/2009/11/on-femme-invisibility/.
49 Blewett and Law, "Sex Work and Allyship."

50 Eva Pendelton, "Love for Sale: Queering Heterosexuality," in *Whores and Other Feminists*, ed. Jill Nagle (New York: Routledge, 1997), 76.

51 Kate Read, "Queering the Brothel: Identity Construction and Performance in Carson City, Nevada," *Sexualities*, Vol. 16, No. 3–4 (2013), 476.

52 "HIV and Sex Workers," *Be in the Know*, www.beintheknow.org/understanding-hiv-epidemic/community/hiv-and-sex-workers.

53 "HIV and Sex Workers."

54 "The Homophobia and Transphobia Experienced by LGBT Sex Workers," Briefing Paper: Global Network of Sex Work Projects, https://nswp.org/sites/default/files/bp_homophobia_transphobia_mpact_nswp_-_2018.pdf.

55 J.T. Parsons, J.A. Koken and D.S. Bimbi, "The Use of the Internet by Gay and Bisexual Male Escorts: Sex Workers as Sex Educators," *AIDS Care*, Vol. 16, No. 8 (2004).

56 "How Porn Can Misrepresent and Fetishize LGBTQ+ Individuals and Relationships," *Fight the New Drug*, https://fightthenewdrug.org/porn-can-misrepresent-and-fetishize-lgbtq-individuals-and-relationships/.

57 "How Porn Can Misrepresent and Fetishize."

58 Carolyn M. West, "Racism in Pornography: Why I Care and You Should too," *Fight the New Drug*, https://fightthenewdrug.org/why-does-the-porn-industry-get-away-with-racist-portrayals-of-black-people/.

59 "How Mainstream Porn Perpetuates Racist Stereotypes of Black Men," *Fight the New Drug*, https://fightthenewdrug.org/how-mainstream-porn-perpetuates-racist-stereotypes-of-black-men/.

60 Maya Khamla, "8 Depictions Mainstream Porn Shies Away from, But Shouldn't," *Bellesa*, www.bellesa.co/collective/456/8-depictions-mainstream-porn-shies-away-from-but-shouldnt.

61 West, "Racism in Pornography."

62 Sandra Song, "Meet the Couple Fighting Porn's Race Problem," *Paper* (November 2020), www.papermag.com/royal-fetish-porn-race-problem-2648632642.html#rebelltitem30.

63 Lisa Speidel and Micah Jones, "Introduction," in *The Edge of Sex: Navigating a Sexually Confusing Culture from the Margins* (New York: Routledge, 2019).

64 Jessamyn Bowling and Niki Fritz, "Binegative Myths in Pornography: An Examination of Sexual Behaviors and Aggression by Sexual Identity Categories," *Journal of Bisexuality*, Vol. 21, No. 2 (2021), 262–280.

65 Speidel and Jones, "Introduction," 16.

66 Speidel and Jones, "Introduction," 8.

67 Dustin Jones and Jonathan Franklin, "Not Just Florida: More Than a Dozen States Propose So-Called 'Don't Say Gay Bills'," *NPR* (April 2022), www.npr.org/2022/04/10/1091543359/15-states-dont-say-gay-anti-transgender-bills.

68 Mark McCormack and Liam Wignall, "Enjoyment, Exploration and Education: Understanding the Consumption of Pornography Among Young Men with Non-Exclusive Sexual Orientations," *Sociology*, Vol. 51, No. 5 (2016), 975–991.

69 Bowling and Fritz, "Binegative Myths in Pornography."

70 Tristan Taormino, Celine Parrenas Shimizu, Constance Penley and Mireille Miller-Young, in *The Feminist Porn Book: The Politics of Producing Pleasure* (New York: University of New York and The Feminist Press, 2013), 9–10.

71 Song, "Meet the Couple Fighting Porn's Race Problem."

72 Song, "Meet the Couple Fighting Porn's Race Problem."

73 Preeti Varathan, "Gay Men Now Earn More Than Straight Men in the US," *Quartz* (December 2017), https://qz.com/work/1147659/gay-men-now-earn-more-than-straight-men-in-the-us-according-to-a-vanderbilt-study.

74 "Lesbian, Gay, Bisexual and Transgender Persons and Socioeconomic Status," American Psychological Association Website, www.apa.org/pi/ses/resources/publications/lgbt.

75 "Lesbian, Gay, Bisexual and Transgender Persons and Socioeconomic Status."

76 Julia Corey, Marian Duggan and Aine Travers, "Risk and Protective Factors for Intimate Partner Violence Against Bisexual Victims: A Systemic Scoping Review," *Trauma, Violence and Abuse*, Vol. 24, No. 4 (2023), 2130.

77 Corey et al., "Risk and Protective Factors for Intimate Partner Violence," 2130.

8

RELATIONSHIPS

Dating, Marriage, Monogamy, and Consensual Non-monogamy

There are various challenges with biphobia and monosexism when navigating relationships as a bisexual person, including the delegitimization of bisexuality, being told it is just a phase or an excuse to be sex-crazed and promiscuous (which monosexual identities can be without needing an excuse if that is how they choose to live). Others believe that attraction to more than one gender means that bisexual people are automatically cheaters. Additionally, there are assumptions that bisexual people in different-gender relationships are straight, but when in a same-gender relationship they are gay or lesbian, which is a major factor in bi-erasure. Furthermore, cis-bi men face the stereotype of being super spreaders of HIV while cis-bi women often face "pervasive hyper-sexualization and objectification from straight men in an attempt to use their sexuality for their own entertainment and pleasure."[1] In reality, bisexual people are in various types of relationships, whether they are hooking up, dating, married, monogamous, or non-monogamous, just like anyone else. Bisexuality is, however, often perceived as a threat that results in potential relationship misunderstandings, miscommunications, erasure, violence, and the pressure to constantly explain, justify, and come out as bisexual.

For gender-diverse bisexual people there are extra layers of discrimination in the world of dating and relationships. One study conducted with multiple gender identities and sexual orientations concluded that 87.5% of the participants would not date a transgender person.[2] This is based in the politics of desirability and the perception of gender-diverse people as "undesirable" (see Chapter 3: "Gender-diverse Identities" for more details on this). Transphobia, biphobia, and monosexism not only impact the ability to meet people but can also increase vulnerability to violence. Moreover, racist

DOI: 10.4324/9781003242659-9

and ableist ideologies add even more layers of marginalization and potential harm. This chapter explores various intersecting identities for bisexual people in the world of dating apps, dating, and different relationship structures including marriage and monogamy/consensual non-monogamy.

Dating and Dating Apps

The popularity of dating apps and online dating has grown over the years, particularly during the Covid pandemic lockdowns.[3] Once viewed as socially unacceptable, the use of dating websites and apps has become normalized as a viable option to meet new people.[4] Some of the original websites still exist, like match.com and e-harmony, while apps like Grindr, Tinder, Hinge, Bumble, and HER, to name a few, are some of the most frequently visited. There are now over 1,500 dating apps and websites operating worldwide, and this market is projected to reach $9.2 billion by 2025.[5]

For many LGBTQ+ people, dating apps have evolved into a common resource for meeting new people, in fact, some research indicates that many in this population use dating apps more often than their heterosexual counterparts.[6] Dating apps allow for transparency, the ability to self-identify sexual orientation and gender identity, along with the usual listing of interests.[7] Disclosing identities ahead of time decreases the of number of times they might have to come out when dating in person and there can be some level of safety through the screening process. Apps specifically designed for LGBTQ+ people can also empower like-minded people to create queer community. Through "constructing app profiles, interpreting others' profiles, and managing app-based interactions," queer people can negotiate "their feelings of responsibility to and for other users, alongside other concerns such as personal security and exploring their own desires and interests."[8]

Of course, dating apps are not perfect and it can be a painful process to find a partner. The experience of potential discrimination is common, particularly when users select "preferences" such as "no femmes" or make body shaming comments like "you would be more attractive if you lost weight."[9] Within gay dating apps "masc 4 masc"—masculine men looking only for masculine men—is another profile descriptor that perpetuates the belief that only certain types of gay men are desirable.[10] There are also constant issues with racist "preferences" such as "no rice" or "not into Black guys," while the promotion of whiteness is set as the ideal and most desirable characteristic for a partner.[11] When people of color are desired, it can be hard to decipher if there is genuine interest or if they are being exoticized and fetishized. For example, young Black men who are gay are often stereotyped as being dominant tops with large penises.[12]

For bisexual people, there are unique challenges, as monosexuality dominates many dating apps that often do not allow users to pick a preference for more than one gender.[13] Although there is some improvement on some apps, there are still limitations in users actually understanding bisexuality. As Stodart et al. explain, "the bisexual community has an inside joke that describes what it's like to date as a bi person: People think it means double the options or double the fun, but it really just means double the rejection."[14] All of the stereotypes listed previously often lead to rejection as bisexual people are perceived as too problematic as a potential partner. On the flipside, predominately heteronormative apps may hypersexualize and fetishize bisexual people, particularly bisexual women, an issue that is addressed further in Chapter 4: "Cisgender Women and Femininities."

Another challenge is the numerous straight couples perusing dating apps to go "unicorn hunting" as they search for a bisexual woman with whom both partners in the couple could be involved.[15] According to Sky Lea Ross, it is estimated around 86% of bisexual people have experienced being sought after to join a threesome.[16] DeCapua's research corroborates this finding, as she writes, "Upon finding out a woman was bisexual, men expressed excitement and greater interest in the woman. They would immediately ask for threesomes, for the bisexual women to make out with another woman, or inquire about their sexual history."[17] Much of this kind of solicitation also involves "catfishing," where straight couples have the woman present herself as a single, queer person searching for another queer woman but then slowly introduce the male partner into the mix with the only intent of having a threesome.[18] This kind of deception can lead to coercive behaviors that are nonconsensual and is based in biphobic stereotypes that objectify bisexual women.[19] In addition, unicorn hunting is mired in heteronormativity, as the straight cisgender man's fantasy of being with two women motivates this behavior.[20]

Queer dating apps can also perpetuate biphobia, such as the belief that bisexual people are somehow tainted for having been in heterosexual relationships and are not "gold star lesbians" or "gold star gays." Some profiles reveal the preference of "gold star only," which may lead to rejection once it is discovered a bisexual person has been involved in straight presenting relationships before.[21] The concept of qualifying sexual identities with the term "gold star" not only perpetuates biphobia but also creates a divisiveness and competition within queer community, as if there is a right and wrong way to be gay or lesbian. This can ostracize the many queer people who do not have the ability or privilege of avoiding heterosexual interactions before being able to come out.[22] In addition, bias exists when bisexual people are perceived as just wanting to experiment[23] or are criticized for being "straight passing," which perpetuates the idea that they are not queer enough.[24]

As of 2024, there are two dating sites specifically designed for bisexual people: BiCupid and Bindr. Started in 2003, BiCupid claims to be the largest bisexual dating platform in the world. There are mixed reviews about BiCupid, particularly the monthly cost required to message people and the

rate at which straight couples are using the site to go unicorn hunting.[25] Bindr
was created in 2022 by Mary Richardson, a bisexual person who "didn't feel
like there was anywhere that was really fluid dating" or where she could be
herself.[26] HER, a dating app specifically designed by queer women for queer
women, has a fairly inviting special section on dating as a bisexual woman,
but it is not designed for bisexual men. OKCupid, Tinder, and Hinge have
all been credited as creating safter spaces for LGBTQ+ people, with more
options to choose from that have enabled more bisexual folks to meet.[27] Tinder in particular, which has a reputation for being a hookup app, is credited by bisexual writer Breena Kerr as a place to explore her sexuality. She
felt hookups allowed her to learn about herself, where other sites added the
pressure of figuring out a long-term relationship with someone.[28] Not every
bisexual person is going to want to approach their sexuality in this way, but
for many, dating apps can create a space for exploration, community, and
finding partners in a way that may be easier than in person.

Marriage

Similar to dating as a bisexual person, marriage can also be fraught with various challenges in a monosexist, biphobic world. The supposed permanence
of traditional marriage and having a life partner "until death do us part"
can often erase bisexual identity. As writer Mary Jayn Frisk discusses, "Once
I got married, my sexual orientation was masked by a list of other titles. I was
seen as a wife and mother, rather than a bi woman. During this time, it felt
like my bisexuality wasn't a big part of my identity anymore. I allowed myself
to ignore the bi part of my identity."[29] Because of the intended monogamy
behind traditional marriage, many bisexual people can feel like they are not
allowed to identify as bisexual anymore, particularly if their marriage is heterosexual.[30] This is a fairly common struggle, especially since approximately
88% of partnered bisexual people are with someone of a different gender.[31]
Robert Cohen maintains that this is likely due to a few factors, including the
fear of homophobia, downplaying their same gender attraction for safety,
and, with 90% of the population identifying as heterosexual, the LGB adults
make up a smaller pool of potential partners.[32]

Being married and bisexual is so common that "married bisexuality" is
listed in Etserberg's work as a typology of bisexuality. According to Esterberg, married bisexuality is "a form of bisexuality that exists when individuals who are (heterosexually) married take same-sex partners as lovers."[33]
There are other configurations of married bisexuality that do not entail
taking lovers, and two powerful and significant books written on this commonality are Carren Strock's *Married Women Who Love Women* and Robert Cohen's *Bisexual Married Men: Stories of Relationships, Acceptance, and
Authenticity.* (A discussion with Cohen is later in this chapter.) According to

Strock, there are various factors for women that may result in being married to men but still having feelings for women. When she first started exploring this topic—because of her own personal experience of being married to a man and falling in love with a woman—the women in her research described a lack of information about lesbianism, being socialized to believe lesbianism was a sickness or wrong and denial of their feelings for women as key factors.[34] In addition, there were many women who just simply believed they were heterosexual but, since getting married, fell in love with a woman, thus discovering their bisexuality.[35]

Robert Cohen's book delves into these realities for married men who face similar challenges. According to Cohen's research, while 33% of bisexual women are out, only 12% of bisexual men are.[36] Cohen explains that many men are partnered in straight passing marriages and may be hiding their bisexuality for various reasons, but this can take a toll and may negatively impact these marriages.[37] As Cohen contends, "Bisexual men who are married to women are thus one of the largest but most invisible queer groups in this country. Their experience is uniquely challenging and joyful, but it is barely represented and often erased as 'not queer enough.'"[38] Regardless of why someone is experiencing married bisexuality, both Strock and Cohen emphasize the importance of examining this further and creating a space for married bisexual people to explore the realities of their identities and situation.

Monogamy vs. Consensual Non-monogamy

Bisexual people are often stereotyped as being promiscuous cheaters who are not able to be monogamous. Back in 1991, Lenore Norrgard wrote a chapter in the book *Bi Any Other Name* entitled "Can Bisexuals Be Monogamous?"[39] Her answer was yes, just like monosexual people, but this question continues to be asked today. Just like some monosexual people, however, bisexual people can also practice *consensual non-monogamy* defined as "an umbrella term for relationships in which all partners give explicit consent to engage in romantic, intimate, and/or sexual relationships with multiple people. These are consensual relationships, not to be confused with infidelity."[40] This includes a variety of possible formats for relationships, such as *polyamory*—literally defined as "multiple loves"—swinging, or open relationships.

Similar to bisexuality, non-monogamy is a centuries old practice that spans the globe and both defy dominant western cultural norms about sexuality, relationships, and marriage. Historically, multiple indigenous communities in America had same gender-loving and non-monogamous relationship structures that were "built on mutual respect and emotional bonds, reflecting a more fluid understanding of love and partnership."[41] The settler mindset considered these deviant behaviors, and compulsory monogamy became part of the "state-sanctioned one-on-one lifelong marriage by the settler colonial state."[42] Indigenous professor and researcher Kim Tall-bear explains that the "imposition of heteronormative settler sexuality and family structure"[43] was enforced by dividing indigenous land into western family units: a male head of the household, who could get 80 acres if he had a wife and 40 acres for each child.[44] Tallbear argues that the critique of non-monogamy lacks an understanding of this racist history or the role the church, state, and science played to maintain this settler structure. This does not just impact indigenous communities but harms all of us by reinforcing heteropatriarchal, racist ideals as the norm and all others as deviant.[45]

Today the battle continues between those maintaining "traditional" family values and those embracing the legitimacy of non-monogamy. According to Christopher Gleason, despite the controversy, the last two decades have seen multiple media outlets "bestowing favorable attention on the lifestyle, further attesting to its growing popularity."[46] Academic analysis of non-monogamy has flourished, and in 2016 the American Psychological Association created a task force to conduct research and training "that would lead to increased awareness and acceptance of consensually non-monogamous lifestyles."[47] Despite these efforts, the power of the social investment in compulsory monogamy is similar to the investment in monosexuality, and those who deviate can be ostracized.

An example of this is described by Kenji Yoshino, who argues that gay, lesbian, and straight people can define themselves in opposition to bisexual people through the institution of monogamy.[48] Given that many straight people have historically associated the spread of HIV with gay men's promiscuity, monogamy has been heralded as the best way to avoid disease. In addition, gay men have had to fight stereotypes about promiscuity, and monogamy can be particularly important as a norm to practice in order to be accepted into "mainstream" society. Bisexual people are perceived as a threat to monogamy, even when in monogamous relationships, because their *potential* for attraction to another gender is associated with non-monogamy. Thus, Yoshino asserts, many straight and queer monosexuals have a vested interest in the erasure of bisexuality. Monosexism intersects with compulsory monogamy as social constructs that allow for the demonizing of both non-monogamy and bisexuality.[49]

Despite Yoshino's analysis, there are plenty of queer people that feel consensual non-monogamy is an acceptable practice. For example, the Pew Research Center found that lesbian, gay, or bisexual adults "are far more likely than straight adults to say open marriages are acceptable (75% vs. 29%)."[50] Clearly there are many different ways for people to have relationships, regardless of sexual orientation, but there needs to be a better understanding of how bisexuality does not actually threaten monogamy. The following personal narratives and conversations create an opportunity to witness the beauty of these variations in relationships while revealing unique challenges for bisexual people. Yaiza discusses her experiences dating as a Latina cis-bi woman; Jazmin writes about not being a unicorn for others to chase; Hilary addresses her own challenges of the dating world; and the last two pieces are conversations first with Marissa and then Rob about being married and exploring polyamory.

A Conversation About Dating with Yaiza

L:

Tell me a little bit about your experiences dating.

Y:

It is interesting. I can pass as straight in certain relationships, but keep in mind when I say "pass as straight," I think that being in relationships with cismen as a bisexual person carries a whole other weight. There are other pressures that are not present if both people are straight in the relationship. So, either way it's never going to be non-oppressive or "normal," but to the world you're seen as in a straight relationship.

Dating a straight man as a bisexual person is one of the most difficult things. First is the question of when do I tell them? Do I just slip it out in a first date or wait? Do I have an obligation to tell them? I just kind of say it whenever it feels like the right time. But there's always this fear. What if I'm out with this person and then I tell them that I'm bisexual and then they like get violent because they're homophobic. It's happened to me before where I'm about to go on a date with someone and I'm like, by the way, I'm bi and then they cancel the date. That is an added layer that straight women don't have to deal with.

There is also the issue of nationality when it comes to dating. I think I've definitely noticed that white American people are more okay with dating women who are bisexual. I always get the "we should have a threesome" question, but whenever I've dated men from other nationalities it's different. I'm Latina, and when I have dated any other nationality that is not white American, there's always that kind of pause and they're like, *oh, that's hot*. I feel like throughout the relationship they just label me as a hookup or a short-term thing because who could ever marry someone who's bisexual? This is not something that their families will accept, even though their families would never have to know. I think that the cultural dynamics very much get in the way of being able to date and also present myself as bisexual when in a relationship.

I do enjoy the funny moments where like, we're watching a movie and they say, "oh my gosh, she's so hot." And I'm just like, "I know!" And they always say "What?" Those aspects are kind of entertaining. I feel like there's this backlash from both ends. When you're dating a straight man, it's translated as a straight relationship and then when you're dating a woman there is the whole aspect of people giving you weird looks. It's just kind of a catch 22.

L:
Have you dated a straight cis man before who was cool with it all?

Y:
No, honestly, not really. I don't think I've ever dated a straight guy who has not asked me about a threesome or not put me in the category of "I couldn't marry you because you're bisexual."

L:
Is there any perception of you being hypersexual as far as the intersection of being both bisexual and Latina?

Y:
As a Latina, for sure. I feel like being bisexual and Latina is just very fetishized among guys, which is also very annoying. I know that the second that guys learn that I'm Latina they just look at me and think *spicy*. Then add the bisexual aspect and they're like, you're extra spicy. I'm put into this category where I'm expected to be this image of what a bisexual Latina is supposed to be like.

That gets in the way of them actually getting to know me as a person, because they have this fetish in their head. It's not always obvious, but it becomes apparent when I'm talking to them and they make certain comments. I remember the last guy that I dated we were talking about something like a queer issue that was coming up in the news. I was giving him a background of the community. And he said, "but you're not even that gay." What does that even mean? I think that inevitably when you talk to a person about your sexuality and your ethnic background, they're just going to attach stereotypes regardless of what you do.

I think there is a lot of societal pressures of how straight men are taught to think and view the world. Especially from different cultures. But at the same time, it's just the culture that I come from. Deeply homophobic and deeply colorist and very sexist. But that doesn't mean that I haven't learned to think differently or I haven't taken the initiative to educate myself and to learn how to be inclusive or how to think about the world in a different way.

L:
You've mentioned your own culture; can you tell me a little bit about that?

Y:
I was born in Cuba and then I moved to Spain when I was about five or six. Then I moved to the U.S. when I was a preteen.

L:
Before coming to this country, were you already thinking about your sexuality?

Y:
No. The assumption when I was growing up was specifically that I had to like guys who were tall, blonde, and had blue eyes. I didn't have interest in dating, I was like 12. So, my crushes at the time were like the main character on the American Dragon cartoon

and maybe the Jonas Brothers. I think I was 14 when I started to think about dating. I didn't even know that bisexuality was a thing. I was attracted to men therefore I was straight. I knew there were gay people but I didn't know that there was a whole other spectrum.

My first boyfriend was actually a Black guy and that created havoc among my family. We held hands a total of like three times and it was a huge deal. It got me thinking about dating dynamics and what I was allowed to do. I wanted to date whoever I wanted, but just because I was dating someone didn't mean that my family could know. That specifically started with the ethnicity or race of the people that I dated.

When I was 16, I met this girl at school and we were really close friends and it was one of those things where I liked her, but I liked her in like a different way. We ended up becoming best friends. At the time I was dating someone, and we broke up and she invited me to a stay over with her family because I was so sad. That night we ended up making out and hooking up. I was very happy with what I experienced, but I was also extremely confused. I had no idea what had just happened. I was like, am I gay now? I still liked guys but I also liked this person very much. Our response to that was like this never happened, let's move on. There were so many things happening at the time with school and family that I couldn't add something else. And then in my senior year, I decided to ask one of my friends who was a girl to homecoming, and I did it in a very cheesy way. She was in theater, so I projected the question on the theater screen when they were practicing. I brought her flowers, the whole thing. I just felt like maybe I should follow my instincts. I was going to college the next year. No one cares. Let me just see what happens.

She said yes! I knew that she identified as queer, so I was like, I don't know what this is, but let me see what happens. We went to homecoming and I tried to tell this to my family. I told them that I asked Sophia to homecoming and my family said, oh as friends. I was like, oh, no, no. But no matter how much I insisted, they were just like, oh, it's friends. We went and it was great. We ended up not dating and were just friends, but it was great.

And then when I was in college, I actually started exploring and doing more reading on bisexuality. It also took me a while to realize that I had lost my virginity to a girl, because I think that in my head, virginity was always penetrative sex with a man. But I lost my virginity with her! One time I was thinking about it, it was actually when I took one of your classes, and it is so interesting because I think that things would have been so much different if I had just known and if people had talked about it. If it was more accepted. My family still doesn't know that I'm not straight.

L:

What makes that difficult to tell your family?

Y:

I think that queerness within Cuban society is one of those things where they're not going to kick you out of the house. They're not going to disown you, but they're definitely going to look at you a little bit differently. I definitely think that has added to who I have dated. Whenever I date a straight man, it's kind of easier on my end. If it gets serious, I won't have to deal with my family. It's just a straight guy. Like whatever. They'd definitely rather I be with someone who's white for sure.

L:

What about someone who is Latino?

Y:

As long as they're white. Yes.

L:

That's part of the colorism that you mentioned?

Y:

Yeah, for sure. Whenever I date women, the first thing that crosses my mind is like, oh fuck, if this gets serious, it's going to be a huge deal. Unintentionally over the years, that has caused me to keep things more casual with women just because of that risk of messing up my family dynamics. I fully realized that having that ability to kind of mask my sexuality with my family is a privilege that other queer people don't have. But I think that even as it is a privilege, it also adds so much pressure. I think that other people from the queer community, you come out, that's kind of the one path for you. But with me, there's just so many different variables. If I come out, then I have to deal with all of this, but if I don't come out I can still, live kind of "normally," but then my family is never really going to know who I am. I think it's very complicated.

L:

That sounds really hard.

Y:

Yeah. It kind of feels like being in an in between. It's interesting because I feel like being Latina and having moved around so much, I'm already in an in between when it comes to cultural identity. Cubans don't think I'm Cuban, Spanish people don't think I'm Spanish, and Americans don't think I'm American. I'm just kind of like in limbo with that. I think sexuality adds that extra layer of being in limbo.

I Am Not a Unicorn, I Am a Lioness by Jazmin Bolan-Williams

We can all agree that this age of dating is an . . . interesting one. But before we get into that I want to bring to light the utter fear I felt as someone with very little experience talking with women in an "interested in a relationship" kind of way. I have only dated men, and while I am still not "a master" at the art of flirting, I can hold my own, but I have ZERO experience flirting with women. So, I was not really sure what to expect when I did decide to try online dating. Most of us don't really go out to meet people (especially since the Plague Times) so we have to rely on online dating, queer or otherwise, but when you are queer online dating comes with its own quirks. Case in point: the ever elusive *unicorn*.

I had heard this term thrown around in regards to finding that "perfect" woman and never really gave it much thought until I decided to branch out of my comfort zone and explore dating women. Then I saw that term A LOT! Every other posting was of a woman in a committed relationship with a man that was looking for another woman to either be "just a girlfriend for me" or "our unicorn" meaning a third for their relationship. The word "unicorn" in this context is used because finding someone like this is so rare, like a mythical creature. It was so prevalent that I felt like I was some lamb offering myself to the best butcher. It was overwhelming the number of women and couples that had reached out to me asking me "how open minded I was" or "would I be ok if her boyfriend could at least watch" etc. I was so turned off and disheartened from that experience that I deleted all my profiles. While I have been a third in a short-lived love affair, that was not what I wanted and I had stated as much on my profiles that I was not interested in being in a poly relationship.

That is when I learned that me just stating I was Bi/Pan was some people's fetish. I never really thought about it that way till I heard other queer people talk about their experiences with dating. Some had stories of dating men who thought that threesomes were on the table. Others dated women who omitted that they were in a committed relationship with a man until later when the couple would suggest having a threesome. I learned that this was a stereotype that Bi/Pan folk are only interested in hook ups and not committed relationships and that we are promiscuous and more likely to be willing to do things with other people. It negates our sexuality and strips us of our relationship beliefs and reduces us to just a fetish and not actual people! It makes us a caricature of that ever elusive "unicorn." I am not a unicorn; I am a lioness—fierce, loyal, and willing to put in the work to navigate my love life and to be devoted to one partner at a time—and I deserve more than just to be someone's "bi/pan poly fantasy girl."

A Conversation About Dating with Hillary Duah

LISA:
Can you tell me a little bit about your journey with bisexuality?

HILLARY:
In high school it was not a thought that crossed my mind whatsoever. I entered a heterosexual relationship for a pretty long time—about four years. Generally speaking, thoughts of being attracted to women didn't really arise up until maybe about freshman year of college. Nothing was really acted upon.

I kind of just brushed it off—I just never really thought much of it. Then I kind of recognized it as something that grew over time. At first it was probably a negligible feeling or just a passing thought; then they came more frequently and more intense.

Once I did have my first experience to actually give it a shot and talk to a girl in a *more than friends* way, that kind of confirmed that for me. Because prior to that point it was only thoughts and curiosities.

L:

Were you still involved with the boyfriend from high school?

H:

Yeah. I had been having those curiosities and so after a little while it was something that was discussed and he was open to me exploring that side of myself. He was very much supportive. It took a lot of conversation and a lot of honesty. Obviously in any relationship that's required, especially with a topic that's sensitive like this. His only concerns were more from a jealousy standpoint and when you're in a monogamous relationship, you want your partner to be faithful to you. So that was just something that had to be discussed. But with him, it was never necessarily a "oh, that's so hot kind of thing." Although it may have been a subliminal *plus* that probably was what helped it along, but primarily, he was interested in my self-discovery.

It wasn't anything that was ever going to occur while we were together. But since that relationship has ended and I've put myself in context with different kinds of guys, I kind of have to be very discerning or be very selective as to whom I disclose that I also am attracted to women. Because generally the response is going to be something superficial. Like, oh, well *you must want a threesome*, or, oh, *well that's hot, I would love to see that*.

L:

Do you feel like you've faced bias or bi-erasure at all?

H:

I can definitely recount several experiences in which
people will just assume it's a phase. I think that
there's a different dynamic between a bi male and a
bi woman. Being a bi woman, there is this automatic
assumption that all girls go through this exploratory phase and it turns out that's just not their
thing. If I was with my ex who was a male, a comment
might be like, "well are you straight now? Or do you
really like women since you're with a man?"

It's ignoring the fact that the definition of being
bisexual is to be attracted to more than one gender. I definitely have experienced those comments of
oh, well you're straight now if I'm talking to a
guy. Or *are you fully lesbian now*? if I'm talking
to a girl. There's this "one or the other mentality" that lots of people have, which I never really
understood. There's just this assumption that eventually I'm going to move out of this phase and
be straight again. It just mitigates the identity
itself by saying that it's not going be permanent.
And then I would say also within the LGBTQ+ community, there's this lack of respect for bisexual
women in which the common attitude is that they
don't really belong in the community. There's this
exclusion from that community because you're not
queer enough.

L:

Is it different to talk to straight people about
bisexuality?

H:

If I'm talking to a woman and just having a conversation, the response is generally positive. Like,
"oh, that's awesome for you. It's great that you
can be comfortable with it. It's great that you can
have new experiences," and it's generally almost a
feminist perspective of, "this is very positive,
I'm happy for you." From a guy's perspective, it's
almost always physical. It's notable to me because
learning more about yourself as a person, all of the
deeper conclusions don't really come to light when

having a conversation with a guy about it. They're just kind of like, "Oh, well then have you had a threesome?" Or something very superficial and physical. Now, if it's a good friend, I think they might have a response that mirrors more of what I would get from probably any woman.

L:
What has dating been like?

H:
There are two different types of relationships for me if I am involved with a guy or a girl. Generally, a relationship with a girl is more personable, intimate, and more connection on an emotional level, whereas those things may exist with dating a guy, but there's a lot of physical aspects involved as well, in a more pronounced way than it would be with a woman. So dating, I just take different approaches.

In the context of dating a man, I think that the disclosure of being bisexual, there can be a positive reaction just because I think that it's immediately internalized how they can benefit from the situation or how they can gain pleasure from the situation. Unless it's a little more involved, I'd say the little aspects of not wanting to share your partner with anyone else or feeling insecure or jealous about anything else kind of come into play there.

Hypersexualization of bisexual women in the media is training boys from a young age to think that this is the ultimate dream you can achieve. . . . I'm sure in porn the most popular category is FFM [two females and a male]. That's just so applauded that they're kind of taught that if you're having sex with two females, they are having sex with you and they wouldn't want to be having sex with each other. The focus is always on the man. I think that media has played a big role in not helping guys realize that there is a world outside of them where, for example, these two women might also be interested in each other.

L:

They aren't learning that women's pleasure matters!

H:

Exactly!

A Conversation About Marriage and Polyamory with Marissa Conniff

LISA:

Tell me a little bit about discovering your bisexuality.

MARISSA:

It's one of those things where I always knew, but I have just started to claim it. I knew I was bi at a young age when most of my friends were googly-eyed after Jack on *Titanic*, I was just as excited for Rose as I was Jack. I learned to cover up my attraction to women, while biphobia reinforced my unintentional tactic to stay closeted. I heard things like, "Being bisexual is just a pathway to being gay" or "All women experiment in college," or "Being bi is just being greedy." I never thought my attraction to women was a big deal because I thought everyone felt that way. But the ultimate reason that it took me so long to come out and to fully own my bisexuality was a lack of emotional security. I never felt safe to be openly bi. Being queer never felt like an option for me, and I leaned on my attraction to men to protect myself from being hated for my queerness. But as I have gotten older and have built a loving family for myself, I have felt safer to be who I am.

Being married to a man, it's complicated how to own being bi. I consider coming out to my husband as the first step for truly owning being bi. My husband has shown me many times that he's an accepting person who loves me. I know I can be myself. Ironically, my queerness came out after we were married. I feel really secure and comfortable in my life, which has allowed me to be myself, queerness included. There was a period of time where I felt like there's no point in coming out because I am married. But one year I promised myself I was going to come out to my husband and best friend during Pride month. One day we're sitting at the table eating lunch while our son's playing in the other room. Bisexuality or queerness just kind of came up in conversation. And I said, "That's me too." I could tell that he was kind of like, wait a minute, what is she saying? And then he said, "I mean, I've always kind of considered you bi." We kept talking about it after that. That was pretty much the gist of that conversation. Just like, okay. Cool. Hooray!

L:

Once you told him, what did you feel like was the next step?

M:

He told me he understood if I wanted to try to date women and was open to it. There had been a consensual non-monogamous moment in the past while we were dating. I met some girl while I was out of town; everything was open and honest. I didn't have a great experience with her, so it made me feel like maybe I wasn't bi. When I officially came out to my husband years later, he said, "I know that you didn't get to be this way when you were younger so you should explore this side of yourself if you want to." My relatives were abusive and conservative, and it wasn't on the list of my priorities to live openly queer. It just wasn't that important to me, when my safety was in question. I think too, if you're bi, you can more easily hide those feelings and live a non-fully authentic life. I enjoy hetero relationships, obviously, I'm in love with a man. It was easy to ignore that side of myself. My husband is my confidant and he knows about my childhood and knows I am evolving as I am healing.

I got a Bumble account and started talking to a lot of women who were actually really similar to me. Bisexual women who were married to men, looking for a woman to be with. And it wasn't all threesome stuff. It was wanting to be with women without their husband. This was during Covid, and it was interesting because everybody was looking to connect through their phones. Everybody was getting very introspective. Everything was changing. I deactivated my Bumble account at some point, but once Covid lockdowns started coming to an end, I went on Bumble again and there really weren't as many people out there, especially in the same situation as me.

L:

It's really interesting to think about there being so many more married women using Bumble at that time. What was going on?

M:

It didn't seem like people were saying "Covid is making me crazy, so I'm getting on Bumble." I think it was more that all of us were just trying to use our phones in any way we could to connect with people. A lot of people at that time went through a lot of introspection. So, a bunch of women started owning that they were queer, bi, or pan and had only their phones as a way to express it.

L:

It basically created a safe space to explore it.

M:

Yes, and I am truly grateful I was able to fully explore this side of myself. But ultimately, I remembered how hard it is to date people. I did not have many wonderful experiences with the women I met at this point in my life, so I just kind of got tired of it. It was becoming more of a distraction at that point, trying to date. And we also realized that being actively non-monogamous is more complicated than we thought. It did not seem fair that I was going out on dates with new people and my husband was not. We couldn't figure out a fair dynamic that worked for us.

L:

How do you feel about him seeing other women?

M:

We did explore it. It never came to fruition, but he was talking to women and stuff, but it also seemed like the women were way less interested in being with a married man. It seemed like I had an easier time finding women who wanted the same things I wanted.

We had jumped right into it and then we pulled back and we were like, you know what? This is complicated. It took me time to realize if I'm with people who don't have a problem with it, then other people's opinions don't matter. So, I did start seeing women again, but then once my son was diagnosed with autism, that shook everything up. You are kind of reborn in a way as a parent once you learn that. I didn't know how seeing women fit into my life anymore. I would go on a date and I was just thinking about my kid. I was so raw and just not in a place to be seeing people. So, in terms of non-monogamy, our door is always just a little open. If that opportunity comes up, then let's explore. And the same goes for my husband with women.

I'm tired at the end of the day with taking care of my son and all that stuff. And I'm focused on my music a lot right now. I'd honestly rather work on gigs than go on dates. That just gives me more right now. And I have reached a new level of understanding for myself that I do not need to be dating women to be bi. There are so many ways I can express my bi-ness that bring me joy.

L:

What do you think of the common narrative for a lot of folks questioning, "Am I bi enough?"

M:

The last gal I went on a date with said to me, "We don't have to prove our queerness to each other. Let's not let that pressure us into getting physical with each other. Rather, let's just let things unfold naturally." That was so sweet and it really took the pressure off. There is some anxiety in our community of wanting to prove queerness. And when she said that to me too, I was wondering, am I doing that? I hadn't even considered it. Once she said

that I just started looking at a lot of things differently regarding my queerness. I started telling
myself that I am bi, that's enough. I don't have to
have a girlfriend for people to believe me.

I understand why people are protective on what is
"queer enough" due to the challenges queer people
have faced throughout history and to this day. It can
be a risk to live openly. As a woman who is married
to a man, I do not have to openly struggle that way.

I'm actually more of the textbook pansexual, but
I enjoy saying I'm bi because I didn't know what
pansexual was growing up. Bi was the only word
I had to describe the way I have always felt. And
then pansexual came and was like, oh, I guess I can
claim that too. But then I get joy out of saying
I am bi because that's the label I have always
wanted to claim. What I've even really come to
learn about being bi is that there is this sort of
heteronormative projection onto that word because
you're then assuming that what it means is that I'm
attracted to men and women, but what it means is
that I'm attracted to my gender and all other genders. So, there's the "bi." I'm interested in the
same gender as myself and I'm interested in other
genders.

L:

I haven't heard it described that way because we're
so focused on it being separate genders. That is
very cool.

M:

I think that made me forever comfortable with saying I am bi. It does make sense that people are
protective, especially when we're talking about the
gender binary, but it's unfair to assume bi people
are harmful to gender freedom.

A Conversation About Marriage and Polyamory with Robert Brooks Cohen

LISA:
How do you make sense of non-monogamy and marriage?

ROB:

I almost never felt like I had to make sense of non-monogamy because monogamy never really made sense to me. I always felt like I was struggling to make sense of monogamy. Why is that so great? And why does everyone want that? And also, why does everyone pretend that that's what's happening? Because actually most people are non-monogamous.

They're either exploring multiple relationships to find someone to marry or they're married and they cheat. So many people cheat and divorce over the cheating, and when I learned the statistics of that, it's just so many. The idea of only being sexually intimate with one person forever just felt to me like setting yourself up for failure. I personally just never desired that. Sex seems very important to me in a relationship and foundational. I mean, there are asexual people, but I feel like it's something very important within a relationship. I also don't think it's this sacred thing that can only be shared by life partners. It's something nice to share with other people. It's like playing tennis. Why can't I have multiple tennis partners? You know, my game changes based on who I'm playing and I learn how to be a better player myself by playing lots of different people. And then when I play tennis with my primary partner, we have a better match.

When I think back to why I think like this, it goes back to my family and sister who's adopted. They adopted my sister when I was 11 years old and she was 18 months old. We went to Hungary and adopted her, and when my parents first brought that up to me as a 10- or 11-year-old, I didn't like that idea, because I'd been an only child for ten years. I liked it, and I got upset when they told me they wanted to do that. The way they explained it to me was that their love wouldn't be divided between me and another child, their love would grow to include another family member. And that mine would, too, and I would see that. That made sense to me, and it was what helped me get over the initial shock. It was exactly what happened. I never thought about that with non-monogamy until years later, but it

just made sense to me that why does love for one
person affect your love for another person?

L:
We're so invested in monogamy it can be so difficult
to understand.

R:
It's so pervasive, the pressure to be monogamous.
It's this cultural ideal that everyone seemingly
desires, and people who are non-monogamous usually
keep it hidden, to avoid the stigma. It's just this
self-fulfilling cycle of invisibility and pretending.

L:
Do you feel like there's an intersection with bisexuality and polyamory when it comes to invisibility?

R:
Yeah. It's definitely misunderstood in a similar
way. I know people who will be out as bi but not
out as non-monogamous because of the questions or
assumptions they'll get. It's similarly invisible
and stigmatized, and there is a lot of crossover
between non-monogamy and the bi community. People
stereotype bi people as needing to be with more than
one gender all the time to be satisfied, which is
not true.
  Both heterosexuality and monogamy are these cultural defaults. It's the only thing we're taught as
what's acceptable. If you're a person who thinks
outside the box on one of those two things, and it
works for you, then you're more likely to think
outside the box on the other one, too. I've seen
bi people come out and then start to realize, oh,
maybe non-monogamy is also for me. You see non-monogamous people who are straight, like swingers or
people who are open but not fully poly and a lot
of them start to think about sexual fluidity, too,
because they're already not conforming to monogamy.
I understand the crossover, but they shouldn't be
conflated. There's a stereotype that all bi people
are non-monogamous but actually, statistics show

that bi people are still mostly monogamous, just slightly more non-monogamous than straight people.

L:

There's also the stereotype that bisexual people want to have sex with lots of different people, or they're greedy, so they are into non-monogamy or they're going to be cheating.

R:

I do think bi people are more likely to be non-monogamous, but I also think they're less likely to cheat. Both of those things force you to be more open and vulnerable with your partner. Straight people are the ones who may get used to hiding things about themselves and being afraid to talk about stuff with their partner. Whereas if you're non-monogamous and you talk about that with your partner, there's no cheating whatsoever. There can be disagreements and people getting upset or jealous or things you have to work through, but cheating is lying. Non-monogamy is not cheating. Cheating is non-monogamy and lying about it. And many queer, non-monogamous people—they're just more likely to be open about it and with someone who's okay with that.

L:

I find it interesting when I teach about polyamory the reaction often is, "I just would get too jealous." We can all get jealous no matter what kind of relationship.

R:

Right. Non-monogamy actually forces you to talk about jealousy and think through those feelings, whereas monogamy you're pretending to avoid jealousy or a certain type of explicit jealousy. That doesn't mean it's never going to come up or you can't be jealous of other things about your partner or other things they're doing that aren't sex, there are really so many ways to be jealous. But then if you're in this monogamous structure, it can just hide that fact and obscure it so you don't talk about it.

I actually think non-monogamy forces stronger relationships to develop. Or it can force a breakup. But if two people aren't right for each other, better for that to come to a head and figure it out, rather than be in this perceived safety of monogamy, but actually you're just ignoring the issues. So non-monogamy forces you to talk about things and ultimately strengthens the relationship.

L:

There's often this idea that something must be wrong with your relationship and that you're opening it, to solve a problem. People often think there is a deficit. Why can't it be additive? We're so invested in monogamy that we go to something must be wrong.

R:

Right. It's just so common and accepted that monogamy is the way to be that it's hard for people to think about why that is. Sex is a fun, pleasurable thing. Why not do it with more people if you're all consenting and talking about it? I do think some people try it to solve issues in their marriage, and that usually doesn't work out well. And then that's all everyone sees and so they think it always fails. But when both people are interested in it, it can absolutely work. I think people have this perception about marriage: your spouse should be everything for you in terms of your love and sex life. We don't think like that in any other area of our lives besides marriage. We don't put all that pressure on one relationship or one person. How could one person be everything for another person?

They should take care of themselves first. If you can't love yourself, how are you going to love somebody else? As RuPaul always says: Your first priority should be to yourself, and then you can give a lot to your partner. But the idea that your needs and what they can offer line up a hundred percent is just impossible. It's also not just about sexual needs but about so much pressure put on a partner to fulfill all your needs and vice versa. I think that's way too much pressure for a marriage forever. In addition to sex, there's raising kids and affording a home, childcare, pet care, all these other life things that in human history has not always happened under one roof with a nuclear family.

L:
When did you realize that you were poly?

R:
I actually think it's similar to bisexuality where it's a separate spectrum. There's a monogamously oriented to poly-oriented spectrum, and we're all somewhere on it, and it can be fluid over time, over our lives. But wherever you are on it, you still get to choose how you identify. I think I've always been more poly oriented, but for a long time I didn't realize that because I was locked into a binary and I assumed I was straight and monogamous. I didn't have enough experience to step out of those boxes. But looking back, in my twenties, I had a lot of short relationships with women. I was often dating multiple women at a time, which so many people I know do that who are monogamous. And that's just playing the field. But then I also had a few more serious relationships, but none of them lasted very long. I do wonder if that's partially because I didn't really want monogamy, but I couldn't fully express that or open up about that.

I think coming out as bi helped me feel comfortable about coming out as poly and talking about that. I'm already stepping out of this box in one way, so I might as well think about this and talk about that, too. It kind of happened simultaneously. It's like once you're willing to step outside the box and identify as a queer minority group, you get the courage to do that, then you start to examine other aspects of sexuality and other spectrums that are related.

L:
When you met your partner were you both poly already?

R:
I don't know if at the time I called myself poly, but I definitely was talking about non-monogamy and

didn't want to be exclusive when we were dating. Then there was a time my partner had identified as comfortable with non-monogamy, but also not poly, and she wanted to try monogamy for a short time, so we kind of went in and out of it. Then the pandemic made us go back to monogamous. Something I'm still trying to figure out is: Where are we both on this spectrum? Because I think we're both poly, but maybe in slightly different ways. So, we're still kind of figuring that out and navigating it. Since we've been vaccinated, we've been very open and exploring other relationships and I think it's been good for both of us. In many ways it has strengthened our relationship and helped us. Sometimes when she's with other partners, it makes me want, desire, and appreciate her more. Because someone else is appreciating her, and it reminds me why I was so attracted to her in the first place.

We're four years into a relationship. . . . Let's say, we're fighting about something. But then she goes on a date with a new person and I almost see her through their eyes again. And I like talking about what did they do and talk about, and how did she feel about it?

I like hearing what she did and did not like about this guy. Sometimes she'll come home and say, it was fun and I liked this, but the guy wasn't as something as you or wasn't as good at this as you . . . I like knowing that, too. It helps me know myself better, through someone else's eyes. I also feel like people are afraid of non-monogamy because it's a threat to the partnership. What if you meet someone who you like better and you want to be with and you want to break up or divorce. But that happens in monogamy too! I feel like if that happened, I would be really sad, especially if it's not what I wanted at the time, and it was my partner's and not my decision. But I don't want to be in a monogamous relationship where my partner wishes she could be with someone else but can't because we're married. The lies and the delusions of that are a lot worse than breaking up.

My partner and I, we're primary partners now. We've acknowledged that could change and we may not be primary partners forever, but because we've talked about that, we've also talked about how we want to be in each other's lives forever. And I feel pretty clear about that. I can't think of anything that would make me never want to see my partner again, even if we weren't primary partners. I feel that's this real deep special connection that is hard to get out of monogamy.

Notes

1 Samantha R. DeCapua, "Bisexual Women's Experiences with Binegativity in Romantic Relationships," *Journal of Bisexuality*, Vol. 17, No. 4 (2017), 468.
2 Karen Blair and Rhea Ashley Hoskin, "Transgender Exclusion from the World of Dating: Patterns of Acceptance and Rejection of Hypothetical Trans Dating Partners as a Function of Sexual and Gender Identity," *Journal of Social and Personal Relationships*, Vol. 36, No. 7 (2018), 2074–2095.
3 Fortune Editors, "Activity on Dating Apps Has Surged During the Pandemic," (February 2021), https://fortune.com/2021/02/12/covid-pandemic-online-dating-apps-usage-tinder-okcupid-bumble-meet-group/.
4 Aaron Smith and Monica Anderson, "5 Facts About Online Dating," Pew Research Center (February 2016), https://internet.psych.wisc.edu/wp-content/uploads/532-Master/532-UnitPages/Unit-06/Smith_Pew_OnlineDating_2016a.pdf.
5 Gosia Szaniawska-Schiavo, "Love in the Age of AI Dating Apps," (March 2024), www.tidio.com/blog/ai-dating-apps/.
6 Ryan M. Wade and Matthew M. Pear, "A Good App Is Hard to Find: Examining Differences in Racialized Sexual Discrimination Across Online Intimate Partner-Seeking Venues," *International Journal of Environmental Research and Public Health*, Vol. 19 (2022), 8727.
7 Kristine Johnson, M. Olguta Vilceanu and Manuel C. Pontes, "Use of Online Dating Websites and Dating Apps: Findings and Implications for LGB Populations," *Journal of Marketing Development and Competitiveness*, Vol. 11, No. 3 (2017).
8 Tinonee Pym, Paul Byron and Kath Albury, "'I Still Want to Know They're Not Terrible People': Negotiating 'Queer Community' on Dating Apps," *International Journal of Cultural Studies*, Vol. 24, No. 3 (2021), 381.
9 Justin Clay, "Discovering 'Masc 4 Masc'," *MTV* (November 2016), www.mtv.com/news/4zii0u/discovering-masc-4-masc.
10 https://quchronicle.com/77672/arts-and-life/my-gripe-with-grindr/.
11 Wade and Pear, "A Good App is Hard to Find," 8727.
12 Wade and Pear, "A Good App is Hard to Find," 8727.

13 Kitty Knowles, "The Bisexual Problem: When Dating Apps Aren't for You," *Forbes* (May 2018), www.forbes.com/sites/kittyknowles/2016/02/16/bisexual-dating-apps-transgender-lgbt-dating-apps/?sh=4e5c5577305d.

14 Leah Stodart, Bethany Allard, Tabitha Britt and Stace Datskovska, "The Best Dating Apps for Bisexual Folks to Find Non-Judgmental Matches," *Mashable* (April 2024), https://mashable.com/roundup/best-dating-apps-for-bisexual-people.

15 Sky Lea Ross, "Unicorn Hunting: Online Dating While Bi," bi.org Website (February 2021), https://bi.org/en/articles/unicorn-hunting-online-dating-while-bi.

16 Ross, "Unicorn Hunting."

17 DeCapua, "Bisexual Women's Experiences with Binegativity in Romantic Relationships," 451.

18 Aditi Murti, "Couples Looking for Bisexual Girlfriends—AKA Unicorn Hunters—Often Commodify Queer Women," *Swaddle* (January 2020), www.theswaddle.com/unicorn-hunting-commodifies-queer-women.

19 Murti, "Couples Looking for Bisexual Girlfriends."

20 Murti, "Couples Looking for Bisexual Girlfriends."

21 Stodart et al., "The Best Dating Apps."

22 David Kaufmann, "Praising 'Gold Star' Gays Isn't Just Silly—It's Ignorant and Divisive," *Quartz* (December 2017), https://qz.com/quartzy/1164834/why-gold-star-gays-arent-a-good-thing.

23 Taylor Bruce, "Biphobia on Dating Apps," *The Daily* (March 2022), www.dailyuw.com/arts_and_culture/wellbeing/biphobia-on-dating-apps/article_12dbed50-a095-11ec-946f-472500752902.html.

24 Stodart et al., "The Best Dating Apps."

25 Stodart et al., "The Best Dating Apps."

26 Atiya Irvin-Mitchell, "Dating App Championing Inclusivity and Fluidity Joins Pittsburgh's AlphaLab Accelerator," *Technical.ly* (April 2024), https://technical.ly/startups/bindr-bisexual-dating-app-alphalab-accelerator/#:~:text=%E2%80%9CI%20didn't%20feel%20like,'Let's%20just%20do%20it'%20%E2%80%A6.

27 Liz Schumer, "10 Best Dating Apps for Bisexuals and Pansexuals," *Good Housekeeping* (April 2023), www.goodhousekeeping.com/life/relationships/g36462437/bisexual-dating-apps/.

28 Breena Kerr, "I Spent Years Ignoring My Bisexuality, Until Tinder Helped Me Come Out," *New York Magazine* (June 2017), www.thecut.com/article/how-using-tinder-helped-me-come-out-as-bisexual.html.

29 Mayk Jayn Frisk, "Maintaining My Bi Identity While Married," bi.org Website (February 2021), https://bi.org/en/articles/staying-bi-while-married.

30 https://sexualbeing.org/blog/can-i-still-be-bisexual-if-i-married-a-man/.

31 Anna Brown, *Bisexual Adults Are Far Less Likely Than Gay Men and Lesbians to Be 'Out' to the People in Their Lives* (Washington, DC: Pew

Research Center, 2019), www.pewresearch.org/fact-tank/2019/06/18/bisexual-adults-are-far-less-likely-than-gay-men-and-lesbians-to-be-out-to-the-people-in-their-lives/.

32 Robert Cohen, "Introduction: The Hidden Lives of Bi+ Married Men," in *Bisexual Married Men: Stories of Relationships, Acceptance and Authenticity* (New York: Routledge, 2024), 11.

33 Kristen G. Esterberg, "The Bisexual Menace: Or, Will the Real Bisexual Please Stand Up?" in *Handbook of Lesbian and Gay Studies*, ed. Diane Richardson and Steven Seidman (London: Sage Publications, 2002), 219.

34 Carren Strock, *Married Women Who Love Women* (New York: Routledge, 2023).

35 Strock, *Married Women Who Love Women*.

36 Cohen, "Introduction," 11.

37 Cohen, "Introduction."

38 Cohen, "Introduction," 15.

39 Lenore Norrgard, "Can Bisexuals Be Monogamous?" in *Bi Any Other Name: Bisexual People Speak Out*, ed. Lani Ka'ahumanu and Loraine Hutchins (Riverdale, NY: Riverdale Avenue Books, 1991).

40 "Background: Psychological Research on Consensual Non-Monogamy," Committee on Consensual Non-Monogamy APA Division 44, www.div44cnm.org/.

41 Julie Harris, "Love Multiplied: A Historical Perspective on Polyamory," *Medium* (December 2023), https://medium.com/conscious-relationship-design/love-multiplied-a-historical-perspective-on-polyamory-a32b5c328d13#:~:text=Polyamory%20in%20tribal%20and%20indigenous%20cultures&text=In%20many%20of%20these%20societies,embedded%20in%20their%20social%20fabric.

42 Kim Tallbear, "The Polyamorist That Wants to Destroy Sex: Interview by Montserrat Madariaga-Caro," Interview on Critical Polyamorist (February 2021), www.criticalpolyamorist.com/.

43 Tallbear, "The Polyamorist That Wants to Destroy Sex."

44 Tallbear, "The Polyamorist That Wants to Destroy Sex."

45 Tallbear, "The Polyamorist That Wants to Destroy Sex."

46 Christopher Gleason, "Introduction," in *American Poly: A History* (New York: Oxford University Press, 2024), 2.

47 Gleason, "Introduction," 2.

48 Kenji Yoshino, "The Epistemic Contract of Bisexual Erasure," *Stanford Law Review*, Vol. 52, No. 2 (2000), 420.

49 Yoshino, "The Epistemic Contract of Bisexual Erasure," 420.

50 Kim Parker and Rachel Minkin, "Views of Divorce and Open Marriages," Pew Research Center Website (September 2023), www.pewresearch.org/social-trends/2023/09/14/views-of-divorce-and-open-marriages/.

9

KINK AND BDSM

Bisexuality is no stranger to kink and BDSM spaces, according to the National Coalition for Sexual Freedom, whose research estimates 35% of people in the kink and BDSM communities are bisexual.[1] *Kink* is an umbrella term that refers to "a heterogenous set of pleasurable leisure activities that often overlap with sexual or erotic activities, although kink is not synonymous with sex."[2] Kink includes a variety of practices, including bondage, domination/submission and sadism/masochism (BDSM), which allows for a space to consensually explore power differentials and the use of "materials or objects that afford a heightened sensory experience associated with pleasure (fetish), and the giving and receiving of intense sensations, such as pain."[3] It is often misunderstood, stigmatized, perceived as mysterious, enshrouded in misconceptions, and conflated with abuse. In addition, kinky people are often accused of perpetuating the heteropatriarchy.[4] In a culture where mainstream images of sex flood the media but open dialogue is discouraged about human sexuality, the perception of kink's deviation from traditional sexuality norms leads to pathologization. Kwon and Greenwell, editors of the groundbreaking anthology *Kink: Stories*, explain how kink and BDSM are often "flattened, simplified, and turned into a joke, a cause for only shame. In movies, television shows, and popular books, kinky people are often also serial killers, emotionally stunted plutocrats, and other stock villains or exaggerated figures of fun."[5] In reality, kink is a "complex, psychologically rich act of communication" and a way of processing joy, trauma, and "expressing tenderness and cruelty and affection and play."[6] It also can be an epicenter for identity exploration, particularly for queer sexualities and gender identities. Given all of these dynamics, what are the connections and intersections between kink and bisexuality?

DOI: 10.4324/9781003242659-10

Kink and BDSM have been heavily debated and contentious topics for decades. With the first edition of the American Psychiatric Association's (APA) *Diagnostic and Statistical Manual* (DSM) in 1952, kink was associated with illness and sexual deviances and labeled a "distasteful" practice. Sadism was placed in the same category as the perpetration of violence, such as rape, sexual assault, and mutilation.[7] By 1980, the diagnosis switched from "sexual deviance" to "psychosexual dysfunctions" and was again connected to acts of violence such as pedophilia.[8] Feminist scholars also heavily debated kink and BDSM at this time, where radical feminists argued about the dangers for women and the more sex-positive feminists emphasized the importance of pleasure.[9] Such anthologies as *Against Sadomasochism* and *Unleashing Feminism* addressed the radical feminist position, which viewed "sexual practices such as BDSM as replicating and reinforcing structural inequalities that harm women."[10] In contrast, the sex-positive authors published anthologies *Pleasure and Danger*, *Powers of Desire*, and *Coming to Power*. *Coming to Power* allowed for an analysis "that women's sexual practices are bound up with power and inequality in complicated ways and that sexual practices, including BDSM, can subvert unequal social structures and create space for new possibilities of experience, particularly in relation to gender."[11] Radical feminists responded to these publications by arguing that the sex-positive position minimized sexual violence and perpetuated "an irresponsible articulation of sexuality that values some women's sexual pleasure at the expense of other women's safety."[12] In addition, a general societal misperception was that normalizing kink and BDSM would allow abusive people to use it as a cover up for actually harming others.[13]

It was not until 2010 when the APA changed the diagnostic codes for BDSM, fetishism, and transvestic fetishism (a variant of cross-dressing) for the next edition of its DSM published in 2013. At this time the DSM made a distinction between behavior and pathology. If consenting adults chose to participate in sexual behavior outside of dominant culture norms, they were no longer diagnosed as mentally ill.[14] Furthermore, research expanded in the last few decades, allowing for a better understanding of kink as a tool to explore identities, embodiment, and dominant culture beliefs about sexuality. Once perceived as a practice for only gay men, researchers documented how kink communities were a space for multiple gender identities and sexualities. In addition, discussions of consent, serious leisure, spirituality, therapeutic spaces for processing trauma, and the expansion of the practice of sexuality became central. More recent kink studies examine the intersection of race and disability, questions of power, privilege, and how systems of oppression impact the experience of kink and BDSM. In a special 2021 edition of the journal *Sexualities* on BDSM, the contributors asked:

> What is BDSM? Is it a sexual practice? A spiritual, or even religious practice? Something else entirely? How does the naturalization of

whiteness in BDSM communities shape participants' experiences? How
does the pillar of consent long taken as axiomatic in the study of BDSM
play out in embodied experiences of BDSM?[15]

Answering these questions or conducting a full analysis of kink and BDSM is beyond the scope of this chapter, which will instead focus on kink and BDSM as a space of exploration, empowerment, and healing for bisexual identity. Compulsory heterosexuality and monosexuality dominate societal norms around sexuality, leaving many queer people particularly ostracized and outcast for not falling into these heteronormative expectations of how one should be sexual, love, and have relationships. Historically many kink and BDSM subcultures were formed to combat dominant culture expectations around both gender and sexual identity. According to writer and sex educator Cameron Glover, these subcultures allowed for communities built outside of the shame and ostracization of mainstream heteronormativity.[16] As Glover states, "Offering this kind of safe space for exploration is one of kink's great virtues, as it provides another option for relationship building and sexual expression that doesn't subscribe to traditional notions of how these structures should exist."[17] Kink includes rather than excludes and is a space that provides new traditions, practices, language, and ways of relating to one another.[18]

Of course, not all LGBTQ+ people participate in kink and BDSM, but various studies do reveal that being LGBTQ+ may make it more likely to be a part of the kink community.[19] For example, The 2016 Kink Health Survey revealed elevated levels of sexual and gender diversity. The report showed 17.49% were transgender, genderqueer, non-binary, and intersex, and for sexual orientation around 76% identified as gay, lesbian, bisexual, pansexual, or queer.[20] It is uncertain if this shows general aspects and qualities of queer sexuality or if this is a consequence of general ostracization from sexual dominant culture.[21] As Sprott asserts, some sexual minorities may participate in kink culture because "they already have had to grapple with other stigmatized aspects of their sexuality."[22] He also argues that the fight against sexual stigma may include exploration of sexuality and the desire to "celebrate sexual diversity in a broader, more expansive way compared to sexual majority cultures."[23]

The typical kink research blends bisexuality into the LGBTQ+ population, but a few studies do show a unique intersection of kink and bisexuality, such as the experience of double discrimination. Both bisexual and kink communities share some common cultural biases resulting in erasure, stigma, and being ridiculed and pathologized. In a monosexist culture bisexuality is often perceived as an invalid sexual orientation, while kink also is often seen as an invalid sexual practice. Because bisexuality is frequently fetishized or stereotyped as kinky, bisexual people who are not part of the kink community may still find that they are stereotyped as being kinky. Those people who are bisexual and actually kinky may experience double discrimination for both their sexual orientation and kink practices, which may lead to limiting how open they are about either identity.[24] The intersection of biphobia, monosexism, compulsory monogamy, and kink shaming can doubly lead to marginalization and silencing.

Regardless of this discrimination, the reality is that bisexual people have long been a part of the kink community. The history of kink practices and communities is extensive and spans centuries, but more contemporary western histories evolve out of the gay male leather communities and rarely include the bisexual heritage that played a role.[25] In the late 1960s and 1970s, the gay-liberation movement's increase in visibility coincided with the visibility of the gay male leather community. Acceptance of bisexual people in these spaces, however, was not any better than it was in the rest of society.[26] Bisexual men who wanted to participate in the leather scene often felt obligated to hide their bisexuality for fear of exclusion if it was known that they played also with women. At the time, many gay men in the leather scene had little interest in interacting socially with lesbians or straight people let alone the desire to play together in kink scenes.[27] Lesbians created their own spaces for kink and BDSM, such as Pat Califia, Galye Rubin, and others who cofounded *Samois*, the first lesbian feminist BDSM organization in the United States.[28]

One example of the bisexual heritage in kink is Steve McEachern and Cynthia Slater in the 1970s. In the basement of McEachern's and Fred Heramb's San Francisco home, the club The Catacombs was created with private BDSM and fisting parties specifically for gay men. What is rarely discussed is that McEachern was bisexual and was credited as one of the people who helped start the contemporary, more integrated queer leather scene. Another player was Cynthia Slater, an openly bisexual educator, activist, and dominatrix, who was in a relationship with McEachern at one point. Slater's activism included fighting for women to be a part of the gay leather scene, and she worked with McEachern to create women-only and mixed-gender BDSM parties at The Catacombs.

This allowed for a unique experience where various gender identities and orientations shared a sexual space, manifested respect for difference, and fostered an atmosphere in which people observed each other, shared in their mutual appreciation for kink, and learned from one another.[29] This format opened up discussion that, for many, certain kinds of BDSM did not necessarily depend on the gender identity or the sexual orientation of the participants. Pat Califia—later Patrick Califia—a bisexual transgender man who wrote the 1980 book *Sapphistry: The Book of Lesbian Sexuality* on butch-femme sexuality and BDSM—writes about his own experience at The Catacombs and what it meant for him. At the time it was prior to his transition, and he identified as lesbian and enjoyed fisting gay men at The Catacombs. He described one interaction as having no affection between him and the man with whom he was playing; however, he felt

Such great love for his body, which had opened, accepted and blessed me; and from his body, waves of gratitude for the pleasure. I was utterly aware of the vulnerability of this man whose legs were locked up and back, his feet waving around his ears, but I was also in thrall to the power of his piggishness, enslaved by the aggressive strength of his wanton hole. There we were, one man and one woman, locked in sexual congress—but nothing could be queerer.[30]

Mixed-gender identities and sexual orientations began to find more ways of participating in kink and BDSM culture together.

Today certain kink communities still desire to be gender exclusive, whether it is simply just preference or safety, but many are credited as spaces of shared erotic identities and acceptance regardless of sexual orientation or gender identity. In addition, kink can be a space to actually explore one's identity and used as a tool for healing.[31] Research has shown that for many, the gender identity of their play partner is "less important than the activity or scene itself."[32] As Sprott and Hadcock contend, "It is noted that gay men might have scenes or ongoing relationships with heterosexual women, or that a person might play with a wide range of genders depending on different scenes or dynamics."[33] According to Newmahr, it "creates a space in which participants achieve a gendered experience; the participants inhabit gender paradoxes of action and service, passivity and strength, powerfulness and powerlessness, but these paradoxes are linked neither to biological sex nor to gender identity."[34]

For bisexual people who are part of a kink community, it can allow for the exploration of their own sexuality, especially when there is a need to escape mainstream culture's biphobia and erasure. Bisexuality is about the potential for attraction to more than one gender, and a kink community that allows for multiple gender identities can be a safe space to experience one's own bisexuality. As Steve Lenius states about this dynamic, "Such a 'pansexual' atmosphere, where it truly doesn't matter to anyone what the gender of one's play partner is, could be just the thing a bisexual or bi-curious person is looking for."[35] For gender-diverse bisexual people, the kink community can be an outlet of acceptance for both their gender identity and bisexuality. In addition, Lenius further conveys,

In sexual matters, members of the kink community tend to be more adventurous and less judgmental. This mindset creates sexual spaces where it's safe to experiment with and stretch personal boundaries, and to experience forms of sexuality and intimacy that have heretofore been kept off-limits.[36]

Not only can kink communities allow for exploration of bisexuality, but Brandy Lin Simula explains how it actually allows for an "undoing" of gender and a move beyond the binary. Since many kink spaces may be a place for experimenting with gender, participants can experience interactions that subvert dominant culture gender expectations. For example, Ritchie and Barker found in their work that BDSM spaces enabled men to feel vulnerable and show emotions or women to partake in dominant positions over male partners.[37] Newmahr asserts that in the community she researched kink was not "especially intertwined with embodiments of masculinity and femininity" but rather "organized around the related but significantly distinct identities built around topping and bottom."[38] As these studies show, kink spaces can be a center for the undoing of gender as a social category, with the BDSM role being replaced as the most important social category. In addition, Simula emphasizes the distinction between "sex" and "sexual" in BDSM interactions. She argues,

> *This distinction also rejects normative linkages between gender and heterosexuality as well as between gender and sexuality more generally; it does so by resisting the conflation of 'sex' (e.g., intercourse, orgasm) with 'sexual' (e.g., arousal, erotic feelings). Similarly, for many participants, this also means that activities and sensations not associated with sexual pleasure or arousal in normative sexual scripts can be experienced as sexual.*[39]

Additionally, BDSM includes sexual practices that are not centered around genitals and allow for a range of both emotional and physical experiences to be sexual. The inclusion of "non-genitally-centered and non-traditionally sexual experiences" reduces the emphasis of gender as central to the interaction. Simula maintains that this creates what she calls a kind of BDSM bisexuality:

> *First, it resists heteronormative linkages between gender and sexuality by creating non-normative meanings of sexuality that extend beyond normative heterosexual sex. Second, it decenters genitals and genitally based sexuality, a shift that also resists normative linkages between gender and sexuality. Third, it reduces the threat of homophobic stigma by allowing participants to define BDSM play with people of the same gender as 'not really sex.' Reducing the importance of gender by distinguishing between 'sex' and 'sexual' also increases the prevalence of BDSM bisexuality.*[40]

BDSM bisexuality can not only undo gender but also can create another kind of bisexuality. When Simula asked participants in her research "how would you describe your sexual orientation?" 46% stated they were bisexual, heteroflexible, bi-curious, pansexual, or queer. When asked about participating in

BDSM activities, 60% reported engaging with a variety of genders and actually identified those interactions as bisexuality.[41] Many of the participants did not identify as bisexual but did experience BDSM bisexuality because of the "greater importance of BDSM role (e.g., top, bottom) than gender (e.g., masculine, feminine) when choosing a BDSM partner(s)."[42] This ties in with Patrick Califia's assertion, "if I had a choice between being shipwrecked on a desert island with a vanilla lesbian and a hot male masochist, I'd pick the boy."[43] The rejection of gender is the result of the importance of a mental connection *regardless* of gender. As one participant stated, "I'll play with a guy as much as I'll play with a girl. . . . For me it doesn't matter if you're a female or male or something in between, making your transition."[44] This creates a space that allows gender-diverse people to also be included in this exploration. This pattern of BDSM bisexuality reflects the "well-known saying among BDSM players that 'leather transcends gender,'" which can include the rejection of the belief that men are natural tops and women bottoms.[45] The differences are less about gender and more about personality, thus reducing the importance of gender and moving beyond the gender binary in the BDSM space.

There are, of course, people in kink communities who are invested in the gender binary, but according to Simula, this still can be a type of BDSM bisexuality. Simula describes this as gender-based switching, where one may take a top role with one gender but a bottom role with another. For example, one participant who identified as a male switch stated:

I've always felt more how should I say—more—I felt safe being a little more sexually aggressive with women. And then more sexually or sensually submissive with other men. So even through college, when I think of that, when I had a boyfriend, he was always on top, he was always the top, I was always bottom.[46]

Instead of the gender role being replaced by a BDSM role, gender actually influences the BDSM role. This kind of BDSM bisexuality not only involves doing gender in normative ways but can be an important part of the BDSM experience that perpetuates the belief that men should be the dominant, aggressive partner while women are passive and submissive. Simula found that, regardless of gender identity, many reported preferring to bottom to men and to top women because of this belief in men as naturally dominant and women naturally submissive. BDSM bisexuality does not always consist of a gender preference, but sometimes it does, and there a variety of ways this kind of bisexuality can exist.[47]

Participating in kink communities allow for some unique exploration of bisexuality, but it also can be used for healing from trauma such as sexual violence, isolation, stigma, and shame. A particularly powerful part of the healing process is the potential connections to community that "provide socialization around consent practices, safety issues related to higher risk practices, and social support for coping with stigma and minority stress."[48] For many, the appeal of kink is the feelings of empowerment, respect, and safety, particularly when collaborative consent is seen as imperative for the practice and is so intentionally negotiated.[49] Even though many outside of the kink community may conceptualize it as a form of abuse, what differentiates kink and BDSM from abuse is consent.[50] Even though kink is not the cure-all for all trauma, and not everyone will find it a healing process, for many it can be a form of spirituality, a space for social connection and a venue for learning coping strategies for neurological dysfunctions and managing of chronic illness and distress. As Cascalheira et al. explain,

> *E*videnc*e suggests that kink relationships are highly structured dynamics in which kink-identified clients may use pain play or power exchange to manage personal problems. . . . Kink scenes and relationships rely on the fundamentals of the BDSM community—safewords, debriefing, aftercare, consent negotiation—to maximize benefit and to reduce risk.*[51]

For bisexual people and other queer identities who may face the impact of multiple marginalizations, finding communities who have these values allow for various empowering benefits in addition to the exploration of identity.

Practitioners of kink and BDSM emphasize the importance of researching and finding a community that will adhere to these values. In addition, not every kink community is going to be inclusive or have a culture that is self-reflective or working against how they may be perpetuating different forms of systemic oppression, such as racism. For people of color, finding safe spaces that allow for a practice that connects to healing, liberation, and autonomy is key. As Black writers Goddess Honey B and Kharyshi Wiginton state about Black kink communities:

> *I*nside these Black kinky communities, we found Black people rejecting white dominant culture's proscriptions on who was worthy of sexual pleasure, who could rule inside the bedroom, or what it meant to powerfully submit. Here we saw Black people using sex and sexuality as a medium to create new realities and praxes, even for those of us at the furthest margins of society.*[52]

Author of *The Body is Not an Apology*, Sonya Renee Taylor, further contends how kink is a celebration of difference and a space of reclamation "where fat folks, disabled folks, Black people, [or] those whose bodies have been labeled deviant might go to find themselves desired, celebrated, and even worshipped for their defiant, glorious bodies. And it is these people, in these bodies, who most often need a refuge where they get to be the authors and agents of their own pleasure, pain, joy, and delight."[53] Given the ways in which bisexual people may face marginalization in both mainstream straight and queer communities, it is not surprising that kink spaces can be a refuge to explore bisexuality and find community. The following conversations with River McMican and Ash Ward reveal their own experiences as bisexual people who practice kink and BDSM, which has allowed for acceptance, exploration, and healing.

A Conversation with River McMican

LISA:
Tell me a little bit about yourself and your bisexual identity.

RIVER:
I jokingly call myself a bad bisexual because I fit all these supposedly negative stereotypes about bi people—that we're promiscuous, kinky, or polyamorous—and we push back against those because they're not true for many bisexuals, but they're absolutely true for me. At the end of the day, I don't see being promiscuous, kinky, or polyamorous as negative. All of those things have fed into my identity as bisexual, non-binary and generally identifies with the queer community.

It's also informed my activism and advocacy in a lot of ways. When you're talking as an advocate, you don't want to accidentally paint your community in a negative light just because you, as a person, happen to fit some of these stereotypes. It can be really challenging to talk around these parts of my life.

L:
That has to be hard to navigate when you know who you are and are comfortable with that. How do you do that?

R:
I keep it kind of quiet. I've been married for 13 years and in a polyamorous relationship for 10. My girlfriend that I've been with for a very long

time, I met her in a fetish club. So, there's that throughline there. But it means there's a chunk of my life that I don't talk about very openly. Even in LGBTQ spaces, I don't often talk about my polyamorous relationships.

I also try to take the temperature of a room before I talk about any of my experiences in the kink community. Sometimes I talk about it in a very abstract sense. I talk about when I was younger and I was a club kid, instead of giving details about my history or talking too much about the places I've been or the communities I've been a part of. It seems a little safer and respectable that way. Polyamory and kink have made my life better, but I don't want to make myself too vulnerable too early if I don't know how people will respond.

L:

How does that make you feel when you have to do that?

R:

It's a very pragmatic choice. I don't like it, but when I'm working as an advocate or an activist, my goal is not necessarily to help myself or represent myself. My goal is to help my community. And when my personal experience might undermine the message for the community, I think it's okay to mask it a little. I see it like code switching to speak to a group, or the way I put on my "educator voice" when I talk at a training versus a casual one-on-one conversation with someone.

L:

Can you tell me a little bit about how you make sense of bisexuality and learning about it in your youth?

R:

The short version is that I've been out since I was 13. That was in the mid-nineties. There has never been a question for me about my sexuality or about who I am attracted to. Effectively, I'm pansexual. I simply do not care. I am sometimes attracted to certain people, sometimes not. I don't care about gender one way or another. But "bisexual" is the term that most people recognize, so it's the term I tend to use when I talk to other folks, and it was the term I used when I was 13 when we didn't really have a lot of other language. But there was never a question for me about whether or not I was bisexual. It was always sort of a given. I never really came out per se because there was no reason to; I never had to make a big deal out of it.

I was really fortunate to grow up in a house that was very progressive. My family just simply didn't care. The friends I had were fine. Everyone was supportive. It was no big deal for me. So, that was how I felt internally about my sexuality.

When I started to look for queer spaces to explore what my identity meant to me, I started looking for youth spaces. Sort of like pride events. I remember going to Boston Youth Pride in high school, but I had a really hard time connecting to community in those spaces. In part, it was because at the time I was in a relationship that looked straight, which immediately puts you at the outskirts of queer community. There's this idea that bisexuality is not an identity you hold; it's something you do. So, a straight-looking relationship, well, guess what? You're not queer anymore, at least as far as a lot of people are concerned. There was a sense that I didn't really belong in those spaces, especially because I wasn't facing the same level of scrutiny or discrimination that some other folks were.

They had real issues with their families, with the places they lived. There were a lot of folks who were really struggling because they just couldn't accept their sexuality. They were struggling to even figure out if they were actually gay. Their entire lives were being upended by this self-discovery process. I didn't have that experience, so I didn't feel like I had a lot to talk about in those spaces. And then there were a lot of spaces that were politically active that were about pushing acceptance for queer folks. People who were arranging events, like the day of silence events, spirit day events, those kinds of things. And at the time, I just didn't care. I thought that activism was pretty cool, but it wasn't really for me. And again, there was no real impetus for my involvement. I wasn't facing any kind of personal struggle. Other people's challenges just didn't register with me in the same way.

I felt like there wasn't a spot for me in queer community. So, at like 17, 18 years old, I knew that I had this identity that was important to me on some level. I knew that I kind of wanted to find out what it meant. It's enough to say I'm bisexual, but what does that mean? Who am I attracted to? What are the things I'm attracted to? What does it mean to be attracted to those things? What makes different kinds of relationships different? You have no idea when you're 17 or 18.

I'm 40 now and I still have no idea what the answer is to those questions! But I wasn't going to find out in those queer spaces; they weren't going to provide that for me. So, I fell back into my other interests. And one of the things that I always loved was new wave and post-punk music. Lots of The Cure and Depeche Mode and catchy synthesizer tunes. That brought me into the Providence goth scene, which was a very close, tight knit little scene that was very closely associated with the kink and fetish scene as well. Goths are pretty sexually liberal. Goth as an aesthetic is pretty fetishy to begin with. A lot of vinyl, fishnets, chains and leather and all those other fun things. And while on the goth side, quite often it's aesthetic, but it translates over.

I became a club kid for several years and I was going out three or four times a week. My entire social circle became focused on this very narrow intersection of the Providence goth and kink scene. And it turned out to be pretty much exactly what I needed. It was a space to explore these ideas of sexual and gender identity. Everyone was already on the margins. There's that joke, that all goths are bisexual. It's not strictly true, but you'd be forgiven for thinking it. Because when you have an aesthetic with that much androgyny and a scene that is so far away from the cishet norm, all those rules of straightness no longer really apply. Even if you were straight, they didn't apply. Because in a fetish or a kink scene, all the straight people that are in that space, they're already on the margins of what is socially acceptable for straight sexuality. That was such a big thing for me because all the queer spaces I had been in up to that point had been defined by navigating straightness. They were spaces for people who had problems navigating straight expectations as they were discovering their sexuality. But I had no interest in navigating straightness. I was much more interested in celebrating queerness.

The kink and fetish scene provided this perfect outlet for exploring what queerness meant. Whether it meant different kinds of partners, self-expression, how I dressed, or different kinds of experiences. There are a lot of things that you don't know if you're going to like them until you try them. Maybe you don't like being whipped, but hey, guess what? In a good open kink scene, there's someone there who wants to help you out and discover what you enjoy. And that was such an incredible thing! There was no judgment, no sense that I had to perform a certain kind of persona to be accepted. That was really powerful. There was no cis straight social structure waiting to punish me for stepping out of line in that space. There's such a need for celebratory queer spaces where queer culture is explored, where straight social norms just simply don't apply. That is incredible. Those spaces don't exist in a lot of places. I was incredibly lucky to find one very early on. I think that that's the kind of thing I would love to make more of as an advocate. More social spaces where people can walk through the door and they leave behind these really restrictive straight social expectations.

L:

I appreciate your honesty about your own experience. What are some other things to know about kink and BDSM?

R:

It's really important to recognize just how little it's about sex. There's this idea that kink is just about when your sex life gets boring, why not try handcuffs or some light bondage or whatever. I think the experience of a lot of people in the kink scene—especially people who are involved in BDSM as a lifestyle long term—sex is the smallest part of it. So much of the kink scene is about trust, vulnerability, exploration, and about learning to communicate really clearly with partners. That was incredibly valuable for me. I was in this scene at 19 and 20 years old, where open, honest, sexual communication was the norm and not the exception. Where you would be free to hook up with whomever, but you were expected to negotiate and talk about what you were into beforehand. And if someone propositioned you and you weren't into it, a polite, "no, thank you" was sufficient. It would be heard!

I think everyone who is involved in BDSM knows that there are unhealthy BDSM spaces. They exist. It's unfortunate, but it's true. I was so lucky to have such a close-knit small safe space that there wasn't enough room for abusive people to really get a foothold. Occasionally we'd get the straight couples coming in unicorn hunting. You could pick them out a mile away. They were these people who would hit on one person inappropriately and then everyone else in the club would know within 15 minutes who they were, what their deal was. They'd leave disappointed because there was just no room for that in that space.

L:

It's a community of support and safety, keeping an eye out for each other.

R:

100%. And I think another really big thing for me about the kink space was the lack of expectation. In a lot of spaces that you go to, like a singles' night at a bar, there's an expectation that you're there to pick someone else up or get picked up yourself. If you go out to a nightclub, if it's not a gay nightclub, there's an expectation that you're straight. In the BDSM scene, a lot of those expectations just don't apply. Maybe you want to get picked up, or maybe you're there because you just like to watch. Or you're dating someone, but you're also at the kink club. That doesn't mean you're cheating on your partner. It could just mean they stayed home that night. There are all of these ways that standard expectations don't apply. And I found that really valuable.

The BDSM community is such an explorative space. You try something to see if you like it, and if you don't, you don't have to do it again. Or people might have a way to help you enjoy yourself more next time. If you've ever spoken to someone who's really into say rope bondage, they want to show you every cool knot they have ever learned. And if you tell them, "Oh, well, I've always had a problem being tied up because it makes my wrists hurt," they'll show you 15 different ways to tie someone up where their wrists aren't even involved. They'll start showing you forearm ladders and stuff. It's incredible. People in the BDSM scene are so generous with their experience. It's this scene where everyone kind of wants everyone else to have fun.

L:

It sounds like you already had an idea of your bisexuality and it was a space to really explore that.

R:

For me, that was the most valuable part of it. This space was to explore sexuality generally, but also gender identity and gender fluidity where there was no repercussion for it. At least my kink scene was very queer. So even though it wasn't technically a LGBTQ community space, for all intents and purposes, it was, even if there were straight people there. There was no one there to challenge my sexuality. Something we hear a lot as bi people is if you're dating a man or you're dating someone of the opposite gender, why do you have to call yourself bi? Like bisexuality is something you do, not something you are. That's the assumption people make. But in the kink scene, no one really cared. I'm dating a man, but making out with a girl, who cares? It just simply does not matter.

L:
There's a lot more going on!

R:
Right. There was a dude in the club whose name was "furniture." The only acknowledgement that anyone gave him was that he was a piece of furniture, use as you see fit. No one is paying attention to what I am wearing or what I am doing in that space. If someone feels so comfortable in that space that they want to be used as a footstool for an hour and a half, that is such a fantastically open space.

When you think about the experiences that most 20-somethings have, there is so much trauma and trying to figure things out. "How do I interact with people I'm attracted to? How do I interact with my own sense of self-identity? How do I want to present myself as an attractive person to other people I am attracted to?" That's really challenging. College-aged people struggle a lot when they experiment with identity. There can be a lot of repercussions. You go to a college party and you mess up. You wear or say the wrong thing to the wrong person, and so on and so on. You try something and you decide you don't like it but that's not socially acceptable. Now you're a social pariah, right? We know that there's a lot of pressure on college-aged youth to engage in sexual behavior that they might not be interested in. True sexual coercion.

That's really sad and unfortunate. You have people who want to explore, but they have no safe space in which to do it. For me, I never had to worry about someone responding violently to me or aggressively to me because of my bisexuality or my gender identity. I never felt like it was a dangerous situation. It's also a public space. Everyone assumes they're being watched. Everyone assumes that it's okay to watch as long as you're not being a jerk about it, basically. It's not like a fraternity party.

L:
What do you feel about kink and BDSM now that you're 40?

R:
It's been a little bit of a throughline through my life, I think because so much of my formative years of sexual experience were defined by that environment of negotiation, communication, experimentation. As I've grown older, even though I'm not involved in it as heavily at this point, it has affected every relationship I've been in. Once you learn how to negotiate, to ask for what you want, to create a judgment-free space to explore what intimacy means, that's really powerful. Even in a non-kink setting, you can create a space where you and your partner or partners can explore what you're interested in. And if it doesn't work out, that's okay. Like you tried, you talked it through, you loved it. Great. Keep going. You didn't like it as much, okay, well now we can talk about that. That is so much more communication than people are used to having around sexuality and intimacy. I carry that into every relationship I've been a part of. Sometimes to the frustration of my partners who maybe didn't have the same experience. I think that's something that I've definitely been really grateful for over the years is the ability to say both what I enjoy sexually, as well as what I enjoy in intimacy. Those experiences have made it so much easier for me to communicate with the people around me.

A Conversation with Ash Ward

LISA:
What are your thoughts on BDSM and kink?

ASH:
One of the things about BDSM and kink is it's just so much more open to people as they are. I think

because consent is so foregrounded in anything kink
related, people are so much more open to talking
about like, what are you okay with? What do you want
to do? And part of that can be I want to be involved
with people of multiple genders. There are fewer
assumptions. There's less of an assumption about
what are you interested in and what you want to do
because there's always a ground rule of having to
talk to people to know what they're interested in
doing.

I think that's how I've always seen it in terms of
the community aspect. With the consent as the foundation, you can't know anything about what someone
wants to do until you talk to them. I don't know if
that's because it's such a marginalized community
or if it's the nature of kink. I don't know where
it comes from. But it's definitely an aspect that's
always been really appealing to me in terms of how
you can step into those spaces and just feel less
pressure to look or perform a certain way.

L:
What's the appeal of BDSM and kink beyond that for
you?

A:
For me it's less specific about me being bi. One of
the things that I've always really struggled with,
especially with the violence I experienced early on
in my life, is just this feeling of having to perform or look a certain way in sex. You should make
these noises or you should like these positions or
this constant surveillance. Where for me, I'm a
sub, I don't really do any dom work. And part of
being a sub, it's really empowering. If I'm tied
up and don't move, I don't have to worry about how
do I move to be attractive to the person. Doms are
normally really vocal about what they want you to
do or what they like about your body or what feels
good for them. I appreciate the view, it's just so
upfront, like, here's what I want to do and here's
what I want you to do, and are you okay with that?
And oh, that feels good and that's what I want you

to do. And I'm sure you could find that in places outside of kink. But for me that's always what's been most affirming.

It just lets me let go of the whole idea of having to look or do things this way. That's what I've found most empowering, especially if you have a dom that gets off on your pleasure. I know that my pleasure is going to be prioritized in that too. And I don't have to ask for that. It's always just going to be there. I feel like I can let go and I don't have to control every single aspect of what's happening in that. I know I'm going be safe. I know there's someone that's taking care of me, looking out for me, making sure that I'm safe and enjoying myself.

One of the things for me too is it helps me stay grounded in what's happening. Because of my trauma I tend to dissociate a lot. And also, with having ADHD, it's really hard for me to focus on one thing that's happening at a certain time. One of the things that's really nice for me about BDSM and kink is there's just more happening. There's more keeping you in that space. It's not just penetrative sex happening. I'm tied up, I can't move, my dom is talking to me and asking me to do things. And it helps ground me there in that moment, in my body and what I want to do instead of having to think about all of those other things.

L:

It's so hard for people to understand that if they don't experience it.

A:

I so often have difficulty trusting people in my day-to-day life just because of trauma or because of people who are just assholes. One of the things that's really nice for me is when I can get to subspaces and this complete and total trust of whoever's with me. Because not only am I feeling euphoria, it's also I know that person isn't going to do anything that I don't want them to do. And that can't happen if I don't completely and totally trust that person. It's almost like this physical proof to myself that that's a person that's safe for me to be around.

L:
You really have to communicate beforehand!

A:
There is just so much more of an understanding of things like aftercare with BDSM. I don't know anyone who's involved in BDSM who doesn't understand that. Like after something's done, you should still make sure that person's okay and spend time with them with snuggles or whatever someone needs after sex. That's always been kind of lacking to me outside of kink spaces. Some people just inherently do it, but there's no expectation or conversation like, okay, what do you need after sex? Even people who are really good about making sure that sex feels good for you. Like, what do you need after sex? What do you want before sex? How do I make sure that you don't feel like you're being used? That's such a huge part of BDSM and kink, and I never hear those conversations outside of it.

For more conversations with Ash, see Chapter 3: "Gender-diverse Identities."

Notes

1 Jillian Keenan, "Is Kink a Sexual Orientation?" *Slate* (August 2014), https://slate.com/human-interest/2014/08/is-kink-a-sexual-orientation.html.
2 Richard Sprott, "The Intersection of LGBTQ+ and Kink Sexualities: A Review of the Literature with a Focus on Empowering/Positive Aspects of Kink Involvement for LGBTQ+ Individuals," *Current Sexual Health Reports*, Vol. 15 (2023), 107.
3 Sprott, "The Intersection of LGBTQ+ and Kink Sexualities," 107.
4 R.O. Kwon, "The Willful Misunderstanding of Kink: What Does It Mean to Conflate a Sexual Practice with Abuse?" *The Cut* (February 2021), www.thecut.com/2021/02/the-willful-misunderstanding-of-kink-by-r-o-kwon.html.
5 R.O. Kwon and Garth Greenwell, "Introduction," in *Kink: Stories* (New York: Simon and Shuster, 2021), xxi.

6 Kwon and Greenwell, "Introduction," xxi.

7 "BDSM & the DSM," KYNK 101 Website, https://kynk101.com/kink-bdsm-facts/dsm.

8 "BDSM & the DSM."

9 Brandy Lin Simula, "Does Bisexuality 'Undo' Gender? Gender, Sexuality and Bisexual Behavior Among BDSM Participants," *Journal of Bisexuality*, Vol. 12, No. 4 (2012), 487–488.

10 Simula, "Does Bisexuality 'Undo' Gender?" 488.

11 Simula, "Does Bisexuality 'Undo' Gender?" 488.

12 Simula, "Does Bisexuality 'Undo' Gender?" 488.

13 Kwon, "The Willful Misunderstanding of Kink."

14 "BDSM & the DSM."

15 Brandy Simula, "Introduction to the Special Issue: BDSM Studies," *Sexualities*, Vol. 24, No. 5–6 (2021), 701.

16 Cameron Glover, "It's Time to Recenter Kink and BDSM as Part of Radical Queer History," *Slate* (November 2018), https://slate.com/human-interest/2018/11/kink-bdsm-radical-queer-history.

17 Glover, "It's Time to Recenter Kink and BDSM."

18 Glover, "It's Time to Recenter Kink and BDSM."

19 Sprott, "The Intersection of LGBTQ+ and Kink Sexualities."

20 Sprott, "The Intersection of LGBTQ+ and Kink Sexualities," 108.

21 Sprott, "The Intersection of LGBTQ+ and Kink Sexualities," 108.

22 Sprott, "The Intersection of LGBTQ+ and Kink Sexualities," 108.

23 Sprott, "The Intersection of LGBTQ+ and Kink Sexualities," 108.

24 Meg Barker, Christina Richards, Rebecca Jones, Helen Bowes-Catton and Tracey Plowman, "Intersections with Bisexuality," in *The Bisexuality Report: Bisexual Inclusion in LGBT Equality and Diversity* (Center for Citizenship, Identities and Governance, Faculty of Health and Social Care), 30, http://oro.open.ac.uk/52881/1/The%20BisexualityReport%20Feb.2012_0.pdf.

25 Steve Lenius, "Bisexuals and BDSM: Bisexual People in a Pansexual Community," *Journal of Bisexuality*, Vol. 1, No. 4 (2001).

26 Lenius, "Bisexuals and BDSM."

27 Lenius, "Bisexuals and BDSM."

28 Sheila Jeffreys, *The Lesbian Heresy* (North Melbourne, Australia: Spinifex Press, 1993).

29 Stephen Stein, "The First BDSM Groups, The 1970s," in *Sadomasochism and the BDSM Community in the United States: Kinky People Unite* (New York: Routledge, 2021).

30 Patrick Califia, "The Necessity of Excess," *POZ Magazine* (October 1998), www.poz.com/article/The-Necessity-of-Excess-12198-6713.

31 R.A. Sprott and B.B. Hadcock, "Bisexuality, Pansexuality, Queer Identity and Kink Identity," *Sexual and Relationship Therapy*, Vol. 33, No. 1–2 (2018).

32 Sprott and Hadcock, "Bisexuality, Pansexuality, Queer Identity and Kink Identity," 217.

33 Sprott and Hadcock, "Bisexuality, Pansexuality, Queer Identity and Kink Identity," 217.

34 Staci Newmahr, "Part 2: Play," in *Playing on the Edge: Sadomasochism, Risk and Intimacy* (Bloomington, IN: Indiana University Press, 2011), 118.

35 Lenius, "Bisexuals and BDSM," 76.

36 Lenius, "Bisexuals and BDSM," 75.

37 Ani Ritchie and Meg-John Barker, "Feminist SM: A Contradiction in Terms or a Way of Challenging Traditional Gendered Dynamics Through Sexual Practice?" *Lesbian and Gay Psychology Review*, Vol. 6, No. 3 (2005), 227–239.

38 Newmahr, "Part 2: Play," 107.

39 Simula, "Does Bisexuality 'Undo' Gender?" 492.

40 Simula, "Does Bisexuality 'Undo' Gender?" 494.

41 Simula, "Does Bisexuality 'Undo' Gender?" 494.

42 Simula, "Does Bisexuality 'Undo' Gender?" 492–493.

43 Pat Califia, "A Secret Side to Lesbian Sexuality: 1979," in *Public Sex: The Culture of Radical Sex*, 2nd Edition (San Francisco: Cleis Press, 2000), 159.

44 Simula, "Does Bisexuality 'Undo' Gender?" 499.

45 Simula, "Does Bisexuality 'Undo' Gender?" 500.

46 Simula, "Does Bisexuality 'Undo' Gender?" 496.

47 Simula, "Does Bisexuality 'Undo' Gender?"

48 Sprott and Hadcock, "Bisexuality, Pansexuality, Queer Identity and Kink Identity," 225.

49 "Healing Through Kink," Embrace Sexual Wellness, LLC: Center for Sex Therapy and Education Website (September 2021), www.embracesexual wellness.com/esw-blog/2021/9/13/healing-through-kink.

50 Sprott and Hadcock, "Bisexuality, Pansexuality, Queer Identity and Kink Identity," 225.

51 Cory Cascalheira, Ellen Ijebor and Yelena Tracie Hitter, "Curative Kink: Survivors of Early Abuse Transform Trauma Through BDSM," *Sexual and Relationship Therapy*, Vol. 38, No. 4 (2021), 4.

52 Goddess Honey B. and Kharyshi Wiginton, "Finding Freedom in Black BDSM," *YES! Magazine* (May 2022), www.yesmagazine.org/issue/ pleasure/2022/05/18/finding-freedom-in-black-bdsm.

53 Goddess Honey B. and Wiginton, "Finding Freedom in Black BDSM."

10

MENTAL HEALTH ISSUES AND THE IMPACT OF VIOLENCE

By Emilia Couture and Lisa Speidel

Plenty of research shows that there are health disparities between LGBTQ+ people and their non-queer peers, but more recent scholarship explores the unique mental health needs of bisexual people.[1] One of the first nationally representative studies found high rates of depression in bisexual youth: 68% of young females and 47% in young males, while suicide attempts were estimated around 35% in females and 22.5% in males.[2] Other research revealed that 59% of cisgender bisexual (cis-bi) women reported mood disorders over their lifetime, in comparison to 44% of lesbians and 30.5% of heterosexual women.[3] In addition, the occurrence of sexual and intimate partner violence is particularly extreme for bisexual people compared to straight, gay, and lesbian people.[4] The CDC National Intimate Partner and Sexual Violence Survey found that 61% of cis-bi women have experienced rape, physical violence, and/or stalking by an intimate partner in their lifetime, in comparison to 35% of straight women and 44% of lesbians.[5] For cisgender bisexual men, it is 37% compared to 26% for gay men and 29% for straight men.[6] Why are bisexual people more vulnerable to violence and mental health struggles?

This is not an easy question to answer, particularly since bisexual people have historically been missing in research and what does exist often combines cis-bi women and men, ignoring the potential for gendered differences.[7] For instance, cis-bi women may manifest more stress related to family relationships where cis-bi men may be more afraid of physical violence.[8] An additional gendered difference is that cis-bi women are more often stereotyped to be "actually heterosexual" whereas cis-bi men are stereotyped to be "actually gay."[9] Since both are presumed to be *truly* interested in men, this can be understood not only as monosexism but as androcentric thinking as

DOI: 10.4324/9781003242659-11

well.[10] This reinforces both cis-bi men and women's identities as invalid, but it uniquely shuts cis-bi women out of the queer community as a whole by deeming them "straight" and focusing their existence around the patriarchy in a misogynistic way.

When considering mental health for bisexual identities, Meyer's minority stress model provides a foundational framework to understand why bisexual people have different experiences than heterosexual, lesbian, or gay peers.[11] Minority stress states that discrimination and stigma can lead to mental health issues, not because of anything inherently true about someone but instead the social conditions within which they exist.[12] The model includes "distal" stress that comes from broader conceptual and ideological bounds, as well as "proximal" stress that encompasses more individual and personal interactions. Hatzenbeuhler expands on Meyer's minority stress theory to emphasize that the interaction between proximal and distal stressors for sexual minorities in particular can result in worsened health outcomes.[13] Furthermore, monosexism can place further stress on bisexual people with the either/or binary thinking and their identities not always being understood or validated.[14]

In general, research reveals how gender-diverse people disproportionately struggle with high rates of depression, anxiety, and overall psychological distress.[15] These mental health issues are not a manifestation of gender dysphoria but rather distress associated with stigma.[16] For gender-diverse bisexual people, the intersection of bi-erasure, biphobia, monosexism, and transphobia can increase negative health outcomes from the multiple layers of minority stress.[17] So few studies are done on gender-diverse bisexual people's mental health and even fewer for bisexual people of color, who face the complex intersection of racism with the challenges addressed earlier.[18] According to the literature on minority stress, those with multiple marginalized identities are at the highest risk for poor health outcomes; however, these are the people who are typically neglected from the research.[19]

This chapter addresses some of these unique complexities by dividing this conversation first into three sections with an intersectional examination of each group; cis-bi women, cis-bi men, and gender-diverse bisexual identities. In addition, a fourth section explores the impact of sexual and intimate partner violence and the fifth section examines ways in which mental health practitioners can improve the services they provide when working with bisexual people.

Cisgender Bisexual Women and Mental Health

When examining the experience of minority stress of cis-bi women, it is important to consider that they face systemic sexism on the basis of their sexuality *and* their gender[20] and also the possibility of other oppressions such as racism, classism, and ableism. The impact of this for cis-bi women includes suffering from certain conditions—such as anxiety and depression—at higher rates than their heterosexual[21] and sometimes lesbian and gay peers.[22] They also encounter elevated rates of substance abuse,[23] eating disorders,[24] and sexual violence in their lifetimes.[25] In addition, cis-bi women can face particular social barriers to gaining adequate mental health care.

An intersectional framework allows for further analysis, particularly with the intersection of social class and race. For example, bisexual people are more likely to be poor than their monosexual peers, even those in the queer community.[26] In one study, lesbians and heterosexual women had a poverty rate of about 14%, while cis-bi women had a rate of 27%.[27] In the same study, cis-bi men had a poverty rate of about 23%, which is still high but lower than cis-bi women.[28] This shows how bisexuality can intersect with social class, and the potential of lower income reducing access to resources such as mental health assistance. Additionally, cis-bi women of color may face the intersection of racism, but most research only examines the difficulties of queer women of color in general, like the work of Calabrese et. al. Their research found that Black sexual minority women reported higher frequency of discrimination and lower social and psychological well-being than white sexual minority women and Black sexual minority men.[29] The multiple layers of marginalization that cisgender women of color face interact with the unique oppressions of being a bisexual person, but it is hard to know exactly in what way because the effects are interactive, not necessarily additive. For example, a recent study examined these complexities and concluded that the highest rate of suicidal ideation was with non-Hispanic Black and Hispanic bisexual women who live in rural areas, but more research is needed to truly understand these unique issues for cis-bi women of color.[30]

Cis-bi women's mental health is also influenced by the constant discourse of "heterosexual privilege." Often bisexual people are told that being in a seemingly straight relationship makes them less oppressed than their lesbian and gay peers.[31] While the sentiment of this may be true on the surface, this also functions to erase part of bisexual identity. For cis-bi women there may be a sense of not feeling "queer enough" if in a relationship with a man, which also means being perceived as ascribing to "feminine" gender norms. This can impact coming out as bisexual, as one study revealed that cis-bi women were out to their communities at a rate of only about 50%, while about 70% of lesbians were out.[32] In general, higher levels of outness has been connected to better mental wellness, specifically, less anxiety, greater lifestyle satisfaction, and better outlook on the self.[33] The benefits and risks of outness for a bisexual individual's context are unique because there are concerns of general acceptance but also the challenge of possibly not being accepted in queer spaces.

Stereotypes about bisexual illegitimacy and promiscuity also affect bisexual people's mental health. For cis-bi women, delegitimizing terms like "barsexual"—women who kiss women in public as only a performance for male enjoyment—erase the women's bisexuality and potential attraction to each other.[34] Cis-bi women also face microaggressions that can increase depression and suicidality.[35] Phrases like "I'm sure it's just a phase" or "Oh, you're bisexual? Would you like to kiss my girlfriend?" or "That's hot, do you want to be in a threesome?" potentially harm cis-bi women's mental wellness. Additionally, cis-bi women can experience hypersexualization and fetishization due to the *perceived* non-normativity of their sexuality.[36] Hypersexualization and exoticization particularly impact cis-bi Black women, resulting in higher levels of psychological distress,[37] along with potentially poor diets that risk deadly conditions such as hypertension and diabetes.[38] Cis-bi women of color also have a higher risk of isolation due to alienation from both queer communities and their racial/ethnic communities, which may prevent necessary social support for mental well-being.[39] Again, more research is desperately needed to understand the relationship of how racism, sexism, and biphobia interact to impact the mental health of cis-bi women of color.

Cis-bi women also suffer from high rates of body image issues and eating disorders are a common response.[40] Some research has suggested that cis-bi women suffer from disordered eating at higher rates than heterosexual women as well as their queer peers.[41] In one study, cis-bi women were two times more likely to have an eating disorder than lesbians,[42] which may be due to many lesbians' decreased likelihood to endorse heteronormative expectations and beauty standards.[43] Eating disorder research has largely not placed specific attention on cis-bi women, so it can be difficult to draw conclusions and understand the nuances that are faced by them within that space.[44]

Cisgender Bisexual Men and Mental Health

What research is available suggests cis-bi men struggle with lower rates of self-worth, self-esteem, and higher rates of depression and anxiety than gay men.[45] The impact of the specific gendered stressors of negative stereotypes described in Chapter 5—cis-bi men are confused, in denial of being *actually* gay, spread HIV at high rates, or the belief that, because they are men and bisexual, they have a higher propensity to cheat—all contribute to these struggles. In addition, Chapter 5 reveals the unique ways cis-bi men feel the pressures to conform to masculine expectations. These stereotypes often lead to a lack of bisexual spaces of support in both straight and gay communities and a high sense of isolation.[46] This can also cause cis-bi men to question the legitimacy and acceptance of their bisexuality especially in a world that does not fully recognize their existence.[47]

Dodge et al. found that bisexual men often feel inauthentic and a way to cope is by compartmentalizing their sexuality "into 'heterosexual' or 'homosexual' versions based upon the setting they were in" while also trying to distance themselves from the "stereotypes associated with bisexual men, as a way to be able to function within social settings."[48] The internalized pressure to fit into the category of either "gay" or "straight" requires a form of code switching, described by Hyde as a "morphing into whoever one needs to be in order to escape censure or increase our chances of desire fulfillment."[49] Hyde further explains,

> *The ability to be perceived as straight in front of parents and fabulously gay at particular nightclubs can seem like a superpower—like getting the best of both worlds. When we are rejected by both the gay and the straight communities, a mask can seem like a refuge.*[50]

There is a plethora of research of the impact of inauthenticity on mental health, particularly how it relates to depression.[51] The combination of fitting into the binary of straight and gay plus masculine expectations can only exacerbate this challenge for many cis-bi men to be true to themselves.[52]

The intersection of racism adds another layer for cis-bi men of color who face unique mental health challenges related to biphobia, monosexism, and racism. Cis-bi men of color face specific racialized stereotypes around bisexuality, for example, the belief that cis-bi Black men practice the "down low" and are spreading HIV at high rates. In actuality, cis-bi men make up only a small percentage of the spread of HIV, but this stereotype still impacts feelings of being able to be out or authentic about their sexuality. In addition, hyper-masculine expectations for cis-bi men of color can impact accessing services and discussions around mental health. As one participant in a bisexuality study by Williams et al. stated, "African American men, they never talk about anything . . . they won't [go to counseling]. We as black men need to be masculine . . . slap a band aid on, keep it moving. That type of attitude."[53] Survival within a racist culture for cis-bi men of color can lead to pressure to comply with heteronormative concepts of masculinity, particularly since deviation from these expectations can result in violence, harassment, or social isolation from their communities.[54] Furthermore, if there are any mental or physical struggles, there can be distrust of health care providers given the historical medical atrocities Black men have faced.[55]

For many cis-bi men the isolation and lack of authenticity and access to support can mean the use of alcohol and drugs. Substance abuse is a common coping mechanism for men struggling with the pressures and expectations of masculinity that may evolve into mental health issues in general, but cis-bi men report higher rates of alcohol abuse relative to heterosexual and gay men.[56] Although there are higher rates of substance abuse for both cis-bi women and men in comparison to monosexual individuals, cis-bi men in particular have higher rates of "other" drug use and dependence compared with both gay and heterosexual men.[57]

Gender-diverse Identities and Mental Health

Gender-diverse people who are bisexual face stereotypes such as potentially impermanent identities, as well as general "othering" within queer and straight communities that privilege binary norms when it comes to sexuality and gender.[58] While cis-bi men and women report the impact of minority stress and worse health scores than monosexual peers, gender-diverse bisexual individuals report the worst scores.[59] According to one study, 47% of pansexual transgender people and 39% of bisexual transgender people reported at least one suicide attempt.[60] Another study of transgender bisexual people concluded that they often felt unsupported by mental health providers. One participant explained, "The general stereotype is that if you're bisexual, you're probably not transsexual, you're just confused. And that if you really are a transsexual and you really are a woman, then you should only be attracted to men."[61]

Williams et al. found that transgender bisexual men who had gender-affirming procedures felt their bisexuality erased, ignored, or misperceived afterward especially if they dated cisgender women. Their sexual identity, which may have been seen as queer before, was erased and presumed to be heterosexual.[62] The participants discussed how this caused immense anxiety as they constantly needed to prove the validity of their sexual identity and defend their queerness. Another finding consisted of the coming out process, which alone can lead to the fear of stigma and rejection, but for gender-diverse bisexual people, they must decide if they should conceal or disclose more than one minority identity. One participant revealed that his family already knew he was a transgender man, but having to come out again as bisexual caused even more stress. Other gender-diverse participants described mental health struggles such as feelings of isolation and not having social support that understood the complexities of these multiple layers of marginalized identities.

The Impact of Violence

It is estimated that bisexual people—regardless of gender identity—experience higher rates of violence in comparison to their monosexual peers. As stated earlier, research indicates that cis-bi women report rape, physical violence, and/or stalking at nearly double the rate of heterosexual women and more frequently than lesbian peers.[63] Cis-bi men also experience violence at higher rates,[64] in addition to bisexual and pansexual transgender people. According to the U.S. Transgender Survey, 51% of pansexual and 41% of bisexual transgender people reported being sexually assaulted in their lifetime, compared to 37% of gay and lesbian transgender people and 35% of heterosexual transgender people.[65] It is clear that bisexual people are particularly vulnerable to this kind of violence.

A comprehensive examination of violence against bisexual people is very limited and most research is on cis-bi women. Misogyny, objectification, and hypersexualization all serve to dehumanize cis-bi women, which may be used as justification for violence in the eyes of perpetrators.[66] For women of color, these numbers can be even higher, particularly for Black bisexual and lesbian women who report higher rates of lifetime victimization as compared to White lesbian women.[67] For cis-bi women of color, racialized fetishization intersects with biphobia, bi-erasure, monosexism, and sexism, which only increases dehumanization and violence.

In addition to the higher rates of sexual violence, there is also evidence of unique ways the aftermath impacts mental health.[68] For example, people could be more likely to victim-blame a bisexual survivor because of stereotypes about promiscuity or temptation of the male gaze.[69] Cis-bi women can experience a particular pressure to "prove" their sexuality for cis men by engaging in same-sex relations, either in public or in private, due to their hypersexualized position.[70] In addition to rape, cis-bi women may be at an increased risk of verbal sexual coercion potentially at double the rate of monosexual women.[71] Disclosure of identity can result in harassment to engage in unwanted sexual acts because people may assume that it means that cis-bi women are willing to partake in any kind of sexual activity at any time.[72] In addition, internalized biphobia may add pressure to prove their sexuality is legitimate, such as engaging in unwanted sexual activity as a subconscious affirmation of the stereotype that cis-bi women are perceived as promiscuous.[73]

Not only are the rates of sexual violence disproportionately high, but bisexual people are also more likely than any other sexual orientation to experience intimate partner violence (IPV).[74] Gender-diverse bisexual people again experience the highest rates but are very underrepresented in the research.[75] It is unclear why the rates are so high, but one study explains that jealousy may be a common contributing factor.[76] Stereotypes about bisexual people as incapable of monogamy can fuel a distrustful partner who has issues with self-confidence, power, and control.[77] Other stereotypes of bisexual promiscuity and perceived infidelity may be used as excuses to use violence as a way to control a bisexual partner.[78] Although IPV is most commonly understood as a dynamic between two people in a straight relationship, it can also be within the context of same-gender loving or queer relationships.[79]

Bisexual survivors of sexual and intimate partner violence are often not believed and victim blaming is rampant, which causes underreporting and even more barriers to seeking help. They often receive relatively fewer supportive responses when disclosing sexual violence, which can increase depression and trauma responses.[80] Bisexual survivors may also be reluctant to disclose for fear of having to out themselves to family, friends, or the police. Gender-diverse bisexual people may be especially afraid to report given the estimation that around 58% of transgender people have been harassed or assaulted by police officers.[81] Other barriers can include the possible fear of perpetuating any negative, biphobic stereotypes, such as being highly promiscuous or unable to be faithful and monogamous.[82] Furthermore, seeking help or leaving a violent relationship is often a time when violence can escalate, which can leave a bisexual victim isolated and unable to escape. Queer informed support is often unavailable and the combination of not understanding the dynamics of IPV, along with limited knowledge about bisexuality, creates even more barriers. In addition, the belief that violence between same-gender loving relationships cannot exist, especially between two cisgender women, further isolates someone who may be seeking help.[83]

Mental Health Providers and Clinicians

It is evident that bisexual people require interventions oriented towards their unique needs. Multiple barriers can exist to accessing mental health care, not just for bisexual survivors of violence but also bisexual people in general. Bi-erasure, biphobia, and monosexist attitudes can pose a potential lack of competency of mental health care providers. Although there are some bi-friendly service providers, many therapists do not receive training about bisexuality. This creates potentially harmful interactions, invalidation, and microaggressions in therapeutic scenarios that limit the benefit of mental health care.[84] Recent studies reveal that 39% of bisexual men and 33% of bisexual women reported not disclosing their sexual orientation to any medical provider, compared to 10% of gay men and 13% of lesbians.[85] Another study found that bisexual people feared that their mental health providers would judge them based on their identities, attractions, and sexual practices.[86] Many experienced negative reactions such as being told their identity was just a phase, not a valid orientation and that they would need to decide whether they were gay or straight. Others disclosed that they were often asked prying questions about their bisexuality that were not helpful or required in providing them care.[87] Bisexuality was often treated as a symptom or the cause of their mental health issues, without an analysis of how social oppression *against* them was actually the main factor. Instead, their bisexuality was pathologized, which can happen even in supposedly LGBTQ+ friendly spaces.[88] Zora Stone elaborates on her own problematic experience with her mental health care provider in the following interview.

As researcher Johnson states, the violence, mental health issues, and suicide rates among bisexual people means that the "situation is dire."[89] Efforts are being made to expand on the research and training around these issues, such as the 2018 special issue of the journal *Sexual and Relationship Therapy* entitled "Shining a Light into the Darkness: Bisexuality and Relationships."[90] The Movement Advancement Project collaborated with multiple bisexual organizations to create an extensive report entitled *The Invisible Majority*, which addresses the multiple issues and struggles of bisexual people. It is full of recommendations for federal and state governments such as the need for more research, cultural competence training for mental health professionals, and better medical school training on bisexuality.[91]

There are multiple resources that one can find to learn more, including books, organizations, and websites included in the resource section of this book. One such excellent tool is The Trevor Project's *How to Support Bisexual Youth*.[92] Another powerful resource was created by The Human Rights Campaign, along with BiNet USA, the Bisexual Resource Center, and the Bisexual Organizing Project. This includes a list of suggestions for bisexual people, advocates, and health care providers:

- what bisexual people can do

  Find a culturally competent health care provider using the Bisexuality-Aware Professionals Directory or HRC's Healthcare Equality Index, which measures LGBT-related policies and practices at U.S. hospitals. While individual providers at these facilities may not be fully versed on bisexual health, they are more likely to be LGBT-friendly than other providers.

  Visibility matters in many settings. If it is safe and you feel confident enough, be "out" to your provider and stand up for yourself. If your provider doesn't offer inclusive paperwork or assumes that you only have relationships with people of one gender, let them know that you are bisexual and that they should avoid making such assumptions
- what advocates can do

  Be an ally to the bisexual community by using inclusive language (i.e., say "LGBT" instead of "gay and lesbian") when you talk about the LGBT community.

  When using community examples to make a case, use a bisexual person as an example, or quote a statistic that highlights a health disparity for the bisexual community.

  Avoid stereotyping bisexual people and call others out when they make biphobic statements.

  Help raise awareness about the health disparities bisexual people face by sharing resources like this brief.

  Advocate for and participate in better and more inclusive research about the bisexual community. A large portion of the transgender community—a group that already suffers major health disparities—describes their sexual orientation as bisexual (25%) or queer (23%), suggesting that some members of the bisexual community may be particularly vulnerable to disparities

- what health care providers can do

  Avoid making assumptions about a patient's gender identity or sexual orientation based on the person's sexual history or gender expression. Also avoid making assumptions about someone's sexual behavior based on their bisexual identity. Assumptions like these can make bisexual patients feel unseen and uncomfortable and therefore less likely to be honest about their health needs.

  Make your intake forms and other paperwork inclusive of people with diverse gender identities and people who have relationships with people of more than one gender. Also, ask patients what kinds of sex they are having so that you can more effectively assess any related sexual health risks.

  Provide sex-positive resources on sexual health and safer sex practices that are inclusive of bisexual and transgender people, like our Safer Sex Guide.

- Become bi-competent and encourage your provider networks to do so as well. Reach out to bisexual organizations that can help you educate yourself and others about bisexual community needs and ways to improve programs and services[93]

This chapter concludes with two interviews with health care providers Janis Luna and Zora Stone. Both discuss their own experiences of violence as bisexual people and also working in the health care system themselves. These two interviews also elaborate on better ways we can provide support to bisexual people that can decrease the mental health disparities.

A Conversation with Janis Luna

LISA:
Why do you think sexual violence rates are higher for people who are bisexual?

JANIS LUNA:
I think it's a couple of things. Bisexual people exist in a position that is vulnerable to a lot of harmful cultural narratives about sex, both within heteronormative spaces and within the queer community. That vulnerability is connected to purity culture and amatonormativity, which is defined as "the assumption that all human beings pursue love or romance, especially by means of a monogamous long-term relationship." It's a term I first learned from my sex therapist friend Rachel Kletchevsky,

which is from Elizabeth Brake's 2011 book *Minimizing Marriage: Marriage, Morality, and the Law.*

From a sex work perspective, the biphobic violence femmes specifically are subjected to is connected to the Madonna/Whore complex (which is something that all femmes are subjected to under purity culture, not just bisexual femmes). When you're "pure" (that is, when you're having sex within a monogamous marriage) you're—just barely—in that "good" category (though there's no real way to succeed at being "good," to be honest. If you abstain from sex for too long, you're considered a prude. And if you're asexual into adulthood, you're perceived as having something "wrong" with you—you're immature, you're stunted or broken in some way). But once you have sex outside of a monogamous marriage or relationship, under patriarchy all bets are off and it's a free for all on femme bodies. This is echoed even within the queer community, in biphobic stereotypes about the supposed "sluttiness," "greediness," "disloyalty," and/or "untrustworthiness" of bisexual folks among queer people who really highly prioritize monogamy. Queer spaces are not a perfect sanctuary from patriarchal gender norms and bisexual femmes are often on the receiving end of this.

And then the other way that I think about it is through the lens of asexuality and how asexuality stands in opposition to compulsory sexuality. I think what happens for a lot of bi folks—and bi femmes in particular—is corrective rape, which is something that asexual folks also experience as part of being perceived as a "deviant" sexuality, both within straight and queer spaces. Whether you're asexual and you are subjected to corrective rape because it's just incomprehensible to people that you don't want sex, or if you're bisexual you have to be exactly 50/50 in your sexual desire/attraction, or you're always available for sex, or whatever biphobic assumptions are being made.

L:

Can you explain a little bit what you mean by "corrective rape?"

JL:

Corrective rape is the term that I've been reading about in Sherronda J. Brown's book *Refusing Compulsory Sexuality: A Black Asexual Lens on
Our Sex-Obsessed Culture.* It is sadly something
that queers have experienced for generations, like
men trying to correctively rape lesbians to "turn
them straight." Brown talks about corrective rape
as something that happens to ace spectrum folks
within straight *and* queer spaces, because *sexuality itself* is what is compulsory in our culture. This can look like being forced to have the
"right" kind of sex, having heterosexual sex forcibly in order to correct for being queer, or having sex forcibly *in general*, because to be asexual
is, again, inconceivable within a culture of compulsory sexuality. That's definitely something I'm
parsing out within my own sexual history right now:
the way that my lack of desire for sex, my lack of
desire for the same frequency of sex, or whatever
was incomprehensible to my partner and seemed to
be experienced as specifically damaging to his ego
or sense of self. Was that due to my demisexual-
ity or my bisexuality? Probably both. And so, the
sentiment behind a corrective rape is, "you don't
know what you want or what you're talking about.
This is something wrong with you. And the thing
that's going to solve it or fix it is sex." And
I think that's something that is not just limited
to sex with cishet men but also occurs within the
queer community, and it's absolutely connected to
compulsory sexuality and internalized heterosexual norms.

L:

Are there also certain stereotypes about bisexual
people that perpetuate this?

JL:

Yeah. That bisexuals are horny all the time, or
really slutty, or can't be trusted, or won't be
loyal in relationships. There's this narrative of a
pathological hypersexuality.

L:

If you're feeling entitled to someone else's body, then it's that idea of, you're there *for me* to do whatever I want.

JL:

Yeah, and people project a lot of fantasies onto bisexual femmes specifically. I think that is part of it too. I remember when I was solo polyamorous and dating in my twenties and being approached really regularly, usually by straight couples for a three-some, and people being very bold about saying like, "we only want to fuck, we don't want any kind of emotional connection to you. We just want to have this experience."

At one point, a couple on *OkCupid* reached out to me, to request a threesome for the boyfriend's birthday like it was an item, a gift. And I was like, this is something that you can certainly *pay* for, for sure, and I might even be into that. But that was not the context with which they were reaching out to me. They were basically like, "we want to give a threesome to my boyfriend for his birthday and we want you to be in it." And it was just like, "well, what's in it for me?"

L:

You were a commodity as a bisexual person.

JL:

Yeah. And then, in another relationship, my ex was almost disappointed that I was reluctant to have a threesome. He ran out of patience. The idea that we were going to have a threesome was almost a given. And I had talked about it as something that I would be open to, but I wanted our relationship to be in a really secure place before we entertained something like a sex party or threesome, because I remember what it was like to be a single femme interacting with couples in my twenties. And I never want to treat another femme the way I was treated. I never want to expose someone to the very vulnerable position of being a "third" to a relationship that I'm in that is unhealthy or where they're being approached as a commodity for my cishet boyfriend's fucking *birthday*, get out of here. There's no way that she wouldn't feel that, or that our behavior wouldn't indicate that to her in some way. And I remember him just complaining to me about our sex life at one point. He was like, "We haven't even had a three-some!" It was absolutely a given that because I am bisexual that would be something we would one day do and that I was withholding from him.

L:

Again, there was this entitlement and expectation about how you were *supposed* to be.

JL:

Yeah. It's entitlement and an assumption. It's something that, again, exists both within the queer community and among heterosexual people too, that bisexuals are just to be projected upon. The girl-on-girl and one penis policy fantasy. Single bisexual femmes just exist to fulfill these fantasies and projections, but don't actually have any emotional interiority, desires, preferences, emotional needs, or vulnerabilities of our own. That's a lot of how I was treated.

It goes back to this Madonna/whore complex and the assumption of hypersexuality and complete sexual accessibility/availability. Because, of course, the same thing happens to sex workers. We are assumed to perpetually be consenting because of the nature or stigma of the work that we do. In that relationship, it certainly had to do with sex, but it also had to do with feeling very entitled and demanding,

For example, my ex's insistence that I send him nudes—it was not framed as, hey, this is maybe part of my love language, or it makes me feel really special, but was just him saying "Why don't you ever do this?" And for me my answer was, well, because it feels like my sex work. It was in the middle of the pandemic, and I would rather sit around in my pajamas and focus on getting through the fucking day. After a full day of supporting folks as a trauma therapist through a damn pandemic, I don't actually want to shave and put on a full face of makeup and send you sexy photos because that's a lot of work. (*Janis Luna expands on this dynamic and violence in their personal narrative "Spoiling The Fantasy" in Chapter 7: "Pornography and Sex Work.")*

L:
I think about the victim blaming, like, "that's because you're bisexual and you're having sex with everybody."

JL:
It's wild because it's always about the views of the perpetrator. And the norms that encourage those views and the stereotypes. I'm bisexual, but I'm also demisexual. I'm on the ace spectrum. I experience attraction in all of these different directions and the lived experience that I'm operating in right now is that I haven't had much sexual contact probably in over a year and I don't really want to. Well, that's not true. I'm like three months pregnant, so I've had some sexual contact in the past three months *(laughing)* But that was a little different.

L:
That was a different desire for that sex.

JL:
Yeah. It was specifically to conceive, and it wasn't with a partner in a recognizably normative way, though it was certainly an intentionally erotic experience in terms of, as Audre Lorde says, the erotic as creative life force energy. But you know that that narrative doesn't exist, the fact that I can be a bisexual and asexual and play in the erotic in order to conceive and all of that is my sexual subjectivity. And that doesn't mean that it's open season on my body right now. It's actually quite the opposite.

L:

I think of the role of all of those stereotypes like hypersexuality, assuming bisexual people are promiscuous, greedy, all polyamorous . . .

JL:

Who cares if someone is "promiscuous?" I don't know what it means—what does *greedy* mean? These are judgments that don't make any sense. And in terms of polyamory, so what? If you're not polyamorous, don't date a polyamorous bisexual, right?

L:

This idea of how you're "supposed" to be acting as a bisexual person, as a woman, as a femme and how people treat you based on these expectations.

JL:

That's the part Sherronda J. Brown is really talking about when they use the term compulsory sexuality. Because they don't use compulsory heterosexuality. From an asexual standpoint, it's compulsory *sexuality*. And the similar types of violence that bisexual people face, both within the queer community and outside of it, are very similar to the ones that asexual people face. It is about the idea of compulsory sexuality. You *have* to want partnered sex, because the idea that you don't means that you're sick or broken or immature—like not fully developed. Then of course, the shades of compulsory sexuality are going to be different based on one's gender and sexual orientation. The shades of that for a bisexual person are different than the shades of that for an asexual person.

L:

Could we say compulsory monosexuality too?

JL:

That's one shape that it takes and a reason why the violence against bisexual people looks the way it does. I was using Madonna/Whore Complex, but I think compulsory monosexuality is a more inclusive word for it. Just because Madonna/Whore is such a gendered way of describing it and it specifically speaks to the way that femmes experience it. But with compulsory monosexuality, the idea that you are deviant, which comes from people conflating non-monogamy and cheating. And the additional emotional and symbolic significance of that of cheating—that "rejection"—that sort of ego attack implied in infidelity and the resultant doubling down on violence in a specific way. I think cheating is definitely a shitty thing to do (and I have experienced being cheated on) but I also know—having experienced it—that it didn't really have anything to do with me and was more about that person's inability to be honest with me or their own manipulative tendencies rooted in their trauma.

L:

Compulsory monosexuality also means that you should only be attracted in this one way or to only one gender. All those stereotypes are perpetuating the idea that bisexual people are lesser than in some way.

JL:

Lesser than and deviant. I think specifically the moral implication of deviance, especially under a purity culture under the sort of Christo-fascist environment that is the United States. To say you're lesser than but lesser than specifically in this really harmful way, implying you're doing some type of moral harm by being the way that you are.

L:

What role do you think this all plays in mental health disparities for bisexual people?

JL:

It comes down to experiencing compounding stigma in these communities that we navigate and walk through. Mainstream, institutional medicine that isn't great for queer health to begin with, but then the more marginalized you are within that community the less funding for research is done. There's something about lesbian, gay, and cis that is easily put into categories, but I think when we exist in spaces that are more non-binary . . . it's hard for people to wrap their heads around it. They really like the simplicity of gay or straight or cis, rather than trans, non-binary, two-spirit, all of these different forms of gender and sexual fluidity.

When you do exist in that more liminal space and in a very embodied way, it's uncomfortable for other people. I remember going to a gynecologist who I was like, oh my God. I had one visit when I was dating a guy. The next time I was there I was dating a girl and I told her and I was like, we're not monogamous. And she kind of just looked me up and down and said, "you know, you can get STDs from women too, right?" And I was like, yeah. But it's kind of your job to tell me which are the ones I'm more likely to get? What are the ways that I can protect myself with people who have one set of genitals versus another? It is the doctor's responsibility to connect them to information and resources and we really fail in those spaces. It's the same thing in therapy, with the emotional intimacy and vulnerability, if you feel like this is someone who at a foundational level cannot understand this aspect of your experience, it's very hard to feel safe.

L:

It also sounds like feeling really judged, that comment from the doctor wasn't coming from a place of kindness. You are being treated like you are "promiscuous."

JL:

Yeah! It's very prescriptive. Bisexual masc-presenting people often experience the flip side of that, which is that they're presumed to be gay. The space to honor bisexuality as an experience is not there if the assumption is that you're either going to end up straight or gay. And it's really sad and hard because it's dehumanizing. It feels like on some level people refuse to see you as the person that you say that you are.

L:
It sounds like that can create barriers to *accessing* services.

JL:
Yeah. It's very discouraging. There are definitely pockets of queer affirming providers and there's more now than there were ten years ago. I've gone to Planned Parenthood for most of my gynecological care throughout most of my twenties and that always felt like a safer place. They were making more of an effort and that was clear from stuff like the forms that I filled out including options with regard to how you identify and seeing that they knew to include bisexuality, to include non-binary identity, went a long way to just being like, okay, I can say that here people won't look at me out of the corner of their eye and be like "you can also become sick that way."

L:
In the context of providing services in general, what are other ways that people could do better when it comes to bisexuality?

JL:
On a material, tangible level, just knowing what your documentation looks like and who it includes and who it excludes and what it says about you, your knowledge and awareness.

Also being well-read—but not just well-read but knowing bisexual people, even if it's not like knowing someone personally—like don't go out and make a bisexual person your best friend purely because they're bisexual—but just asking what is this community like, what are the things that they're talking about? Who can I learn from? What do I need to know about this community to be able to identify when something stigmatizing is happening and to intervene? Trying to figure out what are the resources, what are the options. Who are the people who are already doing this work.

L:

People may say they offer LGBTQ+ affirming care but they don't really understand bisexuality or know their bias.

JL:

Yeah. Bisexuality being in that both/and space, it's difficult for people to wrap their heads around and we have a lot of feelings about that. I think that existing in a liminal space is very triggering for a lot of people. It's a very anxious space to be in, like it is a somatically difficult space to hold because it is uncertain. Whereas the certainty of gay or straight feels, superficially, better, easier to understand. I think that kind of dedication to certainty is also a form of denial.

L:

We're very invested in binaries, so anybody who's providing services—how do they self-reflect in their investment in the binary too?

JL:

Yeah. Again, it's that both/and/neither space that people really struggle with. And that's the tie-in I see to asexuality because asexuality is kind of saying "no" to partnered sex (though of course, there is a spectrum of experience within asexuality as well; asexual people are not a monolith). There exists within asexuality a solo sexuality or an autosexuality. And so, it's the "no" to partnered sex that is very challenging for people. But that varies from person to person. It could be "no" to partnered sex, but for me, for example, I have a solo sexuality practice, a very erotic practice; that's confusing to people that I actually prefer not to have partnered sex, even though I experience attraction to people of all genders. But my sexual practice often is a solo one and I feel very comfortable with that. I've found a lot of joy and healing in my asexuality, too, and I don't believe I'm asexual because I've been "broken." It's just another way I'm experiencing human sexuality right now, and it doesn't have to be fixed or changed.

A Conversation with Zora Stone

LISA:
You said you had a story about your own experience with therapy.

ZORA:
This company that I get therapy through, I specifically asked for someone who was trauma informed and LGBTQ+ friendly. I remember, I had just gotten out of a relationship with my girlfriend at the time. And a few weeks after that I had sex with a man. It's important to note that I am still coping and working through my sexual history and trauma. So, I told my therapist, "Look, I felt really uncomfortable having sex with somebody. It brought up a lot." Honestly now thinking about it, it was really PTSD, where I was remembering old scenarios. And instead of listening to that and her hearing me, she instead said, "Well, no, are you sure it's not you being confused because you went from being with a woman to a man?"

No, in fact, I was explicitly telling you where my discomfort was coming from and you just completely disregarded that and thought it's me "switching" from a woman to a man. And I just paused for a moment, because I was in shock. I've never heard that before, especially coming from a therapist. I think I had asked her something along the lines of "why do you say that?" And she said, "Well, at the end of the day, if you get married, you have to choose one or the other, you have to choose either being with a man or being with a woman." I was so perplexed by that whole sentence. What we just discussed, being with a man or a woman as confusing. And then that whole idea of marriage! My parents were never married, but they've been together longer than marriages that I've known have ever lasted. Marriage in general for me is such a fairytale.

After hearing her say that, the therapy was no longer trauma informed. I shared what trauma I'm experiencing, and now you're just perpetuating a stereotype on me. It honestly scared me and I was telling myself, "Okay, this is one of the many signs that this isn't a good space for me." This was strike three because she had also mimicked stereotypical words and behaviors to portray Black women in previous sessions. I knew I needed to change therapists, but it scares me because I know she's out there still doing this work. I don't know if in her description she still has LGBTQ+ friendly in it. God forbid there's somebody who's not that confident in their sexuality. And she says something along those lines, and this is someone you're supposed to trust in a non-judgmental space.

That terrifies me. For someone who just isn't there yet and still trying to figure out who they are. With my master in social work program (MSW), those are things that I'm pinpointing now. Just because you say you are anti-racist, inclusive, for transgender rights or women's rights, that doesn't mean that you are or that you're going to practice that in social work. You can talk all you want to, but when it's time to show up, how are you going to approach these situations? Seeing interactions in MSW classes, we would be discussing scenarios and people's immediate biases just start coming out and they don't even realize it. I guess in that same sense, it motivates me to continue to pursue this degree because we need some sort of representation out here to call people out on their bullshit and also authentically be there for folks that need that because not everyone gets it.

L:

It's so sad because this person's supposed to be helping you and they're potentially causing more trauma and more damage.

Z:

We often trust them to have the answer. If you have the knowledge and agency to challenge it and be like, you're full of shit, but the person might not be able to do that. Imagine the amount of people who are pushed down because of all of these other pressures of being bisexual and what that looks like and we don't know how isolated people feel. To

have someone that you're supposed to be vulnerable
with and have a nonjudgmental space will ultimately
perpetuate that same harm. It's just scary. And
I have no other way of really explaining it. Now
my current therapist is amazing. She's pretty much
all about having a social constructionist sort of
thing. Like asking questions like "what does this
mean for you? What does that look like? What do you
want to do?" and will ask these questions whether
she agrees with my views or not.

I think that is the most liberating thing. Those
people that are in the LGBTQ+ community that still
don't have that framework and are pushing bisexuality to be one thing or the other and being so
defined. Why not just let people feel loved and let
them be?

L:
Thinking about the intersection with racism, were
there perceptions with your previous therapist of
you as a woman of color?

Z:
Yeah. She was an older white cis woman who, I believe,
specialized in substance abuse. I had mentioned to
her that I was in an organization where it was primarily Black women. I remember, it was my first or
second appointment with her. And I said that this is
the root of my trauma. This is where things really
started going downhill with her. I'm explaining
this interaction with all of these black women.
And she said something along the lines of, "Why
wouldn't any of them go . . . nuh, uh, girl," with
finger pointing and head shaking, like very, stereo-
typically mimicking a Black woman. And I remember
distinctly when she did that, I said to myself in
my head, "I don't know if this is how you talk or
if this is you being racist". . . . I paused for a
moment.

And I remember she said something along the lines
of, "Oh, I'm sorry. I probably shouldn't have done
that." She said something indicating I knew what she
just did. When I was looking for a new therapist,

I gave myself permission to be as picky as I needed to be because this just did not work out at all. And I specifically told the company, "I now want *a Black woman* who is trauma informed and LGBTQ+ friendly. I don't care if she is telehealth. I don't care if she's in person. I do not care, but these are the specific things I need to feel safe." Now, I have a Black woman therapist who has a mixed-race daughter. So even though she's not mixed herself, when I would mention a lot of the things that come with bisexuality and being biracial and bicultural, she gets it to some degree and it's just been so much better. Even in those moments where she doesn't understand, it still feels better because she's not questioning it and allows me to figure it out with her support.

When you're not able to meet a practitioner that's going to be wholeheartedly there for you as a person, how do you confront that? It's hard. And I shouldn't have to explain to that same practitioner what bisexuality means. I shouldn't have to educate you on that. Like, why is that a thing? Even if you don't understand it, why am I paying you for this hour to talk about what bisexuality means?

I think there's a common misperception of just because you're in the community that doesn't necessarily mean that you're also supportive of everyone under that umbrella. You could be a gay man and completely be against transgender rights, you know? It's like, I could be Black, but not agree with immigration. Just because you're in this little umbrella, we can't sit there and excuse behaviors because, "Oh, I'm gay, too." Or, "Oh, I'm part of this little acronym." Again, here is the perpetuation of not allowing people to be who they are. And now I'm scared to say to my gay friends that I'm bisexual because now I feel like they're not going to think that it's a real thing.

L:

You don't have to understand bisexuality to be empathetic and accepting. Also, there are just so many stereotypes that people buy into.

Z:

Right. Like the fact that bisexual stereotypes mean that I'm having sex with twice as many people. I am very sex positive. I love sex. And I will tell you that, but my bisexuality has nothing to do with that or that I want to have a threesome with you. I don't want that. I've had people say that as like an icebreaker-joke sort of thing: "Oh, I must like threesomes" and at the end of the day, I know it's because they're uncomfortable. And it's also show-ing that you're really childish and annoying for thinking that's the immediate thing that I want do with you. I'm bisexual, so now I must be having unsafe sex and don't know how to control myself? Why does it equate to that? That's weird to me.

L:

Why did people think that it's about doubling your options or doing it more because you have an increase in choice? That's not how it works!

Z:

Also, the promiscuity stereotype where I have to be the freak in the bedroom and have unsafe sex. And the assumption that I'm open to all of these pos-sibilities because I'm open about my sexuality and to being with two different genders. And it's not just about being more sexually active, but now I'm this freaky deaky person that's gonna be wearing the mask and be carrying the whip. And no that's not true because, first of all, I deserve consent, like any consent, but that's not even a thing here.

One thing I know, with being biracial, (my mom's white, my dad's Black) there's a whole mental health crisis with biracial adolescence. Society is very monoracial and forces you to pick one culture or race over another, especially if the two races you identify with conflict because one is marginalized and the other is privileged. There's identity con-fusion that comes out of being biracial because of those social pressures and stereotypes and it is similar with being bisexual because of all the things that we've talked about. When it comes to

being biracial *and* bisexual, not only am I trying
to figure out who I am racially and culturally, but
now there's compounded distress with figuring out
who am I sexually. I am consistently asking myself,
"Hold on, is this person right? Do I have to choose
between cisgender versus transgender in my definition of bisexuality?" This reiterates the confusion
that can come with it all because of what society's
telling you.

L:

You do work with sexual and relationship violence.
Can you tell me how that ties in with bisexuality?

Z:

With bisexuality and relationship violence, there's
a harmful stereotype that same-sex relationships
are always healthy and power dynamics don't happen.
That's not reality and makes it harder to believe
people when they say it's happening. Something that
I don't think is touched on enough is that relationship and sexual violence usually . . . [are] only
ever depicted between a dominant cisman and submissive cis woman. Reasonably so, because data shows
that it is usually men using their power and control over women. But I do not think there's enough
conversation around how power dynamics are also
happening in same-sex relationships. When two people in a romantic relationship hold the same gender identity, there's the assumption that there's a
balance of power.

If all we're focused on is these power dynamics
as it relates to someone's sex or masculinity, how
are we supposed to figure out whether or not this is
a healthy relationship? If all I know is what a man
does to a woman and how he becomes aggressive in a
relationship and uses his masculinity and muscular
physique against me . . . then how do I respond when
there's someone who is a feminine cis woman doing
the same behaviors? Do I hold them just as accountable? It's almost as if my mind can't process it
as abuse. It just gets back to that identity and
role confusion piece. For example, I've been in an

emotionally abusive relationship before when I was in college. And that was really hard to understand, especially with me trying to navigate a new relationship and find who I was and what my values were. I eventually was able to learn and identify the relationship as emotionally abusive because I came to recognize the "red flags" that are normally seen in an abusive heterosexual relationship. It was more complex in my same-sex relationship. I had to pick up on different things that I wasn't used to picking up on. For example, I felt like I was pretty established. I had my own job, my own car, my own apartment, paid my own bills as soon as I left college. I could do what I wanted on my own time and I held pride in my hard work and independence. My girlfriend, however, had just moved from another state and she did not have her own car. She did not have her own place. She didn't take on all of these responsibilities the same way I had. And so subconsciously I began to feel a power over her. There was one day she took an Uber to a restaurant midday while I was at work. When I got home and she mentioned that she left the apartment, part of me was put off by it. Cause I'm immediately questioning her, "wait, you left the house today?" I'm not like yelling at her or anything, but for me I felt uncomfortable. I began reflecting on why I was feeling weird that my girlfriend left the house. She's her own person and she should be able to do that, but I realized I felt a dominance over her. I had all this stuff for myself and she didn't, so I implicitly felt that I was the only one who could control where she went. It took a while for me to notice and accept it for what it was because I only saw dynamics like this in heterosexual relationships.

Intimate partner violence, especially with bisexuality and same-sex relationships, it gets more complex and frustrating. If I leave a same-sex relationship and then my next relationship is with the opposite sex, I question, how does that look different? Am I holding myself accountable to the harm I might be causing my partner despite their identity? Would I be acting this way if it were with a woman vs. a man? If we don't think that relationship violence or sexual violence could be happening in the same-sex dynamic, does that increase vulnerability in some way? Does it make it even more impossible to identify it as abusive because we think women can't do this kind of thing? I'm trying to do a better job of holding myself accountable as a cis woman. It has sparked some really vulnerable things that I've had to work through and continue to work through. I'm grateful that I have that knowledge because of my social work background.

Notes

1 "Understanding Bisexuality," The Trevor Project Website (August 2021), www.thetrevorproject.org/resources/article/understanding-bisexuality/.
2 Lindsay Taliaferro, Kari Gloppen, Jennifer Muehlenkamp and Marla Eisenberg, "Depression and Suicidality Among Bisexual Youth: A Nationally Representative Sample," *Journal of LGBT Youth*, Vol. 15, No. 1 (2018), 16–31.
3 Wendy Bostwick, Carol Boyd, Tonda Hughes and Sean Esteban McCabe, "Dimensions of Sexual Orientation and the Prevalence of Mood and Anxiety Disorders in the United States," *American Journal of Public Health*, Vol. 100, No. 3 (2010), 388–573.
4 "Understanding Bisexuality."
5 Jieru Chen, Mikel Walters, Leah Gilbert and Nimesh Patel, "Sexual Violence, Stalking, and Intimate Partner Violence by Sexual Orientation, United States," *Psychology of Violence*, Vol. 10, No. 1 (2020), 110–119.
6 Chen et al., "Sexual Violence, Stalking and Intimate Partner Violence."
7 Robin J. Lewis, Tatyana Kholodkov and Valerian J. Derlega, "Still Stressful After All These Years: A Review of Lesbians' and Bisexual Women's Minority Stress," *Journal of Lesbian Studies*, Vol. 16, No. 1 (2012), 30–44.
8 Lewis et al., "Still Stressful After All These Years."
9 Thekla Morgenroth, Teri Kirby, Maisie Cuthbert, Jacob Evje and Arielle Anderson, "Bisexual Erasure: Perceived Attraction Patterns of Bisexual Women and Men," *European Journal of Social Psychology*, Vol. 52, No. 2 (2021), 249–259.
10 Sapna Cheryan and Hazel Rose Markus, "Masculine Defaults: Identifying and Mitigating Hidden Cultural Biases," *Psychological Review*, Vol. 127, No. 6 (2020), 1022–1052.
11 Ilan Meyer, "Prejudice, Social Stress, and Mental Health in Lesbian, Gay, and Bisexual Populations: Conceptual Issues and Research Evidence," *Psychological Bulletin*, Vol. 129, No. 5 (2003), 674–697.

12 Meyer, "Prejudice, Social Stress, and Mental Health."

13 Mark Hatzenbuehler, "How Does Sexual Minority Stigma 'Get Under the Skin'? A Psychological Mediation Framework," *Psychological Bulletin*, Vol. 135, No. 5 (2009), 707–730.

14 Melissa Legge, Corey Flanders and Margaret Robinson, "Young Bisexual People's Experiences of Microaggression: Implications for Social Work," *Social Work in Mental Health*, Vol. 16, No. 2 (2018), 125–144.

15 Walter Bockting, Michael Miner, Rebecca Swinburne Romine, Autumn Hamilton and Eli Coleman, "Stigma, Mental Health, and Resilience in an Online Sample of the US Transgender Population," *American Journal of Public Health*, Vol. 103, No. 5 (2013), 943–951.

16 Bockting et al., "Stigma, Mental Health and Resilience."

17 Sabra Katz-Wise, Ethan Mereish and Julie Woulfe, "Associations of Bisexual-Specific Minority Stress and Health Among Cisgender and Transgender Adults with Bisexual Orientation," *The Journal of Sex Research*, Vol. 54, No. 7 (2017), 899–910.

18 Monica A. Ghabrial and Lori E. Ross, "Representation and Erasure of Bisexual People of Color: A Content Analysis of Quantitative Bisexual Mental Health Research," *Psychology of Sexual Orientation and Gender Diversity*, Vol. 5, No. 2 (2018), 140.

19 Ghabrial and Ross, "Representation and Erasure of Bisexual People of Color."

20 Lewis et al., "Still Stressful After All These Years," 30–44.

21 Sarah Ehlke, Abby Braitman, Charlotte Dawson, Kristen Heron and Robin Lewis, "Sexual Minority Stress and Social Support Explain the Association Between Sexual Identity with Physical and Mental Health Problems Among Young Lesbian and Bisexual Women," *Sex Roles*, Vol. 83, No. 5–6 (2020), 370–381.

22 Lori E. Ross, Travis Salway, Lesley Tarasoff, Jenna MacKay, Blake Hawkins and Charles Fehr, "Prevalence of Depression and Anxiety Among Bisexual People Compared to Gay, Lesbian, and Heterosexual Individuals: A Systematic Review and Meta-Analysis," *The Journal of Sex Research*, Vol. 55, No. 4–5 (2018), 435–456.

23 Genevieve Weber, "Using to Numb the Pain: Substance Use and Abuse Among Lesbian, Gay, and Bisexual Individuals," *Journal of Mental Health Counseling*, Vol. 30, No. 1 (2008), 31–48; Dawn Szymanski, Lauren Moffitt and Erika Carr, "Sexual Objectification of Women: Advances to Theory and Research," *The Counseling Psychologist*, Vol. 39, No. 1 (2011), 6–38.

24 Melanie Brewster, Brandon Velez, Jessica Esposito, Stephanie Wong, Elizabeth Geiger and Brain TaeHyuk Keum, "Moving Beyond the Binary with Disordered Eating Research: A Test and Extension of Objectification Theory with Bisexual Women," *Journal of Counseling Psychology*,

Vol. 61, No. 1 (2014), 50–62; Audrey Koh and Leslie Ross, "Mental Health Issues: A Comparison of Lesbian, Bisexual and Heterosexual Women," *Journal of Homosexuality*, Vol. 51, No. 1 (2006), 33–57.

25 Chen et al., "Sexual Violence, Stalking and Intimate Partner Violence," 110–119.

26 M.V. Lee Badgett, "Left Out? Lesbian, Gay, and Bisexual Poverty in the U.S.," *Population Research and Policy Review*, Vol. 37, No. 1 (2018), 667–702.

27 Badgett, "Left Out?"

28 Badgett, "Left Out?"

29 Sarah Calabrese, Ilan Meyer, Nicole Overstreet, Rahwa Haile and Nathan Hansen, "Exploring Discrimination and Mental Health Disparities Faced by Black Sexual Minority Women Using a Minority Stress Framework," *Psychology of Women Quarterly*, Vol. 39, No. 3 (2015), 287–304.

30 Lauren Forrest, Ariel Beccia, Cara Exten, Sarah Gehman and Emily Ansel, "Intersectional Prevalence of Suicide Ideation, Plan and Attempt Based on Gender, Sexual Orientation, Race and Ethnicity, and Rurality," *JAMA Psychiatry*, Vol. 80, No. 10 (2023), 1037–1046.

31 Ross et al., "Prevalence of Depression and Anxiety."

32 Koh and Ross, "Mental Health Issues," 33–57.

33 Ariella Tabaac, Paul Perrin and Michael Trujillo, "Multiple Mediational Model of Outness, Social Support, Mental Health, and Wellness Behavior in Ethnically Diverse Lesbian, Bisexual, and Queer Women," *LGBT Health*, Vol. 2, No. 3 (2015), 243–249.

34 Pamela Lannutti and Amanda Denes, "A Kiss Is Just a Kiss? Comparing Perceptions Related to Female-Female and Female-Male Kissing in a College Social Situation," *Journal of Bisexuality*, Vol. 12, No. 1 (2012), 249–262.

35 Selime Salim, A. Alex McConnell and Terri Messman-Moore, "Bisexual Women's Experiences of Stigma and Verbal Sexual Coercion: The Roles of Internalized Heterosexism and Outness," *Psychology of Women Quarterly*, Vol. 44, No. 3 (2020), 362–376.

36 Christine Serpe, Chris Brown, Shawnalee Criss, Kelly Lamkins and Laurel Watson, "Bisexual Women: Experiencing and Coping with Objectification, Prejudice, and Erasure," *Journal of Bisexuality*, Vol. 20, No. 4 (2020), 456–492.

37 Dawn Szymanski and Destin Stewart, "Racism and Sexism as Correlates of African American Women's Psychological Distress," *Sex Roles*, Vol. 63, No. 3–4 (2010), 226–238.

38 Yamile Molina, Keren Lehavot, Blair Beadnell and Jane Simoni, "Racial Disparities in Health Behaviors and Conditions Among Lesbian and Bisexual Women: The Role of Internalized Stigma," *LGBT Health*, Vol. 1, No. 2 (2014), 131–139.

39 Ghabrial and Ross, "Representation and Erasure of Bisexual People of Color."

40 Koh and Ross, "Mental Health Issues."

41 L.B. Watson, B.L. Velez, J. Brownfield and M.J. Flores, "Minority Stress and Bisexual Women's Disordered Eating: The Role of Maladaptive Coping," *The Counseling Psychologist*, Vol. 44, No. 8 (2016), 1158–1186, https://doi.org/10.1177/0011000016669233.

42 Koh and Ross, "Mental Health Issues."

43 R. Engeln-Maddox, S.A. Miller and D.M. Doyle, "Tests of Objectification Theory in Gay, Lesbian, and Heterosexual Community Samples: Mixed Evidence for Proposed Pathways," *Sex Roles*, Vol. 65, No. 7–8 (2011), 518–532, https://doi.org/10.1007/s11199-011-9958-8.

44 Brewster et al., "Moving Beyond the Binary with Disordered Eating Research," 50–62.

45 Ashleigh Rich, Heather Armstrong, Zishani Cui, Paul Sereda, Nathan Lachowsky, David Moore, Robert Hogg and Eric Roth, "Sexual Orientation Measurement, Bisexuality and Mental Health in a Sample of Men Who Have Sex with Men in Vancouver, Canada," *Journal of Bisexuality*, Vol. 18, No. 3 (2018), 299–317.

46 Brian Dodge, Phillip Schnarrs, Michael Reece, Omar Martinez, Gabriel Goncalves, David Malebranche, Barbara Van Der Pol, Ryan Nix and J. Dennis Fortenberry, "Individual and Social Factors Related to Mental Health Concerns Among Bisexual Men in the Midwestern United States," *Journal of Bisexuality*, Vol. 12, No. 2 (2012), 223–245.

47 Dodge et al., "Individual and Social Factors."

48 Dodge et al., "Individual and Social Factors," 232.

49 John Hyde, "The Chameleons of Sexuality," *The Queer Majority* (September 2023), www.queermajority.com/essays-all/the-chameleons-of-sexuality#:~:text=Existing%20in%20the%20void%20created,our%20so%2Dcalled%20feminine%20side.

50 Hyde, "The Chameleons of Sexuality."

51 Anna Sutton, "Living the Good Life: A Meta-Analysis of Authenticity, Well-Being and Engagement," *Personality and Individual Differences*, Vol. 153, No. 15 (2020).

52 Sutton, "Living the Good Life."

53 Deana Williams, Brian Dodge, Bria Berger, Alex Kimbrough and Wendy Bostwick, "Self-Reported Health Concerns and Healthcare Experiences Among Diverse Bisexual Men: An Exploratory Qualitative Study," *Journal of Bisexuality*, Vol. 20, No. 3 (2020) 320.

54 Williams et al., "Self-Reported Health Concerns and Healthcare Experiences."

55 Williams et al., "Self-Reported Health Concerns and Healthcare Experiences."

56 Brian Feinstein and Christina Dyar, "Bisexuality, Minority Stress and Health," *Current Sexual Health Reports*, Vol. 9, No. 1 (2017), 42–49.

57 Sean McCabe, Tonda Hughes, Wendy Bostwick, Brady West and Carol Boyd, "Sexual Orientation, Substance Use Behavior and Substance Dependence in the United States," *Addiction*, Vol. 104, No. 8 (2009), 1333–1345.

58 Jonathan Alexander and Karen Yescavage, "Bisexuality and Transgenderism: Intersexions of the Others," *Journal of Bisexuality*, Vol. 3, No. 3–4 (2003), 1–23.

59 Katz-Wise et al., "Associations of Bisexual-Specific Minority Stress," 899–910.

60 Movement Advancement Project, "A Closer Look: Bisexual Transgender People," (September 2017), 2, https://www.lgbtmap.org/file/A%20Closer%20Look%20Bisexual%20Transgender.pdf.

61 Lori Ross, Cheryl Dobinson and Allison Eady, "Perceived Determinants of Mental Health for Bisexual People: A Qualitative Examination," *American Journal of Public Health*, Vol. 100, No. 3 (2010), 497.

62 Williams et al., "Self-Reported Health Concerns and Healthcare Experiences."

63 Chen et al., "Sexual Violence, Stalking and Intimate Partner Violence," 110–119.

64 Chen et al., "Sexual Violence, Stalking and Intimate Partner Violence."

65 Movement Advancement Project, "A Closer Look," 3.

66 Nicole Johnson and MaryBeth Grove, "Why Us? Toward an Understanding of Bisexual Women's Vulnerability for and Negative Consequences of Sexual Violence," *Journal of Bisexuality*, Vol. 17, No. 4 (2017), 435–450.

67 Serpe et al., "Bisexual Women," 456–492.

68 Johnson and Grove, "Why Us?"

69 Johnson and Grove, "Why Us?"

70 Johnson and Grove, "Why Us?"

71 Salim et al., "Bisexual Women's Experiences with Stigma," 362–376.

72 Emilie Doan Van, Ethan Mereish, Julie Woulfe and Sabra Katz-Wise, "Perceived Discrimination, Coping Mechanisms, and Effects on Health in Bisexual and Other Non-Monosexual Adults," *Archives of Sexual Behavior*, Vol. 48, No. 1 (2019), 159–174.

73 Salim et al., "Bisexual Women's Experiences with Stigma."

74 Susan Turell, Michael Brown and Molly Herrmann, "Disproportionately High: An Exploration of Intimate Partner Violence Prevalence Rates for Bisexual People," *Sexual and Relationship Therapy*, Vol. 33, No. 2–3 (2018), 113–131.

75 Autumn Bermea, Brad van Eeden-Moorefield and Lyndal Khaw, "A Systematic Review of Research on Intimate Partner Violence Among Bisexual Women," *Journal of Bisexuality*, Vol. 18, No. 4 (2018), 399–424.

</>

76 Turell et al., "Disproportionately High."
77 Turell et al., "Disproportionately High."
78 Turell et al., "Disproportionately High."
79 Bermea et al., "A Systematic Review of Research."
80 Susan Long, Sarah Ullman, LaDonna Long, Gillian Mason and Laura Starzynski, "Women's Experiences of Male-Perpetrated Sexual Assault by Sexual Orientation," *Violence and Victims*, Vol. 22, No. 6 (2007), 684–701.
81 Bermea et al., "A Systematic Review of Research."
82 Bermea et al., "A Systematic Review of Research."
83 Luca Rolle, Giulia Giardina, Angela Caldarera, Eva Gerino and Piera Brustia, "When Intimate Partner Violence Meets Same Sex Couples: A Review of Same Sex Intimate Partner Violence," *Frontiers in Psychology*, Vol. 9 (2018), 1506.
84 Kimber Shelton and Edward Delgado-Romero, "Sexual Orientation Microaggressions: The Experience of Lesbian, Gay, Bisexual, and Queer Clients in Psychotherapy," *Journal of Counseling Psychology*, Vol. 58, No. 2 (2011), 210–221.
85 Hannah J. Johnson, "Bisexuality, Mental Health, and Media Representation," *Journal of Bisexuality*, Vol. 16, No. 3 (2016), 378–396.
86 Johnson, "Bisexuality, Mental Health, and Media Representation."
87 Johnson, "Bisexuality, Mental Health, and Media Representation."
88 Johnson, "Bisexuality, Mental Health, and Media Representation."
89 Johnson, "Bisexuality, Mental Health, and Media Representation," 381.
90 Jennifer Vencill and Tania Israel, "Shining a Light into the Darkness: Bisexuality and Relationships," *Sexual and Relationship Therapy*, Vol. 33, No. 1–2 (2018), 1–5.
91 Movement Advancement Project, "Invisible Majority: The Disparities Facing Bisexual People and How to Remedy Them," (September 2016), www.lgbtmap.org/policy-and-issue-analysis/invisible-majority.
92 "How to Support Bisexual Youth: Ways to Care for Young People Who Are Attracted to More Than One Gender," The Trevor Project, www.thetrev orproject.org/wp-content/uploads/2020/09/How-to-Support-Bisexual-Youth.pdf.
93 "Health Disparities Among Bisexual People," Human Rights Campaign, https://assets2.hrc.org/files/assets/resources/HRC-BiHealthBrief.pdf?_ ga=2.85333465.1178755513.1696807685-1876651369.1696807684.

11

DISABILITIES

By Katelyn Friedline

R esearch is only beginning to scratch the surface at the intersection of disability and bisexuality. Within disability studies, a significant examination of broader societal constructions has been conducted, such as the "normate," a term coined by Rosemarie Garland-Thomson that describes how able-bodiedness contrasts with disability to define itself. Other scholars, like Allison Kafer and Robert McRuer, have employed queer theory to define the disability experience. This includes Kafer's concept of crip time, which posits that disabled people live outside of able-bodied timelines and "recognizes how expectations of 'how long things take' are based on very particular minds and bodies."[1] Additionally, McRuer discusses compulsory able-bodiedness—which expands upon the queer theory of compulsory heterosexuality—and argues that it "functions by covering over, with the appearance of choice, a system in which there actually is no choice."[2] There is also the work of Dolmage on disability myths and media tropes[3] along with Mitchell and Snyder's examination of negative stereotypes reinforced through media representation. Mitchell and Snyder address how disability does not suffer from a lack of representation within media; it instead lacks *positive* representation that does not showcase disability as tragedy.[4] Even though there is a great deal of research about disabilities, there is a lack of specific theoretical work on how bisexuality and disabilities work in tandem. This chapter aims to address this intersection more specifically and to foster continued study of this overlooked area of research. In order to properly investigate how exactly disability and bisexuality overlap, it is important to have a general understanding of the history of disability before examining how ableism—a system of oppression "that places value on people's bodies and minds based on societally constructed ideas of normality, intelligence,

DOI: 10.4324/9781003242659-12

excellence, desirability and productivity"[5]—intersects with biphobia, bi-erasure, and monosexism.

What Should a Body Be Able to Do? A Brief Intro to Disability

Traditionally, disability has been viewed through a concept known as the *medical model*. This model constructs disability as an individual problem that must be solved or managed through medical intervention. As Kafer describes in her book *Feminist, Queer, Crip*, the medical model

> *F*rames atypical bodies and minds as deviant, pathological, and defective, best understood and addressed in medical terms. In this framework, the proper approach to disability is to 'treat' the condition and the person with the condition rather than "treating" the social processes and policies that constrict disabled people's lives.[6]

Since the medical model views disability as an individual experience to be addressed only with a doctor, at its very core, it is antithetical to solidarity and disability community-making. Without any room in this model for discussion of shared experience or societal factors, there is no common ground for disabled people to meet and share. By framing disability as a personal defect that needs to be "solved," the addition of shame discourages people from speaking about their lived experiences.

Comparatively, theorists of social model of disability argue that it is the fault of society and its lack of accessibility that disables people, not their disabilities. The Union of Physically Impaired Against Segregation defined the social model in their 1975 statement:

> *I*n our view, it is a society that disables physically impaired people. Disability is something imposed on top of our impairments by the way we are unnecessarily isolated and excluded from full participation in society. Disabled people are, therefore an oppressed group in society.[7]

The framing of the social model as a systemic issue has been incredibly foundational in establishing disability movements and allowing the formation of political groups that fight for societal change. The theory that society only allows certain citizens access to all facets of life, instead of there being a moral failing of disabled people, has been essential for this kind of organizing. Unfortunately, while the social model is a great tool for social change, a main criticism is that it is too simplistic and fails to account for chronic pain or non-mobility-related disabilities. Many scholars have proposed improved models, such as Kafer's political relational model, but the social model is a useful tool for beginning to conceptualize how society and ableism interact to oppress disabled people.[8]

One must note the change in language surrounding the disability community as the push for less medicalized and offensive terms was implemented to move away from the medical model. There is often discussion over person-first language such as "people with disabilities" vs. disability-first language like "disabled people."[9] In this chapter, the style used is disability first language, but that is my own preference when referring to myself as a disabled person. Disability is a major part of my identity and so naming myself as a disabled person has always felt right, but this does not mean that person-first language is incorrect. Many disabled people prefer person-first language as it recognizes their humanity before their disability, and their preference should be respected.

Disability and Sexuality—Infantilization and Eugenics

When addressing disability's relationship to sexuality, it is essential to consider how society infantilizes disabled people. Disability is often portrayed in viral videos on social media or news outlets as deeply inspirational.[10] It is through this lens that disabled people are seen not as people just living their lives but as inspiration porn[11] reminding able-bodied people to be grateful for their lives. It robs disabled people, however, of their autonomy to live and do great things without the narrative of overcoming disability. Furthermore, many parents often capitalize off of viral videos of their disabled children, which either consist of inspiration or a moment of distress to show other people "what it is like." Neither video format allows for the autonomy of the disabled person to choose whether they are presented as being successful "for a disabled person" or that their personal life is broadcast to the entire public.[12]

Another example of infantilization is the experience of many disabled people: able-bodied people assume that they need help.[13] This can manifest as a person walking around the grocery store with a mobility aid and a stranger taking things out of their hands, a wheelchair user being pushed by someone without asking, or a blind person being led without speaking to them. These assumptions that disabled people cannot care for themselves have a common thread of lacking consent and that they should be grateful for the help.[14] An additional contributing factor is "disability organizations" that claim to be fighting against ableism, without any disabled people in their leadership or organization, such as autism advocacy. These organizations often claim to advocate for autistic people, yet they refuse to involve them in any decision making, let alone serving on their boards.[15]

This speaks to a broader societal view of disabled people as nonautonomous adults, unable to make decisions for themselves or provide consent. While this topic is significant on its own, this kind of infantilization feeds into the narrative that they are not sexual in any way, which in reality is totally untrue.[16] Media portrayals perpetuate this stereotype by rarely showing disabled people as sexual beings. Although there is plenty of representation of disabled people, they are rarely depicted as nuanced, living full lives, or making their own choices. As Dolmage discusses, there are instead several disability myths that commonly pop up as tropes within media, such as: "disability as pathology"; "kill or cure"; and "disability as an object of pity or charity."[17] All of these tropes further societal perceptions that disabled people are not fully complex individuals but rather plot points to be acted upon for other people's gain. As Mitchell and Snyder argue, disabled people are presented as static characters, acted upon and used to showcase the main character's growth. The disabled person is not shown as experiencing growth, able to make choices, or having bodily autonomy.[18]

Today there are some better portrayals of disability within media, but rarely does a disabled character mention sex or have a love story of their own. One show in recent years that portrays a disabled character as a fully complex person and as a sexual being is the HBO show *The Sex Lives of College Girls*. Jocelyn, portrayed by disabled actor Lauren Spencer, is a power wheelchair user and is a deeply cool individual who goes to naked parties and is a kind of a sexually informed older sister figure for the main characters in the show. Additionally, in the show *Sex Education* there is a recurring character named Issac, a wheelchair user who is sexually involved with other characters on the show.

While infantilization is a negative phenomenon in and of itself, this cultural narrative did not appear in a vacuum. The roots of the desexualization of disabled people stem from the history of eugenics. Eugenics, within its definition in U.S. history, was a series of systematic and governmental decisions designed to optimize human reproduction towards a certain ideal human state.[19] One of the main purposes of eugenics was to eradicate disability, along with attempting to "improve" the racial makeup of the U.S. This state-sanctioned plan for designing an ideal populace was executed through several policies, including the sterilization of racial minorities, as well as anyone suspected of having any disability at the time. For years, disabled people, on top of being institutionalized, criminalized, and separated from public life, were also subject to sterilization and other surgeries that they did not consent to in order to prevent them from contributing to the population.[20] Although the state-sanctioned effort to prevent disabled people from contributing to the population no longer exists, this infantilization and desexualization of disabled people is a holdover from a eugenics-based mindset. As Kafer discusses, a future for disabled people is not imagined. The only way disability is ever seen in the future is with scientific and technological advancement or the showcasing of "progress" by demonstrating a cure for a certain disability.[21] Furthermore, it is precisely this cultural obsession with removing disability that feeds and perpetuates these narratives that disabled people cannot make decisions for themselves and, therefore, should not be treated like adults with autonomy or sexuality.

Bisexuality and Disability

A couple of patterns emerge when analyzing the intersection of disability and bisexuality, including the refusal to be placed into the singular binaries of the dominant cis-hetero patriarchal culture.[22] Disability is such a widely varied experience that it cannot be categorized into a singular box to oppose able-bodiedness, while bisexuality refuses to conform to the binary enforced by monosexism. The visible existence of both challenges the binaries of able-bodied/disabled and straight/gay that society is so invested in.[23] Disability and bisexuality undermine the dominant power structures in society, which has not been successful in eradicating either disability or bisexuality. Dominant culture has a vested interest in erasing, suppressing, and stigmatizing disability and bisexuality in mainstream existence. This suppression is where biphobia, bi-erasure, and the stigmatization of disability intersect as tools of cis-hetero patriarchy used not only to restrain the ways in which bisexuality and disability challenge binaries but also to inhibit living with joy and fulfillment while being bisexual and disabled.

When bisexuality or disability are seemingly allowed to be visible, these identities are still framed within able-bodied and heterosexist narratives. Disabled bodies can be displayed as entertainment in freak shows and medical theater or as test subjects for medical success, while bisexuality is depicted as a hypersexual performance for a cis-hetero patriarchal gaze. These instances define these moments of visibility through the mindset of the dominant culture. This prevents people from being able to see the truly nuanced existence of these identities and, therefore, still erases them as identities that can be whole, full, and joyful.

In a similar vein, both the disability and bisexual communities experience fetishization. Bisexual fetishization often manifests as being asked by a couple to be in a threesome or a partner automatically assuming that bisexual people all want to be in threesomes.[24] This is not to say that all situations like this are fetishization, but if a person's attraction to a bisexual person is based *solely* on the potential for a threesome, this fetishizes that person's bisexuality. Conversely, while society assumes that many disabled people are not sexual, the other end of this spectrum is the fetishization of disabled people specifically for their disability. The prevalence of pornographic websites specifically dedicated to different types of disabilities, such as amputees, points to a demand for disability fetish content.[25]

These experiences are further amplified if an individual is both disabled and bisexual, as suppression, erasure, and fetishization often compound each other. Since society does not allow for complex narratives around disabled or bisexual people, these identities can be used to invalidate or cancel out the other. For example, if someone is physically disabled, people will infantilize and desexualize them and therefore invalidate their bisexuality. This is exacerbated by the fact that representation of bisexual, disabled people is nonexistent within media or cultural narratives, which becomes a self-fulfilling prophecy and further perpetuates erasure of both identities.

Beyond Visibility

Since one of the main goals of dominant culture has been to erase or suppress both bisexuality and disability from mainstream culture, the seemingly obvious response to combat this is through visibility. There have been multiple movements within both bisexual and disability activism to push for awareness and visibility of these identities. Some examples that come to mind are Bi Visibility Week, which is one week out of the year dedicated to seeing, appreciating, and celebrating bisexuality, as well as the Disability Visibility Movement. The Disability Visibility Movement is both an incredible essay collection edited by disability activist Alice Wong and a larger disability pride movement both online and in person to celebrate the multi-varied forms of disability and make it seen.[26]

This is not to say that visibility is not important within these movements. Visibility is an incredibly useful tool for building community, promoting positive representation and identifying language that fits who they already are. Visibility alone, however, does not take the fight far enough to dismantle the societal structures that marginalize disabled, bisexual people in the first place. In addition, visibility without the breaking down of structures originally designed to erase the existence of bisexual and disabled people increases the chances of further marginalization. As Shiri Eisner notes when analyzing the bi visibility campaign "I Am Visible":

> *The very outset of this campaign assumed that invisibility is the most burning issue for bi people. Given this presumption, it also assumed that the solution for this problem is straightforward visibility. By doing so, the campaign engaged with bisexuality on a superficial level. Instead, it could have asked questions such as: What does invisibility cause? What causes it? What are the material results it creates in the lives of bi people, and especially young bisexuals?*[27]

It is essential to question and analyze the types of organizing done for both the Bisexuality and Disability Movements and scrutinize whether the movements actually address the structural issues that contribute to the marginalization of these communities. Additionally, the goal of visibility-based movements can often be acceptance, but it is not the place of the dominant culture to choose whether to accept bisexual and/or disabled people.

Bisexual and disabled people are worthy of rights and deserve to live their lives fully without stigmatization. For our movements to push solely for acceptance, without larger structural change in mind as well, it places bisexual and disabled people in the position of asking the dominant culture for rights that should have always been their own to begin with. Therefore, while visibility and awareness can be useful tools for bringing people to the cause, this alone will foster movements that lack the imagination of collective liberation. These can seem like lofty goals, but small acts of resistance can foster bigger movements, which is why space must be made within the communities and circles for bodies and minds to be as they are. Whether that means supporting bodies that are outside of "normative" expectations or embracing the fluidity of attraction and love, these smaller actions paired with broader organizing and activism can permit even more people to inhabit all these intersections that once seemed impossible.

Overall, it becomes clear that the experiences of erasure, stigmatization, and fetishization are amplified for individuals who are both disabled and bisexual. The societal perceptions of each identity can also be used to further erase the individual's other identity, leading to further marginalization. Furthermore, while there have been community-led efforts to increase visibility of each of these identities, there has been little community work to specifically acknowledge and address individuals at the intersection of these identities, and if continued progress is to be made, then broader goals beyond visibility need to be fought for.

A Conversation with Shiri Eisner

LISA:
How you do see ableism, monosexism, and biphobia intersect?

SHIRI:
That's a huge question. I mostly look at it from my own vantage point. I have fibromyalgia and endometriosis and a few other things, which so happen to be very prevalent among bi women and non-binary people. They're also very closely linked with trauma and especially sexual trauma, which is also very prevalent among bi women and enbies. I think misogyny is something that is very much in common to all three. There are a lot of parallels.

For example, one way in which fibromyalgia and endometriosis parallel bisexuality (being illnesses that affect AFAB [assigned female at birth] people)

is the misogyny that comes along with that. You
are treated as hysterical, like you're imagining
things, you're not actually in pain or having symptoms, it's all in your head.

That kind of attitude is very common both for
these illnesses and bi experiences—especially the
experiences of bi women not being considered a reli-
able narrator of your own life and experiences. All
these statements about how it's all in your head,
you're imagining things, it's going to pass, you
just have to decide, or it's just a phase.

For example, I used to live on disability for a
few years, because I was unable to leave my bed most
of the time. I was disabled enough to get benefits
from the government, but my mom still didn't believe
that I was truly ill and still doesn't to this day.
I've had fibromyalgia since 2010. She still thinks
that I'm only making it up, that it's all in my head
and I just have to decide to be healthy and boom,
I will be.

It's very much similar, in the way that I feel
my bisexuality is treated, not just by my family,
but also in a lot of other contexts. You know, constantly being questioned on your own life or people not believing you when you say things about
yourself.

L:
They aren't visible disabilities, so people aren't
believing it.

S:
Absolutely. In the book I was talking about having no way to prove or to show that you do have a
physical disability and people's assumptions. These
are all different facets of one, monstrous sort of
ableism and many kinds of oppression that intersect in that way. The way you're treated is affected
by how you're perceived, which is, of course, the
entire problem, the primacy of visibility to the
exclusion of all else.

Just to give an example, I had a really difficult
experience at the emergency room about a year ago.

I was having a really bad episode, really serious endometriosis pain, and I went, in the middle of the night, to the emergency room. Looking at the comparative pain scale, I was at an eight out of ten. That's where my pain was. And they actually gave me opiates, to the vein, like for an IV. Oh my god. And the doctor who berated me for going there after giving me opiates. Even after she offered me morphine and I refused. She berated me for being there at all, for seeking treatment at all.

L:
What were you supposed to do?

S:
According to her I was supposed to just stay home and suffer through it.

L:
Take some Advil and go to bed.

S:
Basically, yeah. That was horrible. That's the thing about visibility, because I carry pain very well. I'm used to it. So, when my pain is truly terrible and excruciating, and I'm hardly functioning, I frown a little, I become quieter. And that is the only external sign you would have of it. And the medical summary of the visit actually stated that I "basically looked fine," that's what they wrote.

There's this enormous gap between what you experience and what your environment perceives, and this general disbelief of what you say about yourself. It's a really seminal experience, I think, for bi people and for invisibly disabled people. It's where we intersect. And of course, the links between these specific sorts of disabilities and poor health in general, being very prevalent among bi people. It creates a situation where all of these experiences are very close together, like facets of the same experience being expressed in different ways and in different locations in our lives.

L:

When you talk about mental and physical health disparities or higher rates of sexual violence for bi people, is there a level of people not believing that too?

S:

Yes. In so many ways. First of all, the dearth of research is a really big factor here. I was recently updating my entry on monosexism in the SAGE LGBTQ Encyclopedia. I think I originally wrote it in 2015. And one of the things I found was that almost no new research has been published in all of these years since then.

This data has been publicly known for a decade now, but no one's talking about it. So many people don't know about the very specific and concrete ways that bi people experience oppression. I feel that when people hear this data, it doesn't even compute; they immediately disregard it. Because it doesn't fit in with how they perceive bisexuality and the social treatment of bisexuality. I've been talking about these things for ten years, and it really feels like nobody listens. There are bi activists who have been talking about these things for years. For example, a lot of people on Bi Twitter, as well as the late and beloved Bi Tumblr. Bisexual activists have been trying to create this discourse, but no one seems to be taking it on.

L:

Bisexuality isn't seen as a valid sexual orientation, is that part of it?

S:

I feel that it's more advanced, like people perceiving bisexuality as inherently privileged. Or there is a very broad scale assumption that bisexuals don't experience oppression to the same level (or at all) and that we only experience oppression to the extent that we pass as gay or lesbian in public. So, it's mainly the perception that there

is no oppression that is specific to bi people that
I think is more responsible for that.

L:

I don't think I knew to what extent that it was
dismissed.

S:

Yeah. Those of us who write, we write about it and
we talk about it—but the broader community. . . . It
always kills me. For example, on Bi Twitter, we talk
a lot about bimisogyny and sexual violence against
bi women. And no one takes it up or retweets it,
but say one thing about bisexuality being binary or
not and everyone is flocking to your yard. It really
kills me. Wherever you are, if you want to do stuff
or talk about bisexuality, like if you don't do it,
it just doesn't get done. No one's going to talk
about it if you don't talk about it.

L:

What are your thoughts on bi visibility?

S:

I have a complicated relationship with bi visibility. I really take issue with visibility being at the
forefront of the bi movement. I don't think it should
be a goal in and of itself. Visibility is like, it's
a tool. It's not a purpose. It's not a cause.

L:

Does it feel a little buzzwordy?

S:

I mean, yes. But also . . . if only it was just a
buzzword and not a deeper practice. A lot of people treat bi visibility as if it was the purpose in
and of itself, but visibility without liberation is
dangerous and makes you a target for violence and
oppression.

We're really seeing that right now with the backlash against the trans movement. For years, the

trans movement was always talking about visibility.
I remember when we were talking about bi and trans
invisibility, bi and trans erasure. It's incredible
to read those texts from the past because now it's so
very different. I remember this cultural moment where
the trans movement was like finally getting its hard-
earned visibility. And we were all very happy. There
was (the very brilliant) Laverne Cox coming into
popular culture, who was bringing really important
things into public consciousness. And then there was
Caitlin Jenner, and this whole wave of trans people
coming to the forefront. But what we're seeing now
is this terrifying, dystopian fascist backlash trying to eradicate trans people from existence.

I really want the bi movement to be very careful
of that. Because insisting on visibility, again,
without liberation, means that we're insisting on
becoming targets of hate.

Visibility is not enough. I also feel when we're
talking about visibility, we're really accepting
all the ways in which society is built, the current power structures and structures of oppression.
Talking about visibility just takes all of it and
normalizes it, because it says the world is basically okay, the problem is that we're not being
seen. But the problem isn't that we're invisible,
the problem is we're actively erased and are suffering from tangible oppression. What we need is to
break down all of these oppressive power structures
that also not only affect us but also a lot of other
groups. And we can build from there, but our starting point can't be visibility.

L:

Do you feel similarly about the disabilities justice movements?

S:

I don't feel there's that much insistence on visibility within disability movements. At least the
ones that I'm exposed to, which I guess is the more
radical part. When I think about liberal disability

movements locally, they are much more focused on
accessibility, like tangible forms of discrimination. They do lobbying with the government and legislation. I'm not a fan of lobbying, government, or
legislation, but even when we just look at the liberal part of the movement, without even considering
the radical parts, I don't think they focus that
much on visibility. They focus more on the actual
issues that are killing us.

Which is what the bi movement should be focused on.
It's disturbing. We're being killed; we're becoming
ill. We have poor mental health; we're exposed to
sexual and intimate partner violence, to bullying
and a long, long line of problems with poverty,
with discrimination. Why don't we talk about these
things? Why are we talking about visibility?

L:
You wrote about the hierarchy of visibility. How
people are treating you based on even being able to
see your identity or disability or not. What do you
think about that and ableism within queer spaces?

S:
The major issue I'm having right now with queer
spaces and ableism is Covid. The world is in complete collective denial. Covid still exists; it is
still a pandemic, but the community has followed
suit with this denial in a way that truly breaks my
heart. The community that I thought of as inclusive, especially radical queer communities, that
are supposed to be aware of inclusion, accessibility, and disability, they're completely fine with
excluding us categorically, because events with no
masking are taking place in enclosed spaces, and
people like me can't participate in them. That is
actually the strongest barrier to my activism right
now. That I can't meet with other people in the same
room.

That really bothers me in a way that I don't even
think I can even feel fully, because if I did,
it would break me. Society is perfectly okay with
high-risk groups either being completely excluded

from participation in public life or alternatively
having to risk our lives. I don't want to be given
this choice. My choice is not to risk my life. And
the fact that the queer community has followed suit
with this kind of approach, this deeply eugenic
politic of literally making disabled people disposable within queer spaces, it is just horrible and
it breaks my heart.

L:

As far as people are concerned in the U.S., it is
pretty much over.

S:

Same here [in Israel/Occupied Palestine], absolutely. People in public spaces see me wearing a
mask and some of them are like, "Oh my god, I hav-
en't seen a person wear a mask in so long. Why are
you still wearing it? COVID is over."

L:

That idea of not having that level of awareness or
being treated as disposable, like you said, that's
huge.

S:

It's enormous. I think it's probably some sort of
collective trauma for disabled people and people in
high-risk groups, being told that you don't matter
and that your life has no value to society. Literally that protecting your health and your life is
unimportant. It is a very strong message, I would
say even visceral. A lot of people are experiencing that right now, and nobody's talking about it
or acknowledging it. The lack of acknowledgement
speaks even more loudly. Covid is literally expanding the disabled population. But it doesn't matter
because once you cross the line, you don't matter
anymore.

L:

That's intense. Are there other thoughts about
ableism in queer spaces?

S:

Actually the original question did make me remember back when I was using a cane. I had a girlfriend at the time and she told me once that when we were out holding hands, she really felt like my cane made people interpret our handholding as a caregiving relationship rather than us being girlfriends. So, I was reminded of that.

L:

That's interesting, how people see people or what they're putting on people.

S:

It's very othering. Specifically, wheelchair users are so often objectified. I had this experience once; I was flying to the U.S. and had a connection flight in London. I was using a wheelchair between the flights because flights really mess up my body. At one point, one of the attendants at the airport was pushing me in the wheelchair. I felt that for her, I was just cargo. I wasn't even a person. She didn't look at me, smile, address or acknowledge me in any way. I felt like I was just a suitcase that she was carrying from one place to another. And that is just a tiny taste that I had of it. I'm not a wheelchair user in everyday life, but from testimonials of people who do use wheelchairs on a regular basis, this is the kind of treatment that they constantly have to suffer.

L:

We have a such long way to go.

S:

Yeah, for sure.

Belonging by Katelyn Friedline

Being both bisexual and disabled has always come with a feeling of begging to be believed. Whether that be by doctors or my peers, I have always felt like I had to plead with someone to trust that I know myself and my body. Growing up, I strongly remember a feeling of not being "normal," both in the feelings I had for my peers and the way my body worked (or didn't), but

I never had words to describe what I was feeling. It wasn't until my early twenties that I was able to name what I was experiencing, both with my sexuality and the diagnosis of my disability. Whether that was through cultural narratives that bisexuality was just a phase or multiple doctors writing off my physical symptoms as "just anxiety," I always felt like people assumed that they knew me better than I knew myself. Even though I lived in my body and with myself my whole life there was this assumption that I somehow was too young or naive to have any clue who I was and a condescension that they knew better.

When I finally started to come to terms with my bisexuality as label that fit me, I remember being both terrified and relieved. Relieved because I finally had the words to describe my own experience to other people in a way that communicated that I was serious. Terrified for what this meant for how people may treat me. At the same time, I was experiencing a large amount of medical trauma that I have only begun to grapple with. After years with multiple misdiagnoses and ineffective treatments that left me feeling worse rather than better, I felt so out of control. I decided to try to explore what I could control and sought out queer spaces.

I went into my first gay bar in a college town in Alabama when I was a senior in college, and while the bar was called a "gay bar," it really served as one of the few queer safe spaces in the area. It was a little hole in the wall tucked away in the downtown area with blacked out windows, one grungy bar top, and a stage. They would host drag shows on the weekends, which attracted their usual queer clientele but also brought in some seemingly straight girls and couples wanting to see the drag queens perform. The first time I went was with a couple of my sorority sisters on one of these drag show weekends, and I was nervous as all hell for what was to come. When we walked in, I was both excited and anxious to possibly embrace this part of myself, but then I ran into some acquaintances from clubs on campus who were gay. We waved at one another, and I walked over to chat. One of the first things they said was, while they were excited to see me, they were growing tired of all the straight sorority girls coming to their bar, including me. They of course did not know my inner turmoil, and I was not anywhere near confident enough to tell them otherwise at the time. Instead, I finished up our conversation and did not stay particularly long out of anxiety that others viewed me the same way. I did work up the courage to come back to that bar a few more times before I graduated and got bolder at telling people I was bisexual, but that initial feeling of being an intruder in queer spaces still stuck with me.

When I graduated and moved to DC, I was in a new place with plenty more queer spaces, but I was afraid of going to the many different gay bars and being seen as a straight intruder. The first few months of living there were marked with some loneliness. While I had great friends, I really longed to be in community with other queer people. Luckily, after a few months, through a chance Instagram connection, I made a couple of queer femme friends who brought me under their wings and assured me that these queer spaces were also for me. No matter how straight I looked, I still belonged. This acceptance and encouragement increased my confidence enough to start experimenting with my style and presenting a bit more androgynous. When I felt like my presentation matched what I wanted to look like—which was fairly queer—enjoying myself in queer spaces became a lot easier. With this new appearance and confidence, I went to one of my favorite queer bars in Adams Morgan. I found myself a lot less worried what others thought and if they were speculating about whether I belonged there or not. I actually allowed myself to just enjoy being in community, dancing and drinking with both my friends and strangers.

It was after a year of living in DC and enjoying the feeling of comfort in queer spaces that my health began to decline. I finally received a diagnosis that seemed to answer and explain my myriad symptoms by which so many specialists previously were baffled. As my health became worse, I moved in with my family and began to use mobility aids—first a cane and then forearm crutches—and had my first experiences with navigating the world as a visibly disabled person. I had expected some of the obstacles, access barriers and mobility challenges, but what really caught me off guard was how other people treated me. I suddenly was subjected to continual stares and intrusive questions of "what happened?" or "what's wrong with you?" Honestly, it messed with me and my sense of self. I was once again plagued with feeling like others were constantly watching and judging me, similar to how I felt when I first started entering queer spaces but now on a significantly larger scale.

In trying to feel less alone with this adjustment of identifying as disabled and navigating the world as a visibly disabled person, as well as grapple with my isolation from my queer community while staying with my family, I turned to movies and shows for solace and solidarity. I tried to seek out shows that maybe had disabled or bisexual characters, not to mention bisexual disabled characters. Once I actually began watching these shows and movies, I found myself sorely disappointed. Disabled characters all lacked stories of their own and only existed to aid the character growth of the main able-bodied characters, or the only ending for many disabled characters was either dying or being miraculously cured. In addition, so many shows barely hinted at characters being bisexual but refused to name them as such. It was gutting to be dying to connect with stories that could in any way reflect my own experiences, only to be confronted with more reminders of how parts of my identity are viewed as things to be hidden or fixed. On the front of any bisexual disabled representation, I still have yet to see that on screen in any way, let alone a portrayal of disabled people as adults who want to date, meet people, and fall in love without infantilizing them in the process.

When my health stabilized a bit, I moved back to DC and there, along with where I am currently in life, I have often been struck that navigating these two different identities can feel like a comedy of errors. While being bisexual can often come with a feeling of wanting to be seen or recognized, being visibly disabled can come with feelings of wanting to be anonymous. For example, when I went back to some of my favorite queer bars in DC with friends, I had markedly different experiences than I previously described, and the big shift was around my disability. First, accessing these spaces was much harder with the number of internal and external stairs and lack of elevators, never mind what happened when I got up to the bar. I was no longer a stranger to these spaces, and yet suddenly I was being handled with velvet gloves. People offered me chairs, bouncers brought in seats from outside, strangers came up and offered help while mentioning their disabled family members, and I was shielded onto the dance floor. The people meant well, but for all of this to happen in one evening really demonstrated just how much my life had changed. Before, I moved through this same bar as just another queer person in the crowd. As much as these people were motivated by kindness it began to feel that their focus and attention on me was less about actually wanting me in the space and instead wanting to make themselves feel better about "helping." All this help would have been great if I had asked for it, but to have it thrust upon me without my consent began to feel deeply infantilizing and othering. I tried my best to power through these evenings and enjoy myself like I used to, but it was hard to approach a person who caught your eye and try to flirt when their first instinct was to say "Oh do you need my seat?" Not to mention when I tried to dance and heard so many comments of "good for you for getting out there!" I suddenly could no longer let myself loose in the crowd and have fun. I left those nights grieving the safe and comfortable spaces I previously had being in community with other queer folks. I was not a peer anymore, rather a hazard to be managed. The loss of comfortability would not have hit as hard if only so many queer spaces were not centered around bar and nightclub scenes in the first place, which are always harder to access for disabled people like myself.

When I think about what it is to be both bisexual and disabled, I can't give a clear answer. While so many of my experiences with each identity feel similar, they each seem to deny me the ability to experience the other. The surveillance, anxiety, and fear of not belonging ring true from my experiences with both identities. Yet, my disability keeps me from being able to enjoy some queer spaces while my bisexuality and queer presentation can hinder the type of medical care I receive from doctors with implicit or explicit biases. If I am being honest, it is on my darkest nights that I often fear that the combination of my identities will just be too much trouble for people to love, too many things to navigate, and I won't be worth the work. While these are my own insecurities, they are fed by all the experiences I've named earlier, including media that shows disability in need of a cure to be palatable or doesn't name bisexuality on screen, let alone that disabled people can be bisexual at all. In spite of all of this I've been working to prove to myself that those fears are false, and I am lucky to have friends and family around me that have shown me that not only is learning to love and understand all my complexities not too much trouble, it's a joy. Now to get the rest of the world to see that too.

For more on disabilities see Chapter 12: "Aging and Older Adults."

Notes

1 Allison Kafer, "Time for Disability Studies and a Future for Crips," in *Feminist, Queer, Crip* (Bloomington, IN: Indiana University Press, 2013), 27.
2 Robert McRuer, "Introduction," in *Crip Theory: Cultural Signs of Queerness and Disability* (New York and London: New York University Press, 2006), 8.
3 Jay Dolmage, *Disability Rhetoric* (Syracuse, NY: Syracuse University Press, 2014).
4 David Mitchell and Sharon Snyder, *Narrative Prosthesis: Disability and the Dependencies of Discourse* (Ann Arbor: University of Michigan Press, 2001).
5 Talila A. Lewis, "Working Definition of Ableism," www.talilalewis.com/blog/working-definition-of-ableism-january-2022-update.
6 Kafer, "Time for Disability Studies and a Future for Crips," 5.
7 Tom Shakespeare, "The Social Model of Disability," in *Disability Studies Reader*, ed. Lennard J. Davis (New York: Routledge, 2010), 268.
8 Emily Ladau, "Understanding Disability as Part of a Whole Person," in *Demystifying Disability: What to Know, What to Say, and How to Be an Ally* (Emeryville, CA: Ten Speed Press, 2021), 39.
9 Ladau. "Understanding Disability as Part of a Whole Person," 13.
10 Beth Haller and Jeffery Preston, "Confirming Normalcy: 'Inspiration Porn' and the Construction of the Disabled Subject?" in *Disability and Social Media*, ed. Katie Ellis and Mike Kent (New York: Routledge, 2016), 42.
11 Stella Young, "Inspiration Porn, and the Objectification of Disabled People," Disability Visibility Project Website, https://disabilityvisibilityproject.com/2014/10/16/stella-young-inspiration-porn-and-the-objectification-of-disabled-people/.
12 Katie Ellis and Gerard Goggin, *Disability in the Media* (London: Red Globe Press, 2015).
13 Ladau, "Understanding Disability as Part of a Whole Person," 104.
14 Ladau, "Understanding Disability as Part of a Whole Person," 95.

15 Pamela Saunders, "Neurodivergent Rhetorics: Examining Competing Discourses of Autism Advocacy in the Public Sphere," *Journal of Literary & Cultural Disability Studies*, Vol. 12, No. 1 (2018), 1–17.

16 Eunjung Kim, "Asexualities and Disabilities in Constructing Sexual Normalcy," in *Asexualities* (New York: Routledge, 2014), 250.

17 Jay Dolmage, "Disability Studies of Rhetoric," in *Disability Rhetoric* (Syracuse, NY: Syracuse University Press, 2014), 34.

18 Mitchell and Snyder, *Narrative Prosthesis*.

19 Lennard Davis, "Introduction: Disability, Normalcy, and Power," in *Disability Studies Reader* (New York: Routledge, 2010), 4.

20 Elizabeth Tilley, Jan Walmsley, Sarah Earle and Dorothy Atkinson, " 'The Silence Is Roaring': Sterilization, Reproductive Rights and Women with Intellectual Disabilities," *Disability & Society*, Vol. 27, No. 3 (2012), 413–426.

21 Kafer, "Time for Disability Studies and a Future for Crips," 29.

22 Kate Caldwell, "We Exist: Intersectional In/Visibility in Bisexuality & Disability," *Disability Studies Quarterly*, Vol. 30, No. 3–4 (2010).

23 Caldwell, "We Exist."

24 Shiri Eisner, *Bi: Notes for a Bisexual Revolution* (Berkeley, CA: Seal Press, 2013); Christine Serpe, Chris Brown, Shawnalee Criss, Kelly Lamkins and Laurel Watson, "Bisexual Women: Experiencing and Coping with Objectification, Prejudice, and Erasure," *Journal of Bisexuality*, Vol. 20, No. 4 (2020), 456–492.

25 Per Solvang, "The Amputee Body Desired: Beauty Destabilized? Disability Re-Valued?" *Sexuality and Disability*, Vol. 25 (2007), 51–64.

26 "The Disability Visibility Project is an Online Community Dedicated to Creating, Sharing and Amplifying Disability Media and Culture," Disability Visibility Project Website, www.disabilityvisibilityproject.com/about/.

27 Shiri Eisner, "Bisexuality and the GGGG Movement," in *Bi: Notes for a Bisexual Revolution* (Berkeley, CA: Seal Press, 2013), 307.

12

AGING AND OLDER ADULTS

By 2050 The Census Bureau estimates that the number of people over the age of 65 in the United States will double to approximately 83.7 million (from 43.1 million in 2012).[1] At present there are more than 2.7 million LGBTQ+ adults over the age of 50 living in the United States[2] and a large portion of this population are bisexual.[3] In a culture obsessed with youthfulness and being able-bodied, however, we often render older adults as invisible. At some point in life, there is an aging out of the narrow parameters of what is noticed or represented in the media, leaving many older adults feeling as if they are not valued in society. Feeling invisible can happen no matter what the gender identity of the person, but women often feel the impact the most, as one study showed, where 70% of the women participants felt invisible in comparison to 32% of the men.[4] According to Sue Westwood, "older women's positive contributions to society are less likely to be recognized than those of older men, and they are more likely to be regarded as a 'burden' or a 'problem' needing attention."[5] Treating older adults as non-existent, particularly those over the age of 65, is a part of systemic ageism—the prejudice and discrimination against older people based on negative stereotypes—which often results in unequal treatment, hostility, rejection, lack of care, and isolation.[6] Aging starts to change the body in various ways that dominant culture deems undesirable, and for bisexual older adults ageism intersects with ableism, biphobia, and bi-erasure, leaving them multiply marginalized.

The study of aging often spans an age range of 30 years or more, from mid-life to older adulthood, with little focus on the variations of these experiences.[7] What a 55-year-old faces can be very different from someone who is 80, yet research often tends to generalize under an umbrella of

DOI: 10.4324/9781003242659-13

"older adult." Diane Whaley, in the *Journal of Aging and Physical Activity*, encourages researchers to use subgroups to differentiate between lived experiences: 65–74 as the "young old," those 75–84 as "old," 85–99 as "old-old," and 100+ as the "oldest old."[8] As Whaley states, "it is time to stop treating older adults as a homogeneous block. We must consider the variability across individuals, as well as investigate in more detail the capacity for an older adult to change over those years."[9] This is a challenge for this chapter when the research on bisexuality and aging is so limited and what does exist generalizes older adults as one group, but specific ages are addressed when possible. In addition, given the ages of the personal narratives at the end of this chapter, a large focus is on those who are 75–84 years old.

Ageism manifests in America through a society socialized to dread and fear aging. For centuries scientists have searched for the ideal "fountain of youth," and in recent years, new technology is working towards "cellular reprograming" that will supposedly allow for the reversal of aging.[10] Globally the anti-aging market—valued at approximately 62 billion dollars in 2021 and estimated to increase to 93 billion by 2027—is booming.[11] Arlene Weintraub asserts that anti-aging "medicine" is a large part of this market that wrongly treats aging as if it is a disease. She writes,

> Getting old is not a disease. The U.S. Food and Drug Administration (FDA) has never approved any therapy to treat aging. And although mainstream medical organizations have issued plenty of guidelines for preventing illnesses that commonly occur late in life, such as heart disease and cancer, none has ever fully endorsed the treatment regimens that the anti-aging industry embraces.[12]

Furthermore, the media enables this industry by bombarding society with images of beautiful, young, able-bodied people as the ideal, only further perpetuating the belief that becoming old is repugnant.

In contrast, anti-ageism advocates argue that aging is indeed a privilege, as one care program for older adults states, "In a world where many people are not fortunate enough to live long enough to experience the full range of life's challenges and rewards, aging is indeed a gift."[13] Longer life creates new opportunities, such as possibly pursuing more education, new careers, new passions, and connections to family.[14] It allows for the passing on of knowledge to future generations, the time for deeper connections to people, and a "unique opportunity to continue expanding our horizons and become our best selves."[15] In addition, there can be a greater sense of "acceptance of self and of others; desire for connection and the means to create it; life experiences that help us make smart decisions; wisdom and empathy."[16] Unfortunately, these ideals are not typically promoted in mainstream culture. Many older adults are left to suffer health disparities and lack of quality care, which are particularly high for those who experience the intersection of other forms of oppression like ableism, racism, classism, transphobia, homophobia, and biphobia.

Each person experiences aging differently, but it generally consists of a reduction "in function of the senses and activities of daily life and increased susceptibility to and frequency of disease, frailty, or disability."[17] A major change is the reduction of hormone production in *menopause*, "an abrupt loss of estrogen and progesterone production in women at mid-age following the cessation of ovarian function."[18] Menopause can impact sexual intimacy due to decrease in vaginal lubrication and elasticity, hot flashes, sleeping issues, and mood changes. Men experience *andropause*, a gradual decline in testosterone that actually starts around 20–30 years of age and continues until death.[19] In addition, erectile dysfunction is common, causing a decrease in the ability to have and keep an erection. Furthermore, the increase in possible health conditions can impact how intimacy or sex is practiced and add to a fear that partner(s) will no longer find them attractive.[20]

These sexual changes in the body contribute to the belief that older adults are not sexual, which for many is untrue. According to the National Social Life, Health and Aging Project, sexual interest remains alive among older adults, as "only one in four 75–85-year-old men report a complete lack of interest in sex, and only about half of 75–85-year-old women say the same."[21] These numbers are not much different than those for 57–64- and 65–74-year-olds.[22] Many older adults are not just interested in being sexual but actually are sexually active, even if there needs to be certain modifications in *how* sex occurs because of bodily changes. The discovery of multiple ways of being sexual outside of penetration contributes to sexual satisfaction, with about one in three placing a high value on some form of sex.[23] Other benefits include "increased life satisfaction and marital quality" with some research indicating that satisfying sex "may in fact delay mortality."[24] Clearly there is a need for more awareness, representation, and discussion about the importance and positive implications of sexuality for older adults; however, ageism creates a barrier. As Flesia et. al state, "ageism certainly represents a significant threat to sexual health and sexual satisfaction among older adults" and few studies are actually conducted to explore this.[25] In addition, the lack of understanding of sexuality for older adults contributes to increased rates of sexually transmitted infections and a reluctance to discuss sexual issues with doctors for fear of disapproval.[26]

The insufficient research on older adults and sexuality also means that sexual orientation is rarely considered, particularly bisexuality.[27] When bisexual people are included, their perspectives are often combined with gay and lesbian identities rather than examined for their unique experiences.[28] For bisexual older adults, there is invisibility as a sexual being and bi-erasure. Terri Clark writes about her own experiences when she states,

What kind of behavior would I, as an aging bisexual, have to engage in for other people to see me as bisexual? Should I walk into the room with a man and a woman on each arm? Should I have multiple partners? Maybe I could leave someone for someone of a different sex (interestingly, in this scenario people still might not read me as bisexual, but rather as having finally "finished" coming out or "gone straight" or, as in my case, "having gone to the other side").[29]

In addition, there can be some gendered differences when it comes to invisibility, particularly as older women are no longer considered desirable in mainstream culture. This is a double-edged sword, for on the one hand, it means escaping the male gaze and not being objectified, but as bisexual writer Sue George contends about her own experience with aging, this can be a difficult experience:

For me, it feels very strange that no one cares any longer whether I am bisexual. As a younger woman, I felt my sexuality was policed, or at the very least monitored, by everyone. This came particularly—though not exclusively—from the lesbians I knew, who had strong views about how I should be living and what my attitude towards men should be. Heterosexual friends and casual acquaintances felt free to pass all kinds of comments about bisexuality in general, and about me personally, about what they imagined I did and who I did it with. At some point, this stopped.... This feels harder to tackle than hostility, because at least I can fight against that.[30]

How people treat George is not actual acceptance of her bisexuality but rather indifference and erasure towards her bisexuality because she is now seen as old and no longer as a sexual being.

Navigating physiological transitions in the body is one challenge, but another is making sense of identities changing. In a society where ageism thrives, it is often an arbitrary timeframe not decided by an individual—but by others—as far as when one is perceived or treated as old. Some may fight this by trying to appear younger, such as dying one's hair, using anti-aging cream, or attempting to thwart the symptoms of menopause through making life changes. Jan Sinnott ponders this issue in a *Journal of Bisexuality* special issue on aging and bisexuality when she describes her own experience of being called "ma'am" for the first time while buying an ice cream cone. She states, "I had been mildly threatened by a stray word that whispered a suggestion of age-related limits to what I could do, or should do.... That was the small start of an identity shift that would demand attention, the shift into being an 'older adult.'"[31] For bisexual people already struggling with the experience of biphobia and bi-erasure, the addition of ageism creates more challenges. As Sinnott writes,

Facing dual stigmas, a person is forced by contradictions to build a more complex concept of identity to remain healthy and relatively unconflicted. . . . The creation of a concept of one's identity that is more inclusive and can rise above simple stigmatized identities cannot happen quickly, and there may be many false 'almost integrations' that are only partial fixes for the identity problem.[32]

Additionally, bisexual older adults are one of the groups that are heavily impacted by ageism. In general, there are health disparities of sexual minority adults with higher rates of "psychological distress, poorer physical health, and reduced access to health care resources" in comparison to heterosexuals.[33] According to Karen I. Fredriksen-Goldsen et al., however, there is an increase in evidence that bisexual older adults specifically have "poorer mental and physical health compared with lesbians and gay men of similar age."[34] The present generation of bisexual older adults grew up in a time when same-gender loving interactions were heavily stigmatized and criminalized but also experienced rampant bi-erasure in both queer and straight communities. Invisibility meant limited access to support and resources, which has continued for many into old age. Fredriksen-Goldsen et al. also discovered that bisexual older adults had higher levels of "internalized stigma, lower levels of identity disclosure" and difficulty finding community.[35]

In Burleson's work, the struggle to find community occurs because bisexual older adults are often "whipsawed by two competing forces."[36] In a world of erasure, finding support is often a challenge for bisexual people in general, but older bisexual adults may not be as familiar with accessing certain resources, such as internet communities. According to Burleson, in the past, people could call service hotlines, hear by word of mouth, or see flyers to find out about social events and support groups. With the change of communication and the internet, it is easy to access that information online, and if there is not an in-person meeting available, there are often virtual meetings. Although there is an increase in internet use for older adults—in 2000 only 14% of 65+ people used the internet in comparison to 2021 at 75%—[37] this older generation may not be as familiar with internet resources for connecting to community.[38] If a physical community is found, as Burleson's case studies revealed, bisexual older adults often felt isolated because activities were designed or dominated by younger people, and their needs were not addressed.[39] Lani Ka'ahumanu, an 80 year-old leader of the bisexual rights movement in the U.S., addresses this reality when she states:

Social isolation and invisibility of elders in the U.S. society is common. Bisexual elders within the LGBT and mainstream elder communities, senior services, and facilities are socially marginalized, stigmatized and isolated. I am worried about the emotional well-being of my community

*and disheartened by the casual and sometimes callous disregard shown by
people and agencies who serve us. Coming out, staying out, and speaking
out are a constant reality for bi+ people of all ages.*[40]

Fredriksen-Goldsen et al. also found that bisexual older adults experienced
disadvantages in socioeconomic status, with high rates of poverty, which
often is an indicator of more age-related health disparities.[41] Surprisingly,
47% of bisexual older men and 48% of bisexual women live at or below 200%
of the federal poverty level.[42] Moreover, this report revealed that bisexual
older adults, "with the same educational attainment as their gay and lesbian peers still had significantly lower income levels, though all groups fair
worse than their heterosexual counterparts due to a lifetime of employment
discrimination."[43] These struggles with aging may exist for any identity, but
the historical experience of invisibility and bi-erasure through a lifetime
increases the "risk for experiencing these adverse processes, with meaning-
ful implications for health and aging."[44]

The institution of marriage is another factor in the experience of aging for
bisexual older adults. Many grew up in a generation where marriage was a
common practice—-in 1960, 72% of all adults ages 18 and older were married[45] in comparison to 2019; 53% were married[46]—and felt that they had to
be in straight marriages. Rampant homophobia, biphobia, bi-erasure, and
the illegality of gay marriage all contributed to this, and many married bisexual people have had to downplay their bisexuality. Additionally, marriage
often erases the fact that there can be attraction to more than one gender,
and those who have been able to live in same-gender loving relationships
but may want to explore other-gender attractions often fear being accused of
"going to the other side."[47] Many believe that married bisexual people "pass"
as heterosexual, but as Terri Clark contends, "In truth, to 'pass' for straight
and have to deny your bisexuality is as painful as it is for gay and lesbian
seniors to have to live in (or go back into) the closet."[48]

Being married, older, and coming out as bisexual creates multiple challenges, including the reactions of adult children and spouses. This does not
necessarily mean that bisexual older adults coming out for the first time want
to end their marriages but that they may be hoping to live more authentically
with the people they love.[49] For those whose marriages have ended and are
interested in new relationships, there can be other challenges. According to
Tim R. Johnson, if a bisexual older adult who was in a straight-appearing
marriage for many years does choose to enter a same-gender loving relationship, for whatever reason, the switching to a partner with the same gender
may render the straight relationship as "inauthentic, unsatisfying or decep-
tive."[50] In reality, the potential attraction to the same gender has always been
there, just not acted upon.[51] As Johnson states, "Imposing these expectations
onto a bisexual person does damage to his or her previous relationship and

can strain relationships with that previous partner or children who now question the quality of their parents' relationship."[52]

What is glaringly missing in the research is the intersection of ageism, biphobia, and bi-erasure with other forms of oppression. There are a few examples, such as Tarynn Witten's work on transgender bisexual older adults. Her study addressed how the participants were fearful of the loss of control due to dementia, the potential lack of access to health and medical care, the treatment from nursing home workers, and potential abuse, along with worries about the ability to live as their authentic selves.[53] This is not unique to just bisexual transgender people, but what did stand out was that the main fears were about their gender identity more so than sexual orientation,[54] which may mean that transphobia dominates in those spaces to a point that bisexuality is not even considered, rendering it invisible once again.

Another area that is missing in research is the intersection of ageism, biphobia, bi-erasure, and racism. Sarah Jen and Rebecca Jones reveal in their work a sample of issues related to race, such as when one participant addressed the role of her Asian identity. Due to the lack of any bisexual Asian older adults or mentors, she was left feeling particularly isolated as an older adult. Instead, she was always the oldest one in queer spaces, and "her age prompted her to take up the positioning of an elder, responsible for the education and support of younger queer individuals which she had not benefited from."[55] Jen and Jones also discuss Black bisexual older adults, who felt pressure to be "representative of all Black people" in predominantly white spaces and the difficulty of finding communities that recognized the intersection of their identities based on age, sexual orientation, and race.[56] Regardless of these challenges, these participants admitted to pulling from a sense of resilience, acknowledging that "growing up as a racial minority helped them to be 'self- sufficient' and to deal with the experience of coming out as non-heterosexual later in life."[57] If there was more discourse and understanding of the intersection of these identities, less energy would have to be put into resilience and more into thriving throughout the aging experience.

There are so many ways that American society could improve support, care, and understanding of bisexual older adults. The intersections of different kinds of discrimination can mean the difference between what is called "successful and unsuccessful aging."[58] Although there is not consensus on what successful aging actually means, the term promotes support of older adults so they can "manage the specific challenges of this stage of life in a prosperous and satisfactory way, with good functional, physical, and cognitive capacity, and an active involvement in psychosocial life."[59] This concept also defies the misinformed notion that aging is about deficiencies or a disease in need of a quick fix or cure.[60] The conventional approach to successful ageing, however, is "limited in its ability to account for the experiences of people who have faced intersectional discrimination throughout their lives" and needs to do better.[61] Bisexual older adults have "specific needs and disparities" and "they deserve, competent, tailored care, including mental health care, starting with the acknowledgment that they exist."[62] Everyone can work to enact change around this, but bisexual older adult Terri Clark particularly asks aging-services providers to consider the following:

- believe that I exist. Bisexuality is a valid sexual orientation
- don't try and talk me into redefining my identity into something more comfortable for you. Or tell me that it is "just a phase"
- celebrate bisexual culture. We have a rich history and many daring voices who have expressed love beyond the monosexual confines. Remember the "B" in LGBT programming, services, and diversity
- ask me, if appropriate, about my other-sex and same-sex relationships. Bisexuals live our lives in multiple ways. Some of us would like to talk about our relationships without feeling judged
- speak up when bisexual people are being excluded or defamed. We all know that our silence speaks loudly. Often, bisexual people (young and old) need each other for support and for community, if for nothing more than the relief that comes with being among others to whom we don't have to defend ourselves[63]

An essential part of Clark's mandate is that people listen to bisexual older adults. The opportunity to start listening is available here, with the rich, powerful narratives of some of the original bisexual activists in the United States: Loraine Hutchins, ABilly Jones-Hennin, and his husband Cris Jones-Hennin. Their stories convey their own realities of growing up bisexual when it was particularly taboo and what it means to be a bisexual older adult today.

A Conversation with ABilly Jones-Hennin

This conversation happened in the spring of 2023. Sadly, ABilly passed away in January of 2024 before this book was published. A powerful tribute to ABilly can be found in the Washington Post at www.washingtonpost.com/ obituaries/2024/01/24/abilly-jones-hennin-dead/.

LISA:
So, you and your husband met through a gay married men's support group?

ABILLY:
Christopher and I met through a gay/bisexual support group called *Gamma Gay/Bi Married Men Association*. And these were men who were in heterosexual

relationships. Their wives were straight women and the men were either gay or bisexual. And I was one of the founding members. This was to be an alternative to the bars, but also just a group of men that had similar lifestyles who were all married. I just stepped up to the front to help get the group going and help organize. At that point I had no problem being public. I had already been the founder of a counseling service called *Growth and Support for Alternative Lifestyle*. This was a counseling service for youth whose parents were LGBTQ and the parents who were dealing with their kids. At that time, it was very unique to be there in the seventies.

We clearly had men who defined themselves as bisexual, whose wives were comfortable with them, and they stayed in their relationship. In fact, I'm friends with a couple still from that group, but it's only recently that the group expanded its name to gay/bisexual married men. So, I met my husband Cris through that group. We actually met by telephone first. He was trying to get clarity if these men were married to men.

LISA:
But he was married to a woman at that time?

AB:
Yes, he was married to his wife who was bisexual. And my wife is still heterosexual. And now Cris and I together, we have ten grandchildren and ten great-grandchildren.

L:
Wow! That's amazing! So, you give Loraine Hutchins credit for helping you recognize your own bisexuality. (*Loraine's interview follows.*)

AB:
Yes. She has been and still is my mentor. Politically she's definitely a force to be reckoned with but on a one-on-one level she is very gentle, and she's clear that people should define themselves as they perceive themselves. Fortunately, we don't think about sexuality as being fixed anymore. Back

then we were talking about one sexuality, which was fixed, and you were what you were. And now we talk about sexuality as fluid. I've always felt like what you are today is not what you were ten years ago in terms of your sexual expression, your sexual orientation, or even gender identity. Now that it is seen as fluid, ten years from now, if I should be around, I may feel different. If something should happen with Cris, who knows if I enter another relationship, it could very well be with a woman or a trans person. A non-binary person. Who knows! I'm ready!

L:

I love your vision and attitude! It is so positive!

AB:

Well, Cris and I entered our relationship with an understanding that it would be an open relationship. How could it not? Since we were both married and neither of us really were into initiating a divorce from our wives. Both of our wives were the ones who decided it was time for them to move on. But we still have a loving relationship with our wives. In my case, I'm sure it's because of the kids. Kids have a way of keeping you together if you wish to be connected to the kids. I'm happy to have that option.

But being in a relationship with someone else that is bisexual, that is an open relationship . . . I clearly fit under bi+ and sometimes I define myself just as being queer. Sometimes it is queer/bisexual. So even how I define myself, it just depends on how I feel about myself at the time. I like being able to say I'm bi+ because that's what I am. You know, being 81, people don't think of us elders as being sexual. A lot of it is how you define sexuality or intimacy. But my take is we can be sexual right up to death. So, if I live to be a hundred, I'm sure I'll still be flirting! I have at least sexual fantasies and I can choose to act on them or not. Depends on what's available for me and what I choose to act on. And also, my health and what my physical stamina allows me to do, but my head will always be there. I have Parkinson's and my mobility is crap right now. It is difficult if I need to move.

But people also don't think of people with disabilities as being capable of being sexual. Or think we should not have sex because of our disability. That's also unfortunate.

L:

I'd love to hear about some of your experiences with activism particularly around issues for bisexual people of color.

AB:

There's more of a presence now of people of color in the LGBTQ community as well as the bi community. It's slowly evolving even if it's still predominantly a white movement. I am part of a black bi male group that I find very rewarding. And I'm very involved with the National Association of Black and White Men Together. I was a former co-chair. But what I find is the richest part is the Black caucus.

We still have to deal with the issue of racism and sexism within our own communities, among ourselves. And the struggle is, while we are dealing with homophobia and biphobia, we also have to acknowledge the issues of sexism, racism, and ableism. It's all there. And the more identities you have, the more struggles you have to deal with. It's exhausting. There are some days I just don't have the energy to deal with any of it. Some days I select what I want to focus on. I'm still going through friends in organizations that will say the "B" in LGBTQ, but then they go right back to just being the L and the G. Folks are still feeling like it is just a fad. They say, "He'll get through it" or "he is just being fashionable." I'm now 81 years old and it's just a *fad*??? Come on! You're joking, right?

L:

Seriously!

AB:

And I think a challenge for people is the fact that Cris and I are in a same-gender loving relationship. Because we present as both cis males, they see us as a gay couple. That is a visual thing. And I think with bisexuals, many are not in a same-gender relationship. People only know of two types of relationships, either same-gender relationships or male/female relationships, gay or straight. If you define yourself as bisexual and that relationship ends and your next relationship looks different, then you get these people that say "I don't trust them." Or they say, "I don't know if they're going to stay with me. First, they're gay, and then they're straight." Then they say, "what am I to believe?" I think it is important for more people in male/female relationships who define themselves as bisexual to be more open and visible about it to the extent that they can safely do so.

L:

What do you feel is the benefit of more bi folks in male/female relationships coming out?

AB:

I think it would be the same benefit of anyone coming out. I think you first have to weigh what's the benefit to the individual, to oneself. If you are internalizing things and not out to at least those who are most important to you and those who you interact with then that's a stress and mental health factor. I'm not saying you have to raise a flag and I don't feel everybody needs to be super active. I think of my dad and the fact that he was bisexual even though there was no name for it. I remember when he passed that all three of the Kinsey books were on his bookshelf.

L:

Oh, wow! Really?

AB:

Yes. He was an MD so I think it got his attention as research. He was a big reader. But it was good that I had him as a role model. Then I had a bubbling—they referred to her as my bubbling lesbian sister—she was very clear that she was just into girls and didn't want to have anything to do with men.

They were supportive of it. We talked about sexuality issues, but interestingly, the word bisexual just never came out and we never talked about it. I think in some circles, I'm sure it was talked about, but not in circles that I was in. I was seven years in the Marine Corps, went through college and I never heard the word bisexual. So, there's still the belief, you are either straight or you're gay. Nothing else in between. Everything is either/or. You are a Republican or you're a Democrat. Nothing else. What's this Green party thing? And don't even think about calling yourself a socialist.

L:

What do you feel like the younger generation can learn from the older generation?

AB:

The key is that both the younger generation can learn from us older folks and us older folks can continue to learn from the younger generation and to be there for them. I'm also part of a grandparent group that is designed to help be supportive of children or grandchildren who may be LGBTQ. I would like to continue to do this work and to recognize that before them, there were folks like my dad. There were lots of people and even organizations in California, pushing the button and expanding our language from seeing ourselves beyond just being homosexual. As I said before, just because we say LGBTQ and that seems to be the trendy thing to say, they don't really focus on the B.

L:

So that's been part of your activism for a long time. How do we pay better attention to the B?

AB:

I'm constantly working with organization and events. Even with the month of March, which is Bisexual Health Awareness month, every Zoom call I'm on, I bring it to people's attention. Or when it is Bisexual Awareness Week. There's a big health conference in DC and one of my friends wanted to know what we wanted to discuss and I said, oh, this is great. It's Bi+ Health Awareness Month. Please make sure they talk about suicide and mental health issues as it relates to us. I think it's important that for men we have focused for decades on the issue of HIV/AIDS and rightfully so, but also, we still deal with other health issues. And the older I get, the more aware I am of gay and bi men and women dealing with other issues, such as heart disease, brain cancer, Parkinson's, or MS. I don't think we're addressing the range of health issues that affect us. And I have concern of anyone living by themselves. What kind of support are they getting? Are the folks checking on them? And are people going into assisted living programs or nursing homes and going back into the closet? Are they becoming invisible because of the way they are treated by other residents and by the caregivers in these facility? Defining themselves as bisexual or any sexual minority can sometime create more stress. And will we be able to have our partners with us, continue to live with us, continue to be with us? So, it's a challenge.

L:

Also, if there are of all these stereotypes or biases against older people being sexual, how is that erased in those spaces? That can be so harmful.

AB:

The other thing is, we also have to look at the damage that religion has done to so many LGBTQ folks. It's just been awful and traumatic and I think that's one of the issues that keeps bisexuals and others closeted. I think we're slowly addressing that. And at least in large cities, we're able to find LGBTQ affirming churches. But it's been a long time coming. And I know even with my church in DC, Metropolitan Community Church, I support that because it was the first affirming church that I was aware of. Troy Perry being the founder of that church. But even with them, every now and then I have to go, "What about the B?" But I noticed the last time I was at

the church, they had some LGBTQ flags, including the
transgender flag, the newer version of the LGBTQ flag
with the black and brown, and a bisexual flag. And
they had a bisexual flag because I gave it to them!

                              L:
Right on!

                              AB:
Sometimes people don't even know what the bisexual
flag looks like. The last LGBTQ event that Cris and
I went to, the 50th anniversary of Stonewall, and
I said, where's the bi flag? And it wasn't there.
It was not there. And somebody pointed one out. It
just wasn't visible, which I found upsetting. But
then I said, well, 50 years ago, it wasn't a very
visible movement.

                              L:
But we have to do better!

                              AB:
Yes. We gotta do better.

                              L:
It sounds like bi-erasure is happening in many
spaces.

                              AB:
Yes. It's sad. The lesbian and gay comrades often do
not speak up for bisexuals. And we often find ourselves having to call out our national organization
and national leaders about bisexuality, bringing it
to their attention ahead of time, not just once a
year for bisexual awareness week but hello! We are
here all year!

                              L:
Why does bi-erasure happen in queer spaces?

                              AB:
You know, that's a good question. I think it's
just historical. The acronym LGBTQ just rolls off

your tongue. But it's a level of consciousness about inclusion that's not there. The importance of including bisexuals in the decision making and it starts at the top. We need to be present at events and be a part of the planning process. I'm inspired that the National Task Force has a bisexual African American that is in leadership. If I was in leadership, I would be asking them what's their position on bisexual and transgender interests. I mean, I want to know the whole gamut, how they feel about the people they will be representing.

L:

It sounds like an ongoing struggle to raise that awareness and include bi+ people.

AB:

And I think we can no longer accept, the excuse, "well we couldn't find one." Uh, *hello*. I'm standing in front of you. Also, part of it is that we do need to have ongoing research, not just one study, many studies, to assess our opinions on a range of issues and to identify what barriers are there in terms of being able to access health care. And as we age, what are the health issues and barriers in terms of transportation, housing, or mental health?

L:

Also, the isolation folks are experiencing!

AB:

Yes!

L:

One last question, how do you find joy in bisexuality?

AB:

Oh, I'm lucky. I live with my joy. I am enjoying the fact that my network of friends continues to expand. My joy is being able to reach out to more and more friends, identifying more and more people. Whenever I read that some young person is coming out, especially if that person is a person of color, someone that looks like me, I get really excited. I will share it. I'll put it on Twitter and I'll put it on Facebook. You know, it does my heart good. To know that I'm not alone. That there are folks claiming their identity at this moment, are sharing it, and are willing to come out. And there's my joy that there is less stigma today than there has ever been before. People are evolving and that means they're open. I'm convinced as people get to know us, they'll get to love us and we'll learn to understand. I think that's how people come to accept us. I don't want someone just tolerating us but actually accepting us. I like to think of the Sly and the Family Stone song. . . . So I'll close with his lyrics when he says, "I wanna thank you, for lettin' me be myself again!" That's my message!

A Conversation with Cris Jones-Hennin (ABilly's Husband)

LISA:
Tell me a little bit about yourself and discovering your bisexuality.

CRIS:
I know that growing up, it was rather confusing, wanting to have relationships with both women and men. And not only having them be contradictory in the sense that I do believe that we're basically made up of four components. We are body, mind, emotion, and spirit. And the challenge with that is balancing equal parts of all four of those. And how we grow each one of those aspects of ourselves and how those integrate. So, if you're growing up and physically you are bisexual and you're running into conflicts, like prejudice, negative emotions, status quo kinds of issues, it begins to stunt your own growth.

In my personal case I started having very early sexual experiences right from the age of five. I kept bumping against things like "you can't wear dresses" or "you can't play with dolls" and "you can't have long hair." Also "you can't be cute if you're a boy or too cute," all these things. But you go through all these phases and you simply are who you are until you sort of get suppressed or traumatized. I do know that I'm fortunate. My early experiences were really positive sexually, and a lot of it had to do with just growing up partly on a farm during the weekends and in an urban area during the week.

And being the youngest for a long time and having two very busy parents and siblings, and being out there exploring in a neighborhood where I was able to spend a lot of time on my own. In kindergarten through second grade, I only went to school from eight to one, so it gave me plenty of time to wander. I still remember doing things that were never mentioned to my parents, but that I would just spontaneously do, like going to my sister's closet and wearing a dress. And then I would run around the neighborhood in a dress until right before they came home and changed quickly.

L:

That's awesome.

C:

I don't know if it was scared out of me, but I'm not a transvestite or anything like that anymore, but I went through that phase. So, I quickly became aware that if I was going to be honest to myself sexually and be bisexual, that it was going to be very difficult. It wasn't until I was in college that I met a woman who was also bisexual who really helped me process not only the theory but just the whole phenomenon of navigating and being honest. And a lot of it has to do with dialogue.

L:

What year was that?

C:

That was 1969.

L:

Was there much discourse around bisexuality at that time?

C:

I went to Antioch, which was definitely all about discourse. I think from a young age I had a number of different sexual experiences with both girls and boys that by the time I was in college I really needed to make sense of it. I was really fortunate that I met this girl who's the daughter of an Epis-copalian bishop. I come from a pretty conservative background, so I needed to have other people from conservative backgrounds try to break through all these prejudices. She was in college to figure out this whole sexual thing. She was aware that she had relationships with men and women and realized the only way that she could really grow and be honest about it was to find other men and women that were also willing to be disciplined in the dialogue and be good sexual, emotional, and spiritual partners. That for me was incredibly liberating. I learned to be a good sexual partner with a woman and with a man because of the *possibility*, and actually the opportunity and the context.

L:

What was happening in the mainstream discourse around bisexuality? Was it accepted?

C:

You know what's really interesting, I would say that Antioch then was where the current generation is now. That it was a context where all of this could be, but people were just beginning to scratch the surface. Just to give you an idea, I met this girlfriend in a philosophy class, and she was sort of a Greta Garbo type person. Very androgynous, in a lot of ways. And I noticed when she was flirting with me, I was sort of not ready to jump into anything. And a week later she was flirting with somebody else and a week later she was flirting with one of my roommates. The reason I'm telling you the story is that into our relationship, one of the guys that she had been flirting with—in the middle of making love on the third floor of the Victorian dorm—burst in through the fire escape and declared her to be a cruel seductress and God knows what else. And it just happened that he was also the son of another Episcopalian Bishop. And he came in and gave us a sermon, a good half hour, indicating that, because of their backgrounds, that she was a wicked woman, going to hell and taking me with her.

L:
He interrupted you all having sex?

C:
Right. He just burst into the room.

L:
That's quite an experience!

C:
It was definitely very dramatic! We spent an hour trying to calm him down and explain to him what our reality was. By that time, she and I had had a lot of dialogue, and I tend to be a doer. If I think something is interesting, I want to actually put it into practice and see it through. So, she and I had done a lot of work and talking about the technical, emotional, and spiritual aspects of sex. She put me onto a lot of literature. It's interesting that a lot of being bisexual is learning not to be jealous. Learning how to deal with possessiveness, dealing with the fact that when relating to one another, it isn't in order to dominate them or to be dominated. It's about sharing, understanding, not feeling insecure. Building a sense of security and confidence in what we're doing. And all of that is a lot of work.

L:
Well, it sounds like polyamory and open relationships also!

C:
Absolutely.

L:
Why do you think bisexuality is still so threatening to people?

C:

In a sense it's always going to be threatening until it is practiced and people learn enough to do it responsibly. And that is a lot of work. I guess you need to have a critical, massive experience where you can say, I'm mature enough to find balance in my sexuality. I remember that when I decided to have children with a lesbian couple, my own sister, who's an educator, was incredibly critical. She felt that it was bringing kids into a messed-up world and it would be messing them up, making them victims to all kinds of things. And what helped me during that period of time was my relationship with my partner in that we were both incredibly happy, and at the level of what we were experiencing, emotionally, spiritually and sexually, I felt confident enough that my sister's fears were bullshit. I definitely didn't confront her and tell her to go to hell. I went about my business and ended up raising two fantastic kids!

L:

Right on! There is often discussion of feelings of isolation for those that are bisexual and they may not realize to what extent people have been challenging norms for decades. They're also very invested in monogamy. What's your perspective on that?

C:

Well, that happened to me. I ended up marrying a bisexual woman who convinced me that we would be monogamous until she was ready not to be. And I ended up having a nervous breakdown. It had to do with relating to somebody who was so sexually and emotionally monogamous. She could only really relate to one other person or that person was the center. And I think my modality of surviving being bi is having a support system of people of all ages and sexes, as diverse as possible. I do feel that in diversity one is constantly opening up possibilities and learning from other people's experiences. I need that for balance. And over eight years, I just became more and more alienated. She and I became so close that we were almost the same mind, same body, same everything. And it just ended up being a trainwreck. I think that one does have to challenge the whole concept of monogamy, if one wants to be honestly bisexual.

L:
But there are folks who are bisexual who do choose to be monogamous too.

C:
Right. I think you can definitely be monogamous. But there are definitely challenges. I think I was fortunate to realize it had to do with the theoretical framework experience with that girlfriend. I had to figure out how I was going to make emotional sense and have confidence in having an open relationship.

L:
Is it easier to be non-monogamous if your partner is bisexual?

C:
Well, my ex-wife who was bisexual and girlfriend from college was bisexual, the other women that I've had long-term relationships with were not. The conflict that arose was theoretically, I have never related to a woman who was not aware of my bisexuality and also was not aware of my relationship with my partner and him being my primary. And I have to say long term relationships that I've had, that were not bisexual, after some time, issues arose where they just wanted me to be their primary relationship.

L:
That does happen, no matter what your sexual orientation or gender identity is. Again, that's that investment in monogamy. That makes that difficult.

C:
It takes figuring out how to mature and how one relates to another. Does one relate to another out

of insecurity or out of trying to grow and figure out
how to be more successfully integrated?

L:
What are some generational differences that you see?

C:
I sense that we all face similar processes of things
like, why are we here? How do we exist? This newest
generation has enormous advantages. I often wonder if the angst that we experienced isn't what
they need to experience but it may make them not as
motivated. The sexual part is like, let's jump into
this experience, but I think to sustain all of that
in developing, supporting, deep bisexual emotional
and spiritual relationships takes a lot of work.
It's exciting because every time you meet somebody
new, you are opening up to an entirely new world.
That new world demands a lot of respect, patience,
fortitude, and caring. But it seems as if people
are feeling able to experience their sexuality much
better today than they were in the fifties when people were basically bipolar in their sexuality.

L:
How do you feel the struggle may be different?

C:
The thought that comes to mind is first not to judge.
Their context is totally different than mine. It's
all their own process. I was an immigrant with a sort
of French background thrown into a very Anglo type
of environment, in the United States and in Canada.
  I think that those challenges, those types of
confrontations, cultures and languages and ways of
being, values were very cataclysmic, very moti-
vating to try to figure out what made sense to me.
I find it really interesting how my kids, who were
born into a really different type of situation, how
quickly they seem to have limited complications in
their lives that I definitely had. I don't know if
it was just that they were more comfortable with

themselves than I was. Initially I had this concept of having kids that were going to be ten times
better than me because they had more opportunities
than I did. I'm not saying that they're not ten
times better than me, but they're definitely not an
extension of me. When my kids were literally becoming adolescents, I definitely had to stop myself and
say, they are not an extension of you, you're here
to support them to be who they are, not who you are.
Let it go. Being a co-parent with several other parents, one of the requirements was that we were all
there to support our kids.

L:

You had two kids with the two moms, correct?

C:

Yes. And because of my open relationship they pretty
much ended up having three long-term dads. It ended
up working really well because I think each one of
us had something very different to contribute. And
we made an effort not to get in each other's way. At
some point the kids did play us against one another,
but I think quickly they realized it didn't make any
sense since we each had something to contribute.
For me it's been kind of fascinating. Particularly
since my sisters have had very challenging kids
and my kids have been very challenging in a lot of
ways, but they've been relatively, what can I call,
successful? Well centered. Because of our openness
and also being careful of how they were being raised
as far as their education, their schools, they were
both very positive. Not only have they been very
open to diversity, but they have been proponents of
it. And in a lot of ways, there were times where
I felt like my kids were more comfortable about
bisexuality than I was.

L:

That's cool. When talking about aging, we often
assume that older people are not sexual any more.
What do you think?

C:

When I first met ABilly, he was definitely into educating me. One of the things that we did was a men's group with an eminent sexologist. We had this really interesting week-long retreat discussing all aspects of male sexuality. We asked the sexologist who was in his early seventies, what's your sexual health like? And he looked at us and he said, "Well, if you don't use it, you're going to lose it." Personally, I have experienced the highest, deepest levels of sexual satisfaction in the last few years, now decade. And a lot of it has to do very simply with having more time to really focus on it. I was working like a dog and both of us had positions that were really exhausting. And you know, we went through HIV, which definitely stopped my exploration for me for years.

But I do think that we are sexual beings until the day we die. There are two things that are happening now. One is that we are aging much later. A lot of it has to do with building good sexual experiences, realizing how important sexuality is to one's well-being. And, there's no doubt that if I did not experience the level of sexuality experiences I would not be as active.

Also, I think understanding and being in one's body is so important. It is something to discipline. I'll give you an example. I've been going through sciatica in the last few weeks, and this is the second bout I've had in three years. And you know, you get older and you think, this will never happen to me, but boom, it happens. And last time I thought, oh well this is an anomaly but this time I said, shit! This is something that's going to be happening. And the last time that I went through this, it definitely put a dent in my sexuality. This time I worked through it and realized that one of the things that sex does is circulates endorphins. It helps with healing. I have found that just masturbating a couple times a day, periods where my sciatica came up, it makes it bearable.

L:
That's powerful.

C:
I have spoken to a number of people that are open to talking about sexuality and who are both my age and older, and it's always been vital to all of them. We have to talk about it to normalize it.

A Conversation with Loraine Hutchins

LISA:
Looking at the history of bisexual activism, you can find information on Kinsey and Klein and then I feel like there's not as great of a historical account right after Klein.

LORAINE:
I knew Klein and he did an incredible gift for the bisexual community by helping to set up the American Institute on Bisexuality, which is based in San Diego. I think they're tapping out of most of their money, but they supported the *Journal of Bisexuality* and some other projects. Between Klein and more of a grassroots movement growing, there were actually people like Maggie Rubenstein, who's still alive in her nineties in San Francisco, and she did a Ph.D. on bisexuality way back before the word was even used. Beth Firestein and Lisa Diamond have also made significant research contributions on bi identities.

And certainly, when it wasn't touched by the American Psychological Association or other big organizations like the Society for the Scientific Study of Sexuality or AASECT, there were people like Rubenstein that helped create some of the foundations and of course my amazing co-conspirator Lani Ka'ahumanu who was mentored by Maggie in San Francisco.

There was a big bisexual center in San Francisco, during the 1980s, that Abilly Jones-Hennin was a part of for a while when he was out there. Then there was the scourge of AIDS and everything . . . but how did I get involved? I always felt that without any words or labels that I felt naturally bisexual. It was just being me. It was just being normal, being natural. I'm not going be arrogant and say everyone is bisexual, but I am going to say that a lot of us have bi potential or capacity that we either explore or don't. I'll just say that when it came to my mother and father, neither of them identified as bisexual, but it was easier for me to identify as bi than to try to replicate their kind of marriage.

I have never replicated any kind of marriage, but I have had deep and significant relationships with men and women in my life. Then there is my primary relationship right now with myself and being my own best lover in every way is what I'm working on. And that is part of me making sense of my mortality and my viability as a being in this world, regardless of who I have sex with and whether it's genital or not.

L:

Right on! When you were getting started with activism, you had mentioned that the word bisexual may not have been used yet, so how did that get established?

LH:

Well, the first groups I found were gay married men support groups. [And that meant gay/bi men married to women, not what it could/would mean now which would simply be men married to men. Whole different thing.] That's where I started. And then I was like, oh God, I'm so tired of being around these men because they focused things on themselves and their needs, and mostly they didn't know how to create cooperative support energy among us.

And so, more and more women found each other. And I worked with a women's journal, a feminist newspaper in Washington DC that was incredibly biphobic, but they allowed me to be a freelance reporter doing some reviews of conferences and books that were just beginning to come out. I started developing with other women a sense of what bisexuality meant from a feminist point of view. We started doing regional and local conferences and emerged with a big national conference in 1990 in San Francisco, which is chronicled in our book *Bi Any Other Name*. There have been a lot of national conferences since then, although not recently.[64]

L:

So that was part of BiNetUSA?

LH:

BiNetUSA was born at the 1990 conference and it was first called the North American Bisexual Network. I was on the first board of directors of BiNet and we had a big regional newsletter where we reported on what was happening in different states around the country. And everything was geographically represented, but we stopped doing that. We stopped being membership based and started being more grant and big donor based in funding autonomy.

Which makes me really cynical because it's dependent on the proclivities of people with money. And it's not accountable to a membership. And the same thing happened with BiNet; there's a longer story about that.

Our book *Bi Any Other Name* catalyzed and mobilized a lot of other books and a lot of other local groups. And it catapulted me into being a media star when I didn't know what I was doing and I was winging it. And for 15 years I spoke at college campuses as the out bisexual person, with leadership, authority, a published author, representing local, regional, and national bi groups, coming to town. I also worked with student groups who sometimes had money, sometimes didn't, and we just negotiated what can they pay me and I would go to a friendly class as well and sometimes meet with the gay student group. I just learned a lot from traveling around. And after I got my Ph.D. I spent over a dozen years teaching mostly undergraduate courses on sexuality and gender and women's health studies.

L:

I was just reading part of the 25th anniversary edition of your book and what I appreciated was

that you had added to the definition of bisexuality
the word *fantasy*. It's not just the potential for
attraction to more than one gender but also could
be the fantasy.

LH:
What we find out when we're bi activists and gay and
straight people come up to us privately and confess
and come out, they will all tell you that they have
fantasies about the other sex or the opposite sex
or the same sex, but it's closeted.

L:
Speaking of activism, what were the issues at that
time and how are they similar or different to today?

LH:
The issues are actually a lot the same. Because we
haven't come that far as a culture. When you sent
me this question for this interview, I wrote down
"still callous disregard." *Callous disregard* is a
phrase that Loni came up with and it has to do with
people's inability to see bisexuality as a natural,
ordinary way of being and to continue to bifurcate
the world into gay verses straight. To say that
those of us who assert that there is something different going on in humanity, we're crazy, deluded,
too idealistic and lost in fantasy. We need to get
with the program and take sides. And if you look at
the opening to *Bi Any Other Name*, the quote says,
"we don't want to take sides."

L:
That seems to be an ongoing challenge!

LH:
Yeah. The thing that irritates us the most is that
bi is totally ignored. Every time I write a let-
ter to the editor or the radio program producer or
whatever, people will say, gay and transgender. And
not only does that erase lesbians, but we're like,
hello. Why are you eclipsing it down to gay and
transgender? It's a journalistic thing though. If

you talk to journalists, they love it. The *New York Times* does it the worst, but they're not the only people. It's like everybody tries to make something smaller than LGBTQIA, you know?

L:

Right. It's like, are you that lazy? It's really not that complicated. We use acronyms, all the time. Can you tell me some other thoughts you may have about aging and generational differences?

LH:

I am a person living with disabilities. The older I get, the more of a disability justice advocate I become. In fact, I've been learning a lot from Black Lives Matter writers who are disability activists. A lot of them have written books about *making a way out of no way and surviving.*[65] And of course, we need more legislation, we need more money. But really, it's about making a way out of no way in a poor community with what you have. It's like putting more water in the soup so that the soup can go around.

So, what's it like to be older? For me, it's really isolating and lonely because there's not enough queer space for me to age in queer space. I'm very aware of every LGBT-oriented, small, retirement project that's trying to start in New York, Houston, or San Francisco, but they're tiny. And they're not well supported. I worked for 25 years in the philanthropy community, part-time as a grant administrator for small family foundations. And I'm very aware of how philanthropists allocate money and how they never touch the principle. And it's only that tiny little bit of interest that the IRS requires them to spend.

There's not the grant money available for regular old people and certainly not for queer old people. And it ain't gonna change. I'm having a meeting tomorrow with some young people in their forties, in the local community, who are African American descendants from the freed black community that was partly created here before the Civil War and around the Civil War by abolitionist Quakers in Maryland. These young people, two of them are coming out as queer after having been socialized to be heterosexual and to make babies and have kids and families and stuff. Not that you can't do that as a queer identified person as well, but they are asking me for advice about how to set up some kind of a group foster home housing setting for queer people of color, particularly young men who can't live at home. And I'm going to say to them, I did that back in the seventies and it's 20 times worse right now in terms of getting funding. And I don't know how they're going to do it. And I love that they're trying.

But what it's like being older for me is feeling lonely, feeling invalidated, feeling like I'm really fed up with heterosexual couples that I'm surrounded by. Even though I love them, they don't get it. They patronize me. They always send their grandchildren to me. I just did a bunch of trans resources for somebody's friend who's the mother of a 15-year-old trans woman in high school and doesn't understand what's going on and I gave her a bunch of resources.

L:

But that's not supporting you.

LH:

No, that's not supporting me and it's not giving me any love or care. And, you know, I have a blog essay that I haven't written yet, that is going to be about Covid being worse than HIV and how it interrupts therapeutic touch. Especially among people who are already isolated.

I've been saturating myself with a lot elder care, assisted living/nursing, senior housing industry research, pre and post Covid. Before Covid, there was research on loneliness and depression, which can be exacerbated by hearing loss. Loneliness and depression are the equivalent on the body burden of smoking 25 cigarettes a day. Now I don't know how they calibrated that, but it's all related to the stress that we're seeing. The fact that people of color generationally experience more and more stress that is multi-generationally passed down. We can quantify this stress and people of color are being disproportionately affected.

L:

Those layers of isolation from being queer, Covid, and for folks who are bisexual, biphobia, bi-erasure, and the intersection of ageism. Also, this idea that older people are not sexual.

LH:

I haven't been successful at breaking down that stereotype. I live in a faith-based, nonprofit continuing care retirement community and I've been in a women's group here that is semi feminist, but every time I bring up sex education, the response is "Oh, no, no, no, no." We can't talk about pussies, pussies, pussies. But I'm scheduling the movie *Women Talking* for next month. It's amazing. It was created by a bunch of women filmmakers who would stop production and process if there were things that were awkward. They had an intimacy coach and a therapist who was there for the cast.

Anyway, I used to say this in the polyamory movement, I was a leader and a speaker there. I would say genitals and sex are the least of it. To me, being sexual is about emotional intimacy and it's about touch. And yes, it can be about orgasm if the parties involved want to orgasm, but to me being sexual is about emotional intimacy and vulnerability and sharing that or not. What I'm trying to say is that with sex as we age, penile/vaginal sex is the least of it. Although it's wonderful and we should all have it and we should use lube and we should enjoy it. But if we don't have it, fingers and hands and everything is better than not having anything. And to me, sex is whatever level of sharing you achieve together or with yourself. I studied a lot as a sex educator and it is true that people with disabilities can orgasm with their wrist or their bicep, or their cheek because it's how you run erotic energy in your body and how you breathe.

L:

I appreciate your honesty about that. Can you tell me some more about what it is like for people living in your community?

LH:

I don't have the financial resources to walk away from this community, but I see this community as a metaphor for where we're stuck with social injustices that polarizes. Us/them. I don't want to be us/them. I want to figure out a new "common language," as Adrienne Rich says, a new common language for how we can make it better together. With all my skills of 70 years of communication, collaboration, and organizing, I don't know how to do it.

And that's part of my challenge here because I feel like everything in my life that I did as an organizer has prepared me to be here. Working with asshole lawyer powerhouses in DC at the federal government and all those levels prepared me for dealing with the board of directors and the CEO here. The people who think that they have the power to decide how elderly people who are declining live well. And it's exhausting. I need to do a lot more personal work on shielding because I've been sticking my neck out.

L:

It sounds like people are lucky to have you do that! Going back to bi-erasure, it makes me think of the idea of invisibility. For people who are bisexual, older with disabilities. We often don't talk about how invisibility can be so harmful.

LH:

I appreciate you bringing all this up because we need to be having these conversations. I think a lot of the talk about bisexuality in general, we focus on the polarizing. Robyn Ochs and us all call it getting beyond the binary, both/and, not either/or polarities that divide.

It makes me think of how we talk about feminism. When I taught women's studies and LGBT studies,

I taught health sexuality, and I taught women's health and in all those classes, when I tried to bring in feminist theory, which was sometimes really well done in the textbooks, my students didn't get lesbian separatism at all. They didn't understand it. It didn't compute with anything in their personal experience. It's like they'd never been exposed to black separatism or Black Panthers or anything about what happened in the Civil Rights movement. There was a separatist time in history and there are women aging today who still feel very separatist. And my students would look at me like, "Professor, what are you talking about? This doesn't make any sense. We're all happy, we're all queer." I'm like, there's something you need to understand about this theoretically and historically.

A good thing that Robyn Ochs does is this *Bi Women's Quarterly*.[66] She had a young intern that was working with me and they were editing a piece I had written. I was brought up by lesbian separatists in the women's movement who taught me about feminism. I understood their inherent biphobia, but they were my abusers and they were cruel to me because of my bisexuality. But I also understood their need for separate space and how it helped them to grow, feel safe, healthy, and develop their analysis so that they could, if they chose, go back into mixed spaces. That sounds like a very privileged statement, which it is because people with less resources can't choose. They have to deal. Anyway, I had written the piece and the intern was basically trying to edit it and censor me because she felt like a lot of the stuff I had written was transphobic, unintentionally. I started dialoguing with her and I found out that she wanted to change my word choices, my sentences, because she didn't want me to offend anybody who was trans. I worked with her and I changed everything she wanted changed, but I ended up out of that experience feeling there was a weird generational disconnect where my language was inappropriate. And considered incorrect and that I had to change to be accepted. It is about generational differences and it's about understanding our history

and our theoretical basis for how we approach identity orientation or gender or both. And that's where
some of this disconnect still is for me between
generations.

LS:
It sounds like we need to be better about learning
from each other, from each generation. Where do you
find joy in bisexuality?

LH:
I don't find much joy in bisexuality. I find a lot of
joy in being myself and real and whole. Bisexuality
is part of that. But it's not bisexuality in a little box that makes me joyful. It's being alive and
being fully alive is being bisexual. I wish I could
find more joy. Joy is there in the living and in the
aliveness. And I wouldn't be any other way. I can't
see being forced to choose between women and men
and every other gender. I mean, there's no choice.
I choose to be me.

Notes

1 Jennifer Ortman, Victoria Velkoff and Howard Hogan, "An Aging Nation: The Older Population in the United States," Current Population Reports (U.S. Census Bureau, May 2014), www.census.gov/content/dam/Census/library/publications/2014/demo/p25-1140.pdf.

2 Karen I. Fredriksen-Goldsen, "The Future of LGBT+ Aging: A Blueprint for Action in Services, Policies, and Research," *Generations: Journal of the American Society on Aging*, Vol. 40, No. 2 (2016).

3 Movement Advancement Project, "Invisible Majority: The Disparities Facing Bisexual People and How to Remedy Them," (September 2016), www.lgbtmap.org/file/invisible-majority.pdf.

4 Heidi Syropoulos, "Coming to Terms with Invisibility and Ageism," Independence Blue Cross Website (November 2023), https://insights.ibx.com/coming-to-terms-with-invisibility-andageism/#:~:text=70%20percent%20of%20respondents%20said,until%20the%20age%20of%2064.

5 Sue Westwood, " 'It's the Not Being Seen That Is Most Tiresome': Older Women, Invisibility and Social (In)Justice," *Journal of Women and Aging*, Vol. 35, No. 6 (2023), 558.

6 Kristen Weir, "Ageism Is One of the Last Socially Acceptable Prejudices," *Monitor on Psychology*, Vol. 54, No. 2 (2023), www.apa.org/monitor/2023/03/cover-new-concept-of-aging.

7 Diane Whaley, "An Argument for a Development Approach in Studying Older Adults' Physical Activity," *Journal of Aging and Physical Activity*, Vol. 22, No. 3 (2014), 301.

8 Whaley, "An Argument for a Development Approach," 301.

9 Whaley, "An Argument for a Development Approach," 301.

10 Antonio Regalado, "How Scientists Want to Make You Young Again," *MIT Technology Review* (October 2022), www.technologyreview. com/2022/10/25/1061644/how-to-be-young-again/.

11 Matej Mikulic, "Anti-Aging Statistics and Facts," Statista Website (February 2024), www.statista.com/topics/10423/anti-aging/#:~:text=The%20 global%20anti%2Daging%20market,some%2093%20billion%20by%20 2027.

12 Arelene Weintraub, "Physician, Heal Thyself!" in *Selling the Fountain of Youth: How the Anti-Aging Industry Made a Disease Out of Getting Old—and Made Billions* (New York: Basic Books, 2010), 4.

13 "The Privilege of Aging: Its Impact on Health and Longevity," Amada Senior Care Website, www.amadaseniorcare.com/2023/10/the-privilege-of-aging-its-impact-on-health-andlongevity/#:~:text=Aging%20 affords%20us%20the%20opportunity,with%20the%20people%20 around%20us.

14 "Ageing and Health," World Health Organization Website (October 2022), www.who.int/news-room/fact-sheets/detail/ageing-and-health.

15 "The Privilege of Aging."

16 Brenda Lange, "The Benefits of Aging," Columbia University Irving Medical Center Website (August 2022), www.cuimc.columbia.edu/ news/benefits-aging.

17 "Understanding the Dynamics of the Aging Process," National Institute on Aging Website, www.nia.nih.gov/about/aging-strategic-directions-research/understanding-dynamics-aging.

18 Mark Pataky, William Young and K. Sreekumaran Nair, "Hormonal and Metabolic Changes of Aging and the Influence of Lifestyle Modifications," *Mayo Clinic Proceedings*, Vol. 96, No. 3 (2021), 789.

19 Pataky et al., "Hormonal and Metabolic Changes of Aging," 789.

20 "Sexuality and Intimacy in Older Adults," National Institute on Aging Website, www.nia.nih.gov/health/sexuality/sexuality-and-intimacy-older-adults.

21 Michael McFarland, Jeremy Uecker and Mark Regnerus, "The Role of Religion in Shaping Frequency and Satisfaction: Evidence from Married and Unmarried Older Adults," *The Journal of Sex Research*, Vol. 48, No. 2–3 (2011), 297.

22 McFarland et al., "The Role of Religion in Shaping Frequency and Satisfaction," 297.

23 McFarland et al., "The Role of Religion in Shaping Frequency and Satisfaction," 297.

24 McFarland et al., "The Role of Religion in Shaping Frequency and Satisfaction," 297.

25 Luca Fesia, Merylin Monaro, Emmanuele Jannini and Erika Limoncin, "'I'm too Old for That': The Role of Ageism and Sexual Dysfunction Beliefs in Sexual Health in a Sample of Heterosexual and LGB Older Adults: A Pilot Study," *Healthcare*, Vol. 11 (2023), 459.

26 Fesia et al., "I'm too Old for That."

27 Sarah Jen, "Beyond the Binary: Bisexual Sexualities in Later Life," *Generations Journal*, Vol. 46, No. 4 (Winter 2022–2023).

28 Karen Fredriksen-Goldsen, Sarah Jen and Anna Muraco, "Iridescent Life Course: LGBTQ Aging Research and Blueprint for the Future—A Systemic Review," *Gerontology*, Vol. 65, No. 3 (2019), 253–274.

29 Terri Clark, "Oh 'Bi' the Way…Don't Forget About the 'B' in LGBT Aging," *Philadelphia Gay News* (October 2016), https://epgn.com/2016/10/26/oh-bi-the-way-don-t-forget-about-the-b-in-lgbt-aging/.

30 Sue George, "Is Anyone Else Out There? My Experiences as an Older Bi Woman," Opening Doors Website (September 2021), www.openingdoors.lgbt/news/is-anyone-else-out-there-my-experiences-as-an-older-bi-woman.

31 Jan Sinnott, "Introduction to the Special Issue on Aging and Bisexuality: Can These Complex Life Patterns Be an Impetus for Identity Flexibility and Growth?" *Journal of Bisexuality*, Vol. 16, No. 1 (2016), 4.

32 Sinnott, "Introduction to the Special Issue on Aging and Bisexuality," 13.

33 Karen Fredriksen-Goldsen, Chengshi Shiu, Amanda Bryan, Jayn Goldesn and Hyun-Jun Kim, "Health Equity and Aging of Bisexual Older Adults: Pathways of Risk and Resilience," *The Journal of Gerontology Series B: Psychological Sciences and Social Sciences*, Vol. 72, No. 3 (2017), 468.

34 Fredriksen-Goldsen et al., "Health Equity and Aging of Bisexual Older Adults," 469.

35 Fredriksen-Goldsen et al., "Health Equity and Aging of Bisexual Older Adults," 469.

36 William E. Burleson, "Bisexuality: An Invisible Community Among LGBT Elders," in *Handbook of LGBT Elders: An Interdisciplinary Approach to Principles, Practices and Policies*, ed. Debra Harley and Pamela Teaster (New York: Springer, 2016), 317.

37 "Internet, Broadband Fact Sheet," Pew Research Center Website (January 2024), www.pewresearch.org/internet/fact-sheet/internet-broadband/.

38 Burleson, "Bisexuality," 317.

39 Burleson, "Bisexuality," 317.

40 Movement Advancement Project, "A Closer Look: Bisexual Older Adults," 3, www.lgbtmap.org/policy-and-issue-analysis/bisexual-older-adults.

41 Fredriksen-Goldsen et al., "Health Equity and Aging of Bisexual Older Adults," 469–470.

42 Movement Advancement Project, "A Closer Look," 2.

43 Movement Advancement Project, "A Closer Look," 2.

44 Fredriksen-Goldsen et al., "Health Equity and Aging of Bisexual Older Adults," 475.

45 D'Vera Cohn, Jeffery Passel, Wendy Wang and Gretchen Livingston, "Barely Half of U.S. Adults Are Married—A Record Low," Pew Research Center Website (December 2011), www.pewresearch.org/social-trends/2011/12/14/barely-half-of-u-s-adults-are-married-a-record-low/#:~:text=The%20share%20of%20Americans%20ages,and%2015%25%20were%20never%20married.

46 Richard Fry and Kim Parker, "Rising Share of U.S. Adults Are Living Without a Spouse or Partner," Pew Research Center Website (October 2021), www.pewresearch.org/social-trends/2021/10/05/rising-share-of-u-s-adults-are-living-without-a-spouse-or-partner/#:~:text=Americans'%20marital%20and%20living%20arrangements,to%209%25%20in%202019).

47 Clark, "Oh 'Bi' the Way."

48 Clark, "Oh 'Bi' the Way."

49 Burleson, "Bisexuality."

50 Tim R. Johnson, "Bisexual Aging and Cultural Competency Training: Responses to Five Common Misconceptions," *Journal of Bisexuality*, Vol. 16, No. 1 (2016), 101.

51 Johnson, "Bisexual Aging and Cultural Competency Training."

52 Johnson, "Bisexual Aging and Cultural Competency Training," 101–102.

53 Tarynn Witten, "Aging and Transgender Bisexuals: Exploring the Intersection of Age, Bisexual Sexual Identity, and Transgender Identity," *Journal of Bisexuality*, Vol. 16, No. 1 (2015), 58–80.

54 Witten, "Aging and Transgender Bisexuals."

55 Sarah Jen and Rebecca Jones, "Bisexual Lives and Aging in Context: A Cross-National Comparison of the United Kingdom and the United States," *The International Journal of Aging and Human Development*, Vol. 89, No. 1 (2019), 31.

56 Jen and Jones, "Bisexual Lives and Aging in Context," 31.

57 Jen and Jones, "Bisexual Lives and Aging in Context," 31.

58 Movement Advancement Project, "A Closer Look," 3.

59 Henrique Pereira and Debanjan Banerjee, "Successful Aging Among Older LGBTQIA+ People: Future Research and Implications," *Frontiers in Psychiatry*, Vol. 12 (2021), 2.

60 Pereira and Banerjee, "Successful Aging Among Older LGBTQIA+ People."

61 Elisabeth Langmann and Merle Wessel, "Leaving No One Behind: Successful Ageing at the Intersection of Ageism and Ableism," *Philosophy, Ethics, and Humanities in Medicine*, Vol. 18, No. 22 (2023), 1.

62 Movement Advancement Project, "A Closer Look," 3.

63 Clark, "Oh 'Bi' the Way."

64 The only exception is the BECAUSE conference, annually, in the Midwest; often in Minneapolis/St. Paul, hosted by the Bisexual Organizing Project in the Twin Cities.

65 See Leah Lakshmi Piepzna-Samarasinha, Care Work: Dreaming Disability Justice; Ai-Jenn Poo's work on domestic care workers organizing and eldercare, etc., as well as all the work of adrienne maree brown and Shira Hassan's Saving Our Own Lives: A Liberatory Practice of Harm Reduction and Kazu Haga's Healing Resistance: A Radically Different Response to Harm, and a handbook by the Foundation for Intentional Community—The Cooperative Culture Handbook: A Social Change Manual to Dismantle Toxic Culture & Build Connection by Yana Ludwig & Karen Gimnig.

66 A national bi women's newsletter based in New England that has been going for many, many decades.

RESOURCES

Websites

ambi
www.ambi.org/
American Institute of Bisexuality
www.bisexuality.org/
BECAUSE Conference
www.becauseconference.org/
bimedia.org
bi.org
The Bisexual Index
www.bisexualindex.org.uk/
Bisexual Organizing Project
www.bisexualorganizingproject.org/
Bisexual Resource Center
https://biresource.org/
GLAAD: Celebrate Bisexuality+
https://glaad.org/bisexual
HRC: Resource Guide to Coming Out as Bisexual
www.hrc.org/resources/resource-guide-to-coming-out-as-bisexual
LGBT Foundation: We Celebrate Bi People!
https://lgbt.foundation/get-involved-with-our-bi-spaces/
PFLAG: Bisexual+ Resources
https://pflag.org/resource/bisexual-resources/
The Trevor Project: Understanding Bisexuality
www.thetrevorproject.org/resources/article/understanding-bisexuality/

Hotlines: (From PFLAG's webpage)
https://pflag.org/resource/support-hotlines/

Crisis Intervention/Suicide Intervention

The Trevor Project: (866) 488–7386. www.thetrevorproject.org/
National Suicide Prevention Lifeline: (800) 273–8255 (online chat available). https://988lifeline.org/
Crisis Text Line: Text START to 741–741. www.crisistextline.org/

Youth Information

The Gay, Lesbian, Bisexual and Transgender National Hotline: (888) 843–4564
The GLBT National Youth Talkline (youth serving youth through age 25): (800) 246–7743
Trans Lifeline: (877) 565–8860
The National Runaway Safeline: 800-RUNAWAY (800–786–2929). www.1800runaway.org/youth/nrs_can_help/
The True Colors United: (212) 461–4401 https://truecolorsunited.org/
Self-Abuse Finally Ends (S.A.F.E) https://selfinjury.com/

HIV/AIDS Information

AIDS in Prison Project Hotline: (718) 378–7022 (English and Spanish)
This hotline provides HIV and AIDS information for prisoners and accepts collect calls.
National AIDS Hotline (800) 342-AIDS/(800) 344–7432 (Spanish)/(800) 243–7889 (TDD) www.thebody.com/index/hotlines/other.html

Other Hotlines

U.S. National Domestic Violence Hotline: (800) 799–7233 (English and Spanish) (800) 787–3224 (TTY). www.thehotline.org/
Rape Abuse and Incest National Network (RAINN): (800) 656-HOPE/(800) 810–7440 (TTY) https://rainn.org/
Pride Institute: (800) 547–7433 24/7. https://pride-institute.com/

Books to Read

Bi Any Other Name—Bisexual People Speak Out by Lani Ka'ahumanu and Loraine Hutchins
Bi: Notes for a Bisexual Revolution by Shiri Eisner
Bisexuality and The Western Church: The Damage of Silence by Carol Shepherd
Bisexuality, Religion and Spirituality by Alex Toft and Andrew Kam-Tuck Yip.
Bisexuality: The Basics: Your Q&A Guide to Coming Out, Dating, Parenting and Beyond by Lewis Oakley
Bi: The Hidden Culture, History, and Science of Bisexuality by Julia Shaw

Bi the Way: The Bisexual Guide to Life by Lois Shearing

Bisexual Married Men: Stories of Relationships, Acceptance, and Authenticity by Rob Cohen

Bisexual Men Exist: A Handbook for Bisexual, Pansexual and M-Spec Men by Vaneet Mehta

Blessed Bi Spirit: Bisexual People of Faith by Debra Kolodny

Boyslut: A Memoir and Manifesto by Zachary Zane

Claiming the B in LGBT: Illuminating the Bisexual Narrative by Kate Harrad

Getting Bi: Voices of Bisexuals Around the World by Robyn Ochs and Sarah Rowley

It Ain't Over Til the Bisexual Speaks: An Anthology of Bisexual Voices by Lois Shearing and Vaneet Mehta

Life Isn't Binary: On Being Both, Beyond and In-Between by Meg-John Barker and Alex Iantaffi

Married Women Who Love Women by Carren Strock

Recognize: The Voices of Bisexual Men Robyn Ochs and H. Sharif Williams

Sexuality, Religion and the Sacred: Bisexual, Pansexual and Polysexual Perspectives by Loraine Hutchins and H. Sharif Williams

The Edge of Sex: Navigating a Sexually Confusing Culture from the Margins by Lisa Speidel and Micah Jones

The People's Book of Human Sexuality: Expanding the Sexology Archive by Bianca Laureano

Trans Sex: Clinical Approaches to Trans Sexualities and Erotic Embodiments by Lucie Fielding

INDEX

For Product Safety Concerns and Information please contact our EU
representative GPSR@taylorandfrancis.com
Taylor & Francis Verlag GmbH, Kaufingerstraße 24, 80331 München, Germany

www.ingramcontent.com/pod-product-compliance
Lightning Source LLC
Chambersburg PA
CBHW050330270326
41926CB00016B/3385

9 781032 151298